The Global
Etiquette Guide
to Mexico and
Latin America

The Global Etiquette Guide to Mexico and Latin America

Everything You Need to Know for Business and Travel Success

Dean Foster

John Wiley & Sons, Inc.

This book is dedicated to my parents, Joseph and Sylvia, who first showed me the world

Published by John Wiley & Sons, Inc., New York
Published simultaneously in Canada

This publication is designed to provide accurate and authoritative information in regard to the subject matter covered. It is sold with the understanding that the publisher is not engaged in rendering professional services. If professional advice or other expert assistance is required, the services of a competent professional person should be sought.

Wiley also publishes its books in a variety of electronic formats. Some content that appears in print may not be available in electronic books. For more information about Wiley products, visit our web site at www.wiley.com.

Library of Congress Cataloging-in-Publication Data:

Foster, Dean Allen.
    Global etiquette guide to Mexico and Latin America / Dean Foster.
      p.   cm.
    Includes bibliographical references and index.
    ISBN 0-471-41851-X (pbk.)
    1. Etiquette—Mexico—Handbooks, manuals, etc. 2. Mexico—Social life and customs—Handbooks, manuals, etc. 3. Etiquette—Latin America—Handbooks, manuals, etc. 4. Latin America—Social life and customs—Handbooks, manuals, etc. I. Title.

    BJ1838 .F673   2002
    395'.098—dc21

                                2002002966

Printed in the United States of America

10 9 8 7 6 5 4 3 2 1

Contents

Preface   vii

Introduction: Why Getting It Right around the World
                Is So Important   1

Part One   Meso- and Centroamerica:
              Saludos, Salsa, and Simpático   **9**

Chapter One: Mesoamerica: Mexico   13
Chapter Two: The Northern Centroamerican Cultures:
               Guatemala, Belize, Honduras, and
               El Salvador   38

   Guatemala   *38*
   Belize   *58*
   Honduras   *61*
   El Salvador   *63*

Chapter Three: The Southern Centroamerican Cultures:
                 Nicaragua, Costa Rica, and Panama   65

   Nicaragua   *65*
   Costa Rica   *82*
   Panama   *86*

Part Two   South America:
              Conquistadors, Contessas, and Condomble   **89**

Chapter Four: The North Andean Cultures: Colombia,
                Venezuela, and Ecuador   93

   Colombia   *93*
   Venezuela   *115*
   Ecuador   *120*

Chapter Five: The South Andean Cultures: Peru and
                    Bolivia   126

    Peru   *126*
    Bolivia   *131*

Chapter Six: Brazil   136

Chapter Seven: The Western "Southern Cone" Cultures:
                    Argentina and Chile   162

    Argentina   *162*
    Chile   *183*

Chapter Eight: The Eastern "Southern Cone" Cultures:
                    Paraguay and Uruguay   189

    Paraguay   *189*
    Uruguay   *192*

Part Three   The Caribbean:
**   *Mambo, Mosaic, and Manana***   **197**

Chapter Nine: The Hispanic-African Cultures: Cuba,
                    The Dominican Republic, and Puerto Rico   199

    Cuba   *199*
    The Dominican Republic   *217*
    Puerto Rico   *235*

Chapter Ten: The Franco-African Cultures: Haiti   239

Chapter Eleven: The Anglo-African Cultures: Jamaica,
                    Barbados, and Trinidad and Tobago   255

    Jamaica   *255*
    Barbados   *270*
    Trinidad and Tobago   *273*

Index   277

Preface

The idea for this series emerged out of the work that my staff and I, and literally thousands of people from around the world that we work with, have been doing for almost two decades: assisting businesspeople and travelers to better understand their colleagues in other cultures. This work has primarily focused on international business and has taken many forms: helping to prepare families of employees adjust to an overseas assignment; assisting individual businesspeople in their negotiations with colleagues abroad; and helping global organizations to build more effective global teams. As business has globalized, the need for cross-cultural information has grown.

But globalization hasn't affected only the businessperson. While most of the work in the cross-cultural field has developed in response to international business needs, the need for cross-cultural information for the nonbusiness international traveler (both actual and of the armchair variety!) has also grown. Unfortunately, the amount of useful, objective, and applicable information, adapted to the needs of the more casual international explorer, has been limited. In most cases, what information was available usually took the form of anecdotal war stories, overgeneralized stereotypes (always interesting, but of dubious veracity), or theoretical statements about culture that were too removed from the day-to-day adventures of the international traveler. As the gap between useful cultural information for international business and international travelers grew, so did the need to bridge it. Hence, the idea for the Global Etiquette Guide series.

Correction: I embarked on this project at first with the goal of writing one book. But the world, as it turned out, was simply too big, and so was the book. Given my work, I for one should not have been surprised at this development, but at first was concerned about how to handle the dilemma. Nevertheless, under the kind and careful guidance of my editor, publisher, and agent, we expanded the original concept into a series. And I am glad we did. For one thing, it gave me the breathing room to explore all cultures to the degree that was necessary for the reader; for another, it gave me the opportunity to experience just how fine a team I was working with.

My editor, Tom Miller, did double duty, providing patience and insight, through both the serialization of the original book and the actual editorial review of the material. His input, despite my occasional and incorrect misgivings, gave me focus, pause to rethink when it was important to do so, and perhaps most importantly, impetus and space to keep going in the face of demanding schedules and unpredictable events. A good editor provides the professional expertise to fine-tune the work. A great editor also provides faith. Tom never failed to offer both.

Jane Dystel is everything an author can ask for in an agent. On many levels, this series would not have happened without her. She is always available, always on my side, and equally able to manage scrupulously the details of a particular project while helping me to put the pieces in place for the bigger career; I am very grateful to have her support. This is the second time we have worked together on a project, and I look forward to many more.

Bob Stein is the lawyer behind the scenes. Lawyers are, no doubt, overlooked far too often, and easily forgotten once their job is done. Here I have probably been more neglectful than most, for Bob is also a dear and longtime friend who has never failed to support me, even in my most ridiculous moments, and I fear I have taken advantage of that. Forgive me, Bob, and thank you . . . again.

I also want to thank all the professionals in the cross-cultural field with whom I have had the pleasure to work over the years. They have all contributed in important ways to these books. To my colleagues at Berlitz International and at GMAC Intercultural, who, around the world, have given me opportunities to play a leading role in the cross-cultural field, I am eternally grateful. To the many professionals in both competing and supporting organizations whom I have learned from, and worked and played with, many, many thanks. Finally, to the diverse thousands of individuals around the globe, of all cultures and backgrounds, who, in their work with me and my staff, have provided us with the joy and opportunity to learn about their unique part of the world, my very heartfelt thanks. Without your perspectives, experiences, and input, my work, and ultimately these books, would never have been possible.

When exploring cultural differences, one quickly observes that there are some cultures that "work to live," and others that "live to work." Balancing these two perspectives is a constant challenge for both cultures and individuals, and my world would surely be quite unbalanced without the love and support of my wife, Sheryl. She has been my constant, both the wind beneath my wings and my tether to the shore. I know this has not been easy, as she must also balance her own professional demands with our personal life. That she has done both is a testament to her strength and love. These books, as with so much else in my life, could not have occurred without her.

Leah, my daughter, plays a great role in these books. As I've watched her grow into the intelligent and caring young woman she is today, she serves as a constant reminder that the prize we work so hard for should truly be worth something. It needs to be created in love, based on justice, and worth the struggle. As I hope I have given meaning to her life, she continues to give meaning to mine. We have been growing up together all her life, and although she is now "all grown up," I have no intention of stopping.

Finally, after crediting all these worthy folks for their kind and important contributions, I must now credit myself: all the shortcomings of these books are mine. If I overstated a culture too broadly, overlooked an important cultural consideration, or in any way misrepresented or misjudged a particular way of life, the error is mine and no one else's. I only ask that the reader please consider the cause as the "anthropologist's dilemma": that is, the impossibility of describing a culture objectively, due to the fact that the "describer" is viewing the culture being observed ultimately in reference to their own (in my case, the United States). For some, this unfortunate natural law of the social sciences may be an added bonus (for other Americans, perhaps). For others, this may cause some serious and legitimate misgivings. I hear you both. Please take solace in the fact that every effort has been made to minimize the negative effects of this phenomenon whenever and wherever possible. No doubt I have not succeeded completely.

Why Getting It Right around the World Is So Important

Apparently, the world is getting smaller and smaller every day. We can't make it through a twenty-four hour period without the media informing us of something happening in a distant land, without our local bank accounts being affected by a foreign stock market, without our schools having to make decisions about bilingual education, and without the possibility that our friends, coworkers, neighbors, and possibly family, will have come from somewhere else, speak a language we barely understand, and have a perspective on life that may be radically different from our own. As English speakers, isn't it unnecessary that we learn another language . . . or become familiar with another culture? After all, isn't technology spreading the English language and American pop culture so globally that we're all going to understand one another through the medium of Coca-Cola and rock 'n' roll anyway? The answer to all of the above, as anyone who steps off a plane in a foreign land will learn, is a resounding "No."

I like to think that the world is getting bigger, not smaller; that world cultures, perhaps unique among many aspects of life that are indeed being homogenized, will not be; and that cultures more deeply rooted and with far longer histories than that of the U.S. pop culture, along with their languages, will still be with us long after Coca-Cola becomes their favorite soft drink and rock their favorite form of music.

There is no doubt that cultures are in contact with one another to a degree never before experienced in human history. The vastness of human experience, which is the world, is suddenly in our respective faces as never before. Each of us is experiencing not the smallness of the world, but the very bigness of it. For most of us, this is not an easy thing to do. For a variety of reasons, such as the economics of globalization, the development of technology, and the evolution (or devolution, depending upon your point of view) of current political forms, the need to recognize and understand differences in cultures has probably never been more critical than it is today.

Businesspeople traveling the world are learning to appreciate the consequences of the misunderstood gesture, the ill-placed word, the uninformed judgment; workers down the hall are required to communicate effectively with coworkers who may or may not speak their language or understand their ways; world travelers, from tourists to diplomats, evaluate the success of their sojourns more and more according to their ability to understand and appreciate the differences that exist between themselves and their new foreign hosts. Understanding, managing, appreciating, and maximizing the benefits of cultural differences, in fact, have become the most critical factors in the success of the global businessperson, the international diplomat, the manager of a multicultural office, or simply the continent-hopping tourist seeking a vacation of reward and richness. No, the world is not getting smaller—but we *are* being required to act much bigger in order to make sense of it all.

This book can help us to do that. There is no doubt that those forces of economics, politics, and technology that are bringing us in closer contact with one another foster, in some measure, a sense of unity. However, the degree to which understanding is developed simply as a result of cultural contact is questionable. Unfortunately, history provides us with evidence that when cultures collide, through whatever forces and for whatever reasons, the initial results are often disastrous. There is nothing inherent in cultural contact that automatically leads to understanding, homogeneity, peace, love, justice, and universal brotherhood. In fact, the reverse, at least in the short run, has been true. Over time, and only when specific structures such as democratic political forms, legal systems, and economic opportunities are in place, can cultures that once did not understand one another begin to accept one another. All one needs to do to better appreciate this sobering fact is to read the international headlines of any major newspaper any day of the week.

Nevertheless, if we are bound, as we apparently are, to hurtle headlong into one another's cultures, the least we can do is prepare ourselves to understand the other a little better. The forces of globalization carry information that both informs and misinforms one culture about the other. So we cannot depend for truth on what Hollywood tells us about Mexico, what Joe Smith relates to us over drinks about his recent trip to São Paulo, or what our coworker Maria from Caracas tells us about how Venezuelan businesspeople think. Neither the global businessperson nor the casual tourist can afford to make mistakes when abroad, to misunderstand the intent of his or her foreign hosts, or to risk inadvertently offending someone. If we are all now working, living, loving, growing, and having to not only survive but thrive in a universe far larger and more complex than anything we were prepared to handle, it's time, to say the least, to get prepared. And that's the purpose of this book.

What This Book Is . . . and Is Not

This book is one of several in the series of Global Etiquette Guides, each of which focuses on a major world region. Each book follows the same format and structure, so whether you are beginning the series with this book or have already read one of the others, you will recognize a structure that makes the reading fun and provides you with the information you need about the countries in the region quickly and easily.

However, no one book can provide you with everything you've ever wanted to know about any particular culture, let alone the major cultures of even one particular world region. People make lifelong careers out of studying about any one particular culture, and there are sections in most libraries with many books focused solely on one aspect of one culture. Nor can one book provide you with everything you need to know to do business successfully every time in those cultures. But this book will look at most major cultures in Latin America, those with which most people will have some contact or be influenced by in their lifetimes. It will provide important information about the basic day-to-day behaviors in those countries that enable the inhabitants to pursue what they believe to be the best way to live their lives, achieve their goals, and solve their problems; in short, the day-to-day customs, etiquette, and protocols of these cultures that make them what they are, and, perhaps, different from our own.

The information provided about business issues, practical "do's and don'ts" for all travelers, and the underlying values and belief systems of the various cultures will be useful for global businesspeople, casual international travelers, and cultural researchers. Most important, this information will address the one issue we all have in common in the face of our amazing diversity: our need to create a day-to-day modus operandi for living, for dealing with other people, and for communicating our needs and desires. *The Global Etiquette Guide to Mexico and Latin America* is intended to be a practical and relatively thorough guide to the protocol, etiquette, and customs that are the ways of life in one of the world's most important cultural regions.

What Do We Mean by "Culture"?

Culture is the normative way in which groups of people behave and the belief systems that they develop to justify and explain these behaviors. These behaviors can differ between groups, generally as a result of the different experiences that disparate groups have had. In turn, these experiences are usually a combination of history, geography, economics, and other factors, which vary from group to group. What makes all cultures similar, however, are the essentially universal problems of life that we all must address, as individuals and as societies. The problems and questions are the same everywhere, but the answers we come up with as societies can be different. This is what defines our individual cultures. Geert Hofstede, one of the seminal researchers in the field of culture, says, "If the mind is the hardware, then culture is the software," meaning that we are all hardwired pretty much the same, but the programs that we run on can be quite dissimilar. Culture is human software, and the challenge is to make the programs compatible.

I also want to emphasize the normative and group aspects of culture. I am constantly amazed at how from person to person we all can seem so much alike, and yet from society to society, we can be so very different. Culture reveals itself mainly in the group dynamics of the major institutions of society, and not necessarily in the interpersonal behaviors of individuals. In any particular culture, you may run into people, therefore, who behave very differently from the way we describe the culture; in these cases, these individuals are behaving outside the norm. Culture is not a predictor of individual behavior, so when we discuss any cultural protocol, we are talking about general tendencies, expectations, and normative preferences. As someone foreign to a culture, you may be very far from its norm; for that reason, it is important to know what that norm is, respect it, and adjust to it.

This issue of norms also reminds us that the statements we make about any given culture are generalizations. There are certainly situations, individuals, and conditions that would reveal contradictory behaviors within the same culture. When we make a cultural statement, at least in this book, we are speaking of *primary* tendencies; in no way is this meant to imply that contradictory behaviors will not exist. In fact, it is this delicious complexity of cultures that makes them so fascinating and challenging to work with. In most cases, we are usually also referring to situations between strangers, for once personal relationships are established, many formalities fall by the wayside.

Mexico and Argentina provide us with an example of this in Latin America. In fact, there probably are no two cultures that, in many important ways, are more different from each other than Mexico and Argentina. Additionally, within each of those countries, we see great variances of behaviors: Mexicans from northern Chihuahua can be distinctly different from Mexicans from southern Chiapas, and Argentines from Buenos Aires can be distinctly different from Argentines from Tierra del Fuego. Nevertheless, all these people do share some overarching and unifying ideals, values, behaviors, and beliefs that identify them first as Mexicans and Argentines, and that secondarily distinguish them from non-Latinos in general.

So how important is it really to "go native"? The answer: not very. The goal of this book, and the goal of all intercultural understanding, is not to pre-scribe behaviors for you—behaviors that may be uncomfortable or unnatural to your own culture (many no doubt will be). Rather, the goal of this book is to explain unfamiliar behaviors so that you can come to understand them and why they exist, appreciate the benefits they bring to their culture, and adjust to them to the degree that you are comfortable in order to make someone from that culture equally comfortable with you. No one, however, can be someone he or she is not, and the worst thing you can do is to act inauthentically. There is no greater offense than an awkward and uncomfortable U.S. American, for example, giving his Mexican colleague an *abrazo* (a customary embrace) for the first time, simply because he read in a book that he should. The greater benefit from such information comes when the U.S. American understands the meaning of the Mexican embrace, is prepared for it, and does not respond to it in a way that offends the Mexican. Wherever you are, be yourself and be true to your own culture, but be true as an enlightened, informed, and respectful cultural being.

How the Book Is Organized

When you approach a world region, such as Latin America, from a cultural per-spective, there are first megacultures, and to varying degrees, variations on these megacultural themes, which are usually grouped geographically within the region. For example, there is the megacultural category of Hispanic cul-tures, which can be found from the Rio Grande in the north of Mexico right on down to the tip of Tierra del Fuego at the southern end of the South American continent. While many countries in this broad geographical swath are Hispanic (with their roots in Spain), such as Cuba, Mexico, Panama, Colombia, Peru, and Argentina, many are not, such as Brazil, Jamaica, and Barbados. Yet all are technically Latin American. Much of what is said about the protocols and eti-quette of any one Hispanic Latin American culture will also be true for most other Hispanic Latin American cultures; nevertheless, there can also be many differences among them. Yet all of the Hispanic countries are technically, in many key ways, more similar to one another than they are to countries within a different megacategory, such as, for example, the Anglo-African cultures of Belize, the Bahamas, and Jamaica, or the Luso-African culture of Brazil. And since the protocol and etiquette *topics* that are discussed for any one country are generally the same for all countries, the Latin American cultures are organized according to these main Latin American megacultural or regional groups.

Each group begins with a discussion of those cultures that provide the foundations for all the countries within the group, followed by further explorations of the countries within that cultural region and how they differ from one another. This has been done in order to highlight the distinctions that make each country within a cultural region unique and different without having to repeat information that is common to all the countries. Nevertheless, many readers will probably want to dip into the book country by country, rather than read it as a whole. If that's your style, rest assured that important cultural behaviors and facts are repeated country by country when necessary, so you won't miss too much if you want to read about one country without referring to others in the same region. To make finding specific countries easy, the contents page lists each country, so you can go straight to the page listed for information on that country's protocol and etiquette if you so desire.

The topics explored for every country are generally the same. Each chapter begins with "Some Introductory Background" on the culture, and "Some Historical Context," followed by a quick "Area Briefing," which usually talks about politics and government, schools and education, and religion and demographics. This should give you a good appreciation for the forces that have shaped the culture. "Fundamental Cultural Orientations" explores the belief systems that justify the behaviors people reveal to one another on a day-to-day basis, giving you an understanding of why the protocols and etiquette exist as they do. The rest of the chapter takes an in-depth look at the actual customs of the country: greetings and verbal and nonverbal communication styles; protocol in public; dress; dining and drinking; how to be a good guest or host; gift giving; how to celebrate the major holidays; and important aspects of the business culture. For each of these topics there are subtopics that explore aspects of the culture in relation to men and women, younger and older generations, and both business and social circumstances.

This book does not look at all nations and all cultures within Latin America. The world is a dynamic and changing place, and one of the difficulties about writing about culture at this point in world history is the fact that countries and cultures do not necessarily line up. While there is no one country representing the distinct Mayan culture, for example, there is most definitely a Mayan culture in Centroamerica. And while Mexican culture extends deep into the geographic west of the United States, exploring Mexican culture in the United States requires a book of a different focus. For these, and other thorny reasons, the book explores only those countries in the region that are, in the judgment of the author, distinguishably different from one another and of greatest interest to the reader. My apologies if I have not included a country or a culture of interest: it is not out of disrespect or malice, but merely because of space, knowledge, and time limitations.

The Meaning of the Information

In order to understand why the protocol, manners, and etiquette of any particular country are as they are, it is critically important to understand the belief systems and fundamental values that are at the heart of the culture. This is why every country includes a brief description of "Fundamental Cultural Orientations."

These orientations, of course, change country by country, but the categories themselves remain the same. For example, it is common for lunch not to begin before 2 P.M. in Mexico. This protocol is based on a more fundamental cultural orientation in Mexico around the issue of time. In Venezuela, lunch is more commonly served at noon; this different protocol results from a different fundamental cultural orientation in Venezuela around the same issue, time. (Of course, it's important to remember that Mexicans *can* take their lunch at noon, and Venezuelans *can* take their lunch at 2 P.M.; it's just that there is, from a cultural point of view, a difference in the concept of what constitutes timeliness.) Therefore, let's briefly explore those fundamental orientation issues around which all cultures can differ, because we will be referring to them again and again with each country we visit.

As the example stated earlier illustrates, cultural orientations revolve around some very basic concerns shared by all cultures:

1. What's the Best Way for People to Relate to One Another?

Societies are all about people, and how we organize ourselves in relation to one another is an issue that every culture must sort out for itself. Cultures might insist on honoring a societal hierarchy, structure, and organization, and they do so with all sorts of perks: titles, rank, different signs of respect, different roles for men and women, younger and older, and so on. Other cultures deemphasize the importance of such things, preferring to treat everyone as equals. So we have cultures that are *hierarchy* and *organization* oriented, and on the opposite end of the spectrum, cultures that are *egality* oriented. Some cultures might reward individuals for standing out, empowering them to make decisions on their own, while other cultures insist that individuals fit into the group, making sure that no one does anything without the consent and support of others. So we have cultures that are *other-independent,* and on the opposite end of the spectrum, cultures that are *other-dependent.* A culture might place a value on devising systems for organizing life, creating interconnected rules and regulations that must apply universally to all, while another culture might place more emphasis on the personal relationships that exist between people as the determinant of how to do things. So we have cultures that are *rule* oriented, and others that are *relationship* oriented. All of these orientations have to do with what a culture believes to be the best ways by which people can relate to one another.

2. What's the Best Way to View Time?

All societies have to handle moving through time, creating a way of understanding and simultaneously managing the flow of things. Cultures might place a great deal of importance on managing and controlling time. For these *monochronic* cultures, clocks, agendas, calendars, and deadlines determine what and when things are done, and time is a limited commodity that must be carefully managed. For other cultures, time exists, of course, but it is not the determinant of people's actions. For these *polychronic* cultures, time remains in the background, there is usually plenty of it, and relationships and immediate needs usually determine what and when things are done. Some cultures might move quickly with a limited amount of information, while other cultures need a great deal of information in order to make even a small decision. Therefore, cultures may be *risk-taking* or *risk-averse*. Finally, do the people put more of their energy into maintaining what they already have, or do they value change for change's sake? A culture may be *past* oriented (and often more fatalistic), while another may be more *future* oriented (and often more controlling).

3. What's the Best Way for Society to Work with the World at Large?

All societies must make decisions about how they fit into, process, and deal with the larger world. Essentially, this means how a culture communicates, thinks, and plans. Some cultures might create, analyze, and communicate information very directly; they depend upon the meaning of the word and don't embed information in the larger context of the situation. These cultures often place a high value on confrontation and absolute truth: they are *low-context* communicators. However, other cultures value the importance of communicating indirectly—with actions, not words—and have subtle systems in place for exchanging information appropriate to the situation and the environment, through nonverbal behavior. These cultures place a high value on the maintenance of smooth interpersonal relationships; they are *high-context* communicators. One culture might place the greater emphasis on the process by which goals are achieved, while another culture places the greater emphasis on the goal itself, regardless of how it's achieved. Therefore, cultures can be *process* oriented (relying often on deductive logic), or *results* oriented (relying often on inductive logic). In addition, cultures may be more associative in their thought processing; that is, they do things based on the way they know things always have been done, or how they are already being done in a similar situation. Finally, cultures might value the formal, established, reliable, and in some cases almost ritualized way of doing things, while other cultures might value change, informality, and spontaneity. Therefore, cultures may be *formal* or *informal* in their general orientation toward protocol itself.

It's important to remember that very few cultures are either absolutely one way or the other in their orientation. Most fall somewhere in between, and are simply more or less inclined to one way than the other. In Latin America, many countries share many of the same orientations. It's also important to remember that any one culture is a profile made up of all of these orientations, so be careful not to prejudge what one culture's orientation might be in one area just because of its orientation in another: you might be very surprised at the diversity and complexity of the combinations that exist when we tour the Latin American region! All world regions, Latin America included, provide us with the opportunity to explore an enormous diversity of cultural behaviors; the range, especially in what is considered correct and incorrect, can be staggering. Remember, the only constancy is change and the only absolute is complexity. What is correct in one culture may be incorrect in another, and what works in one can be a disaster in the other. As the old saying goes, "When in Rome, do as the Romans," and in Latin America, when in Guadalajara we must also do as the Mexicans, in Rio de Janeiro as the Brazilians, in Havana as the Cubans . . .

<table>
<tr><td>**PART
ONE**</td><td>## Meso- and
Centroamerica</td></tr>
</table>

Saludos, Salsa, and Simpático

An Introduction to the Region and Our Special Relationship with Latin America

A colleague remarked to me once that the capital of Latin America, if there is one, is Miami. He reminded me that most multinational companies, and not just those based in North America but those based in Europe and Asia as well, have their Latin American headquarters located there. He then went on to ruefully remark that the difference between Miami and Cancún is that in Cancún, they speak English. Being from Caracas, he then admitted that he loves to come to Miami whenever he can because it's just like Caracas, "except that everything works." As with all humor, it was funny because there was a significant element of truth to his statements, and it points up the very special role that Latin American culture plays in the Americas, as well as in the world. For starters, there is perhaps no other world region that currently has a greater cultural influence on North American culture. By 2010, it is estimated that almost one-third of the population in the United States will be of Hispanic origin; at present, almost 20 percent of the population of the United States claims Spanish as their first language. Of all the cultures explored in this book series, only two actually share borders with, and thus claim the title of "neighbor" with the United States; and unquestionably, Mexico is one of the leading countries within the Latin American region. In fact, a strong argument could be made for redefining the geography of Latin America to include major population areas of Toronto, Chicago, New York, and other northern American cities, not to mention vast tracts of land from the Pacific coast eastward to the Mississippi River. "Latino" culture, that unique version of Hispanic culture from the Latin American region (as opposed to other Hispanic areas of the world, including Spain) has an increasing and profound effect on the larger developing culture of North America, and therefore holds a very special place in this series.

The modern western hemisphere is a reflection of four major cultural influences: indigenous American cultures (Amerindians, Aztecs, and Incas), African cultures (the result of the slave trade that Europeans brought with them when they "discovered" the Americas), northern European cultures (which primarily rooted themselves in North America), and southern European cultures (which primarily rooted themselves in South America). The history of the region is usually divided between pre-Columbian times (meaning before Columbus and the onslaught of the Western conquest), and after the conquest (modern times). In most cases, indigenous cultures could not survive the onslaught, and with some notable exceptions, including Mexico, were reduced to playing a minimal role in the development of the culture from the conquest forward. African cultures, because of their vanquished status in the New World, were typically subordinated to the dominant European-based developing culture, whether integrated into it (as in Latin America) or as a parallel culture standing outside of the mainstream (as in North America). Perhaps the greatest cultural influence on the development of both North and South American culture was the European conquest, no doubt because it was violent, intrusive, and fueled by politics, economics, and missionary zeal. In fact, the New World represented, for both northern and southern Europeans, an opportunity for their own respective fifteenth-century perspectives of man and the world to flower unrestrained by the challenging forces and social constraints of fifteenth-century Europe. The result is a mirroring in both North America and South America of northern European and southern European cultures, but in a way magnified, exaggerated, and generally unrestrained, so that while Europe moved on with its history, those aspects of fifteenth-century Iberia that were transported to South America defined South America from that point forward, just as those aspects of fifteenth-century England that were transported to North America became fundamental to the definition of North America. If you want to see an example of fifteenth-century Castile today, you don't go to Madrid; Madrid and the rest of Spain has moved on with its history, transplanting its legacy of conquistadors to Peru, Ecuador, and Colombia: instead, take a plane to Lima, Quito, or Bogotá, and there you will see the remains of the conquest, alive and (somewhat) well, albeit in a twenty-first–century form. Equally, if you want to see an example of fifteenth-century Puritan England today, you don't go to London; England went on with its history and essentially threw the Puritan radicals out (while incorporating some of their ideas): take a trip to Boston, Chicago, or Silicon Valley instead, and there you will see the remains of the Protestant revolution, literally and furiously, at work. However, the northern European and southern European conquests, while both on a mission, were on very different missions. Northern Europeans, essentially being Puritans, were Protestant—literally protesting the Catholic-type notions that prohibited them from speaking directly as empowered individuals to their God—and when they came to the New World, they were rejecting the old, leaving it behind, and instead became reformist and individualistic, believing in the salvation of individual "good works." Southern Europeans were not, on the other hand, rejecting of the world that sent them across the sea; rather, their mission was to claim the New World in the name of the king and the church; they transplanted, even more vigorously, the traditions of hierarchical and aristocratic Crown and Roman Catholicism. These are the roots of North American and South American culture today, and after four hundred years they continue to define to a significant degree the essence of what it means to be either north or south "of the border." Let's take a closer look at the Latin cultures that are generally south of the border.

Getting Oriented

Defining the parameters of culture is always tricky, and in this region, as we have previously noted, the borders blur easily. For example, some of the Caribbean cultures (Belize, Curaçao, Bonaire, Jamaica, Trinidad, the Caymans, the Bahamas, British Virgin Islands, and Barbados) are not Latin based, while it can be correctly argued that "Latin" America extends well into the United States, including southern Florida, southern California, much of the Southwest, and major sections of U.S. cities. Other terms break down even further: "Hispanic" refers to cultures that have roots in Spain, and while much of Latin America is Hispanic, some key cultures in the region are not. Brazil, the largest country, is a "Luso-African" culture, its roots going back to Portugal and western Africa, not Spain. Therefore, although Portugal is a Latin culture, the significant African influence in Brazil creates a culture that cannot be defined simply as Latin; consequently, Brazilians prefer to define themselves as South American, not Latin American. There is no doubt, however, even with these complexities, that the overwhelming majority of cultures in this region have been substantively defined by Latin culture and identify with Latin culture. With these considerations in mind, and using the culturally blind criteria of geography, for our purposes, the region consists of the following groups:

- Meso- and Centroamerica: Mexico, Central America (Belize, Guatemala, Nicaragua, Honduras, El Salvador, Costa Rica, and Panama)
- The Andean Cultures: Peru, Ecuador, Bolivia, Colombia, and Venezuela
- Brazil
- The Southern Cone Cultures: Argentina, Chile, Paraguay, and Uruguay
- The Caribbean Cultures: Greater Antilles (Cuba, Haiti, Dominican Republic, Jamaica, and Puerto Rico) and Lesser Antilles (the multicultural island chains from the U.S. Virgin Islands in the north to Trinidad in the south)

Finally, an important consideration for readers from the United States: all inhabitants of the western hemisphere, from Alaska in North America to Tierra del Fuego on the southern tip of South America, are technically Americans. Americans from the United States need to be particularly careful not to appropriate the term "American" for themselves, as many countries in the region also see themselves as American. (Canadians typically refer to U.S. citizens as Americans, but usually only when distinguishing themselves from their immediate neighbor south of their border.) If you are from Brazil, you are Brazilian, if you are from Mexico, you are Mexican, and if you are from the United States, you are a U.S. American (avoid the catchall "North American" to distinguish the U.S. American, as North American technically includes Canadians, and many Mexicans may apply a strict geographical definition to define themselves as "North American" as well, despite their cultural links to the rest of the Latin American region).

CHAPTER ONE

Mesoamerica: Mexico

Some Introductory Background on Mexico and the Mexicans

In the center of Mexico City (the world's largest city, with approximately 20 million people, and growing at an average rate of about 4,000 people per month) is the largest public square in the Americas: it is called the *zócalo,* and its focal point is the great Roman Catholic Metropolitan Cathedral. Directly underneath and to the back of the Cathedral, however, you can visit the unearthed remains of the top of an enormous Aztec pyramid, perhaps the most sacred of all Aztec monuments to their gods. And surrounding the square are the government offices of the modern Mexican Republic. These elements reflect the complexity of the Mexican culture, which combines pre-Columbian "indígena" (indian or indigenous) culture, Roman Catholic "conquistador" culture, and modern "European secular" culture.

This mixture in the people has created *"la raza,"* or "the race," of which most Mexicans are very proud, and this is one of the primary distinctions between Mexico and much of the rest of Latin America: Mexicans do not reject their Indian roots, but incorporate them as an essential part of Mexican culture. But as the great Mexican author Octavio Paz has stated, these conflicting traditions have also left the Mexican with a divided soul, never quite knowing his or her parentage, both personally and as a member of the culture in a constant struggle for identity. Mexicans want other North Americans to understand and appreciate the rich nature of Mexican culture: it is not tacos and *cerveza;* it is the four-thousand-year-old history of ancient and advanced civilizations ripped from their moorings, overtaken by newer gods from the East in shining armor, who were themselves later challenged by aggressive "gringos" from the North.

Today, there are three Mexicos geographically as well. The Mexico of the north is similar to the United States, with a climate and topography that is flat, dry, rugged, and desert. In the middle, we have the volcanic plateau, rimmed east and west by vast north-south mountain ranges, with the great center of Mexico City (Mexico, D.F., or Distrito Federales—"Federal District"—as it is known in Mexico) as its heart; this region is ancient, conservative, landed, and agricultural. Finally, in the scrub and subtropical south of Chiapas and the Yucatán, we have Mayan-influenced, pre-Columbian Mexico, the poorest and perhaps the most disenfranchised.

Some Historical Context

Mexicans, maybe more so than members of any other Latin American culture, are very sensitive to people from the United States calling themselves "American." Mexicans will quickly tell you that they are Americans, too. It is important, therefore, for Americans from *Estados Unidos* to refer to themselves as "Americans from the Unites States" or "U.S. Americans" when speaking with anyone else in the western hemisphere, but especially so when speaking with Mexicans. By the way, the term "gringo" (said to refer to the green uniforms of the U.S. troops during the U.S.-Mexican war, and the resulting Mexican protest, "Green, go") can be either positive or negative in its connotation depending on the context: When used to describe a U.S. American whom a Mexican does not know, it is usually used pejoratively; if it is used to describe a U.S. American with whom a Mexican has a good relationship, it is being used affectionately.

Mexico was for thousands of years a region of competing and advanced Indian civilizations, beginning with the Olmecs and Toltecs and moving on through many others—the most familiar of which were the Mayans—ending with the last great indigenous Mexican civilization, the Aztecs. The greater of these civilizations, at their height, surpassed contemporary civilizations in Europe and Asia; for example, when Cortez "discovered" Tenochtitlán (the capital of the Aztec Empire, upon which Mexico City was built), it had more canals than Venice and more people than Paris or London at the time. Suddenly, and literally overnight, their civilization was swept away by conquistadors from a strange land, and in one of history's great coincidences, an event that was predicted by their own Aztec cosmology and therefore accepted as inevitable. In one cataclysmic blow, the gods of a thousand years, and the accompanying beliefs and worldviews, were overturned and replaced by the new Catholic God and his emissaries. Mexico became one of two major centers for Spanish rule (a viceroy, or representative of the king, was installed in both Mexico and what was then known as Grancolombiana, or the present region comprising Ecuador, Colombia, and Peru) and subsequently became the consolidating heart of Spanish power in the Americas. Quickly, the Castilian court carved up the vast landed wealth of the region, parceling it out in massive sections to the relatively small handful of royal representatives of the Castilian court. At the same time, the government bureaucracy, justified by a rigid Catholic hierarchy, imposed itself across the land with a heavy-handed authority that was unchallengeable at first, and that was uprooted over three hundred years later only through massive and bloody revolutions. The system, imposed from above, ensured that massive wealth remained in the hands of the privileged few and created a rigidly defined class system throughout Latin America based on land ownership that set the stage for political instability, limited democracy, and revolution based on land ownership reform in the centuries to come. (The fruits of this legacy live on today as Mexico, and the rest of the region, continues to struggle with poverty, concentrated wealth, powerful oligarchies, and sometimes unstable, unrepresentative governments.) The situation was exacerbated by the rapid advancement of North American conquest, as the Puritans themselves developed into a major European-based culture to the north. By the time the *gringos* established themselves in California, almost one-third of Mexico was lost to the United States, a fairly recent historical fact of life that continues as a background source of difficulty in Mexico-U.S. relations. While Latin America struggled with its own legacies, it also had to contend with an economically powerful and occasionally militarily intrusive neighbor to the north. As the Mexican dictator Porfirio Díaz once said, "Pity poor Mexico; so close to the United States, so far from God."

An Area Briefing

Politics and Government

The government of Mexico today is technically a federal republic, with a president who serves a nonrepeatable six-year term and a bicameral legislature. The 2000 presidential election marked a sea change in the political history of Mexico, being the first time since the Mexican Revolution—the hard-fought battle for independence from Spain—that the candidate from the PRI (the Partido Revolucionario Institucional, or Institutional Revolutionary Party) lost the presidential election. The PRI, until then the singular ruling party in the country, is still extraordinarily powerful and retains control over much of Mexican politics. It remains to be seen if the new parties represent a more democratic Mexico, if they can solve some of the apparently intractable problems from the past, and if the PRI will reinvent itself for the future.

Schools and Education

Schooling is compulsory through high school; however, in poorer rural regions and difficult urban neighborhoods, maintaining quality education and children's attendance through these grades is a challenge. Many children are pressed into working to help the family survive instead of attending school. The wealthy send their children to private schools, including universities in Europe and the United States. Many of Mexico's elite have been educated at Les Grandes Ecoles in France and at Ivy League institutions in the United States.

Religion and Demographics

Most Mexicans are Roman Catholic, with minority populations of Jews, Protestants, Muslims, and others. In fact, it is a Marian culture, in that Mary is a central figure of devotion for many Mexican Roman Catholics, and the patron saint of Mexico—the Virgin of Guadalupe—is female. Recall that in its effort to establish a secular democratic republic, the government disestablished the church's authority, and there is still an uncomfortable relationship between the power of the church in Mexico and government authority. Mexico today is demographically an extremely young country, with more than 60 percent of the population under the age of thirty. There is still a rigid separation of the genders in Mexico, more so in the less urbanized and more conservative areas; even in the urban centers, women struggle with the glass ceiling at work and the need to perform "two jobs"—that of homemaker and societal nurturer, as well as businesswoman—and to do each twice as well as the Mexican male. Non-Mexican businesswomen must take extra care in order to not be judged as overly aggressive, yet must maintain extreme professionalism in order to not have their authority questioned. Consider too that Mexico, like most of the region, is economically a developing nation and struggles with all the challenges associated with that status, including substantial poverty, inadequate and ill-serving infrastructures, and corruption. Nevertheless, Mexico has made great strides recently, and the younger generation is facing the future with renewed optimism and hope.

Fundamental Cultural Orientations

1. What's the Best Way for People to Relate to One Another?

OTHER-INDEPENDENT OR OTHER-DEPENDENT?   As is the case with most countries in the region—due in part to the heavy influence of Roman Catholicism—Mexican behavior can be viewed as significantly other-dependent, with strong individual action being taken to demonstrate responsibility to the larger group. Most individuals will seek, either formally or informally, the opinions and support of family, friends, and coworkers before venturing off to do or say something on their own. People are most comfortable in the "bosom" of others, and individuals are simply not part of society unless they can claim membership to or affiliation with some group, neighborhood, town, or business organization. A consequence of this, of course, is a resistance to the outsider, and a need for all outsiders to become associated with members of the in-group as soon as possible in order to be accepted. This is often demonstrated through the need to build strong and enduring personal relationships. There is an old Spanish saying that children live at home until they are old enough to have their parents live in their home with them. To be alone in Mexico is to live a dangerous and difficult life. Causing someone to lose face, or experience embarrassment, public ridicule, or criticism of any kind, is a great insult in this other-dependent culture; here, how one is thought of by others is one of the most important concerns in life. Despite this strong need to look good in the eyes of others, the individual must bear responsibility for him- or herself in the world. In Hispanic culture, every individual is unique, and has the right to advance in his or her own way in the world, as long as it is done with consideration for others; the proof of the value of one's individual behavior is whether and the degree to which it positively affects the lives of others. Therefore, individual Mexican pride, based on one's role, achievements, and level in society, is strong, a representation of one's role in the larger society, and can easily be insulted.

HIERARCHY-ORIENTED OR EGALITY-ORIENTED?   Certainly the younger generation, especially in the cities, feels more empowered as individuals than their elders, but the traditions of the Roman Catholic hierarchy still play a powerful role in determining who does what and when. Subsequently, the Mexican workplace is typically rigidly layered, with the individual at the top (*el jefe* or *el patrón*—"the boss") having supreme decision-making authority (but only in a way that honors his role as leader in the group) and the support staff being required to follow step, challenge as little as possible, and solve all problems before they surface at the top. In civic life, this means that government, which is supposed to be democratic, often fails to be. A practical example of this is the role of policemen on the street: they typically represent authority, not assistance. Women and men are rigidly separated in their social roles, as is the case more or less throughout all of Latin America, which is a very macho culture; women traditionally play the nurturing role in society, while men play the public leaders, in government and business. Of course, there are women who achieve high levels in both, but they do not represent most women. While their public role may be limited, however, women in Mexico are far from devalued. To the contrary, they are entrusted with the most important work for the most important institution in society: nurturing the family.

RULE-ORIENTED OR RELATIONSHIP-ORIENTED? Despite the fact that Mexico (and the rest of the region) has tried valiantly to establish civil governments with rules and regulations that would apply to all, the reality mirrors the historical imprint of the Roman Catholic Church, in which authority and its rules could always be circumvented by those clever enough or with connections. One of the lasting legacies of Latin cultures is the rigid social hierarchy and the value people place on finding ingenious ways around rules and regulations in order to live their lives. Most of the time, the way one circumvented the authorities was to rely on the only true source of dependability in an otherwise cruel and difficult world: one's family, proven friends, and loyal business associates. Therefore, relationships—not rules—rule. Situations, if involving the right people and the right issues, will most always determine the behaviors of individuals, not bland laws or bureaucratic fiats. This can lead to corruption, which is a major difficulty in Mexico and throughout the region. (Historically, *la mordida,* or "bite," has been an accepted facet of Mexican life: some form of payment needs to be made in order to get something done, whether it's to void a traffic ticket or win government approval for a project. In its most innocuous form, *la mordida* represents the need to build personal relationships in order to get things done; in its more common form, it represents the expectation on the part of some poorly paid government bureaucrats that they need to be compensated more appropriately for providing a valued service; and in its most insidious form, it is out-and-out extortion.) This cultural dependence on personal relationships (and personal trust, or "confianza," or a feeling of "simpatico") means that Mexicans will need time to get to know you before they will be ready to talk business. Attempts to discuss the terms of the deal or the immediate task at hand without having built the necessary personal trust and understanding is often a waste of time. Which takes us to our next concern.

2. What's the Best Way to View Time?

MONOCHRONIC OR POLYCHRONIC? Outside of the major cities, time is circular, and very polychronic; it is more monochronic in Mexico City, but even there, old agrarian patterns die hard, even if people aren't waking up and heading for the fields in the morning. In rural areas, it is easiest to work in the fields in the cool of the early morning and late afternoon; the midday heat is usually too oppressive, and provides a good opportunity to stoke up on a filling meal and a siesta before heading back out until the sun sets.

Working on the Paseo de la Reforma (one of the two main axis roads in Mexico City) today still means showing up at the office around 9 A.M., but sometimes not really getting started until 9:30 or 10 (drinking coffee, checking the news, and catching up with coworkers may take precedence). Lunch occurs around two o'clock, and can either be a quick bite at the local sandwich shop or last for several hours at an elegant restaurant (those are postlunch, not predinner, cigars they are smoking at 5 P.M. in the restaurant lounge). After returning to the office (people would, in an earlier time, retire for a short nap after having gone home for the large main midday meal; this, by the way, is still done in some areas), workers stay as necessary, perhaps up to eight or nine o'clock. At that point, they return home or meet friends at a local bar for some drinks. Dinner, in either case, is usually not before 10 or 11 P.M. (especially in the summer) and can last till midnight or later.

On weekends, Friday and Saturday night revelries more often than not can last until after the sun comes up Sunday morning. If you really want things to occur punctually, it is perfectly okay to identify the time as *"a la gringa"* or *"Norteamericano,"* as opposed to *"a la Mexicana."*

RISK-TAKING OR RISK-AVERSE?   Latin cultures, in general, are risk-averse, and that is one of the driving reasons for the creation of structure and hierarchies. Mexico is no exception. Decision making can be slow and tedious, as various levels of the hierarchy need to be consulted, and as information must be made available to many, in order for it to occur. The belief is to do it right the first time; analyze everything carefully—several times, if necessary—and debate all aspects of a decision until everything is clear and agreed upon. After all, a risk, if it turns out wrong, results in a mistake that can have unredeemable consequences for the individuals involved. Even when individuals are empowered to make a decision, there can be a reticence to take the required final step. Nevertheless, there is a growing impatience among new entrepreneurs with the tedious risk-avoidance, and in Guadalajara and Monterrey especially, there can be a palpable frustration with the traditional risk-averse attitudes.

PAST-ORIENTED OR FUTURE-ORIENTED?   Latin American cultures, especially Mexico, have seen their world turned upside down more than once with their having little or no ability to control the events. First it was volcanoes and earthquakes, then conquistadors from the east, then the U.S. presence from the north. In Mexico, there is a strong doubt in the ability to control what happens, but the effort is always there, for to struggle is to live. Mexicans look back to their roots for stability and are generally wary about the ultimate outcome of things. Their efforts, therefore, will as likely be to personal aggrandizement in a situation as in the success of the mission, and this is especially true with outsiders whom they may not have grown to trust (especially unknown people from the United States, who come to Mexico, knowingly or not, with the baggage of a reputation of exploitation). Mexicans have a strong desire to believe in their own ability to overcome the odds, but there is an equally strong acceptance of the inevitability of setbacks and failures, almost a fatalistic expectation of it, and a resistance to identify individuals for blame when and if things go wrong.

3. What's the Best Way for Society to Work with the World at Large?

LOW-CONTEXT DIRECT OR HIGH-CONTEXT INDIRECT COMMUNICATORS?
Most Mexicans are high-context communicators; depending upon the rank and status of those present, and the situation, Mexicans will be careful about what

they say and how they say it. The importance of hierarchy and other-dependency requires careful speech; in any but the most private moments with trusted family and friends, speaking one's mind is done carefully—especially at work. Mexicans, like most Latinos, want smooth interpersonal working relationships, especially with outsiders, and will go the distance to reassure you that everything is okay and that all is in order—even when it may not be. This is not based on a desire to deceive, but rather on a need to appear capable, and not to lose face in the eyes of people from cultures with great resources. It is critical, therefore, to always confirm information; to have multiple, independent, and reliable sources to verify or interpret what you are being told; and to be able to read between the lines. "There are as many truths as there are bananas" goes a Mexican saying; in a culture that has seen one truth replaced by another again and again, there is a strong tolerance for, in fact dependence on, the subjective interpretation of events and reality (this is revealed in the unique Latin American art, in both books and paintings, known as "magical realism," where fantastical events are treated with everyday acceptance). This tendency also makes for complimentary and respectful introductory conversation, and an avoidance of anything that may strike you as unpleasant; at first, Mexicans will always try to say what they think you want to hear.

PROCESS-ORIENTED OR RESULT-ORIENTED? As with other Latino cultures, there is a strong reliance on the deductive process: how things are being done is as important as the final result. But Mexicans are also very subjective, and will also often fall back on what they personally believe in order to make or justify a decision. Because there is great admiration for the process (after all, if the process is correct, the result will be good), coupled with a sometimes serious lack of resources in what still is a developing country and a cumbersome and byzantine bureaucracy, Mexicans may not be able to follow through with the actions necessary to put the plans in place. Yet they may be reticent to admit this or inform you when problems develop. It is therefore that much more important for non-Mexicans to stay involved with them, helping them to implement what has been agreed to. This must be done, however, with sensitivity toward the pride that Mexicans feel in being able to handle things on their own; therefore, never be intrusive, but always be available; always be open to learning about their ways, while providing them with the resources and information they need, whenever possible, to assist them in making things happen. Mexicans can be very clever about making the end result happen, but the way they get there, if they get there at all, may be very different from the original plan.

FORMAL OR INFORMAL? In Mexico, there are definitely "correct" and "incorrect" ways to get things done, which tends to formalize human relationships, both socially and in business. Mexico has a formal culture. Family members relate to one another according to formal rules that respect traditional family roles. *El papa, la madre, el niño, la niña, mi amigo:* no matter the role, there is a formal way of relating between the actors. This does not have to be artificial or contrived; in fact, it is often loving and spontaneous. But it is respectful and prescribed. Even the language is divided into formal and informal forms and phrases, and personal behaviors are ruled by etiquette and protocol. Maintaining honor and personal pride is critical, and this requires a bit more formality. *Never* insult the honor, pride, or personal beliefs of a Mexican or his or her family, colleagues, or associates.

Greetings and Introductions

Language and Basic Vocabulary

Spanish is the language, but about a third of the population also (and in some cases, only) speaks an indigenous Indian language, such as Nahuatl (the language of the Aztecs) or Mayan (spoken by many in the Yucatán). The Spanish in Mexico is a pure, not a Castilian, Spanish. Be sure to use any Spanish you do know, even if you learned it from a neighbor or in school: Mexicans love it when you try to speak Spanish, and they will help you get it right; this often becomes a relationship-building event and can be a more important activity in the formative stages of the relationship than any substantive discussions you can have.

Here are the basics:

Buenos días	Good morning
Buenas tardes	Good afternoon
Buenas noches	Good evening
¡Hola! ¿Que tal?	Hello, how are you? (informal)
¿Como está usted?	How are you? (formal)
Adiós	Good-bye
Por favor	Please
Gracias	Thank you
Con permiso/¿Mande?	Pardon me
De nada	You're welcome
Muy bien	Very well
Con mucho gusto	Pleased to meet you
Un placer	A pleasure
Señor	Mr.
Señora	Mrs.
Señorita	Miss
Ingeniero(a)	Engineer
Abogado(a)	Lawyer
Doctor	Doctor
Gerente	Manager

There is the charming use of the diminutive in Mexican Spanish to indicate familiarity and closeness: you sequentially add the suffix "ito," so "momento" becomes "momentito" or even "momentitito." Remember, in written Spanish, questions and exclamations are also indicated at the beginning of the sentence, with an upside-down exclamation point or question mark.

Honorifics for Men, Women, and Children

You must use *señor* (Mr.) and *señora* (Mrs.) plus the family name when introduced to strangers. Unless and until your Mexican colleague specifically invites you to use first names, and despite how he or she might refer to you, you must always use the family name plus the correct Spanish honorific (*señorita*— Miss—is still required for a young, unmarried woman). If you do not know whether a woman is married, use *señorita* (please note: this is the reverse from what is done in Spain, where *señora* is used when the marital status of the woman is unknown). *Don* (*doña* for an unmarried woman) is a special title of respect, typically used before the *first* (given) name only, and usually used only by people who know each other well and desire to show great respect. Married women are not necessarily "safe" from machismo, so wearing a wedding band does not always protect a woman alone. However, being a mother virtually ensures that a man will remain at a distance: Bring pictures of your children. Children in Mexico are expected to be respectful and not overly conversational when speaking with adults, and should always use honorifics when referring to adults. In situations where a title is known or used, the honorific plus the title is usually employed, either with or without the name (e.g., Señor Ingeniero, or Señor Ingeniero Cortez). *Licensiado* is a "title" generally used for anyone with a skill requiring some sort of diploma. "Doctor" may be safely used as a way to give respect to anyone with a university degree; as an honorific, it does not have to refer only to a Ph.D. For casual contacts (e.g., with waiters, store help, etc.), just use *señor* or *señorita* without the name. It is very important to greet people at work or in stores and restaurants with an appropriate greeting for the time of day—*buenos días, buenas tardes,* or *buenas noches*—and *adiós* upon leaving. If you speak any Spanish at all, it is important to use it, but be sure to use the formal pronoun, *usted,* in the beginning and do *not* switch to the *tu* (informal "you") form unless and until your Mexican colleague has specifically invited you to or does so him- or herself.

Spanish family names are often hyphenated, with the mother's family name added after the father's family name. In formal speech and in written correspondence, the fully hyphenated name is used; in face-to-face introductions, usually only the father's family name is used. For example, José Ramón Mendez-Rodriguez is Señor Mendez in face-to-face introductions, with Mendez being José's father's family name and Rodriguez being José's mother's family name. Women often keep their family name when they marry, but add their husband's father's family name with the preposition *de.* For example, Señora Maria Isabel Gonzalez-Sanchez de Rodriguez is married to Señor Rodriguez, her maiden name is Gonzalez (her father's family name), and she retains her mother's family name—Sanchez—as well; in face-to-face communication she is more often referred to as Señora de Rodriguez or, very informally, as Señora Rodriguez.

The What, When, and How of Introducing People

Always wait to be introduced to strangers before taking that responsibility upon yourself. Mexicans are most comfortable with a third-party introduction whenever possible (consider the importance of the *persona bien colocada:* the "well-connected person"). Try to ensure that for yourself ahead of time. You will be introduced to women first, then the most senior men. Do not presume to seat yourself at a formal gathering: if possible, wait to be told where to sit. Shake hands with everyone individually in a group when being introduced and before departing; the U.S. group wave is not appreciated. Avoid ending the conversation with the expression "Have a nice day"; it sounds controlling and insincere. Kissing is a common greeting once you have established a strong relationship, whether between women or men and women; it usually consists of a kiss on two cheeks (actually an "air kiss," first on the left side, and then the right; there can be three kisses between *señoritas,* twice as a greeting, and one more time as a wish for marriage). It is not uncommon to see men and men, and women and women, walking arm in arm down the street; they are good close friends or associates, and it usually means nothing more than that.

The use of business cards is common; if possible, you should have your business card translated into Spanish on the reverse. Be sure to put any advanced educational degrees and your full title or position on both sides of your business card. Such emblems of your status are very important to Mexicans; they want to know they are doing business with an important person.

Physical Greeting Styles

The handshake is common. The Mexican version is a brisk, firm snap: it is done once, quickly and firmly, between two men, but not as robustly between men and women or two women. The handshake should be accompanied by the appropriate greetings (see the list of terms outlined earlier). Smiling and other nonverbal forms of communication need not accompany the handshake when it is between people who have not met previously. Men should wait until a woman extends her hand before reaching for it, and women may take the lead in extending their hand or not. Men must remove their gloves when shaking with a woman, but a woman need not remove her gloves when shaking hands with a man. Between family, friends, or trusted business associates, an extra touch on the elbow or a hug (the *abrazo,* or embrace) will generally occur. This can happen even as soon as the second meeting; do not initiate it, but respond warmly in kind if it is initiated with you. Eye contact during the introduction is important, and should be maintained as long as the individual is addressing you.

Communication Styles

Okay Topics / Not Okay Topics

Okay: politics, current events, anything interesting (but never to the point of being controversial at first), the arts, sports (soccer and bullfighting are both very big), music, history, and philosophy. Be careful about initiating such discussions yourself, however, as the more important art is to discuss interesting things in a way that does not make the other person uncomfortable; a truly cultured person is someone who knows how to do this. Mexicans love to see you demonstrate knowledge of and interest in things Mexican, but you need to know what you are talking about (it seems arrogant and insulting otherwise). Mexicans will do everything possible to "educate" people from the United States about Mexican culture; be a student, go along with the effort, enjoy yourself, be appreciative and admiring, and take the opportunity as a way to build that all-important personal relationship, even when the conversation is about the strained Mexican-U.S. history (your Mexican colleague may not say what you want to hear). *Not okay:* Do not inquire about a person's occupation or income in casual conversation, although that may be inquired of you. Americans often begin a conversation with "So, what do you do?"; this is too personal in Mexico, and is often not the most interesting topic of conversation. Do not give your opinions about Mexican Indians, their treatment or status (while Mexicans are proud of their Indian cultural contribution, they do not like to self-associate themselves with indios—a derogatory term, while indígeno, referring to the culture, is not—since they represent the lower class in Mexico today), or regional or neighboring difficulties, such as Chiapas or Guatemala. Do not talk about drugs and Mexican immigrants, or "Montezuma's Revenge"; keep your health issues to yourself, because no one wants to hear about them. Also not okay: money and inquiring about private family matters (although speaking about the health and other general aspects of family life is very important). Do not go to Mexico (or Latin America) without pictures of your family, and when family is brought up (which it will be almost immediately in the conversation), use it as an opportunity to bring out the photographs. Try to avoid conversations about Mexican politics or the economic situation, and never tell a dirty joke with a woman present.

Tone, Volume, and Speed

Discussions between strangers usually start out politely restrained, but can quickly become animated and very lively, depending upon the nature of the discussion and the circumstances of the developing relationship. At meals, the wine, tequila, and beer flow, and conversation is an art; it is enjoyed, savored, and commented upon, but it never gets out of hand, and is always carried on respectfully. In business, speak softly and with restraint. It garners respect.

Use of Silence

There can be some silence, especially in formal situations, or when confrontation needs to be avoided. In general, it is not that common, except in group discussions where something has been said that can cause someone a public loss of face. Enjoy the simultaneous conversations and frequent interruptions that usually define Mexican conversation style.

Physical Gestures and Facial Expressions

The U.S. "okay" sign, made with the thumb and the forefinger, is considered vulgar and obscene by many: avoid it. In addition, winking and whistling—initiated by either a man or a woman and often accompanied by a positive comment—is meant to be a friendly introduction between men and women; it is known as the *piripo,* and is not an insult. If a woman is not interested, she merely need not acknowledge it. But, if a woman's eyes meet a man's eyes under these circumstances, it is an indication of interest. Never stand with your hands on your hips: it is aggressive (however, there is nothing defensive about folding the arms in front of you). Tapping the bottom of the elbow indicates that the person you are talking about is cheap or making a stingy offer.

Waving and Counting

The thumb represents the number 1, the index finger the number 2, and so on. It is insulting to beckon someone with the forefinger; instead, turn your hand so that the palm faces down and motion inward with all four fingers at once. If you need to gesture for a waiter, subtly raise your hand; never click, call, or whistle. Waving or beckoning is done with the palm down and the fingers moving forward and back in a kind of scratching motion.

Physicality and Physical Space

Mexicans tend to get closer than North Americans are generally comfortable with, but never extremely so. Do not step back when your Mexican associate steps forward. Mexican men may touch each other during conversations, adjust each other's ties, dust off each other's shoulders, and the like. Never speak with your hands in your pockets; always keep them firmly at your side when standing. If men and women must cross their legs, it must never be ankle over knee (the preferred style for women is to cross ankle over ankle). Remember, even in public, formal is always better than informal, until you are informed otherwise: no gum chewing, *ever;* no slouching; no leaning against things.

Eye Contact

Eye contact can be direct, and at times may be disconcerting for many Americans. It is important not to interpret this behavior as a way of intentionally trying to make you uncomfortable. It is the way Mexicans show their interest. Conversely, if you look away, your behavior will say to your Mexican colleague that you are disinterested, rude, or establishing yourself as the subordinate in a hierarchical relationship; none of these is a good idea. Maintain eye contact when it is made with you. If a stranger's eyes meet yours and linger, it can imply romantic interest. Act accordingly!

Emotive Orientation

Mexicans are often animated and physically expressive, but rarely overly passionate in their expression. Therefore, while expressive gesturing is common, until you know people well, you want to indicate restraint, while not seeming lifeless. There is an old Mexican expression that North Americans are like corpses: too rational, too distant. Join in if you like, but keep cool if you can. Mexicans will always admire you if you can remain logical, formal, respectful, and diplomatic—especially at first—while being warm, open, and personable.

Protocol in Public

Walking Styles and Waiting in Lines

It is more important in Mexico to maintain one's face by being first in line (and never last) than it is to maintain a queue. Don't be too distressed if someone walks right up to the front of the line at a bank, a restaurant, or a store, and gets served because of the relationship he or she has with the clerk, while you have been waiting patiently in line for forty minutes. This occurs also in response to rank based on gender and age. People also have a tendency to stand very close in public; this may feel uncomfortable at first. Resist the urge to back away; most of the time, you are not being intentionally crowded. Remember, the need to appear helpful and courteous is strong, and if you ask for directions on the street, you will no doubt be instructed on just where to go . . . whether or not the individual actually knows!

Behavior in Public Places: Airports, Terminals, and the Market

Customer service, as a concept, is catching on, but is not fully institutionalized. Store hours are typically not designed around customer convenience (many stores are closed on weekends, certainly Sundays, and most evenings—except Thursdays, usually), although there are many malls now in Mexico where stores stay open late. Personally thanking store owners, waiters, chefs, and hotel managers for their services is very much appreciated. In food markets, you can touch the produce; in goods stores, it may be difficult for you to return a product unless there is a flaw in it. Because it is a touching culture, when paying for something in a store, do not put the money on the counter; put it into the clerk's hands and they will do the same with your change. In most small shops and in markets, bargaining is very expected. If you don't bargain well, that's okay; put a smile on your face and ask for half of what the listed price is. Stick to it and walk away if you have to, and you'll land somewhere in between. Never get angry, though, since bargaining is a game to get to know you, and it is supposed to make shopping a more pleasant, personal experience.

Many indígenos and poorer people are reduced to begging in the cities, and small children and women may approach you on the street or come up to your taxi window to ask for money. It is always difficult deciding whether or not to give, but remember that the social support systems in Mexico are negligible, and begging is often the only way for these people to sustain themselves.

Smoking is on the decline, believe it or not, and there may be smokeless areas in public places in the major cities; if you do smoke, be sure to always offer a cigarette to everyone you are talking to before you light up. In bathrooms, on the plumbing "C" means hot (*caldo*) and "F" means cold (*frío*).

When answering a phone, use the phrase *digame* (speak to me), *por favor.* The use of cell phones is ubiquitous, and most pay phones—when they work— require a telecard (phone service can be intermittent and haphazard; it wasn't too many years ago that businesses would hire workers to do nothing but sit at a desk and redial a telephone number until the connection was made). Be sure to give both the paternal and maternal last name of the person you are looking for when calling directory assistance, as there are many people with the same last names.

Bus / Metro / Taxi / Car

Driving is on the right, but people pass very quickly on the left. Driving is difficult in the cities, and dangerous in the rural areas, and being a pedestrian is just as risky: both drivers and pedestrians really are very aggressive. Additionally, throughout Latin America, street rules are observed only sporadically (stoplights are viewed as suggestions) and drivers usually do not turn their lights on after dark (it is believed to blind the oncoming traffic), but may have them on during the day for extra safety. The metros shut down after midnight or 1 A.M. The best and safest way to catch a cab is at designated taxi stands (hotels are good places, but often charge more for the same ride: a hotel surcharge is added to the meter fare, in some cases). Bring food and water on board commuter trains if your trip is a long one, as there may not be a café car. The crime situation in Mexico ebbs and flows, and in some cities and on some intercity roads can be a considerable risk. Try to have a contact to keep you up-to-date about the crime situation, and if it sounds serious, it is. In such cases, maintaining security as a foreigner on the street is essential, and you must call a taxi only from the telephone or hotel, not from the street; additionally, try to avoid walking the street alone, especially at night.

Tipping

A 10 percent tip is usually sufficient in restaurants and taxis; more is considered nouveau and gauche. Porters and hotel help get the equivalent in pesos per item or service rendered, theater and bathroom attendants usually a few pesos (and in both cases, tipping in U.S. dollars, as is done throughout much of the region, is perfectly fine, actually preferred). Please double-check the current dollar/ peso exchange rate, as it can vary quickly and significantly. Restaurants usually have the 10 percent tip already included on the bill, but if you are unsure, it's okay to ask if service is included or not. Even if it is, it is still appropriate to leave a few pesos or odd change if service was particularly good.

Punctuality

It is perfectly acceptable—in fact, essential—to arrive at most social events about an hour late. If you arrive sooner, you will be running the risk of interrupting the host or hostess as he or she gets ready. For business meetings, even in Mexico City, being late by five to fifteen minutes or more is usually not a problem, but it is safer for the new employee or visitor to be on time, while not being surprised if others are not. Usually, the meeting will not begin in earnest until all attendees have arrived (or at least until all the decision makers have shown up), and this may not correspond to the time listed in the agenda. Resist questioning the late ones for a reason; they always have one, usually involving an obligation with more important people, like superiors, old friends, or family.

Dress

Until you know otherwise, and especially for business and most social situations between adults, dress is formal, no matter the occasion, at work, in the restaurant, or on the street, for men and women. Good taste is everything, and should be reflected in the clothes one wears. At work, men wear very stylish suits (dark is best), white shirts, and interesting and sophisticated ties; polished shoes are the order of the day, and accessories such as stylish watches, cuff links, and tie clips are common. Women usually accessorize so that even the simplest of outfits stands out for its interest and style. Mexican women may wear more makeup and jewelry than women in the United States, and it is fashionable, especially in summer, not to wear stockings.

On the street, informal may mean jeans and sneakers, though that is more common as clothing to wear at the gym or the beach, or while jogging (women do not wear sneakers to work); for a social gathering, informal more often than not means tastefully coordinated clothes, sometimes including a jacket and tie for men (it rarely means jeans, sneakers, and T-shirts). "Formal" usually means formal evening wear, very dressy by U.S. standards.

Seasonal Variations

It is cooler in the north, and hotter in the south; additionally, the evenings in Mexico, especially in the high central plateau, can be quite cool, so a wrap (consider the historical popularity of the Mexican serape), jacket, or sweater is advised. Mexico City is built in the caldera of an ancient volcano (which, in fact, rumbles from time to time), so the altitude is quite high, and the rim of the caldera traps much of the air pollution; the combination of smog (especially in winter) and altitude can be challenging, so take your time to adjust (no jogging around Chapultepec park . . . really!).

Colors

Bright colors are best reserved for accessories, as offsets to the more sophisticated dark or soft hues and beiges of the outfits themselves.

Styles

Fashion for both men and women, as in many other aspects of life in Mexico, looks to Europe and not to the United States, although few people on the street can actually afford the latest trends. Nevertheless, even the average person has a heightened sense of fashion, and one should dress with the same thought and care that one should put into every aspect of his or her life. Mexicans can combine colors, weaves, textures, and designs, often based on indigenous Indian designs. Both men's and women's shoes can be remarkably stylish. Sometimes Mexican businessmen may wear the Latin American *guayabera,* or formally designed open-collar shirt (it is generally worn outside of the pants, usually without a jacket): although it may appear informal, it definitely is not, and is not an invitation for the non-Mexican to wear a dress shirt without a tie or jacket.

Accessories / Jewelry / Makeup

The right makeup, hairstyle, and accessories are very important for women. Men also accessorize.

Personal Hygiene

In Mexico, personal hygiene is very important. There is a real concern for cleanliness and smelling good; perfumes and colognes are used often. Latin men may sport facial hair, in the form of mustaches. Please note that most rest room and bathroom facilities throughout Latin America do not have plumbing capable of handling paper toilet tissue; it is for this reason that there is a small receptacle next to the toilet for your used tissue: do not flush it down the bowl, but place it in the receptacle, or else you'll face the embarrassment of having to call for help when the bowl overflows.

Dining and Drinking

Mealtimes and Typical Foods

Breakfast (*el desayuno,* or *el almuerzo*) is served from about 7:30 to 9 A.M., and usually consists of the coffee, rolls, butter, and marmalade typical of the quick continental breakfast; sometimes tortillas are served with breakfast. Coffee in the morning can be strong and black, or with hot milk (*café con leche*).

Lunch (*el almuerzo,* or *la comida*) was traditionally the main meal of the day; even today, in busy cities, it can be an elaborate affair lasting several hours (usually an important business lunch)—or it can be a quick sandwich or a salad at a shop on the corner. Because of the altitude of Mexico City, it is wise to eat lightly if you can, although lunch is often the heaviest meal. Lunch is served from 2 to 3:30 P.M. (or beyond). It usually consists of at least three courses, beginning with soup, going on to meat or fish and rice and beans, plus a dessert (usually flan). Even the quick business lunch often will include a main course and a dessert and coffee. On Sunday, the family day, the main meal is supper, which is usually served at lunchtime and can last well into the evening.

If lunch was light, a *merienda,* or snack, is taken around 5 P.M.: this is usually some pastries and coffee.

Dinner (*la cena*) is served from 8:30 P.M. on, with 8 to 9 P.M. the customary time. In major cities, dinner may not start until 9 P.M. or later, even during the week, and on weekends can last till midnight or beyond. If the main meal of the day was lunch, then dinner is light, and this is often the case with families at home; it usually consists of soup, some wraps (like tamales or burritos), cheese, and vegetables, plus dessert. Drinks served with dinner are usually wines—most often imported from either Spain or Argentina/Chile—or beers. Dinner parties tend to end around midnight (but can go much later if all are having a good time).

In addition to restaurants, there are cantinas, which serve mainly drinks and snacks (cantinas are really only for men), and *pastelerías,* where coffee, tea, and pastries are served. Be very careful about the places you go to eat: if they don't look safe or clean, you should avoid them. Do *not* eat food off the street from the street stalls: this can be very dangerous to your health. Be very careful about food and drink in Mexico (and throughout Latin America); there are dangerous bugs around. First, the water: Do not drink tap water anywhere in Mexico (except where *officially* noted as safe, sterilized, or "electrified," as in the resort hotels of Cancún, for example). This means no ice in any drinks (ice cubes may be made from tap water); ask for drinks *sin hielo* (without ice) when ordering. Close your mouth in the shower in the morning, and brush your teeth with bottled water. Drink only bottled water and soft drinks from bottles with intact seals opened in front of you; the fruit juices in Mexico are wonderful, but until your digestive system has adjusted, avoid them: they may have been diluted with water from the tap. Coffee and tea are generally okay, because the water is boiled first. Avoid fresh dairy products, including milk, custards, mayonnaise, and ice cream, because they all usually require refrigeration, which may be questionable in certain parts of Mexico. Definitely avoid raw shellfish and fish (this makes the wonderful ceviche—raw marinated fish salad, one of Mexico's great appetizer delicacies—off-limits, unless you know about its preparation), and do not eat any raw or uncooked vegetables or fruits, unless you can peel them; this means no green salad. On your first few trips to Mexico, you will inevitably get the Mexican tummy . . . it is hard to avoid a drop of water here or there. If you have followed the above rules carefully, it is probably nothing to worry about; it will be uncomfortable for a day or two. Eat lightly, drink lots of safe fluids, stay in or near your room, rest, and it will pass. If a fever or vomiting develops, be sure to seek medical attention immediately.

Regional Differences

Tortillas, or ground baked meal in the form of a round flat pancake, accompany most meals, and serve as the bread. They are really "the spoon you can eat," since you use them to scoop up food and then eat the whole thing. Tortillas are typically yellowish in color (made of corn) but may be white (made of wheat) in the north. They are generally served wrapped in a hot cloth in a small round container with a lid to keep the heat in, and often, each person gets his or her own container of tortillas. Take one out of the cloth, refold the cloth to keep the others below warm, and put the lid back on the container. Tortillas may be topped off and filled with any kind of stuffing, and eaten as a wrap. Plain tortillas help cool down the mouth if you've eaten one too many hot peppers (whatever you do, don't drink beer or water to quench the sting: it only spreads the pain). Mexican cuisine is anything but the sad fast-food Tex-Mex most people in the United States are familiar with: it is a complex and rich cuisine, with variations reflecting the traditions of each individual section of the country. Keep in mind that many foods are wrapped in corn husks (tamales), plantain skins, and other coverings: remember, you eat what's inside, you do not eat the coverings (just peel them away and put them to the side of your plate).

Typical Drinks and Toasting

A drink of mescal will probably be offered to you after a meal as a grappa, or brandy: it is a clear tequila-like liquor made from the Maguey plant. Tequila is a similar liquor made from a different cactus (mescal is the bottle with the worm at the bottom, and the person who gets the last drink out of the bottle is often obliged to also eat the worm!), and *pulque* is a very unrefined, raw form of mescal that must be drunk within a few hours of distillation. To drink tequila properly, you will be served a small plate of salt and a wedge of fresh lime. First, take a pinch of salt with your right hand and put it in the hollow formed in your left hand when you hold your left-hand thumb and crooked index finger together horizontally. Raise your left hand to your lips and lick the salt out of the hollow with one swipe of your tongue. Drink the entire shot of tequila at once. Immediately bite into the lime wedge and suck on the juice. (The lime actually sweetens the flavor in your mouth.) Tequila is ranked according to age, and has degrees of quality, like fine brandy. Occasionally, tequila is served with a *sangrita* chaser: a small shot of tomato juice—sometimes prepared with herbs, salt, and pepper—that you drink right after you drink the tequila. Once the Mexican meal gets under way, tequila or beer will be the drink in most cases. Beer bottles with an indentation on the bottom serve as a bottle opener for the next bottle. Beer comes *clara* (light), *oscura* (dark), or *de barril* (draft). The most common toast is *salud* (to your health).

Table Manners and the Use of Utensils

Do not begin eating until the host says, *"¡Buen provecho!"* Referring to European traditions as they do, Mexicans do not switch knives and forks, as people do in the United States. The knife remains in the right hand, and the fork remains in the left. When the meal is finished, the knife and fork are laid parallel to each other across the right side of the plate. If you put both utensils down on the plate for any real length of time, it is a sign to the waitstaff that you are finished, and your plate may be taken away from you. Alternately, if you lay your cutlery down on either side of the plate it generally means you haven't finished; but if you really are, the host might interpret this as a sign that you were not happy with the meal.

The fork and spoon above your plate are for dessert. There are often many additional pieces of cutlery at a formal meal; if you're unsure of which utensil to use, always start from the outside and work your way in, course by course. Bread, if replacing tortillas (rarely will there be bread and tortillas), is sometimes served without butter; in that case, there usually will not be a butter knife, nor will there be a bread dish: bread is placed on the rim of your main plate or on the table by your plate. There will be separate glasses provided at your setting for water, and white and red wine or beer (after-dinner drink glasses come out after dinner).

When not holding utensils, your hands are expected to be visible above the table: this means you do not keep them in your lap; instead, rest your wrists on top of the table (never your elbows). At the table, pass all dishes to your left. Never cut the lettuce in a salad: deftly fold it with your knife and fork into a little bundle that can be easily picked up with your fork.

As on the Continent, any salad will usually be served after the main course; most formal meals begin with a soup (tortilla soup, a clear soup with strips of tortilla in it, is a national favorite), and move on to either an appetizer (such as ceviche, guacamole—the dip made with mashed avocados, lime, and spices), or a *sopa seca,* or "dry soup," which is really a pasta with a sauce. This precedes the main course, typically meat or fish, and all meals end with a dessert of wonderfully sweet custard (flan) or other sweet puddings or pastries (sometimes white cheese with guava paste is served as dessert; the combination of tart and sweet is compelling). One of the great national dishes of Mexico is mole, which is a complicated sauce (including, among other ingredients, chocolate), over meat, usually chicken or turkey. Rice is a universal staple throughout the country. Along the coast there is wonderful fresh seafood prepared in a variety of ways. Cactus (*nopal*) is often an ingredient in salads, and plantains and their leaves are used for both food and stuffing.

Seating Plans

The most honored position is at the head of the table, with the most important guest seated immediately to the right of the host (women to the right of the host, and men to the right of the hostess). If there is a hosting couple, one will be at each end of the table. In the European tradition, men and women are seated next to one another, and couples are often broken up and seated next to people they may not have previously known. This is done to promote conversation. Men typically rise when women enter the room, and continue to hold doors for women and allow them to enter a room first. Remember, as is the case throughout the Continent, the first floor in Mexico (*PB,* or *planta baja*) is really the second floor, with the first floor usually referred to as the lobby or ground floor.

Refills and Seconds

If you do not want more food, or cannot eat everything on your plate, don't worry; it is perfectly okay to leave some food on your plate in Mexico. You may always have additional beverages; drink enough to cause your cup or glass to be less than half full, and it will generally be refilled. Portions are generally equal to or greater than those in the United States, and there are usually more courses, for both lunch and dinner.

At Home, in a Restaurant, or at Work

In informal restaurants, you rarely will be required to share a table. Waitstaff may be summoned by making eye contact; waving or calling their names is very impolite (although you might see some Mexicans make a kind of *pssst* sound; don't do it). The business breakfast is not common in Mexico, although you do see it creeping into the business life of the major cities slowly. The business lunch (more common than dinner) and dinner are very acceptable, but, depending upon how well developed your relationship with your Mexican colleagues, they are generally not times to make business decisions. Take your cue from your Mexican associates: if they bring up business, then it's okay to discuss it (more often than not, over the coffee and brandy at the end of the meal), but wait to take your lead from their conversation. No gum chewing, *ever,* at a restaurant or on the street. No-smoking sections in restaurants are still a rarity.

When you arrive at a Mexican associate's home for a formal meal, you will be told where to sit, and there you should remain. Do not wander from room to room; much of the house is really off-limits to guests. Use the toilet before you arrive, as it is considered bad form to leave the dinner party, or the table, at any time. Once you (and the group) are invited to another room, most probably the dining room, be sure to allow more senior members of your party to enter the room ahead of you: men should move aside to allow women to enter the room ahead of them. Often drinks and hors d'oeuvres are served in the living room prior to the dinner. In a private home, be careful about what and how you admire things: The host may feel obliged to give it to you! Once at the table, be sure to look for place cards, or wait until the host indicates your seat: do not presume to seat yourself, as the seating arrangement is usually predetermined.

If you invite people to your home, be prepared to always have the invitation accepted, although they may not, in fact, show up; rejecting the invitation is difficult for Mexicans, who seek to not offend. They may indicate their true intentions by simply responding to your invitation with "I will try."

Being a Good Guest or Host

Paying the Bill

Usually the one who does the inviting pays the bill, although the guest is expected to make an effort to pay. Sometimes other circumstances determine who pays (such as rank). Making payment arrangements ahead of time so that no exchange occurs at the table is a very classy way to host. Women, if out with men, will not really be able to pay the bill at a restaurant: if you want to, make arrangements ahead of time, and don't wait for the check to arrive at the table. The only time it is considered appropriate for a woman to pay the bill is if she is a hosting businesswoman from abroad. If a businesswoman invites a Mexican businessman to a meal, she should be sure to extend the invitation to his spouse as well, or may want to consider telling him that her (female) colleague will also be joining them (and be sure to have a female colleague along). Do not allow the Mexican male to suggest bringing one of his colleagues along (remember, the person doing the inviting can refuse the suggestion). If a Mexican male invites a businesswoman to a meeting or a meal that seems to have more than business as the subject, a businesswoman should always insist that she bring her female associate along (someone who is needed because of her role in the company); if you are a businesswoman making your first business trip to Mexico and have not yet established a relationship with your Mexican male counterparts, you are strongly advised to bring a female business associate along on the trip. Unmarried businesswomen may want to consider wearing a wedding band. If you have children, be sure to discuss that fact at some point early in the initial conversations: aggressive macho behavior usually stops when men learn they are dealing with a *madre*.

Transportation

It's a very nice idea, when acting as the host, to inquire ahead of time as to whether your guests will require transportation. If necessary, you should arrange for taxi service at the end of the meal. When the cars arrive, be sure not to leave your spot until your guests are out of sight.

When to Arrive / Chores to Do

If invited to dinner at a private home, do not offer to help with the chores, nor should you expect to visit the kitchen. Middle- and upper-class Mexicans often have household help for the kitchen chores. Do not leave the table unless invited to do so. Spouses do not attend business dinners without a special invitation to do so. Being invited to a dinner party in Mexico is a special honor, and not often extended to new relationships. If such an invitation is offered, accept it as an opportunity to build a new and close relationship: that is what your Mexican associate is looking for. Reciprocate by hosting your colleague in your home when and if he or she comes to your country or at a fine restaurant on another night of your trip.

Gift Giving

In general, gift giving is not common among business associates, although it is nice to bring a small gift from abroad if you are revisiting a business acquaintance (as, at this point, they have probably become a friend). One exception: as is the case throughout most of Latin America, some chocolates or a small gift for the secretary of the person you are visiting can work wonders for future smooth sailing! In this case, always give your business contact his or her gift in a social setting, never in the office. If a man is giving a gift to a woman in a business setting, it is important to present it as a gift to her from his wife or sister. Holiday cards are very appropriate, particularly as a thank-you for your Mexican colleague's business in the previous year, and should be mailed in time to be received the week before Christmas. Mexicans celebrate Three Kings Day (as all Latin American cultures do), January 6, as the time for holiday gift giving.

Gifts are expected for social events, especially as thank-yous for private dinner parties. The best gift in this case is expensive flowers—and be sure to have them sent ahead of time on the day of the dinner (simple floral arrangements are not appreciated). Never send chrysanthemums or yellow-colored flowers (they are used primarily as funeral flowers), red roses (these usually indicate romantic intent; traditionally, it was believed that red flowers can cast a romantic spell!), or white flowers (they are used to remove spells!), and always be sure the bouquet is in odd numbers (an old European tradition). If you must bring flowers with you to the dinner party, unwrap them before presenting them to your hostess. Other good gifts would be chocolates or a good bottle of European (not Californian) wine (do not bring tequila or mescal, no matter how fine). In addition to the gift (and certainly if you did not send or bring one), be sure to send a handwritten thank-you note on a card the very next day after the dinner party; it is best if it is sent by messenger and not mailed.

If you are staying with a Mexican family, an appropriate thank-you gift would be a high-quality item that represents your country and is difficult to get in Mexico, but that is not representative of the United States in general (Mexicans know a lot about the United States already; it's people from the United States who don't know much about Mexico, usually): small U.S.-made electronic gadgets, a set of American bath towels (always a good gift almost everywhere, since they are usually more luxurious), or anything that reflects your host's personal tastes is appropriate. Do not give Mexican silver as a gift. As in other European cultures, gifts are generally opened at the time they are given and received.

Special Holidays and Celebrations

Major Holidays

Most Mexican workers get two weeks paid vacation; August is a popular vacation time. Business slows down from December 15 to January 6, and Holy Week is sometimes a more difficult time in which to accomplish work than Christmas. Office Christmas parties (*posadas*) are very common. In addition, there are many regional fiestas and saints' days throughout the year that usually close down businesses for a day or two; check with your local contacts. As you establish personal relationships with your Mexican colleagues, you may be invited to special family events, such as a wedding, a baptism, or a *quinceañera* (a celebration of a girl's fifteenth birthday, equivalent to the American "sweet sixteen" or a debutante's coming out); be sure to go, and bring an appropriate gift for the girl (money is not appropriate).

January 1	*Año Nuevo* (New Year's Day)
January 6	*Día de los Reyes* (Three Kings Day; this is the gift-giving day, not Christmas)
January 17	Saint Anthony's Day (a favorite saint in Mexico)
February/March	*Carnaval* (pre-Lenten celebration)
March 21	Benito Juarez's Birthday (Benito Juarez was a very popular leader)
March/April	*Semana Santa/Pasqua* (Holy Week and Easter)
May 1	*Día del Trabajo* (Labor Day)
May 5	*Cinco de Mayo* (celebrates the ousting of Maximillian and the French from Mexico; this is not a major holiday in Mexico, and does not celebrate Mexican independence, from either the United States or Spain)
June	Corpus Christi
August 15	*Asuncíon* (Assumption)
September 16	Independence Day
October 12	*Día de la Raza* (Columbus Day in the United States)
November 1–2	*Día de los Santos* (or *Muertos*) (All Saints' Day; a very popular holiday in Mexico where skeletons are paraded, and families go to the gravesites of relatives to make offerings, say prayers, and play music)
November 20	Revolution Day
December 12	Day of the Virgin of Guadalupe (a very important holiday, as the Virgin Mary is said to have made herself visible to a poor peasant farmer in the small town of Guadalupe, and began the Catholicization of Mexico)
December 16	Christmas celebrations usually begin
December 25	*Navidad* (Christmas Day)

Business Culture

Daily Office Protocols

In Mexico, doors are usually closed; knock first (this includes bathrooms) before opening doors, and when leaving a room, close the door behind you. It is not common for women to attain positions of authority in Mexico; in the traditional Mexican workplace, women are usually relegated to lower-level management and administrative support positions. Women do struggle to reach the same levels of achievement as their male counterparts in Mexican business, and it is rare (though not impossible) to see women at the highest levels of business and government in Mexico. People organize their time on a daily basis according to the tasks they must accomplish, and the relationships they must depend upon in order to accomplish these tasks; the clock takes a backseat. Therefore, the day may begin slowly, but there can be much activity by day's end, and people often stay late in the office in order to finish up what needs to be done. This pattern repeats itself over larger blocks of time in regard to the accomplishment of projects and the meeting of deadlines.

Management Styles

Privacy and individual accomplishment of one's tasks are critical; workers provide what their bosses expect of them, and the preparation of plans, methods, and reports can be time-consuming and complicated efforts. Gathering the information required in order to do what your boss expects from you, or creating consensus among your colleagues in order to accomplish a particular goal, can take a long time. All of this occurs in a formal and sometimes very rigid hierarchical structure, which means that deadlines and efficiency are secondary to attention to detail, perfection of form, bureaucratic requirements, and the need to be clever in the face of limited resources in order to be effective. Because of this rigid rank and hierarchy orientation, titles in Mexico are very important; the highest ones (e.g., vice president) are usually reserved for very senior, executive-level positions, and should not be used as casually as they are in the United States. Complimenting and rewarding employees publicly are usually not done. For non-Mexicans, it is essential to try to have a local contact who can tell you what is really going on after you return home, and to have a local intermediary—as well as a local lawyer and *notario* (a very responsible administrative position throughout much of Latin America)—to act as a liaison for you with the people you need to see while you are there. This needs to be set up ahead of time.

Boss-Subordinate Relations

Rank most definitely has its privileges in Mexico. Pride and self-importance require that Mexicans always do business with the most important people in any organization (and this should be the same for the non-Mexican working with them). There is a rigid chain of command that must be heeded. No matter what field you are in, there is a proper way for communicating with particular individuals, and an established procedure one is expected to follow. Deviating from the normal channels will generally make more problems for you, even if the intent is to bypass what appear to be difficulties or obstacles. Bosses are expected to provide guidance, distribute information, and make decisions; subordinates are expected to provide detailed information and follow the decisions made by the superiors.

Conducting a Meeting or Presentation

At meetings of peers, there can be open communication and sharing of ideas; in fact, these sessions often serve as information-sharing and decision-making forums in which all individuals are expected to contribute. Under these circumstances, discussions are usually vibrant, with many people speaking at once; questions are common and interruptions, even of presentations, should be expected. In more formal, conservative organizations, meetings are often gatherings of nonpeers, clearly called together by decision makers in order to gather information from below, clarify goals, and formulate action plans. In these cases, individuals often do not share ideas and are not expected to contribute to mutual problem solving. Remember, because a close personal relationship is often demonstrated through physicality in Latin cultures, the nearer your Mexican colleagues are to you, typically, the better they are responding to your proposal.

Negotiation Styles

Mexicans generally play their cards close to the vest; they do not divulge information easily (it is seen as the source of power). They are usually circumspect in their communication styles, and will indicate their thoughts in indirect ways, at least at first. They will respect someone who comes to them with already established knowledge and experience, and will build relationships based on your level in society and the organization. Whether you are worth knowing and doing business with may be more important than the details of your proposal, and the relationship may, in fact, sustain you, despite occasionally more attractive terms from other competitors. Nevertheless, details are important, and a carefully planned, logically organized, and beautifully presented proposal (including good-looking charts, graphs, and hand-outs) is key. Bargaining is the essence of the negotiation, as a way to build trust; be reasonable, but do not overcompromise, as this shows weakness.

The first meeting is usually formal, with the Mexicans sizing up you and your organization: it will be conducted in the office. Take copious notes afterward, but put on a warm, dignified demeanor during the meeting. Never be condescending. Expect to go out to a restaurant for lunch or dinner as a possible first meeting.

Although the contract must be legal down to the dotted i's, it really is just a legal formality to the Mexicans and can be overcome, by either party, if such a need arises later on. Plan your meetings as carefully and as well in advance as you can, but expect changes. The goal, at least for the first meeting, is the development of a good feeling of respect and mutual trust (simpatico). Remember also that the meeting might start and end much later than you anticipated; nevertheless, as in most polychronic cultures, you should always arrive on time. Coffee is the universal greeting; always accept it, always serve it (in nice china, never in Styrofoam), and drink as much or as little as you can or desire. It is the gesture of acceptance and appreciation that counts (never refuse coffee, or an invitation to go with your colleague to a café and have some). As you should throughout most of Latin America, if you are hosting at a restaurant, choose the finest restaurant you can, at least for the first (and last) meeting; by the same token, stay at the best hotel you can. These things carry prestige and will signal that you are someone worth doing business with.

Written Correspondence

Business letters should be very formal and respectful of hierarchy. Last names are usually written in uppercase; dates are given using the day/month/year format (typically with periods in between, not slashes); and an honorific plus a title is as common as an honorific plus the last name. The time of day is written in military time; weights and measures are given in metric measurements. Monetary amounts are written so that the period breaks up the figure into tens, hundreds, and thousands, and a comma separates pesos from centavos.

The traditional language used in openings and closings is convoluted and formal, and you should write your e-mails, letters, and faxes using a precise formula. Be sure to inquire first, in all communications, about your colleague's health and progress, then move on to the substance of your communication, and close with a salutation and your personal wish for his or her success and well-being (the Latin communication "sandwich"). Some important business abbreviations: "S.A." means "incorporated," a *cia* is a company, and EE.UU. is the abbreviation for the United States. If your colleagues write to you in Spanish, try to respond in Spanish, if you can, or use the services of a translator. Written addresses are usually in the following format:

Line 1: name
Line 2: title/position
Line 3: company
Line 4: street address
Line 5: city, state

The Northern Centroamerican Cultures: Guatemala, Belize, Honduras, and El Salvador

Note: Refer to the preceding chapter on Mexico for information about general Latin American cultural behaviors; the material that follows describes country-specific Centroamerican variations on general Latin American customs.

Some Introductory Background on Centroamerica and the Centroamericans

Centroamerica is a politically, economically, and culturally very unstable zone in Latin America, making traveling, living, or working there alternately challenging, fascinating, frustrating, and enlightening. Although much of Latin America shares these characteristics, what makes Centroamerica remarkable is that in a sense, the difficult history of the larger region has concentrated itself into this crucible of seven small countries that geographically connects North and South America, vividly revealing the larger issues that have challenged and continue to challenge most of Latin America. The region's topography is a metaphor for its cultural, political, and economic condition: a rugged, sometimes impassable tropical landscape, with a climate that periodically unleashes hurricanes and floods, the weather and terrain served to keep both the original indigenous peoples of the region and the modern cultures separated, fractured, and warring with one another over the centuries. In the post-conquest period, Catholicism, rigid oligarchies, and pressure and intervention from the United States only exacerbated the difficulties in the region. Each country has its own issues and difficulties with its own people, its neighbors, and the United States (for example, discuss politics of the region, or the role of the United States in Centroamerica, very carefully, as it is regarded by many in the region as highly exploitative and interventionist), which, despite the similarities between the countries, prove in most cases to be difficult and unyielding.

GUATEMALA

Some Historical Context

While Mexico had the Aztecs, and the area of what is currently referred to as Peru today had the Incas, Guatemala had the Mayans. As the center of one of the Americas' three great pre-Columbian civilizations, Guatemala, like Mexico and Peru, and unlike much of the rest of Latin America, has retained much of its indigenous heritage. In fact, there is perhaps no other country in Latin America that is still so powerfully influenced culturally by its original indigenous culture than Guatemala (even its name, a loose translation of "the land of the greater Maya," reflects this). Unlike its neighbor Mexico, however, for a variety of reasons unique to Guatemala, the influence of its indigenous peoples, the Mayans, is highly stratified, and does not permeate consistently throughout the society as a whole. When the Spanish conquered Guatemala in the sixteenth century, they imposed a rigid authority from above, wielded by a powerful few, keeping themselves and the majority of the rest of the country quite separate. This rigid political and economic stratification has been the source of many of Guatemala's difficulties over the years, most recently expressed in a terrible civil war that lasted almost two decades at the end of the twentieth century. And, as is the case with much of the rest of the region, the problems of such social stratification have mainly taken the form of frustration over political disenfranchisement and economic inequalities. The ruling elite today is still mainly non-Mayan (the descendants of the Europeans), remnants of the oligarchies that developed as a result of the parceling out of the land by the ruling Spanish after the conquest to a handful of Spanish owners (in Mexico, for example, these vast tracts of land were known as *latifundia*). Political issues usually reflect economic issues: the inability of most of the people (in Guatemala's case, mainly Mayan) to be democratically represented in the decisions of the country that affect them, and the failure of the society to provide economic opportunity to the vast majority of the people. Always reflecting the issues of the larger region, in Guatemala too, the theme of economic reform has usually been defined as a struggle between landowners and peasants, with peasants demanding land reform and a redistribution of the wealth as the path to economic justice and landowners resisting. Political groups line up accordingly, and external groups such as the church, the militia, neighboring countries (including the United States), with their own interests to consider, also throw in their support, either overtly or covertly, behind one side or the other. The result, for many of the countries in the region, Guatemala being no exception, has often been a cycle of struggle, coups, corruption, and in some cases, violent civil war.

An Area Briefing

Politics and Government

Guatemala has had border difficulties with its neighbors, Mexico, Belize, and Honduras. When Guatemala first declared its independence from Spain, it became part of Mexico and did not secure its further independence from Mexico without struggle (it went on to become part of the Federation of United Provinces of Centroamerica, a union of the north central American states that declared themselves independent from Spain in the early 1800s; the United Provinces, however, quickly fell apart in the 1830s as disputes and dissention among the participating states prevented unity); even today, there is a border dispute with Mexico that simmers under the surface and erupts from time to time. Additionally, Guatemala has yet to formally acknowledge Belize, a neighbor with whom it has had occasional border skirmishes in the past. The government today is technically under civilian rule, although in the past the military and individual dictators have ruled the country, and terrorists and the militia still pose a strong threat to the establishment of real democracy in the country.

Schools and Education

Schooling is compulsory through the beginning grades of high school; however, in poorer rural regions and in difficult urban neighborhoods, maintaining quality education and children's attendance through these grades is a challenge. Many children are pressed into working to help the family survive in place of attending school. The wealthy send their children to private schools, including universities in Europe and the United States.

Religion and Demographics

Today, Guatemala is the most populous country in Centroamerica. While almost 90 percent of the population is indigenous (about 45 percent is pure indígena—primarily but not solely Mayan—and another 45 percent is mestizo, or mixed European and indígena), and Mayan culture defines almost every aspect of daily life for most of the people in the country, the small ruling elite is still mainly of European origin, and still a separated class. About 5 percent of the people are Asian and African (African populations, manifested in the Garifuna culture, can be found primarily along the entire Caribbean coast of Centroamerica, the result of the slave trade to the Caribbean; for more information about this, please see the section in this book on the Caribbean). The majority of the people speak Mayan, maintain Mayan traditions, and remain even today disenfranchised as the lower class from the political, economic, and cultural elite of the country. Mayan Indians have primarily been converted to Catholicism, resulting in a religion that combines many indigenous and Catholic beliefs. The adoption of Catholicism by the indigenous population also resulted in a rejection of Catholicism by the ruling elite in favor of a form of evangelical Protestantism (usually associated with a church in the United States, and viewed by many Catholics—who have become associated with social change—as just another form of United States colonialism). A small but significant element of the elite are South Koreans (and, to a lesser degree, other Asians): they run many manufacturing plants (*maquilladora*) in the country, and have retained their own cultural traditions strongly.

Fundamental Cultural Orientations

1. What's the Best Way for People to Relate to One Another?

OTHER-INDEPENDENT OR OTHER-DEPENDENT?   As is the case with most countries in the region, Guatemalan behavior can be viewed as significantly "other-dependent." Most individuals will seek, either formally or informally, the opinions and support of family, friends, and coworkers before venturing off to do or say something on their own, and this is especially the case with the indí-gena culture. People are most comfortable in the "bosom" of others, and individuals are simply not part of society unless they can claim membership to or affiliation with some group, neighborhood, town, or business organization. A consequence of this, of course, is a resistance to the outsider, and a need for all outsiders to become associated with members of the in-group as soon as possible in order to be accepted. Again, this is significantly more apparent between the indigenous groups and visitors. This is often demonstrated through the need to build strong and enduring personal relationships. There is an old Spanish saying that children live at home until they are old enough to have their parents live in their home with them. To be alone in Guatemala is to live a dangerous and difficult life. Causing someone to lose face, or experience embarrassment, public ridicule, or criticism of any kind is a great insult in this other-dependent culture; here, how one is thought of by others is one of the most important concerns in life.

HIERARCHY-ORIENTED OR EGALITY-ORIENTED? The Guatemalan workplace is rigidly layered, with the individual at the top (*el patrón*—"the boss") having supreme decision-making authority (but only in a way that honors his role as leader in the group) and the support staff being required to follow step, challenge as little as possible, and solve all problems before they surface at the top. In civic life, this means that government, which is supposed to be democratic, often fails to be, and there is deep resentment between the classes. Women and men are rigidly separated in their social roles, as is the case more or less throughout much of Latin America, which is a very macho culture; women traditionally play the nurturing role in society, while men play the public leaders, in government and business. Wealth and power is demonstrated through conspicuous display of wealth, and the avoidance of work that should be performed by those of the lower classes.

RULE-ORIENTED OR RELATIONSHIP-ORIENTED? Because of the rigid stratification of society, the behaviors of one class can be quite different from those of another, and although rules are supposed to be applied universally, there is no doubt in Guatemala that individuals in different classes are treated differently. (Most behaviors referred to in this chapter on Guatemala, in fact, refer mostly to the nonindigenous classes, as interaction between *indígenas* and outsiders is often limited.) Therefore, relationships—not rules—rule. Situations, if involving the right people and the right issues, will almost always determine the behaviors of individuals, not bland laws or bureaucratic fiats. For non-Guatemalans, this means that your Guatemalan counterparts need time to get to know you before they will be ready to talk business. Attempts to discuss the terms of the deal or the immediate task at hand without having built the necessary personal trust and understanding is often a waste of time. Which takes us to our next concern.

2. What's the Best Way to View Time?

MONOCHRONIC OR POLYCHRONIC? Outside of the major cities, time is circular, and very polychronic; it is more monochronic in Guatemala City, and among the Asian-run *maquilladoras,* but even there, old agrarian patterns die hard, even if people aren't waking up and heading for the fields in the morning. Work begins early, around 8 A.M.; lunch occurs around noon and can last till 2 P.M. and work resumes at 2 P.M. and can last till 5 or 6 P.M., but the pace is often relaxed. Dinner is usually around 7 or 8 P.M. If you really want things to occur punctually, it is perfectly okay to identify the time as *a la gringa* or *Norteamericano,* as opposed to Guatemalan time.

RISK-TAKING OR RISK-AVERSE?   Latin cultures, in general, are risk-averse, and that is one of the driving reasons for the creation of structure and hierarchies. Guatemala is even more so. Decision making can be slow and tedious, even if the decision is being made by a single, powerful leader at the top. Oftentimes, risk-taking, if it turns out wrong, results in a mistake that can have unredeemable consequences for the individuals involved. Even when individuals are empowered to make the decision, there can be a reticence to take the required final step, and this is often demonstrated through impressive discussion and assurances but indeterminate action.

PAST-ORIENTED OR FUTURE-ORIENTED?   Latin American cultures, including Guatemala, have seen their world turned upside down more than once with their having little or no ability to control the events. Guatemalans, therefore, look back to their roots for stability, and are generally wary about the ultimate outcome of things, although the ruling business elite will be quick to assure you of their ability to move forward. Motivating or even basically communicating with the indígena groups will be extremely difficult (language itself can be a significant barrier, as most do not speak Spanish or English).

3. What's the Best Way for Society to Work with the World at Large?

LOW-CONTEXT DIRECT OR HIGH-CONTEXT INDIRECT COMMUNICATORS? Most Guatemalans are high-context communicators; depending upon the rank and status of those present, and the situation, Guatemalans will be extremely careful about what they say and how they say it. The importance of hierarchy and other-dependency, the distrust between the classes, and the instability of the social system require careful speech; in any but the most private moments with trusted family and friends, speaking one's mind is done carefully—especially at work. Guatemalans, like most Latinos, want smooth interpersonal working relationships, especially with outsiders, and will go the distance to reassure you that everything is okay and that all is in order—even when it may not be. This is not based on a desire to deceive but rather on a need to appear capable, and not to lose face in the eyes of people from cultures with great resources. It is critical, therefore, to always confirm information; to have multiple, independent, and reliable sources to verify or interpret what you are being told; and to be able to read between the lines. There is a strong tolerance for, in fact dependence on, the subjective interpretation of events and reality. This tendency also makes for complimentary and respectful introductory conversation, and an avoidance of anything that may strike you as unpleasant; at first, Guatemalans will most always try to say what they think you want to hear.

PROCESS-ORIENTED OR RESULT-ORIENTED? Most Guatemalans process information subjectively, and will often fall back on what they personally believe in order to make or justify a decision. Their experience with similar past situations will often guide their present decision making more powerfully than any evidence or argument you present. Guatemalans may not be able to follow through easily with the actions necessary to put plans in place, yet they will be reticent to admit this or inform you when problems develop. It is therefore that much more important for non-Guatemalans to stay involved with them, helping them to implement what has been agreed to.

FORMAL OR INFORMAL? Guatemala has a formal culture, although the formalities change depending upon the class you are with and from. Family members relate to one another according to formal rules that respect traditional family roles. *El papa, la madre, el niño, la niña, mi amigo:* no matter the role, there is a formal way of relating between the actors. This does not have to be artificial or contrived; in fact, it is often loving and spontaneous. But it is respectful and prescribed. Even the Spanish language is divided into formal and informal forms and phrases, and personal behaviors are ruled by etiquette and protocol. Maintaining honor and personal pride is critical, and this requires a bit more formality when first developing the relationship. *Never* insult the honor, pride, or personal beliefs of a Guatemalan or his or her family (and this means the entire extended family), colleagues, or associates.

Greetings and Introductions

Language and Basic Vocabulary

Spanish is the official language, but most *indígenas* speak their own local language, the main one being Mayan. Most of the ruling business elite speak some competent English. Be sure to use any Spanish you do know, even if you learned it from a neighbor or in school: most Spanish-speaking Guatemalans love it when you try to speak Spanish, and they will help you get it right; this often becomes a relationship-building event and can be a more important activity in the formative stages of the relationship than any substantive discussions you can have.

Here are the basics:

Buenos días	Good morning
Buenas tardes	Good afternoon
Buenas noches	Good evening
¡Hola! ¿Que tal?	Hello; how are you? (informal)
¿Como está usted?	How are you? (formal)
Adiós	Good-bye
Por favor	Please
Gracias	Thank you
Con permiso	Pardon me
De nada	You're welcome
Muy bien	Very well
Con mucho gusto	Pleased to meet you

Un placer	A pleasure
Señor	Mr.
Señora	Mrs.
Señorita	Miss
Ingeniero(a)	Engineer
Abogado(a)	Lawyer
Doctor	Doctor
Gerente	Manager

Remember, in written Spanish, questions and exclamations are also indicated at the beginning of the sentence, with an upside-down exclamation point or question mark.

Honorifics for Men, Women, and Children

You must use *señor* (Mr.) and *señora* (Mrs.) plus the family name when introduced to strangers. Unless and until your Guatemalan colleague specifically invites you to use first names, and despite how he or she might refer to you, you must always use the family name plus the correct Spanish honorific (*señorita*—Miss—is still required for a young, unmarried woman). If you do not know whether a woman is married, use *señorita* (please note: this is the reverse from what is done in Spain, where *señora* is used when the marital status of the woman is unknown). *Don* (*doña* for an unmarried woman) is a special title of respect, typically used before the *first* (given) name only, and usually used only by people who know each other well and desire to show great respect. Married women are not necessarily "safe" from machismo, so wearing a wedding band does not always "protect" a woman alone; however, being a mother virtually ensures that a man will remain at a distance: bring pictures of your children. Children in Guatemala are expected to be respectful and not overly conversational when speaking with adults, and must always use honorifics when referring to adults. In situations where a title is known or used, the honorific plus the title is usually employed either with or without the name (e.g., Señor Ingeniero, or Señor Ingeniero Cortez). *Licensiado* is a title generally used for anyone with a skill requiring some sort of diploma. "Doctor" may be safely used as a way to give respect to anyone with a university degree; as an honorific, it does not have to refer only to a Ph.D. For casual contacts (e.g., with waiters and store help), just use *señor* or *señorita* without the name. It is very important to greet people at work or in stores and restaurants with an appropriate greeting for the time of day—*buenos días, buenas tardes,* or *buenas noches*—and *adiós* upon leaving. If you speak any Spanish at all, it is important to use it, but be sure to use the formal pronoun, *usted,* at the beginning, and do *not* switch to the *tu* (informal "you") form unless and until your Guatemalan colleague has specifically invited you to or does so him- or herself.

Spanish family names are often hyphenated, with the mother's family name added after the father's family name. In formal speech and in written correspondence, the fully hyphenated name is used; in face-to-face introductions, usually only the father's family name is used. For example, José Ramón Mendez-Rodriguez is Señor Mendez in face-to-face introductions, with Mendez being José's father's family name and Rodriguez being José's mother's family name. Women often keep their family name when they marry, but add their husband's father's family name with the preposition *de.* For example, Señora Maria Isabel

Gonzalez-Sanchez de Rodriguez is married to Señor Rodriguez, her maiden name is Gonzalez (her father's family name), and she retains her mother's family name—Sanchez—as well; in face-to-face communication she is more often referred to as Señora de Rodriguez or, very informally, as Señora Rodriguez.

The What, When, and How of Introducing People

Always wait to be introduced to strangers before taking that responsibility upon yourself. Guatemalans are most comfortable with a third-party introduction whenever possible. Try to ensure that for yourself ahead of time. You will be introduced to women first, then the most senior men. Do not presume to seat yourself at a formal gathering: if possible, wait to be told where to sit. Shake hands with everyone individually in a group before departing; the U.S. group wave is not appreciated. Avoid ending the conversation with the expression "Have a nice day"; it sounds controlling and insincere. Kissing is a common greeting once you have established a relationship, and it can occur quite quickly whether between women or men and women; usually, there is a kiss on two cheeks (actually an "air kiss," first on the left side, and then the right). It is not uncommon to see men and men, and women and women, especially indígenas, walking arm in arm down the street; they are family, good close friends, or associates, and it usually means nothing more than that.

The use of business cards is common; if possible, you should have your business card translated into Spanish on the reverse. Be sure to put any advanced educational degrees and your full title or position on both sides of your business card. Such emblems of your status are very important to Guatemalans; they want to know they are doing business with an important person.

Physical Greeting Styles

The handshake is common. The Guatemalan version is often soft, especially between women and men. The handshake should be accompanied with the greetings outlined above. Smiling and other nonverbal forms of communication need not accompany the handshake when it is between people who have not met previously, especially in business. Men should wait until a woman extends her hand before reaching for it, and women may take the lead in extending their hand or not. Men must remove their gloves when shaking hands with a woman, but a woman need not remove her gloves when shaking hands with a man. Between family, friends, or trusted business associates, an extra touch on the elbow or a hug (the *abrazo,* or embrace) will generally occur. This can happen even as soon as the second meeting; do not initiate it, but respond warmly in kind if it is initiated with you. Eye contact during the introduction is important, and should be maintained as long as the individual is addressing you.

Communication Styles

Okay Topics / Not Okay Topics

Okay: your family and background, the arts, sports (soccer is very big), music, history, and philosophy. Guatemalans love to see you demonstrate knowledge and interest in things Guatemalan, but you need to know what you are talking about if you give your opinions on the subject (it seems arrogant and insulting otherwise). Be a student when Guatemalans teach you about their country, go along with the effort, enjoy yourself, be appreciative and admiring, and take the opportunity as a way to build that all-important personal relationship. *Not okay:* Do not discuss the difficult economic or political situation, international relations, or other sensitive issues. Do not discuss religion or the economic and class difficulties with businesspeople (who are generally from the ruling elite). Do not inquire about a person's occupation or income in casual conversation, although that may be inquired of you. Americans often begin a conversation with "So, what do you do?"; this is too personal in Guatemala, is often not the most interesting topic of conversation, and can be a difficult topic for your Guatemalan colleague to discuss. Do not compare Guatemala to any of its neighbors, or talk disparagingly of any aspect of the culture, past or present. Avoid discussions about Centroamerican relations in general. Do not talk about your tummy; keep your health issues to yourself, because no one wants to hear about them. Do not go to Guatemala (or anywhere in Latin America) without pictures of your family, and when family is brought up (which it will be almost immediately in the conversation), use it as an opportunity to bring out the photographs. Never tell a dirty joke with a woman present. Many women, in the company of men, completely defer all conversation to their male partner, so men must be sensitive that Guatemalan men may answer for the woman being addressed.

Tone, Volume, and Speed

Discussions between strangers usually start out politely restrained and most often remain cool and measured. At meals, the beer may flow, and conversation is an art: it is enjoyed, savored, and commented upon, but it never gets out of hand, and is always carried on respectfully. In business, speak softly and with restraint. It garners respect.

Use of Silence

There can be some silence, especially in formal situations, or when confrontation needs to be avoided. In general, silence is not that common, except in group discussions where something has been said that can cause someone a public loss of face. Guatemalan speech patterns are typically not as polychronic and simultaneous as may be the case in other parts of Latin America.

Physical Gestures and Facial Expressions

The U.S. okay sign, made with the thumb and the forefinger, along with the *figa* (thumb between index and middle finger in a fist), is considered vulgar and obscene: avoid it. Never stand with your hands on your hips: it is aggressive (however, there is nothing defensive about folding the arms in front of you). Tapping the bottom of the elbow indicates that the person you are talking about is cheap or making a stingy offer. Women may greet each other by holding onto each other's shoulder or forearm.

Waving and Counting

The thumb represents the number 1, the index finger the number 2, and so on. It is insulting to beckon someone with the forefinger; instead, turn your hand so that the palm faces down and motion inward with all four fingers at once. If you need to gesture for a waiter, subtly raise your hand; never click, call, or whistle. Waving good-bye is done with the palm up at eye level and moving the fingers forward and back together quickly.

Physicality and Physical Space

Guatemalans tend to get closer than North Americans are generally comfortable with, but never extremely so. Do not step back when your Guatemalan associate steps forward. Guatemalan men may touch each other during conversations, adjust each other's ties, dust off each other's shoulders, and the like. Never speak with your hands in your pockets; always keep them firmly at your side when standing. If men and women must cross their legs, it should never be ankle-over-knee (the preferred style for women is to cross ankle over ankle). Remember, even in public, formal is always better than informal: no gum chewing, *ever,* no slouching, no leaning against things.

Eye Contact

Eye contact should be direct but do not be surprised if Guatemalans look down or away when you are speaking with them (this is especially the case with *indígenos*); this is a sign of listening and respect, not of disinterest.

Emotive Orientation

Guatemalans are rarely overly passionate in their expression. Therefore, until you know people well, you want to indicate restraint, while never seeming lifeless. Guatemalans will always admire you if you can remain logical, formal, respectful, and diplomatic—especially at first—while being warm, open, and personable.

Protocol in Public

Walking Styles and Waiting in Lines

It is more important in Guatemala to maintain one's face by being first in line (and never last) than it is to maintain a queue. Don't be too distressed if someone walks right up to the front of the line at a bank, a restaurant, or a store and gets served because of the relationship he or she has with the clerk, while you have been waiting patiently in line for forty minutes. This occurs also in response to rank based on gender and age. People also have a tendency to stand very close in public, and this is often the case between indígenas; this may feel uncomfortable at first. Resist the urge to back away; most of the time, you are not being intentionally crowded. Remember, the need to appear helpful and courteous is strong, and if you ask for directions on the street, you will no doubt be instructed on just where to go . . . whether or not the individual actually knows! Finally, because of the recurrent military situation in the country, it is illegal to photograph any installation, soldiers, or police, or to wear military clothing or carry anything that could be interpreted as a weapon, including a pocketknife.

Behavior in Public Places: Airports, Terminals, and the Market

Customer service, as a concept, is catching on, but is not fully institutionalized. Store hours are typically not designed around customer convenience (many stores are closed on weekends, certainly Sundays, and most evenings—except Thursdays, usually), although there are many local markets that are open at many different hours, some quite late. Personally thanking store owners, waiters, chefs, and hotel managers for their services is very much appreciated. In food markets, you can touch the produce; in goods stores, it may be difficult for you to return a product unless there is a flaw in it. In most small shops and in markets, it is very much expected that you will bargain. If you don't bargain well, that's okay; put a smile on your face and ask for half of what the listed price is. Stick to it, walk away if you have to, and you'll land somewhere in between. Never get angry, though, since bargaining is a game to get to know you, and it is supposed to make shopping a more pleasant experience. And please consider, when you bargain, that the economic conditions in Guatemala are very poor, especially for the makers of those beautiful woven fabrics you are bargaining for. Many indígenos and poorer people are reduced to begging in the cities, and small children and women may approach you on the street or come up to your taxi window to ask for money. It is always difficult deciding whether or not to give, but remember that the social support systems in Guatemala are negligible, and this is often the only way for these people to sustain themselves.

Smoking is on the decline, believe it or not, but if you do smoke, be sure to always offer a cigarette to everyone you are talking to before you light up. In bathrooms, on the plumbing "C" means hot (*caldo*) and "F" means cold (*frío*).

When answering a phone, say your last name. The use of cell phones is ubiquitous, and most pay phones—when they work—require that you press a button under the receiver once you are connected in order for your party to hear you (phone service can be intermittent and haphazard; it wasn't too many years ago that businesses would hire workers to do nothing but sit at a desk and redial a telephone number until the connection was made).

Bus / Metro / Taxi / Car

Driving is on the right, but people pass very quickly on the left. Driving is difficult and dangerous in the cities and off the main highways in the rural areas, and being a pedestrian is just as risky: both drivers and pedestrians really are very aggressive. Additionally, throughout Latin America, street rules are observed only sporadically (stoplights are viewed as suggestions); and drivers usually do not turn their lights on after dark (it is believed to blind the oncoming traffic), but may have them on during the day for extra safety. There are no metros. The best way to catch a cab is at designated taxi stands (hotels are good places, but often charge more for the same ride: a hotel surcharge may be added to the meter fare, in some cases). Bring food and water on board commuter trains if your trip is a long one, as they may not have a café car. The crime situation in Guatemala ebbs and flows, and on some intercity roads can be a considerable risk. Try to have a contact to keep you up-to-date about the crime situation, and if it sounds serious, it is. In such cases, maintaining security as a foreigner on the street is essential, and you must call a taxi only from the telephone or hotel, not from the street; additionally, try to avoid walking the street alone, especially at night and especially in the old section of Guatemala City.

Tipping

A 10 percent tip is usually sufficient in restaurants and taxis; more is considered nouveau and gauche. Porters and hotel help get the equivalent in quetzales of U.S. $1.00 per item or service rendered, theater and bathroom attendants usually half (and in both cases, tipping in U.S. dollars, as is done throughout much of the region, is perfectly fine, actually preferred). Double-check the current dollar/quetzale exchange rate, as it can vary quickly and significantly. Restaurants usually do not include the service charge in the bill. Even when the tip is included, it is still appropriate to leave a few quetzales or odd change if service was particularly good.

Punctuality

It is perfectly acceptable—in fact, essential—to arrive for social events about an hour late. If you arrive sooner, you will be running the risk of interrupting the host or hostess as he or she gets ready. For business meetings, being late by five to fifteen minutes or more is usually not a problem, but it is safer for the new employee or visitor to be on time, while not being surprised if others are not. Usually, the meeting will not begin in earnest until all attendees have arrived (or at least until all the decision makers have shown up), and this may not correspond to the time listed in the agenda. Resist questioning the late ones for a reason; they always have one, usually involving an obligation with more important people, like superiors, old friends, or family.

Dress

Until you know otherwise, and especially for business and most social situations between adults, formal dress is best, no matter the occasion, at work, in the restaurant (although most restaurants do not require ties, but do require jackets for men), or on the street, for men and women. Good taste is everything, and should be reflected in the clothes one wears. At work, men wear very stylish suits (dark is best), white shirts, and interesting and sophisticated ties; polished shoes are the order of the day, and accessories such as stylish watches, cuff links, and tie clips are common. Women usually accessorize so that even the simplest of outfits stands out for its interest and style. Upper-class Guatemalan women may wear more makeup and jewelry than women in the United States.

On the street, informal may mean jeans and sneakers, though that is more common as clothing to wear at the gym or the beach, or while jogging (women do not wear sneakers to work); for a social gathering, informal more often than not means tastefully coordinated clothes, sometimes including a jacket and tie for men (it rarely means jeans, sneakers, and T-shirts). "Formal" usually means formal evening wear, very dressy by U.S. standards.

Seasonal Variations

Evenings in Guatemala, especially in the mountainous country, can be quite cool, so a wrap (for women), jacket, or sweater is advised. The Caribbean coast in the north is typically humid and hot.

Colors

Bright colors are common, as are more sophisticated European styles for the business class. Outside of business, wearing native dress is respected if you know what you are doing: don't do it unless you do (those beautiful embroidered blouses for women are called *huipiles*).

Styles

Guatemalans, as they do with colors, also combine weaves, textures, and designs, often based on indigenous Indian designs. The fabrics, colors, and designs of Guatemalan clothing are world famous.

Accessories / Jewelry / Makeup

For the upper class, the right makeup, hairstyle, and accessories are very important for women. Men also accessorize.

Personal Hygiene

In Guatemala, personal hygiene is very important, although poverty does make it difficult for the poorer people. Latin men may sport facial hair, in the form of mustaches. Note that most rest room and bathroom facilities throughout Latin America do not have plumbing capable of handling paper toilet tissue; it is for this reason that there is a small receptacle next to the toilet for your used tissue: do not flush it down the bowl, but place it in the receptacle, or else you'll face the embarrassment of having to call for help when the bowl overflows.

Dining and Drinking

Mealtimes and Typical Foods

Breakfast (*el desayuno*) is served from about 7 to 8 A.M., and usually consists of the coffee, rolls, butter, and marmalade typical of the quick continental breakfast, or eggs and black beans; sometimes tortillas are served with breakfast. Coffee in the morning can be strong and black, or with hot milk (*café con leche*).

Lunch (*el almuerzo*) was traditionally the main meal of the day; even today, in busy cities, it can be an elaborate affair lasting several hours (usually an important business lunch)—or it can be a quick sandwich or a salad at a shop on the corner. Lunch is served from 12:30 or 1 P.M. to 3:30 P.M. (or beyond). It usually consists of soup, meat or fish, and rice and beans or plantains, plus a sweet dessert. Even the quick business lunch often will include a main course and a dessert and coffee. On Sunday, the family day, the main meal is supper, which is usually served at lunchtime and can last well into the evening.

Dinner (*la cena*) is served from 7:30 P.M. on. If the main meal of the day was lunch, then dinner is light, and this is often the case with families at home; it usually consists of soup, some meats or fish, black beans, and rice or plantains. Drinks served with dinner are usually juice, water, or beer. Dinner parties tend to end at around midnight.

In addition to restaurants, there are *comedors,* which are small restaurants serving fast Guatemalan-style food. *Pastelerías* serve coffee, tea, and pastries, and a *panadería* has baked goods. Be very careful about the places you go to eat: if they don't look safe or clean, you should avoid them. Do not eat food off the street from the street stalls: this can be very dangerous to your health. Be very careful about food and drink in Guatemala (and throughout Latin America); there are dangerous bugs around. First, the water: Do not drink tap water anywhere in Guatemala (except where *officially* noted as safe, sterilized, iodized, or "electrified"). This means no ice in any drinks (ice cubes may be made from tap water); ask for drinks *sin hielo* (without ice) when ordering. Close your mouth in the shower in the morning, and brush your teeth with bottled water. Drink only bottled water and soft drinks from bottles with intact seals opened in front of you; the fruit juices in Guatemala are wonderful, but until your digestive system has adjusted, it is wiser to avoid them: they may have been diluted with water from the tap. Coffee and tea are generally okay, because the water is boiled first. Avoid fresh dairy products, including milk, custards, mayonnaise, and ice cream, because they all usually require refrigeration, which may be questionable in certain parts of Guatemala. Definitely avoid raw shellfish and raw fish and do not eat any raw or uncooked vegetables or fruits, unless you can peel them; this means no green salad. Meats should be prepared well done when possible. You will inevitably get the Latin American tummy if you stay long enough . . . it is hard to avoid a drop of water here or there. If you have followed the above rules carefully, it is probably nothing to worry about; it will be uncomfortable for a day or two. Eat lightly, drink lots of safe fluids, stay in or near your room, rest, and it will pass. If a fever, severe pain, or vomiting develops, be sure to seek medical attention immediately.

Regional Differences

Try anything served with *chirmol,* a sauce made with onions and tomatoes that is often served with meat. *Cuchitos* is a tamale-like husk covering a meat-filled corn dough. Another sauce not to miss is *pepian,* made with ground meat, sesame, pumpkin, and raisins. *Guacamole* (a dip of avocados and spices) is ubiquitous and delicious. Rice, chips, or tortillas help cool down the mouth if you've eaten one too many hot peppers, although Guatemalan food is typically not as spicy as, for example, Mexican food (whatever you do, don't drink beer or water to quench the sting: it only spreads the pain).

Typical Drinks and Toasting

Atole de maíz (made with corn) and *atole de arroz* (made with rice) are popular hot drinks served in most homes. Once the meal gets under way, beer will be the drink in most cases. After the meal, a clear sugarcane brandy, *aguardiente,* can be served. The most common toast is *salud* (to your health).

Table Manners and the Use of Utensils

Do not begin eating until the host says, *"¡Buen provecho!"* Referring to European traditions as they do, Guatemalans do not switch knives and forks, as people do in the United States. The knife remains in the right hand, and the fork remains in the left. When the meal is finished, the knife and fork are laid parallel to each other across the right side of the plate. If you put both utensils down on the plate for any real length of time, it is a sign to the waitstaff that you are finished, and your plate may be taken away from you. Alternately, if you lay your cutlery down on either side of the plate it generally means you haven't finished; but if you really are, the host might interpret this as a sign that you were not happy with the meal.

The fork and spoon above your plate are for dessert. There are often many additional pieces of cutlery at a formal meal; if you're unsure of which utensil to use, always start from the outside and work your way in, course by course. Bread, if replacing tortillas (rarely will there be bread and tortillas), is sometimes served without butter; in that case, there usually will not be a butter knife, nor will there be a bread dish; your bread is placed on the rim of your main plate or on the table by your plate. Remember, if tortillas are served, they can be used to scoop up bits of food on your plate. There will be separate glasses provided at your setting for water and beer (after-dinner drink glasses come out after dinner).

When not holding utensils, your hands are expected to be visible above the table: this means you do not keep them in your lap; instead, rest your wrists on top of the table (never your elbows). At the table, pass all dishes to your left.

Seating Plans

The most honored position is at the head of the table, with the most important guest seated immediately to the right of the host (women to the right of the host, and men to the right of the hostess). If there is a hosting couple, one will be at each end of the table. In the European tradition, men and women are seated next to one another, and couples are often broken up and seated next to people they may not have previously known. This is done to promote conversation. Men typically rise when women enter the room, and continue to hold doors for women and allow them to enter a room first. Remember, as is the case throughout the region, the first floor in Guatemala (*PB,* or *planta baja*) is really the second floor, with the first floor usually referred to as the lobby or ground floor.

Refills and Seconds

It is expected that you eat everything on your plate. Nevertheless, it is a compliment if you ask for seconds, so when being served family style be sure to take small portions so that you can eat everything on your plate and still ask for seconds. You may always have additional beverages; drink enough to cause your cup or glass to be less than half full, and it will generally be refilled.

At Home, in a Restaurant, or at Work

In informal restaurants, you may be required to share a table. Waitstaff may be summoned by making eye contact; waving or calling their names is very impolite (although you might see some Guatemalans make a kind of *pssst* sound; don't do it). The business breakfast and lunch are more common in Guatemala than the business dinner; dinner is usually saved for family, not business guests. The business meal, however, is generally not a time to make business decisions. Take your cue from your Guatemalan associates: if they bring up business, then it's okay to discuss it (more often than not, over the coffee at the end of the meal), but wait to take your lead from their conversation. No gum chewing, *ever,* at a restaurant or on the street.

When you arrive at a Guatemalan associate's home for a formal meal, you will be told where to sit, and there you should remain. Do not wander from room to room; much of the house is really off-limits to guests. Use the toilet before you arrive, as it is considered bad form to leave the dinner party, or the table, at any time. Once you (and the group) are invited to another room, most probably the dining room, be sure to allow more senior members of your party to enter the room ahead of you: men should move aside to allow women to enter the room ahead of them. Often drinks and hors d'oeuvres (*boquitas,* or peanuts, olives, or chips) are served in the living room prior to the dinner. In a private home, be careful about what and how you admire things: the host may feel obliged to give it to you! Once at the table, be sure to look for place cards, or wait until the host indicates your seat: do not presume to seat yourself, as the seating arrangement is usually predetermined.

If you invite people to your home, be prepared to always have the invitation accepted, although they may not, in fact, show up; rejecting the invitation is difficult for Guatemalans, who seek to not offend. They may indicate their true intentions by simply responding to your invitation with "I will try."

Being a Good Guest or Host

Paying the Bill

Usually the one who does the inviting pays the bill, although the guest is expected to make an effort to pay. Sometimes other circumstances determine who pays (such as rank). Making payment arrangements ahead of time so that no exchange occurs at the table is a very classy way to host. Call for the bill (by saying *"La cuenta, por favor"*), and be prepared to pay it when it arrives. Women, if out with men, will not really be able to pay the bill at a restaurant: if you want to, make arrangements ahead of time, and don't wait for the check to arrive at the table. The only time it is considered appropriate for a woman to pay the bill is if she is a hosting businesswoman from abroad. If a businesswoman invites a Guatemalan businessman to a meal, she should be sure to extend the invitation to his spouse as well, or may want to consider telling him that her (female) colleague will also be joining them (and be sure to have a female colleague along). If a Guatemalan male invites a businesswoman to a meeting or a meal that seems to have more than business as the subject, a businesswoman should always insist that she bring her female associate along (someone who is needed because of her role in the company); if you are a businesswoman making your first business trip to Guatemala and have not yet established a relationship with your Guatemalan male counterparts, you are strongly advised to bring a female business associate along on the trip. Unmarried businesswomen may want to consider wearing a wedding band. If you have children, be sure to discuss that fact at some point early in the initial conversations: any aggressive macho behavior usually stops when men learn they are dealing with a *madre.*

Transportation

It's a very nice idea, when acting as the host, to inquire ahead of time as to whether your guests will require transportation. If necessary, you should arrange for taxi service at the end of the meal. When the cars arrive, be sure not to leave your spot until your guests are out of sight.

When to Arrive / Chores to Do

If invited to dinner at a private home, do not offer to help with the chores, nor should you expect to visit the kitchen. Middle- and upper-class Guatemalans often have household help for the kitchen chores. Do not leave the table unless invited to do so. Being invited to a dinner party in Guatemala is a special honor, and not often extended to new relationships. If such an invitation is offered, accept it as an opportunity to build a new and close relationship: that is what your Guatemalan associate is looking for. Reciprocate by hosting your colleague in your home when and if he or she comes to your country or at a fine restaurant on another night of your trip.

Gift Giving

In general, gift giving is not common among business associates, although it is nice to bring a small gift from abroad if you are revisiting a business acquaintance (as, at this point, they have probably become a friend). One exception: as is the case throughout most of Latin America, some chocolates or a small gift for the secretary of the person you are visiting can work wonders for future smooth sailing! In this case, always give your business contact his or her gift in a social setting, never in the office. If a man is giving a gift to a woman in a business setting, it is important to present it as a gift to her from his wife or sister. Holiday cards are very appropriate, particularly as a thank-you for your Guatemalan colleague's business in the previous year, and should be mailed in time to be received the week before Christmas.

Gifts are expected for social events, especially as thank-yous for private dinner parties. The best gift in this case is expensive flowers. Never send chrysanthemums or white-colored flowers (they are used primarily as funeral flowers), red roses (these usually indicate romantic intent; traditionally, it was believed that red flowers could cast a romantic spell!), and always be sure the bouquet is in odd numbers (an old European tradition). When you bring flowers with you to the dinner party, be sure to unwrap them before presenting them. Other good gifts would be chocolates or a good bottle of wine. If you are staying with a family, an appropriate thank-you gift would be a high-quality item that represents your country and is difficult to get in Guatemala, but that is not representative of the United States in general: small American-made electronic gadgets, a set of American bath towels (always a good gift almost everywhere, since they are usually more luxurious), or anything that reflects your host's personal tastes is appropriate. Gifts are generally opened at the time they are given and received.

Special Holidays and Celebrations

Major Holidays

Business slows down from December 15 to January 6, and Holy Week is a more difficult time in which to accomplish work than Christmas. In addition, there are many regional fiestas and saints' days throughout the year that usually close down businesses for a day or two; check with your local contacts.

January 1	*Año Nuevo* (New Year's Day)
January 6	Three Kings Day
March/April	*Semana Santa/Pasqua* (Holy Week and Easter)
May 1	*Día del Trabajo* (Labor Day)
June 30	Army Day
August 15	*Asunción* (Assumption)
September 15	Independence Day
October 20	Revolution Day
November 1	*Día de los Santos* (All Saints' Day, a very popular holiday in Guatemala where family members decorate graves, fly kites, and have picnics in the cemeteries)
December 16	Christmas celebrations usually begin
December 24	Christmas Eve
December 25	*Navidad* (Christmas Day)

Business Culture

Daily Office Protocols

In Guatemala, doors are often closed at senior management level; knock first (this includes bathrooms) before opening doors, and when leaving a room, close the door behind you. It is not common for women to attain positions of authority in Guatemala; in the traditional Guatemalan workplace, women are usually relegated to lower-level management and administrative support positions. People organize their time on a daily basis according to the tasks they must accomplish, and the relationships they must depend upon in order to accomplish these tasks; the clock takes a backseat. Therefore, the day may begin slowly, but there can be much activity by day's end, and people with responsibility can stay late in the office in order to finish up what needs to be done. This pattern repeats itself over larger blocks of time in regard to the accomplishment of projects and the meeting of deadlines.

Management Styles

Workers provide what their bosses expect of them, and the preparation of plans, methods, and reports can be time-consuming and complicated efforts. Gathering the information required in order to do what your boss expects from you, or creating consensus among your colleagues in order to accomplish a particular goal, can take a long time and is a critical requirement in Guatemala. All of this occurs in a formal and sometimes very rigid hierarchical structure, which means that deadlines and efficiency are secondary to attention to detail, perfection of form, bureaucratic requirements, and the need to be clever in the face of limited resources in order to be effective. Because of this rigid rank and hierarchy orientation, titles in Guatemala are very important; the highest ones (e.g., vice president) are usually reserved for very senior, executive-level positions, and should not be used as casually as they are in the United States. Complimenting and rewarding employees individually and publicly is usually not done. For non-Guatemalans, it is essential to try to have a local contact who can tell you what is really going on after you return home, and to have a local intermediary—as well as a local lawyer and *notario* (a very responsible administrative position throughout much of Latin America)—to act as a liaison for you with the people you need to see while you are there. This needs to be set up ahead of time.

Boss-Subordinate Relations

Rank most definitely has its privileges in Guatemala. Pride and self-importance require that Guatemalans always do business with the most important people in any organization (and this should be the same for the non-Guatemalan working with them). There is a rigid chain of command that must be heeded. No matter what field you are in, there is a proper way for communicating with particular individuals, and an established procedure one is expected to follow, although few Guatemalan organizations are large enough for complicated bureaucracies to develop (with the exception of the government). Deviating from the normal channels will generally make more problems for you, even if the intent is to bypass what appear to be obstacles. Bosses are expected to provide guidance, distribute information, and make decisions; subordinates are expected to provide detailed information and follow the decisions made by the superiors.

Conducting a Meeting or Presentation

At meetings of peers, there can be open communication and sharing of ideas; in fact, these sessions often serve as information-sharing and decision-making forums in which all individuals are expected to contribute. In more formal, conservative organizations, meetings are often gatherings of nonpeers, clearly called together by decision makers in order to gather information from below, clarify goals, and formulate action plans. In these cases, individuals often may not share ideas and are not expected to contribute to mutual problem solving.

Negotiation Styles

Guatemalans generally play their cards close to the vest; they do not divulge information easily (it is seen as the source of power). They are usually circumspect in their communication styles, and will often indicate their thoughts in indirect ways. They respect someone who comes to them with already established knowledge and experience, and will build relationships based on your level in society and the organization. Whether you are worth knowing and doing business with may be more important than the details of your proposal. Nevertheless, details are important, and a carefully planned, logically organized, and beautifully presented proposal is key. Bargaining is the essence of the negotiation, as a way to build trust; therefore, be reasonable, but do not overcompromise, as this shows weakness.

The first meeting is usually formal, with the Guatemalans sizing up you and your organization: it will be conducted in the office. Take copious notes afterward, but put on a warm, dignified demeanor during the meeting. Never be condescending. Although the contract must be legal down to the dotted i's, it really is just a legal formality to the Guatemalans and can be overcome, by either party, if such a need arises later on. Plan your meetings as carefully and as well in advance as you can, but expect changes. The goal, at least for the first meeting, is the development of a good feeling of respect and mutual trust. Remember also that the meeting might start and end later than you anticipated; nevertheless, as with most polychronic cultures, you should always arrive on time. Coffee is the universal greeting; always accept it, always serve it (in nice china, never in Styrofoam), and drink as much or as little as you can or desire. It is the gesture of acceptance and appreciation that counts (never refuse coffee, or an invitation to go with your colleague to a café and have some).

Written Correspondence

Business letters should be very formal and respectful of hierarchy. Last names are usually written in uppercase; dates are given using the day/month/year format (with periods in between, not slashes); and an honorific plus a title is as common as an honorific plus the last name. The time of day is written in military time; weights and measures are usually given in metric measurements. Monetary amounts are written so that the period breaks up the figure into tens, hundreds, and thousands, and a comma separates the quetzales from the centavos.

The traditional language used in openings and closings may appear convoluted and formal, and you should write your e-mails, letters, and faxes using a precise formula. Be sure to inquire first, in all communications, about your colleague's health and progress, then move on to the substance of your communication, and close with a salutation and your personal wishes for his or her success and well-being (the Latin communication "sandwich"). Some important business abbreviations: "S.A." means "incorporated," and EE.UU. is the abbreviation for the United States. If your colleagues write to you in Spanish, try to respond in Spanish, if you can, or use the services of a translator. Written addresses are usually in the following format:

Line 1: name
Line 2: title/position
Line 3: company
Line 4: street address
Line 5: city, state

BELIZE

Note: Refer to the previous sections on Mexico and Guatemala for information about general Centroamerican and Latin American cultural behaviors; the material that follows describes specific Belizean variations on general Centroamerican and Latin American customs.

Some Historical Context

Belize is the one Centroamerican country that is not Hispanic: its roots are British and African; therefore, the official language is English, not Spanish (although Spanish is spoken in many places and there is a kind of Creole that is also spoken by some of the more rural Belizeans), and it is British English. The British colonized the region—formerly known as British Honduras—after routing the pirates who roamed the coast (actually the coral reef, second in size only to Australia's Great Barrier Reef), and used the area to bring Africans as slaves into the Americas. Relations between Belize and Guatemala have been stormy in the past, so be sure not to raise this topic in conversation. The major business is agriculture and tourism: do not even attempt to take coral or tropical fish out of the country, as doing so is highly illegal.

Fundamental Cultural Orientations

1. What's the Best Way for People to Relate to One Another?

OTHER-INDEPENDENT OR OTHER-DEPENDENT? While the need for group affiliation is powerful, outsiders can be easily and quickly involved in the group, when there is a reason for them to be. Traditional Latin *individualismo* is not as powerful as it is in some of Belize's Hispanic neighbors.

HIERARCHY-ORIENTED OR EGALITY-ORIENTED? Because most of the people's predecessors were at one time slaves, and the ruling elite historically British (not Spanish), there is little emphasis placed on hierarchy and structure among the general population in Belize. Consequently, this is not an overtly macho culture, and men and women typically do not relate to each other according to machismo-based roles.

RULE-ORIENTED OR RELATIONSHIP-ORIENTED? Typically, rules are respected, although the priority is honoring the social responsibilities that individuals have toward one another.

2. What's the Best Way to View Time?

MONOCHRONIC OR POLYCHRONIC? While time is flexible when it comes to social occasions, it is not significantly so, and punctuality is expected for business appointments. Remember, this culture was influenced by monochronic Northern European British traditions, not polychronic Hispanic traditions.

RISK-TAKING OR RISK-AVERSE? Because the pace of life is slow, decisions can take time, but this generally is not because of any aversion to risk. Belizeans tend to have a higher tolerance for ambiguity and uncertainty than their Latin neighbors, and individual decision makers can move quickly.

PAST-ORIENTED OR FUTURE-ORIENTED? Belize is perhaps neither past- nor future-oriented, but more present-oriented, with a concern for a better future.

Greetings and Introductions

Honorifics for Men, Women, and Children

As is done in all English-speaking Caribbean cultures, maintain formality at first, and use last names and titles whenever possible. Do not switch to the informal first name unless and until your Belizean colleague has specifically invited you to or does so him- or herself. Among good friends and family, Belizeans often refer to one another with nicknames that reflect a physical or personal characteristic, such as "Big Harry" or "Cooking Sarah."

The What, When, and How of Introducing People

Here are some unique Belizean cultural communication considerations: In large groups, do not expect personal introductions; you are expected to introduce yourself to others. Take the time to have an extended conversation with people, even those you meet casually. Because of the significant African population, Americans may be engaged in conversations about life in America.

Protocol in Public

Behavior in Public Places: Airports, Terminals, and the Market

Interestingly, the telecommunications infrastructure in Belize is quite good, and many phones accept telecards, which can be purchased at local shops.

Tipping

Typically, a 10 percent tip is included on the bill in restaurants, so leaving just a few small coins as extra change is all you need to do if you enjoyed the service.

Dining and Drinking

Mealtimes and Typical Foods

Breakfast is typically referred to as "tea," and lunch is typically referred to as "dinner," while the evening meal can be called "dinner" as well, or "supper." By the way, if you are invited to a home for "tea" or to "drink some tea," you are really being invited for dinner, so be prepared! Belize is a very small country, and still heavily agricultural. There is really no urban culture, and therefore, restaurant life is minimal; you may be invited to a home quickly. In this case, consider that desserts and coffee after a meal are rare, as are appetizers before the meal. As a guest in a home, you may be served first, and the family may wait until you are finished to have their meal; in this case, eat everything that you put on your plate, and take small portions, so that you may be offered more and so that there is enough for everyone. When you are finished with your plate, push it slightly away from you, with the silverware lying parallel on the side of the plate. If you are served tortillas with your meal, tear each in pieces as you eat it. If you are lucky, you might be invited to a "boil-up," a special family affair where all sorts of foods are cooked and served family style for many people. Some local specialties include *gibnut* (a kind of rabbit-like rodent), tamales (never eat the husk, just push that aside after unwrapping it), and in some homes, iguana. There are basically two varieties of local beer: light (referred to as "lager") and heavy (referred to as "stout"). Because English is the predominant language the toast is "cheers" or "to your health."

Table Manners and the Use of Utensils

Because of the British influence, your hands are expected, when not holding utensils, to be in your lap at the dinner table.

Special Holidays and Celebrations

Major Holidays

January 1	New Year's Day
March 9	Baron Bliss Day (in honor of a wealthy Englishman who made many philanthropic donations to Belize)
March/April	Holy Week and Easter
April 21	The Queen's Birthday
May 1	Labor Day
May 24	Commonwealth Day
September 10	National Day
September 21	Independence Day
October 12	Columbus Day
December 25	Christmas Day
December 26	Boxing Day

Business Culture

Since Belize is not a Hispanic macho culture, non-Belizean women visitors, whether visiting for business or social reasons, typically do not need to take the same precautions suggested for neighboring Hispanic cultures (although the degree of business opportunity, because of the size and agricultural and tourist orientation of the country, is generally limited in Belize, for women as well as men). While punctuality is important in business, the time frame in which—and pace at which—projects get done can be long and extended.

HONDURAS

Note: Refer to the previous sections on Mexico and Guatemala for information about general Centroamerican and Latin American cultural behaviors; the material that follows describes specific Honduran variations on general Centroamerican and Latin American customs.

Some Historical Context

Honduras is perhaps the poorest of the Centroamerican countries; the irony here is that due to relatively benign disinterest in the province on the part of Castilian Spain in the fifteenth century and the mestizo nature of most of the population, the rigid class distinctions that were put in place by the Spanish aristocracy elsewhere in this region did not evolve in Honduras (nevertheless, the indigenous Mayans and Misquitos put up a fierce—though utimately futile—resistance to the Spanish invaders, and most Hondurans regard the Mayan chief Lempira, who was killed in battle with the Spanish, as a hero). Today, most of the country exists in a desperate economic condition, with a very small business elite, mainly resident foreigners (primarily Arabs and Asians), ruling the economy, but not in a position of political control. At the bottom of the economic ladder are the mestizo Indians of the southeast. Historically, Honduras struggled for its independence from Spain as a member of the Union of Central American provinces, but when these nations were freed from Spain and the Union collapsed, Honduras then had to struggle to remain independent from its neighbor Guatemala and the Guatemalan legacies of rigid social class stratification (which did not fit with Honduran demographics or history). These struggles remain a major source of much of Honduras' difficulties. The situation was exacerbated by the massive hurricane of 1989, which figuratively and literally devastated the country. Family is everything to Hondurans, and the benefits to extended families determine individual action. Politically and historically, Honduras proved again and again an ally to United States interests in the region, and therefore became a receivership state to U.S. aid in the efforts on the part of the U.S. government to avert and dismantle other regimes within the region that it interpreted to be against U.S. interests. Consequently, Honduras has been a pariah state among its neighbors from time to time, increasing its dependence upon the United States and decreasing its power within the region. Because of the significantly homogeneous and generally more egalitarian society (about 90 percent of the people are mestizo, or a mixture of indigenous Honduran Indian and European), Hondurans are not viewed as conservative or resistant to change; in fact, Hondurans, as distinguished from their neighbors, tend toward flexibility and a willingness to see new options and ways of doing things. This generally leveled nature of society reveals itself also in the more casual dress: even in business, men may often go without a tie or jacket, although the Latin American *guayabera* is very popular.

Specific Honduran cultural attributes include a very laid-back response to disagreement and conflict (it is very difficult for a non-Honduran to confirm the meaning of what is said, since there is a very strong tendency to avoid negativity or statements that would indicate problems or difficulties). Additionally, fatalism is particularly strong in Honduras, no doubt as a mechanism for relieving the stress of poverty; rather than focusing on solutions, Hondurans often adopt a more resigned position to a given situation, choosing instead to focus on what is positive about what may be impossible to change. Women, in this strongly macho culture, do not play a significant role outside of the home; when women meet each other, they usually do not shake hands or kiss, but rather gently hold each other's right elbow, or rest their hands on each other's shoulder. Another Centroamerican nonverbal behavior is tapping the underside of the elbow, which indicates that the other person in the dialogue is cheap. Waving an outstretched index finger from side to side indicates disagreement, or "no," and the typical handshake, even between men, may appear soft or limp.

Special Holidays and Celebrations

Major Holidays

The local fiestas and celebrations are perhaps more important than the official holidays in Honduras, so be sure to check with your local contacts to find out when the patron saint may be celebrated, or what other events may be affecting regular daily activity.

January 1	*Año Nuevo* (New Year's Day)
February/March	*Carnaval*
March/April	*La Semana Santa/Pasqua* (Holy Week and Easter)
April 14	*Día de los Americas* (Day of the Americas)
May 1	*Día del Trabajo* (Labor Day)
September 10	Day of the Child (children get treats at home and at school, and there is a charming custom of adults greeting children on the street as they pass them)
September 15	Independence Day
October 3	Birthday of Morazan (the national liberator)
October 12	*Día de Cristóbal Colón* (Columbus Day)
October 21	Armed Forces Day
December 25	*Navidad* (Christmas Day)

EL SALVADOR

Note: Refer to the previous sections on Mexico and Guatemala for information about general Centroamerican and Latin American cultural behaviors; the material that follows describes specific El Salvadoran variations on general Centroamerican and Latin American customs.

Some Historical Context

El Salvador is the most densely populated nation in Centroamerica. After the revolutions against Spanish control in the nineteenth century, the nations of the region were joined together in the United Provinces of Centroamerica; this quickly dissolved as individual countries soon squabbled over their own individual interests, El Salvador leading the dissolution, and almost immediately coming into conflict with its neighbors, Honduras and Guatemala, over borders and land reform. The recurring issues of land reform and economic opportunity again propelled the country recently into an extended civil war, with Marxist revolutionary guerrillas fighting an essentially rightist military government that supported the landed interests and the status quo (and that was, in turn, supported militarily and financially by the United States in its efforts to obstruct Marxist development in the region). The war ended in a shaky truce and left almost 100,000 El Salvadorans missing or dead. The landed oligarchic controlling elite are strictly removed from the poor masses, a direct result of the heavy-handed imposition of aristocratic conquistador culture in the fifteenth century combined with the lack of a powerful indigenous culture (there were Indian cultures in El Salvador when the Spanish arrived, but none of them represented the center of powerful indigenous cultures in Centroamerica as they did in Guatemala or Mexico). Because the Catholic church sided with the peasants in their struggle against the oligarchs, beginning in the 1950s and 1960s, the church immediately became suspect in the eyes of the ruling elite, and many of the business elite today have rejected Roman Catholicism for a kind of neopentecostal Protestantism that preaches that wealth is a sign of faith (and subsequently that the condition of the poor is a sign of their fall from grace due to their faithlessness—read, practice of Catholicism and not Protestantism—and not the result of an oppressive sociopolitical system). The elite are highly educated and familiar with U.S. ways (English is well understood among the elite, although Noah, the most popular indigenous language, is still spoken, along with Spanish, by many of the poorer classes), and even the poor and middle classes have strong contacts with (and family in) the United States; many El Salvadorans seek jobs in the States, and have developed a reputation for being extremely hard workers, with an achievement mentality and an affinity for American values.

Special Holidays and Celebrations

Major Holidays

As is the case throughout the region, local fiestas and celebration of individual town's saints' days are ubiquitous; check with your local contacts.

January 1	*Año Nuevo* (New Year's Day)
March/April	*Semana Santa/Pasqua* (Holy Week and Easter)
May 1	*Día del Trabajo* (Labor Day)
May 10	Mother's Day
June 17	Father's Day
August 1–5	Christian religious holiday period
September 15	Independence Day
October 12	*Día de Cristóbal Colón* (Columbus Day)
December 25	*Navidad* (Christmas Day)

CHAPTER THREE

The Southern Centroamerican Cultures: Nicaragua, Costa Rica, and Panama

NICARAGUA

Note: Refer to the previous chapters on Mexico and Guatemala for information about general Centroamerican and Latin American cultural behaviors; the material that follows describes specific Nicaraguan variations on general Centroamerican and Latin American customs.

Some Historical Context

Perhaps no other country in the region has been subjected to U.S. intervention more than Nicaragua. Soon after its independence from both Spain and the United Provinces of Centroamerica, Nicaragua became the apple of rich American financiers' eyes; Southern Americans saw a source of new cheap labor, replacing the suddenly defunct U.S. slave-based agricultural system, and Northern industrialists (namely Cornelius Vanderbilt) saw an opportunity for a fantastic new venture: a canal across Nicaragua connecting the Atlantic and Pacific Oceans (due to major lakes in central Nicaragua, the amount of land needed to convert into a canal is actually less in Nicaragua than in Panama). Southern Americans financed a mercenary, William Walker, who led a raggle-taggle group of Americans into Nicaragua and managed to claim power and become "president" of Nicaragua (for a New York minute, in any event: Vanderbilt succeeded in funding his own mercenaries in neighboring countries to topple Walker, and destabilized Nicaragua for years to come). Land reform, as it did throughout the region, became a cause célèbre, a way to democratize and enfranchise the poor, with "liberals"—based in the city of Leon—demanding reform and "conservatives"—based in the city of Granada—resisting reform. The two cities became "ground zeros" for either side for years to come, literally pulling the country apart in opposite directions. The United States has intervened militarily in these struggles from time to time, mainly on the side of the conservatives, and the ruling conservative business elite today has a strong familiarity with English and U.S. cultural ideals. As new philosophies emerged and the nineteenth century became the twentieth, the liberals and conservatives became, respectively, Marxist revolutionaries (in the form of Sandinistas, celebrating a famous local liberal hero, Augusto César Sandino, who resisted American troops sent in by Calvin Coolidge in the 1920s to stem a "Communist threat") and supporters of the ruling status quo. Nicaragua only recently united into an unsteady republic, with a neutral capital, Managua, ironically and fittingly made even more unstable by periodic devastating earthquakes. Be sensitive to both revealing a knowledge of the unique and troubling Nicaraguan-U.S. relationship and speaking softly about it: it is a source of great ambivalence and distress. Nicaraguans are proud of their struggles, and will be impressed that you understand the difficult history between the two nations. They are amazed that most Americans, for example, don't even know who William Walker was.

An Area Briefing

Schools and Education

Schooling is compulsory through the beginning grades of high school; however, in poorer rural regions and difficult urban neighborhoods, maintaining quality education and children's attendance through these grades is a challenge. Many children are pressed into working to help the family survive instead of attending school. The wealthy send their children to private schools, including universities in Europe and the United States.

Religion and Demographics

Throughout Nicaragua's struggles, the Roman Catholic church has had limited political influence (compared to the influence it wielded in many of Nicaragua's neighbors), even as it has continued to serve as a source of day-to-day stability during periods of unrest. Many of the ruling conservative elite subscribe to a kind of neopentecostal Protestantism, the theology of which justifies the wealth of the ruling elite as evidence of their faith (Protestantism), and the poverty of the lower classes as evidence of their lack thereof (because they are Catholic).

The country is about 70 percent mestizo (of mixed indigenous Indian and European blood), 15 percent European, 10 percent African, and 5 percent pure indígena.

Fundamental Cultural Orientations

1. What's the Best Way for People to Relate to One Another?

OTHER-INDEPENDENT OR OTHER-DEPENDENT? As is the case with most countries in the region, Nicaraguan behavior can be viewed as significantly "other-dependent," with strong individual action being taken to demonstrate responsibility to the larger group, mainly the family. Most individuals will seek, either formally or informally, the opinions and support of family members, friends, and coworkers before venturing off to do or say something on their own. People are most comfortable in the "bosom" of others, and individuals are simply not part of society unless they can claim membership to or affiliation with some group, neighborhood, town, or business unit. For most of the people, the extended family unit lives together, with aunts, uncles, and cousins all very near (if not under the same roof). A consequence of this, of course, is a resistance to the outsider, and a need for all outsiders to be identified as being on one side of the struggle or the other. However, the influences of present struggles and historical legacies are strong, and individuals are proud of their beliefs and positions; they do not suffer loss of face easily. Their unique historical experience has made Nicaraguans, in this sense as individuals, determinedly independent-oriented.

HIERARCHY-ORIENTED OR EGALITY-ORIENTED? The Nicaraguan workplace is rigidly layered, with individuals at the top having supreme decision-making authority, and staff underneath being required to follow step, challenge as little as possible, and solve all problems before they surface at the top. However, in less-traditional, liberal organizations and businesses, there can be a strong egalitarian ethos running through the entire organization, as a demonstration of their revolutionary and democratic position. Once again, this is a representation of the deep division between the status quo and the liberals. In civic life, this means that government, which is supposed to be democratic, often fails to be, and there is deep resentment between the classes. Women and men are rigidly separated in their social roles, as is the case more or less throughout much of Latin America; however, women in Nicaragua have benefited from the struggle in that the liberal interpretation of the woman's role is far more egalitarian (witness the election of a woman president after the most recent civil unrest in the 1980s), and there is a higher percentage of women in school in Nicaragua than in most of the rest of the region. Demonstrating conspicuous wealth or avoiding manual labor, which is often a sign of privilege in the rest of the region, can engender strong negative responses in Nicaragua.

RULE-ORIENTED OR RELATIONSHIP-ORIENTED? Because of the rigid stratification of society, the behaviors of one class can be quite different from those of another, and although rules are supposed to be applied universally to all, there is no doubt in Nicaragua that individuals in different classes are treated differently. The universal application of law to all is a very sensitive issue in Nicaragua. For non-Nicaraguans, time is well-spent developing a personal relationship with the right person (often an *enchufado,* or an important business intermediary), and revealing yourself and your ideas respectfully; attempts to discuss the terms of the deal or the immediate task at hand without having built the necessary personal trust (*confianza*) and understanding is often a waste of time. Which takes us to our next concern.

2. What's the Best Way to View Time?

MONOCHRONIC OR POLYCHRONIC? Outside of the Managua, time is circular, and very polychronic; it is more monochronic in Managua, but not by much. Relationships take time, so time tends to remain as a secondary issue in the background. Work begins early, around 8 A.M.; lunch occurs around 12 P.M. and can last till 2 P.M., after which work resumes until 5 or 6 P.M. The pace is often relaxed; be on time, but be prepared to wait. Dinner is usually around 7 or 8 P.M. If you really want things to occur punctually, it is perfectly okay to identify the time as *a la gringa* or *Norteamericano,* as opposed to Nicaraguan time.

RISK-TAKING OR RISK-AVERSE?   Latin cultures, in general, are risk-averse, and that is one of the driving reasons for the creation of structure and hierarchies. The instability in Nicaragua, however, acts as a counterweight to this, requiring from time to time fast decision making and the swift seizing of opportunities when and if they arise. Decision making in any traditional organization can be slow and tedious, even if the decision is being made by a single, powerful leader at the top, but may also be surprisingly fast.

PAST-ORIENTED OR FUTURE-ORIENTED?   Latin American cultures, including Nicaragua, have seen their world turned upside down more than once with their having little or no ability to control the events. In Nicaragua, this instability is still a current fact of life, and there is little in their past to guide them securely into the future. Nicaraguans, therefore, while generally wary about the ultimate outcome of things, look hopefully to the future, and are motivated by the possibilities that change can offer.

3. What's the Best Way for Society to Work with the World at Large?

LOW-CONTEXT DIRECT OR HIGH-CONTEXT INDIRECT COMMUNICATORS?
It has been important in Nicaragua to identify yourself, your beliefs, your positions, and your ideas, in order to be affiliated with one group or another. For this reason, Nicaraguans can be quite direct and blunt in their communication style and, depending upon the rank and status of those present and the situation, will either feel entitled to say what they feel or be very careful in their expression. Nicaraguans, unlike others in the region, are less concerned with loss of face, and will be less inclined to sugarcoat bad news or avoid confrontation. Nevertheless, it is critical to always confirm information, to have multiple and independent sources "on the ground" to confirm for you what you are being told, and to be able to read between the lines without directly challenging the veracity of what your Nicaraguan colleague is saying. There is a strong tolerance for, in fact dependence on, the subjective interpretation of events and reality. This tendency also makes for complimentary and respectful introductory conversation, and an avoidance of anything that may strike you as unpleasant at first.

PROCESS-ORIENTED OR RESULT-ORIENTED?   Nicaraguans are very subjective in their decision making, and will often fall back on what they personally believe in order to make or justify a decision. Their experience with similar past situations will often guide their present decision making more powerfully than any evidence or argument you present. Nicaraguans may not be able to follow through easily with the actions required to put plans in place, yet they will be reticent to admit this or inform you when problems develop. It is therefore that much more important for non-Nicaraguans to stay involved with them, helping them to implement what has been agreed to.

FORMAL OR INFORMAL?   Nicaraguan culture is split between a more traditional, Hispanic, formal culture and a newly created (read, "revolutionary"), egalitarian, and subsequently more informal culture. Family members relate to each other according to formal rules that respect traditional family roles. *El papá, la madre, el niño, la niña, mi amigo;* no matter the role, there is a formal way of relating between the actors. This does not have to be artificial or contrived; in fact, it is often loving and spontaneous. But it is respectful and formal. Even the Spanish language is divided into formal and informal forms and phrases. Never insult the honor, pride, or personal beliefs of a Nicaraguan or his or her family (and this means the entire extended family), colleagues, or associates.

Greetings and Introductions

Language and Basic Vocabulary

Spanish is the official language, but Garifuna is spoken by the coastal African population. Additionally, the indígenas speak their own local languages. Most of the ruling business elite speak some competent English. Be sure to use any Spanish you do know, even if you learned it from a neighbor or in school: Nicaraguans love it when you try to speak Spanish, and they will help you get it right; this often becomes a relationship-building event and can be a more important activity in the formative stages of the relationship than any substantive discussions you can have.

Nicaraguan Spanish is extremely colorful, and if you know Spanish, you may be surprised at the extraordinarily vibrant—some would claim to the point of being questionably obscene on the one hand and remarkably poetic on the other—style of language.

Here are the basics:

Buenos días	Good morning
Buenas tardes	Good afternoon
Buenas noches	Good evening
¡Hola! ¿Que tal?	Hello, how are you? (informal)
¿Como está usted?	How are you? (formal)
Adiós	Good-bye
Por favor	Please
Gracias	Thank you
Con permiso/¿Mande?	Pardon me
De nada	You're welcome
Muy bien	Very well
Con mucho gusto	Pleased to meet you
Un placer	A pleasure
Señor	Mr.
Señora	Mrs.
Señorita	Miss
Ingeniero(a)	Engineer
Abogado(a)	Lawyer
Doctor	Doctor
Gerente	Manager

Remember, in written Spanish, questions and exclamations are also indicated at the beginning of the sentence, with an upside-down exclamation point or question mark.

Honorifics for Men, Women, and Children

You must use *señor* (Mr.) and *señora* (Mrs.) plus the family name when introduced to strangers. Unless and until your Nicaraguan colleague specifically invites you to use first names, and despite how he or she might refer to you, you must always use the family name plus the correct Spanish honorific (*señorita*— Miss—is still required for a young, unmarried woman). If you do not know whether a woman is married, use *señorita* (please note: this is the reverse from what is done in Spain, where *señora* is used when the marital status of the woman is unknown). Married women are not necessarily "safe" from machismo, despite the current changes, so wearing a wedding band does not always protect a woman alone; however, being a mother virtually ensures that a man will remain at a distance: bring pictures of your children. Children in Nicaragua are expected to be respectful and not overly conversational when speaking with adults, and must always use honorifics when referring to adults. In situations where a title is known or used, the honorific plus the title is usually employed either with or without the name (e.g., Señor Ingeniero, or Señor Ingeniero Cortez). *Licensiado* is a "title" generally used for anyone with a skill requiring some sort of diploma. "Doctor" may be safely used as a way to give respect to anyone with a university degree; as an honorific, it does not have to refer only to a Ph.D. For casual contacts (e.g., with waiters and store help), just use *señor* or *señorita* without the name. It is very important to greet people at work or in stores and restaurants with an appropriate greeting for the time of day—*buenos días, buenas tardes,* or *buenas noches*—and *adiós* upon leaving. If you speak any Spanish at all, it is important to use it, but be sure to use the formal pronoun *usted* at the beginning and do not switch to the *tu* (informal "you") form unless and until your Nicaraguan colleague has specifically invited you to or does so him- or herself.

Spanish family names are often hyphenated, with the mother's family name added after the father's family name. In formal speech and in written correspondence, the fully hyphenated name is used; in face-to-face introductions, usually only the father's family name is used. For example, José Ramón Mendez-Rodriguez is Señor Mendez in face-to-face introductions, with Mendez being José's father's family name and Rodriguez being José's mother's family name. Women often keep their family name when they marry, but add their husband's father's family name with the preposition *de*. For example, Señora Maria Isabel Gonzalez-Sanchez de Rodriguez is married to Señor Rodriguez, her maiden name is Gonzalez (her father's family name), and she retains her mother's family name—Sanchez—as well; in face-to-face communication she is more often referred to as Señora de Rodriguez or, very informally, as Señora Rodriguez.

The What, When, and How of Introducing People

Always wait to be introduced to strangers before taking that responsibility upon yourself. Nicaraguans are most comfortable with a third-party introduction whenever possible. Try to ensure that for yourself ahead of time. Most of the time, you will be introduced to women first, then the most senior men. Do not presume to seat yourself at a formal gathering: if possible, wait to be told where to sit. Shake hands with everyone individually in a group when being introduced and before departing; the U.S. group wave is not appreciated. Avoid ending the conversation with the expression "Have a nice day"; it sounds controlling and insincere. Kissing is a common greeting once you have established a relationship, and it can occur quite quickly whether between women or men and women; usually, there is a kiss on two cheeks (actually an "air kiss," first on the left side, and then the right). It is not uncommon to see men and men, and women and women, walking arm in arm down the street; they are family, good close friends, or associates, and it usually means nothing more than that.

The use of business cards is common; if possible, you should have your business card translated into Spanish on the reverse. Be sure to put any advanced educational degrees and your full title or position on both sides of your business card. Such emblems of your status are very important to Nicaraguans; they want to know they are doing business with an important person.

Physical Greeting Styles

The handshake is common. The Nicaraguan version can be soft, especially between women and men. The handshake should be accompanied by the appropriate greetings (see the list of terms outlined earlier). Smiling and other non-verbal forms of communication need not accompany the handshake when it is between people who have not met previously. Men should wait until a woman extends her hand before reaching for it, and women may take the lead in extending their hand or not. Between family, friends, or trusted business associates, an extra touch on the elbow or a hug (the *abrazo,* or embrace) will generally occur. This can happen even as soon as the second meeting; do not initiate it, but respond warmly in kind if it is initiated with you. Eye contact during the introduction is important, and should be maintained as long as the individual is addressing you.

Communication Styles

Okay Topics / Not Okay Topics

Okay: your family and background, the arts (especially poetry, which is extremely popular in Nicaragua), sports, music, and history (be careful!). Nicaraguans love to see you demonstrate knowledge and interest in things Nicaraguan, but you need to know what you are talking about if you give your opinions on this topic (it seems arrogant and insulting otherwise). Be a student when they teach you about Nicaragua, go along with the effort, enjoy yourself, be appreciative and admiring, and take the opportunity as a way to build that all-important personal relationship. *Not okay:* Do not discuss the difficult economic or political situation, international or U.S.-Nicaragua relations, or other sensitive issues. Do not inquire about a person's occupation in casual conversation, although that may be inquired of you. Do not compare Nicaragua to any of its neighbors or talk disparagingly of any aspect of the culture. Do not talk about your tummy; keep your health issues to yourself, because no one wants to hear about them. Do not go to Nicaragua (or anywhere in Latin America) without pictures of your family, and when family is brought up (which it will be almost immediately in the conversation), use it as an opportunity to bring out the photographs. Never tell a dirty joke with a woman present. Many traditional women, in the company of men, completely defer all conversation to their male partner, so men must be sensitive that Nicaraguan men may answer for the woman being addressed.

Tone, Volume, and Speed

Discussions between strangers usually start out politely restrained and most often remain cool and measured. At meals, the beer may flow, and conversation is an art: it is enjoyed, savored, and commented upon, but it never gets out of hand, and is always carried on respectfully. In business, speak softly and with restraint. It garners respect.

Use of Silence

There can be some silence, especially in formal situations, or when confrontation needs to be avoided. In general, it is not that common, but interruptions and the discussion of many topics simultaneously are.

Physical Gestures and Facial Expressions

The U.S. "okay" sign, made with the thumb and the forefinger, is considered vulgar (although Nicaraguans familiar with things American will generally correctly understand the American using this gesture), as is the *"figa"* sign (made by placing the thumb between the index and middle fingers in a fist): avoid both. Never stand with your hands on your hips: it is aggressive (however, there is nothing defensive about folding the arms in front of you). Tapping the bottom of the elbow indicates that the person you are talking about is cheap or making a stingy offer. Women may greet each other by holding onto each other's shoulder or forearm.

Waving and Counting

The thumb represents the number 1, the index finger the number 2, and so on. It is insulting to beckon someone with the forefinger; instead, turn your hand so that the palm faces down and motion inward with all four fingers at once. If you need to gesture for a waiter, subtly raise your hand; never click, call, or whistle. Waving good-bye is done with the palm up at eye level and moving the fingers forward and back together quickly (Nicaraguans familiar with U.S. ways also sometimes wave goodbye with the palm facing out).

Physicality and Physical Space

Nicaraguans tend to get closer than North Americans are generally comfortable with, but never extremely so. Do not step back when your Nicaraguan associate steps forward. Nicaraguan men may touch each other during conversations, adjust each other's ties, dust off each other's shoulders, and the like. Never speak with your hands in your pockets; always keep them firmly at your side when standing. If men and women must cross their legs, it must never be ankle over knee (the preferred style for women is to cross ankle over ankle). Remember, even in public, formal is always better than informal: no gum chewing, *ever,* no slouching, no leaning against things.

Eye Contact

Eye contact should be direct when conversing, but do not be surprised if Nicaraguans look down or away when you are speaking with them (this is especially the case between classes); this is a sign of listening and respect, not of disinterest.

Emotive Orientation

Nicaraguans can be passionate in their expression. Nevertheless, until they know you well, you want to indicate restraint and coolness, while never seeming lifeless. Nicaraguans will always admire you if you can remain logical, formal, respectful, and diplomatic—especially at first—while being warm, open, and personable.

Protocol in Public

Walking Styles and Waiting in Lines

It is more important in Nicaragua to maintain one's face by being first in line (and never last) than it is to maintain a queue. Don't be too distressed if someone walks right up to the front of the line at a bank, a restaurant, or a store and gets served because of the relationship he or she has with the clerk, while you have been waiting patiently in line for forty minutes. This occurs also in response to rank based on gender and age. People also have a tendency to stand very close in public, and this may feel uncomfortable at first. Resist the urge to back away; most of the time, you are not being intentionally crowded. Remember, the need to appear helpful and courteous is strong, and if you ask for directions on the street, you will no doubt be instructed on just where to go . . . whether or not the individual actually knows! Finally, because of the recurrent military situation in the country, it is illegal to photograph any installation, public infrastructure, soldiers, or police; due to past civil unrest, even individuals may be reticent to allow you to take their photograph, so be sure to ask permission before clicking away.

Behavior in Public Places: Airports, Terminals, and the Market

Customer service, as a concept, is catching on, but is not fully institutionalized. Store hours are typically not designed around customer convenience (many stores are closed on weekends, certainly Sundays), although there are many markets that are open at many different hours, some quite late. Stores may close from 12 to 2 P.M. for the lunch hour and reopen from 2 or 3 to 7 or 8 P.M. Personally thanking store owners, waiters, chefs, and hotel managers for their services is very much appreciated. In food markets, you can touch the produce; in goods stores, it may be difficult for you to return a product unless there is a flaw in it. In most small shops and in markets, bargaining is very much expected. If you don't bargain well, that's okay; put a smile on your face and ask for half of what the listed price is. Stick to it and walk away if you have to, and you'll land somewhere in between. Never get angry, though, since bargaining is a game to get to know you, and it is supposed to make shopping a more pleasant experience. And please consider, when you bargain, that the economic conditions in Nicaragua are generally very difficult for those who make and market the goods you are buying. Many poorer people are reduced to begging in the cities, and small children and women may approach you on the street or come up to your taxi window to ask for money. It is always difficult deciding whether or not to give, but remember that the social support systems in Nicaragua are negligible, and begging is often the only way for these people to sustain themselves. If you smoke, be sure to always offer a cigarette to everyone you are talking to before you light up. In bathrooms, on the plumbing "C" means hot (*caldo*) and "F" means cold (*frío*).

When answering a phone, say your last name. The use of cell phones is growing but not ubiquitous, and most pay phones are unreliable (phone service can be intermittent and haphazard; many businesses still hire workers to do nothing but sit at a desk and redial a telephone number until the connection is made).

Bus / Metro / Taxi / Car

Driving is on the right, but people pass very quickly on the left. Driving is difficult in the cities, and dangerous off the main highways in the rural areas, and being a pedestrian is just as risky: both drivers and pedestrians really are very aggressive. Additionally, throughout Latin America, street rules are observed only sporadically (stoplights are viewed as suggestions) and drivers usually do not turn their lights on after dark (it is believed to blind the oncoming traffic), but may have them on during the day for extra safety. There are no metros. The best way to catch a cab is at designated taxi stands (hotels are good places, but often charge more for the same ride: a hotel surcharge may be added to the meter fare, in some cases). The crime situation in Nicaragua ebbs and flows, and on some intercity roads can be a considerable risk. Try to have a contact to keep you up-to-date about the crime situation, and if it sounds serious, it is. In such cases, maintaining security as a foreigner on the street is essential, and you must call a taxi only from the telephone or hotel, not from the street; additionally, avoid walking the street alone, especially at night.

Tipping

A 10 percent tip is usually sufficient in restaurants and taxis; more is considered nouveau and gauche. Porters and hotel help get the equivalent of U.S. $1.00 per item or service rendered, theater and bathroom attendants usually half (and in both cases, tipping in U.S. dollars, as is done throughout much of the region, is perfectly fine, actually preferred). Please double-check the current exchange rate, as it can vary quickly and significantly. Restaurants usually do *not* include the service charge in the bill. Even when the tip is included, it is still appropriate to leave some odd change if service was particularly good.

Punctuality

It is perfectly acceptable—in fact, essential—to arrive at social events about a half hour late. If you arrive sooner, you will be running the risk of interrupting the host or hostess as he or she gets ready. For business meetings, being late by five to fifteen minutes or more is usually not a problem, but it is safer for the new employee or visitor to be on time, while not being surprised if others are not. Usually, the meeting will not begin in earnest until all attendees have arrived (or at least until all the decision makers have shown up), and this may not correspond to the time listed in the agenda. Resist questioning the late ones for a reason; they always have one, usually involving an obligation with more important people, like superiors, old friends, or family.

Dress

Until you know otherwise, and especially for business and most social situations between adults, formal dress is best, no matter the occasion, at work, in the restaurant (although most restaurants do not require ties, more expensive restaurants do require jackets for men), or on the street, for men and women. Good taste is everything, and should be reflected in the clothes one wears. At work, men wear suits (dark is best), white shirts, and ties; polished shoes are the order of the day. Women usually accessorize so that even the simplest of outfits stands out for its interest and style. Upper-class Nicaraguan women may wear more makeup and jewelry than women in the United States. On the street or at casual social get-togethers, informal can mean jeans (though not sneakers, which are worn only at the gym or while playing sports or jogging—women do not wear sneakers to work—or tastefully coordinated clothes, sometimes including a jacket and tie for men; it rarely means T-shirts. "Formal" usually means formal evening wear, very dressy by U.S. standards.

Seasonal Variations

Evenings in the mountainous country of Nicaragua can be quite cool, so a wrap (for women), jacket, or sweater is advised. The coasts are typically humid and hot, and the heat and humidity can be extreme throughout the entire country during the summer (a time when lightweight, more casual clothing is typically worn for business and social situations).

Personal Hygiene

In Nicaragua, personal hygiene is very important, although poverty does make it difficult for the poorer people. Latin men may sport facial hair, in the form of mustaches. Note that most rest room and bathroom facilities throughout Latin America do not have plumbing capable of handling paper toilet tissue; it is for this reason that there is a small receptacle next to the toilet for your used tissue: do not flush it down the bowl, but place it in the receptacle, or else you'll face the embarrassment of having to call for help when the bowl overflows.

Dining and Drinking

Mealtimes and Typical Foods

Breakfast (*el desayuno*) is served from about 7 to 8 A.M., and usually consists of either the coffee, rolls, butter, and marmalade typical of the quick continental breakfast or eggs and black beans; sometimes tortillas are served with breakfast. Coffee in the morning can be strong and black, or with hot milk (*café con leche*).

Lunch (*el almuerzo*) is traditionally the main meal of the day; even today, in busy cities, it can be an elaborate affair lasting several hours (usually an important business lunch). Lunch is usually served from 12 to 2:30 P.M. (or beyond). It typically consists of soup, meat or fish, and rice and beans or plantains, plus a sweet dessert. Even the quick business lunch often will include a main course and a dessert and coffee. On Sunday, the family day, the main meal is supper, which is usually served at lunchtime and can last well into the evening.

Dinner (*la cena*) is served from 7 P.M. on. If the main meal of the day was lunch, then dinner is light, and this is often the case with families at home; it usually consists of soup, some meats or fish, black beans, and rice or plantains. Drinks served with dinner are usually juice, water, or beer. Dinner parties usually end at around midnight.

In addition to restaurants, there are *pastelerías*, which serve coffee, tea, and pastries, and *panaderías*, which serve baked goods. Be very careful about the places you go to eat: if they don't look safe or clean, you should avoid them. Do not eat food off the street from the street stalls: this can be very dangerous to your health. Be very careful about food and drink in Nicaragua (and throughout Latin America); there are dangerous bugs around. First, the water: Do not drink tap water anywhere in Nicaragua (except where *officially* noted as safe, sterilized, iodized, or "electrified"). This means no ice in any drinks (ice cubes may be made from tap water); ask for drinks *sin hielo* (without ice) when ordering. Close your mouth in the shower in the morning, and brush your teeth with bottled water. Drink only bottled water and soft drinks from bottles with intact seals opened in front of you; the fruit juices in Nicaragua may look wonderful, but until your digestive system has adjusted, avoid them: they may have been diluted with water from the tap. Coffee and tea are generally okay, because the water is boiled first. Avoid fresh dairy products, including milk, custards, mayonnaise, and ice cream, because they all usually require refrigeration, which may be questionable in certain parts of the country. Definitely avoid raw shellfish and raw fish and do not eat any raw or uncooked vegetables or fruits, unless you can peel them; this means no green salad. Meats should be prepared well done when possible. You will inevitably get the Latin American tummy if you stay long enough . . . it is hard to avoid a drop of water here or there. If you have followed the above rules carefully, it is probably nothing to worry about; it will be uncomfortable for a day or two. Eat lightly, drink lots of safe fluids, stay in or near your room, rest, and it will pass. If a fever or vomiting develops, be sure to seek medical attention immediately.

Regional Differences

There is an interesting dish eaten by many Nicaraguans during the Lenten season, where traditionally meat is prohibited: a paste of iguana is sometimes used as a substitute for the meat, or mixed into soups to enrich them when meat is otherwise not being eaten.

Typical Drinks and Toasting

Once the meal gets under way, beer will be the drink in most cases. The most common toast is *salud* (to your health).

Table Manners and the Use of Utensils

Do not begin eating until the host says, *"¡Buen provecho!"* Because of the significant U.S. influence, Nicaraguans dine both U.S. style (switching the knife and fork) and European style (keeping the knife in the right hand and the fork in the left throughout the entire meal). When the meal is finished, the knife and fork are laid parallel to each other across the right side of the plate. If you put both utensils down on the plate for any real length of time, it is a sign to the waitstaff that you are finished, and your plate may be taken away from you. Alternately, if you lay your cutlery down on either side of the plate it means you haven't finished; but if you really are, the host might interpret this as a sign that you were not happy with the meal.

The fork and spoon above your plate are for dessert. There are often many additional pieces of cutlery at a formal meal; if you're unsure of which utensil to use, always start from the outside and work your way in, course by course. Bread, if replacing tortillas (rarely will there be bread and tortillas), is sometimes served without butter; in that case, there usually will not be a butter knife, nor will there be a bread dish; your bread is placed on the rim of your main plate or on the table by your plate. Remember, if tortillas are served, they can be used to scoop up bits of food on your plate. There will be separate glasses provided at your setting for water and beer (after-dinner drink glasses come out after dinner).

When not holding utensils, your hands are expected to be visible above the table: this means you do not keep them in your lap; instead, rest your wrists on top of the table (never your elbows). At the table, pass all dishes to your left.

Seating Plans

The most honored position is at the head of the table, with the most important guest seated immediately to the right of the host (women to the right of the host, and men to the right of the hostess). If there is a hosting couple, one will be at each end of the table. In the European tradition, men and women are seated next to one another, and couples are often broken up and seated next to people they may not have previously known. This is done to promote conversation. Men typically rise when women enter the room, and continue to hold doors for women and allow them to enter a room first. Remember, as is the case throughout the region, the first floor in Nicaragua (*PB,* or *planta baja*) is really the second floor, with the first floor usually referred to as the lobby or ground floor.

Refills and Seconds

You are expected to eat everything on your plate. Nevertheless, it is a compliment if you ask for seconds, so be sure, when being served family style, to take small portions so that you can eat everything on your plate and still ask for seconds. You may always have additional beverages; drink enough to cause your cup or glass to be less than half full, and it will generally be refilled.

At Home, in a Restaurant, or at Work

In informal restaurants, you may be required to share a table. Waitstaff may be summoned by making eye contact; waving or calling their names is very impolite (although you might see some Nicaraguans make a kind of *pssst* sound;

don't do it). The business breakfast and lunch are more common in Nicaragua than the business dinner; dinner is usually saved for family. The business meal, however, is generally not the time to make business decisions. Take your cue from your Nicaraguan associates: if they bring up business, then it's okay to discuss it (more often than not, over the coffee at the end of the meal), but wait to take your lead from their conversation. No gum chewing, *ever,* at a restaurant or on the street.

When you arrive at a Nicaraguan associate's home for a formal meal, you will be instructed on where to sit, and there you should remain. Do not wander from room to room; much of the house is really off-limits to guests. Use the toilet before you arrive, as it is considered bad form to leave the dinner party, or the table, at any time. Once you (and the group) are invited to another room, most probably the dining room, be sure to allow more senior members of your party to enter the room ahead of you: men should move aside to allow women to enter the room ahead of them. Often drinks and hors d'oeuvres are served in the living room prior to the dinner. In a private home, be careful about what and how you admire things: the host may feel obliged to give it to you! Once at the table, be sure to look for place cards, or wait until the host indicates your seat: do not presume to seat yourself, as the seating arrangement is usually predetermined. If you invite people to your home, be prepared to always have the invitation accepted, although they may not, in fact, show up; rejecting the invitation outright is difficult for Nicaraguans, who seek to not offend. They may indicate their true intentions by simply responding to your invitation with "I will try."

Being a Good Guest or Host

Paying the Bill

Usually the one who does the inviting pays the bill, although the guest is expected to make an effort to pay. Sometimes other circumstances determine who pays (such as rank). More often than not, the bill may be shared among all the table. Making payment arrangements ahead of time so that no exchange occurs at the table is a very classy way to host. Call for the bill (by saying *"La cuenta, por favor"*), and be prepared to pay it when it arrives. Women, if out with men, will not really be able to pay the bill at a restaurant: if you want to, make arrangements ahead of time, and don't wait for the check to arrive at the table. The only time it is considered appropriate for a woman to do this is if she is a hosting businesswoman from abroad. If a businesswoman invites a Nicaraguan businessman to a meal, she should be sure to extend the invitation to his spouse as well, or may want to consider telling him that her (female) colleague will also be joining them (and be sure to have a female colleague along). If a traditional Nicaraguan male invites a businesswoman to a meeting or a meal that seems to have more than business as the subject, a businesswoman should always insist that she bring her female associate along (someone who is needed because of her role in the company); if you are a businesswoman making your first business trip to Nicaragua and have not yet established a relationship with your Nicaraguan male counterparts, you are strongly advised to bring a female business associate along on the trip. Unmarried businesswomen may want to consider wearing a wedding band. If you have children, be sure to discuss that fact at some point early in the initial conversations: any aggressive macho behavior usually stops when men learn they are dealing with a *madre.*

Transportation

It's a very nice idea, when acting as the host, to inquire ahead of time as to whether your guests will require transportation. If necessary, you should arrange for taxi service at the end of the meal. When the cars arrive, be sure not to leave your spot until your guests are out of sight.

When to Arrive / Chores to Do

If invited to dinner at a private home for a formal meal, do not offer to help with the chores, nor should you expect to visit the kitchen. Upper-class Nicaraguans often have household help for the kitchen chores. Do not leave the table unless invited to do so. Being invited to a dinner party in Nicaragua is a special honor, and not often extended to new relationships. If such an invitation is offered, accept it as an opportunity to build a new and close relationship: that is what your Nicaraguan associate is looking for. Reciprocate by hosting your colleague in your home when and if he or she comes to your country or at a fine restaurant as your guest on another night of your trip.

Gift Giving

In general, gift giving is not common in business, although it is nice to bring a small gift from abroad if you are revisiting a business acquaintance (as, at this point, they have probably become a friend). In this case, always give your business contact his or her gift in a social setting, never in the office. One exception: as is the case throughout most of Latin America, some chocolates or a small gift for the secretary of the person you are visiting can work wonders for future smooth sailing! If a man is giving a gift to a woman in a business setting, it is important to present it as a gift to her from his wife or sister. Holiday cards are very appropriate, particularly as a thank-you for your Nicaraguan colleagues' business in the previous year, and should be mailed in time to be received the week before Christmas.

Gifts are expected for social events, especially as thank-yous for private dinner parties. The best gift in this case is expensive flowers—never send chrysanthemums or white-colored flowers (they are used primarily as funeral flowers), red roses (these usually indicate romantic intent), and always be sure the bouquet is in odd numbers (an old European tradition). When you bring flowers with you to the dinner party, unwrap them before presenting them to your hostess. Other good gifts would be chocolates or a good bottle of wine. If you are staying with a family, an appropriate thank-you gift would be a high-quality item that represents your country and is difficult to get in Nicaragua, but that is not representative of the United States in general. Small American-made electronic gadgets, a set of American bath towels (always a good gift almost everywhere, since they are usually more luxurious), or anything that reflects your host's personal tastes is appropriate. Gifts are generally opened at the time they are given and received.

Special Holidays and Celebrations

Major Holidays

Local fiestas and celebrations (typically of local town saints) occur at different times in different locations throughout the year; check with local contacts.

January 1	*Año Nuevo* (New Year's Day)
March/April	*Semana Santa/Pasqua* (Holy Week and Easter)
May 1	*Día del Trabajo* (Labor Day)
September 14	Commemoration of the Battle of San Jacinto
September 15	Independence Day
December 7	Griteria Day (a day of devotion to the Virgin Mary)
December 8	*Immaculada Concepcíon* (Immaculate Conception)
December 25	*Navidad* (Christmas Day)

Business Culture

Daily Office Protocols

Consider the serious division in society in Nicaragua between the traditional conservative sector and the liberal "revolutionary" sector: this will reveal itself in the business organization as well. Traditionally, office doors, at least for senior management, may be closed; knock first (this includes bathrooms) before opening doors, and when leaving a room, close the door behind you. It is not common for women to attain positions of authority in Nicaragua; in the traditional Nicaraguan workplace, women are usually relegated to lower-level management and administrative support positions. People organize their time on a daily basis according to the tasks they must accomplish, and the relationships they must depend upon in order to accomplish these tasks; the clock takes a backseat. Therefore, the day may begin slowly, but there can be much activity by day's end, and people with responsibility can stay late in the office in order to finish up what needs to be done. This pattern repeats itself over larger blocks of time in regard to the accomplishment of projects and the meeting of deadlines.

Management Styles

Gathering the information required in order to do what your boss expects from you, or creating consensus among your colleagues in order to accomplish a particular goal, can take a long time. All of this occurs in a formal and sometimes very rigid hierarchical structure, which means that deadlines and efficiency are secondary to attention to detail, perfection of form, bureaucratic requirements, and the need to be clever in the face of limited resources in order to be effective. Because of this rigid rank and hierarchy orientation, titles in Nicaragua are very important; the highest ones (e.g., vice president) are usually reserved for very senior executive-level positions, and should not be used as casually as they are in the United States. Complimenting and rewarding employees publicly is usually not done. For non-Nicaraguans it is essential to try to have a local contact who can tell you what is really going on after you return home, and to have a local intermediary (*el enchufado*)—as well as a local lawyer and *notario* (a very responsible administrative position throughout much of Latin America)—to act as a liaison for you with the people you need to see while you are there. This needs to be set up ahead of time.

Boss-Subordinate Relations

Rank most definitely has its privileges among the traditional elite in Nicaragua. Pride and self-importance require that Nicaraguans always do business with the most important people in any organization (and this should be the same for the non-Nicaraguan working with them). There is often a rigid chain of command that must be respected. No matter what field you are in, there is a proper way for communicating with particular individuals, and an established procedure one is expected to follow, although few Nicaraguan organizations are large enough for complicated bureaucracies to develop (with the exception of the government). Deviating from the normal channels will generally make more problems for you, even if the intent is to bypass what appear to be obstacles. Traditionally, bosses are expected to provide guidance, distribute information, and make decisions; subordinates are expected to provide detailed information and follow the decisions made by the superiors.

Conducting a Meeting or Presentation

At meetings of peers, there can be open communication and sharing of ideas; in fact, these sessions often serve as information-sharing and decision-making forums in which all individuals are expected to contribute. In more formal, conservative organizations, meetings are often gatherings of nonpeers, clearly called together by decision makers in order to gather information from below, clarify goals, and formulate action plans. In these cases, individuals often do not share ideas and are not typically expected to contribute to mutual problem solving.

Negotiation Styles

Nicaraguans generally play their cards close to the vest; they do not divulge information easily (it is seen as the source of power). They are usually circumspect in their communication styles with outsiders. They respect someone who comes to them with already established knowledge and experience, and will build relationships based on your level in society and/or the organization. Whether you are worth knowing and doing business with may be more important than the details of your proposal. Nevertheless, details are important, and a carefully planned, logically organized, and beautifully presented proposal is key. Bargaining is the essence of the negotiation, as a way to build trust; therefore, be reasonable, but do not overcompromise, as this shows weakness.

The first meeting is usually formal, with the Nicaraguans sizing up you and your organization: it will be conducted in the office. Take copious notes afterward, but put on a warm, dignified demeanor during the meeting. Never be condescending. Although the contract must be legal down to the dotted i's, it really is just a legal formality to the Nicaraguans and can be overcome, by either party, if such a need arises later on. Plan your meetings as carefully and as well in advance as you can, but expect changes. The goal, at least for the first meeting, is the development of a good feeling of respect and mutual trust. Remember also that the meeting might start and end later than you anticipated; nevertheless, as in most polychronic cultures, you should always arrive on time. Coffee is the universal greeting; always accept it, always serve it (in nice china, never in Styrofoam), and drink as much or as little as you can or desire. It is the gesture of acceptance and appreciation that counts (never refuse coffee, or an invitation to go with your colleague to a café and have some).

Written Correspondence

Business letters should be formal and respectful of hierarchy. Last names are usually written in uppercase; dates are given using the day/month/year format (with periods in between, not slashes); and an honorific plus a title is as common as an honorific plus the last name. The time of day is written in military time; weights and measures are usually given in metric measurements.

The traditional language used in openings and closings may be convoluted and formal. Be sure to inquire first, in all communications, about your colleague's health and progress, then move on to the substance of your communication, and close with a salutation and your personal wishes for his or her success and well-being (the Latin communication "sandwich"). Some important business abbreviations: "S.A." means "incorporated," and EE.UU. is the abbreviation for the United States. If your colleagues write to you in Spanish, try to respond in Spanish, if you can, or use the services of a translator. Written addresses are usually in the following format:

Line 1: name
Line 2: title/position
Line 3: company
Line 4: street address
Line 5: city, state

COSTA RICA

Note: Refer to the previous chapters on Mexico and Guatemala for information about general Centroamerican and Latin American cultural behaviors; the material that follows describes specific Costa Rican variations on general Centroamerican and Latin American customs.

Some Historical Context

The anomaly of the region, Costa Rica has rarely been at war with any of its neighbors; it has the highest literacy rate in Centroamerica, it has no official army to guard its borders, and it has been a relatively stable democratic republic since its inception. Costa Rica reserves a higher percentage of its land for preserved national parks than any other nation in the world. It has been called the Switzerland of Centroamerica (incorrectly, in that it is not an armed nation, and Switzerland certainly is) because its overwhelming mountains make the country an isolated island of civility and neutrality in a region of great instability and hostility. Why this Costa Rican phenomenon? Primarily because:

- The indigenous culture did not represent a powerful civilization when the conquistadors arrived.
- The topography dissuaded the Spanish from entrenching themselves in the country.
- The Spanish (and subsequent Europeans) who did come, came late (despite the "discovery" of the country by Columbus, who christened the country "rich coast," or Costa Rica), *after* the Republican revolutions in Europe, meaning that the rigid conquistador traditions of fifteenth-century Spain were not transplanted. More often than not, Europeans who settled in Costa Rica were not there to claim the country for God and Crown, but rather were there seeking land and mercantile opportunities.

There is, therefore, a strong affiliation with the U.S. ideals of hard work and individual effort, represented in part today by the large expatriate retirement communities of U.S. citizens in Costa Rica (many on converted *fincas,* or farms), and the fact that even in local markets, bargaining, that ubiquitous form of shopping throughout most of Latin America, is usually not done. Not surprisingly, Costa Ricans are also relatively monochronic (at least in terms of being punctual, although business projects can move agonizingly slowly since Costa Ricans are also fairly conservative and risk-averse), at least in comparison to most of the rest of Latin America.

Costa Ricans are very proud of the fact that their former president, Oscar Arias Sanchez, won the Nobel Peace Prize for his efforts to halt the Nicaraguan civil war: express pride and interest in this.

Greetings and Introductions

Language and Basic Vocabulary

Relative to other Spanish-speaking countries in the region, the Spanish spoken in Costa Rica has been characterized by some as "passionless" (compared to the Nicaraguan and Panamanian Spanish to the north and south of the country, which is rich in nuance, colorful pronunciation, and the common use of words that would cause many Costa Ricans to blush!). Costa Ricans, unique among Latin Americans, use both the formal pronoun, *usted*, and the reflective *voceo* informal pronoun (not the *tu*), where *vos* replaces *tu,* almost interchangeably (perhaps reflecting the lessened concern of indicating distinction between people based on relationships). Costa Ricans refer to themselves as *ticos* (men) and *ticas* (women), never "Ricans" (this is derogatory). English is spoken by many people, certainly businesspeople.

Physical Greeting Styles

Costa Ricans are relatively non-emotive, reserved, rather individualistic (and very proud and self-respecting: never challenge this in a Costa Rican), and coolly subdued and detached in their interpersonal communication styles. For this reason, the ubiquitous Latin-American *abrazo* greeting is typically not done, and kissing is done only between people who know each other well.

Communication Styles

Eye Contact

The eye contact patterns of Costa Ricans are similar to those of North Americans: they make eye contact, but during the course of a conversation eye contact may shift; do not interpret this as disinterest.

Protocol in Public

Tipping

The tip in Costa Rica is usually included in the bill in a restaurant, and there is no need to tip taxi drivers in this egalitarian culture.

Dining and Drinking

Regional Differences

A dish unique to Costa Rica, a version of which can be found throughout many countries of the region and in South America, is the breakfast/lunch/dinner dish known as *gallo pinto,* a mixture of beans and rice, cooked together, served with or without eggs, meat, onions, cilantro, and other garnishes and vegetables. Another unique Costa Rican culinary tradition is *casado:* this is a set-lunch menu, and usually consists of a main course and dessert with beverage. *Picadillos* is a blended puree of vegetables and meat (note that in Costa Rica *carne,* or meat, really means beef).

Gift Giving

Because of the significant, positive U.S. influence, Costa Ricans are very familiar with things American, so gifts need to be considered carefully, as U.S.-made items are easily available in Costa Rica. (By the way, avoid calla lilies as a dinner gift when visiting a home, as they are typically used as funeral flowers in Costa Rica).

Special Holidays and Celebrations

Major Holidays

January 1	*Año Nuevo* (New Year's Day)
March 19	*Fiesta de San José* (Feast of Saint Joseph)
March/April	*Semana Santa/Pasqua* (Holy Week and Easter)
April 11	Anniversary of the Battle of Rivas
May 1	*Día del Trabajo* (Labor Day)
June	Feast of Corpus Christi
June 29	Feast of Saints Peter and Paul
July 25	Celebration of the Annexation of Guanacaste Province (a small peninsula, once not part of the country)
August 2	Feast of Our Lady of the Angels
August	Mother's Day
September 15	Independence Day
October 12	*Día de Cristóbal Colón* (Columbus Day)
December 8	*Immaculada Concepcíon* (Immaculate Conception)
December 24	Christmas Eve
December 25	*Navidad* (Christmas Day)

Business Culture

Costa Ricans are, perhaps more so than any other Latin Americans, egalitarian, and do not automatically seek or demonstrate blind respect for position and rank; a single powerful high-ranking individual may make the final decision, but usually only after input from most all those involved with the decision, no matter their position. Typically, this means everyone involved in a meeting or presentation, for example, is encouraged to share their views and ask questions, albeit respectfully and in an orderly, non-polychronic way. Nevertheless, machismo between men and women is strong, and women can be restricted in their social roles primarily to nurturing roles at home (however, non-Latin foreign businesswomen can do business in Costa Rica, as long as their authority and credibility is clearly established). At the business table, Ticos can discuss things quite openly; there is far less need to avoid negativity and a greater concern for expressing truth and honesty, even if negative or unpleasant, than there is the need to appear conciliatory and harmonizing. And because of their pride for law and egalitarianism, corruption is minimal, relative to the rest of the region (never offer a payment to any police officer or bureaucrat).

PANAMA

Note: Refer to the previous chapters on Mexico, Guatemala, and Nicaragua for information about general Centroamerican and Latin American cultural behaviors; the material that follows describes specific Panamanian variations on general Centroamerican and Latin American customs.

Some Historical Context

Panama has existed, for most of its history, on the receiving end of U.S. action in the region: when Colombia won independence from Spain, Panama was a part of Colombia; when U.S. plans for a canal failed to materialize in Nicaragua, it turned to Panama, but could not strike a deal with Colombia. Panamanians, however, eager for independence from Colombia, had their cause supported by the United States, in exchange for the rights to build and control the canal. Subsequent to the building of the canal, U.S. military, economic, and political interests became entrenched in Panama. Today, therefore, Panamanians are very familiar with U.S. culture: English is understood (if not spoken) widely throughout the country (certainly among businesspeople). There is a large middle class in Panama, as a result of the disestablishment of any remaining oligarchic forms from Colombia when the United States supported Panamanian independence from Colombia, but the country is still ruled by a very small, sometimes military, right-wing elite, which usually responds to U.S. interests. Because of the American, Indian, and European influences, the majority of the population is mestizo (of mixed Indian and European blood), many of whom were originally brought in to work on the canal from Europe, North America, Asia, and Africa; subsequently, although the society is stratified, there is a tradition of peaceful coexistence between different races in Panama. The degree to which different races and groups coexist in Panama is unique in the region, and is often reflected in Panamanian social and business relationships. It is not uncommon for individuals from any of the Panamanian racial and ethnic groups, for example, to be represented at all levels of Panamanian society. Nevertheless, class distinctions are rigid in Panama, as they are throughout most of the region (the difference is that class is not necessarily associated with one ethnic group or another in Panama). The indigenous peoples, the Cuna Indians, are a distinct group in Panama, who do not generally interact with Latin Panamanians or people from the United States (they are quite independent, and do not appreciate being approached, photographed, or otherwise disturbed). Some unique Panamanian cultural considerations include the need for foreigners to be extremely cautious in day-to-day life in Panama: Colón, on the Caribbean side of the canal (opposite Panama City, on the Atlantic side of the canal—referred to by locals, by the way, simply as "Panama"), for example, is considered as the most dangerous city in the western hemisphere; in general, no one, man or woman, should go out alone at night in Panama.

Communication Styles

Panamanian women will often greet each other by holding onto the other's forearm or elbow, or shoulder, and exchanging kisses (and please consider that familiarity with U.S. ways also means that Panamanians understand the meaning of most U.S. gestures and nonverbal forms of communication).

Okay Topics / Not Okay Topics

Okay: Baseball is a national passion, and a great topic of conversation. *Not okay:* Avoid discussions of the Canal and strained U.S.-Panamanian/Noriega-drug-corruption problems and relations. Also, be sensitive to the ambivalent attitudes held by local Panamanians about Americans (practically speaking, however, Americans and Panamanians in Panama usually do not interact with each other, and this is to the loss of both).

Dress

The Panamanian equivalent of the *guayabera* is called the *panabrisas,* or *camasilla.*

Dining and Drinking

Regional Differences

A typical Panamanian dish you should not miss is *ropa vieja,* or "old rope," which is a dish of shredded beef and peppers, served with plantains and rice. There is a strong influence of West Caribbean cuisine, especially on the Caribbean coast, which naturally includes seafood and fish. Several drinks unique to Panama include *chicha,* which is typically fruit juice and sugar; *arroz con pina* (rice with pineapple, believe it or not!), *chicheme* (made of corn, vanilla, and milk, and said to be very good for your health), and *seco,* a sugarcane liquor mixed with milk and ice that is mainly drunk in the country, not in Panama City. Dinner parties at homes of businesspeople will usually be served by household help: do not invite them to join the meal, or comment on them.

Special Holidays and Celebrations

Major Holidays

January 1	*Año Nuevo* (New Year's Day)
January 9	Day of National Mourning
February/March	*Carnaval* (four days before Ash Wednesday; a very big celebration in Panama, and not a good time to do business)

March/April	*Semana Santa/Pasqua* (Holy Week and Easter; this is not a good time for business)
May 1	*Día del Trabajo* (Labor Day)
May 25	Anniversary of the May Revolution
August 15	Panama City Day
November 1	National Anthem Day
November 2	All Souls' Day
November 3	Independence Day
November 4	Flag Day
November 10	Celebration of First Call of Independence Day
November 28	Independence from Spain Day
December	Mother's Day (celebrated on the second Sunday of the month)
December 25	*Navidad* (Christmas Day)

Business Culture

Especially for Americans, it is always important in Panama to establish *personalismo,* or a personal relationship, in order for business to succeed. Panamanians are impressed with titles and positions and power: stay at the most expensive hotel you can in Panama City when there on business.

PART TWO

South America

Conquistadors, Contessas, and Condomble

Getting Oriented

The Andes provides the backbone to the continent, running along the western rim from Venezuela in the north all the way down to the tip of Chile and Argentina in the south. The Amazon, "the lungs of the world" and the greatest of the world's great rivers, defines greater Amazonas, the rich eco-belly of the continent that, surrounding the massive river, emerges out of the Guyana highlands in the north and stretches out to the plains and swamps of south central Brazil. Finally, the plains of the pampas in Argentina define the remainder of the continent as we move southward toward Tierra del Fuego. These three mega-geographical divisions roughly mirror the megacultures of the continent, Andean cultures in the north and west (Venezuela, Colombia, Peru, Ecuador, and Bolivia), the Southern Cone cultures of Argentina, Chile, Paraguay, and Uruguay, and the Amazonas of Brazil and the Guyanas. For the sake of clarity, we've broken the Andean cultures down into north Andean (Venezuela, Colombia, and Ecuador) and south Andean (Peru and Bolivia), as there are some distinctions that justify the two groupings, as well as the Southern Cone west (Argentina and Chile) and east (Paraguay and Uruguay).

An Introduction to the Region

The conquest provided Spain with an immense new empire, but one that needed to be governed, at least from the perspective of the Crown in Madrid, with an irredeemable iron hand. There was no accommodation to local cultures, beliefs, or civilizations, as all were considered subordinate to, and in fact in need of, the law of the Spanish Crown and the blessings of the Christian God who, through His mercy, brought the conquistadors to the Americas. The conquest achieved in less than a century the almost total annihilation of all that indigenous America had built up over the millennia: the nearly complete destruction of whole civilizations, some in many ways far more advanced than those of contemporary

Europe, a holocaust of unprecedented proportions resulting in the death of millions, from slaughter, displacement, and disease (the Europeans brought new bacteria and viruses that the indígenas were not resistant to), and the replacement of all that was destroyed with a completely new cosmology and political and economic life. The world would never be the same again, especially so for the peoples of that region of the "New World" that would later become known as Latin America.

Making all this happen required total authoritarian control, and the Crown's formula was to establish viceroys, representative offices of the Crown in the New World, in conjunction with the church's efforts to Christianize the population. There were essentially two major viceroys (and a lesser one in what was to become Peru): one in Mexico and one in what was then termed Grancolombia, and which today would be the Colombia/Venezuela/Ecuador region. The viceroy in Mexico had to content itself with the destruction of the great Aztec civilization, and the subordination of all other indigenous groups, including the Mayans, while the viceroy of Grancolombia dealt with the subordination of the remains of the great Incas and other indigenous groups in the Andes. While Aztecs and other groups in Mexico, over time, achieved a role in the creation of *"la raza,"* or the modern Mexicans, Incas and other Andean peoples were either destroyed or so marginalized from what was to become the dominating European civilization as to play a virtually insignificant part in the development of the new countries of Colombia, Venezuela, Ecuador, Peru, and Bolivia. In all of these countries, the indigenous people were either systematically destroyed or ignored, and, to this day, represent an underclass in their own countries. In this sense, the viceroy of Grancolombia more significantly and more successfully transplanted the Crown and church in its region than did the viceroy of Mexico, and destroyed, in the process, the indigenous Andean civilizations and their world. Today, there is no greater legacy of the conquest than the proudly Hispanic cultures of Venezuela, Colombia, Ecuador, Peru, and Bolivia and the lingering rigid and vivid class distinctions that separate these European descendants from the mestizos, Africans, and indígenas of these countries as they live side by side in two very different worlds.

While Spain was establishing its viceroy on the continent in Grancolombia and Peru, the Portuguese were establishing themselves in their territory of Brazil. The Portuguese did not face the advanced indigenous civilizations of the Incas or Aztecs; in a sense, their mission was more easily accomplished, as the need to subjugate whole civilizations of people simply wasn't as necessary in the Amazon, swamps, and plains of what would become Brazil. And since the scale (though not the degree) of slaughter and brutality was less, the Portuguese were able to get on with the business of colonization and exploitation, assisted as they were by a steady stream of slaves from their already existing colonies on the opposite side of the Atlantic, along the coasts of Africa. Portuguese colonies in Africa, such as Angola and what is today Namibia, provided the free labor necessary to run the vast agricultural tracts of land that the Portuguese in Brazil were administering, primarily in the name of commerce and trade. If the destruction of great indigenous civilizations was one of the hallmarks of the Spanish conquest in the New World, the slave trade was one of Portugal's major legacies. Today, Brazil is a mixed, yet stratified, society of Europeans, Africans, and a spectrum of all mixtures in between, with a significant Asian population thrown in, a basically Luso-African culture still struggling to find a way to equitably distribute its rich opportunities to all of its people.

Finally, there is the Southern Cone of Chile and Argentina, Uruguay and Paraguay, cultures in many ways more European than South American, having been established much later in the game by emigrating Italians, Germans, Spaniards, and yes, people from the United States and (in most cases) without a significant indigenous population to rout. Taken as a whole, South American cultures share some very significant similarities, yet have emerged, through their individual histories, with some very unique cultural identities. Let's begin our exploration of the region with the north Andean cultures.

The North Andean Cultures:
Colombia, Venezuela,
and Ecuador

COLOMBIA

Some Introductory Background on Colombia and the Colombians

Among Latin American countries, Colombia is perhaps the most formal, most reserved, and most closely related with the traditions of fifteenth-century "conquistador" Spain. This is largely due to the fact that Spain set up its first viceroy in the New World in what became Bogotá, the current capital of Colombia. The customs surrounding daily social and business life among individuals in the interior of Colombia—where the major cities of Bogotá, Cali, Manizales, and Medellín are found—is extremely formal (Colombians on the coasts, particularly in the northern Caribbean resort areas, are less constrained by these formalities, having been influenced as well by Caribbean cultures—please see Part Three of this book for more information about the Caribbean cultures). It is said that if one wants to learn Spanish, for example, one should take lessons from a Colombian, for the Spanish that Colombians speak has been the least influenced by local culture, and most retains its original "pure" form from Spain (even Spain moved on to alter its Spanish into the Castilian that Spaniards speak today, but Colombia did not). If previously noted region-generic cultural traits, such as reserve, pride, and formality were ever required anywhere in Latin America, it is here in Colombia, and here in Colombia that you will see these behaviors.

Some Historical Context

Not only did the Spanish viceroy set up its New World headquarters in what was to become Colombia, but Colombia was also one of the first countries in Latin America to gain independence from Spain. Led by the Venezuelan Simon Bolivar (the independence hero who led much of South America to independence from Spain), Colombia became a leading nation in the Latin American independence movement, and assumed a major role in unshackling the continent from Spain. After independence, the Republic of Grancolombia, which included

Panama, Venezuela, and Ecuador, was established, with Colombia as the leader (the others subsequently broke away from Colombia, leaving a legacy of unsettled and difficult relations with Colombia that exist still today). The ubiquitous Latin American issue of land reform has repeatedly and dramatically played itself out in Colombia, precisely because of the rigid entrenchment of the privileged classes, exacerbated by the equally unyielding topography: essentially, three challenging pre-Andean mountain ranges divide the country, adding to the already powerful social divisions, and dividing the population into urbanites, coastal peoples, and rural farmers. The resulting stratified and fractured condition has destabilized government after government, the sovereignty of any one government being challenged by homegrown guerrilla groups, whether they were fighting for independence or land reform, on the side of powerful landholders, or, as is the case today, for drug cartel bosses. It is important to note that while cocaine is a major source of (illegal) revenue, the money stays mainly outside of the public coffers in the hands of a drug oligarchy (virtually a state within a state, with its own rules, militia, and ethos), and Colombians are quick to impress upon non-Colombians the fact that the country is, in fact, also the world's largest producer of, believe it or not, carnations (the flower business is very big business in Colombia)! The biggest legal export, in fact, is cotton. Additionally, Colombians see the drug problem in its complexity, being so close to it, and will quickly remind non-Colombians of the fact that Colombia and its policies, as in all Latin American countries, are heavily influenced by pressures from North America (in this case the argument goes that if there weren't so much North American demand, there wouldn't be so much illegal production, and the subsequent flight from the development of less immediately lucrative long-term industries, etc.). Additionally, many Colombians see the drug problem as a current manifestation of the deeper issue of land reform and wealth redistribution, and much of the civil unrest—which reveals itself in the form of guerrilla activity versus government intervention—reflects the more traditional Latin American struggle of conservative oligarchs versus reformists. The drug problem in Colombia is intimately tied to the far more complex sociopolitical problems of the country. Suffice it to say that the current problems make Colombia, among other things, a difficult country in which to do business and travel, and safety should be a major concern for all visitors, especially people from the United States. Kidnapping seems to be a preferred way of garnering everything from money to media coverage; since the kidnapping of U.S. businessmen is an especially popular activity with a variety of guerilla groups, finding oneself in the middle of a civil disturbance in any of the troubled cities, such as Medellín, can be an unsettling experience, to say the least. The U.S. State Department periodically issues warnings to travelers to Colombia; stay informed before and during your trip to Colombia, and know ahead of time what to do if you find yourself caught up in a civil disturbance or a victim of kidnapping. Having stated the necessary, we should also add that despite the required caution, life in Colombia, as in most places experiencing difficulty, goes on relatively smoothly for most people most of the time, and Colombia has a rich and fascinating culture that is well worth exploring. Once you know the rules, and have taken the necessary precautions, your trip to Colombia can be a rewarding and positive one.

An Area Briefing

Politics and Government

Government authority, nominally in the form of a federal democratic republic with a bicameral legislature, a president, and a judicial system, is, in Colombia's present circumstances, often compromised. The government struggles to maintain both its control over drug lords and break-away guerrilla factions on the one hand, and its credibility in the face of a corrupted judiciary and legislature on the other.

Schools and Education

Schooling is compulsory through high school; however, in poorer rural regions and in difficult urban neighborhoods, maintaining quality education and children's attendance through these grades is a challenge. Many children are pressed into working to help the family survive instead of attending school or do not attend due to civil disorder. The wealthy send their children to private schools, including universities in Europe and the United States.

Religion and Demographics

The people are mainly Roman Catholic, with minority populations of Jews, Protestants, and followers of other Amerindian indigenous religions. The rigid separation of classes also exists along racial lines, giving revolutionary movements additional gusto: the European-based ruling elite at the top, mestizos (those with European and indígena blood—about 60 percent of the population) below, with mulatto (those with African and European blood—about 15 percent) below that, and Africans (mainly on the coast, approximately 5 percent of the population) and a very small percentage of pure indigenous people at the bottom.

Fundamental Cultural Orientations

1. What's the Best Way for People to Relate to One Another?

OTHER-INDEPENDENT OR OTHER-DEPENDENT? As is the case with most countries in the region—due, in part, to the heavy influence of Roman Catholicism—Colombian behavior can be viewed as significantly "other-dependent." Most individuals will seek, either formally or informally, the opinions and support of family, friends, and coworkers before venturing off to do or say something on their own. While individuals are responsible for their decisions, the group in all its forms (extended family, coworkers, community) plays a powerful role in the decisions that individuals make, as it does in all Latin cultures. *Roscas,* or informal decision-making groups made up of powerful individuals in their field (be it at work, in the community, or as drug mafia-type bosses), play a powerful role in pressuring individuals to act in particular ways, appropriate to their role in any given situation. Individuals are simply not part of society unless they can claim membership to or affiliation with some group, neighborhood, town, or business organization. A consequence of this, of course, is a resistance to the outsider, and a need for all outsiders to become associated with members of the in-group as soon as possible in order to be accepted.

Causing loss of face, embarrassment, public ridicule, or criticism of any kind is a great insult in this other-dependent culture; here, how one is thought of by others is one of the most important concerns in life. Despite this strong need to look good in the eyes of others, the individual must bear responsibility for him- or herself in the world. In Colombia, every individual is unique and has the right to advance his or her own way in the world, as long as it is done with consideration for others; the proof of the value of one's individual behavior is whether and the degree to which it positively affects the lives of others. Therefore, individual Colombian pride, based mainly on one's role, achievements, and level in society, is strong, a representation of one's role in the larger society, and can easily be insulted.

HIERARCHY-ORIENTED OR EGALITY-ORIENTED? In Colombia, hierarchy and power are still rigidly determined, and unlike other areas in Latin America where the church has played a revolutionary role, the church in Colombia is a particularly conservative institution, tied, as it was at the beginning, to the privileged class. The traditions of the Roman Catholic hierarchy and the viceroy have played a powerful role in determining who does what and when. Subsequently, the Colombian workplace is rigidly stratified, with the individual at the top (*el jefe* or *el patrón*—"the boss") having supreme decision-making authority (but only in a way that honors his role as leader in the group) and the support staff being required to follow step, challenge as little as possible, and solve all problems before they surface at the top. In civic life, this means that government, which is supposed to be democratic, often fails to be, and individuals have allegiance to their immediate local leadership, whatever form that might take. In this most macho of all Latin American cultures, women and men are rigidly separated in their social roles, as is the case more or less throughout all of Latin America; machismo in this "conquistador culture" is perhaps more powerful than in any other Latin American country. Women should not go out unaccompanied at any time (the "chaperone" concept is alive and well in Colombia today, and single women of any age are often required to have one). Of course, there are women who achieve high levels in both government and business (many Colombian women are involved in politics), but they do not represent most women.

RULE-ORIENTED OR RELATIONSHIP-ORIENTED? As in all Latin cultures, but again more so, due to the rigidity of Colombian tradition, formal rules abound in Colombia, but informal ways of getting around the rules abound equally. There is an established pattern of behavior that encourages the circumvention of rules from above by those clever enough or with connections. Therefore, relationships—not rules—rule. This results in everything from minor day-to-day corruption (some form of "payment" needs to be made in order to get something done, whether it's to void a traffic ticket or win government approval of a project) to major insurrection (guerrilla resistance). In Colombia, time is well spent developing the personal relationship (*confianza,* or trust, and *simpatico,* or a sense of implicit agreement and understanding). Energy put into resolving the terms of the deal or dealing with the immediate task at hand without having built the necessary personal trust and understanding is often a waste of time.

2. What's the Best Way to View Time?

MONOCHRONIC OR POLYCHRONIC? Colombia is mainly polychronic, although non-Colombians would do best arriving for business on time. For social occasions, however, it is essential that everyone arrives at least one-half to one full hour later than the stated time. Outside of the major cities, time is circular, and very polychronic. Dinner at home, for example, is usually between 7 and 8 P.M., but a dinner party in someone's home will often not start until 9 or 10 P.M., even though guests may have been invited for 8 P.M. If you really want things to occur punctually, it is perfectly okay to identify the time as *Norteamericano,* as opposed to *a la Colombiana,* although it will be difficult to enforce.

RISK-TAKING OR RISK-AVERSE? Latin cultures, in general, are risk-averse, and that is one of the driving reasons for the creation of structure and hierarchies. Colombia is no exception. The rigidity of the system makes Colombia one of the most risk-averse cultures in the region: this means that repeated efforts must be made to convince and motivate, especially if it means changing the way something is done. This is a culture of entrenchment, and change and movement are generally seen as destabilizing and unwelcome to the status quo. Decision making can be slow and tedious, as various levels of the hierarchy need to be consulted, and as information must be made available to many in order for it to occur. Even when individuals are empowered to make a decision, there can be a reticence to take the required final step.

PAST-ORIENTED OR FUTURE-ORIENTED? Latin American cultures, including Colombia, have seen their world turned upside down more than once with their having little or no ability to control the events. First it was volcanoes and earthquakes, then conquistadors from the east, Venezuelans, the United States, and now drug lords and guerillas. In Colombia, there is a strong doubt in the ability to control what happens, but the effort is always there, for to struggle is to live. Nevertheless, while they look back to their roots for stability, Colombians are hopeful for the future, and will express confidence in the fact that there is a reason to work for change. This sometimes strong desire to believe in their own ability to overcome the odds is often balanced against an equally strong acceptance of the inevitability of setbacks and failures, almost a fatalistic expectation of it, and an inclination to place the blame on others and uncontrollable events when things go wrong.

3. What's the Best Way for Society to Work with the World at Large?

LOW-CONTEXT DIRECT OR HIGH-CONTEXT INDIRECT COMMUNICATORS? The conquistador traditions require high-context communication, where information and truth is embedded in the situation and not necessarily in the words that Colombians use. They will be quick to assure you that all is going as planned or as you desire or that they are eager to do as they agreed. This is not based on a desire to deceive, but rather on a need to appear capable, and not to lose face in the eyes of people from cultures with great resources. It is critical, therefore, to always confirm information; to have multiple, independent, and reliable sources to verify or interpret what you are being told; and to be able to read between the lines. The importance of hierarchy and other-dependency requires careful speech; in anything but the most private moments with trusted family and friends, speaking one's mind, especially at work, is done carefully. In a culture that has seen one truth replaced by another again and again, there is a strong tolerance for, in fact dependence on, the subjective interpretation of events and reality. This tendency also makes for complimentary and very respectful introductory conversation, and an avoidance of anything that may strike you as unpleasant; at first, Colombians will always try to say what they think you want to hear.

PROCESS-ORIENTED OR RESULT-ORIENTED?   As do other Latinos, Colombians rely strongly on the deductive process: how things are done being more important than the final result. This is evident among the well-educated business elite. But Colombians are also very subjective, and will often fall back on what they personally believe in order to make or justify a decision. While many Colombian businesspeople are influenced by facts and logic, persuasion is best when it confirms already existing beliefs.

FORMAL OR INFORMAL?   If there is a correct and incorrect way to get things done, then this also tends to formalize our relationships, both socially and in business. Colombian culture is perhaps the most formal of all cultures in Latin America. Family members relate to each other according to formal rules that respect traditional family roles. Formality is rarely artificial or contrived; in fact, it is often caring and spontaneous. But it can be cool, detached, and respectful. Even the language is divided into formal and informal forms and phrases, and personal behaviors are ruled by etiquette and protocol. Maintaining honor and personal pride is critical, and this means a bit more formality. Never insult the honor, pride, or personal beliefs of a Colombian or his or her country, family, colleagues, or associates.

Greetings and Introductions

Language and Basic Vocabulary

An important note: as is the case throughout most of South America, the term *gringo* is not commonly used in Colombia; people from the United States are more often referred to as *Norteamericanos,* and if they are being spoken of negatively, the term *Yanqui* is used. The Spanish in Colombia is a pure—not Castilian—and very formal Spanish. Be sure to use any Spanish you do know, but recognize that Colombians will seek to identify you and your origins by the Spanish you use. Many businesspeople understand and also speak basic English. Some of the Spanish spoken in certain areas is heavily influenced by local dialects and regionalisms. Additionally, South American Spanish differs in accent, pronunciation, and words, sometimes significantly (and especially so with slang—including scatalogical language—and modern terminology), from Mexican, Centroamerican, and Caribbean Spanish, so be sensitive to the fact that these differences exist if you have worked and traveled in other Spanish-speaking countries outside of South America. Here are the basics:

Buenos días	Good morning
Buenas tardes	Good afternoon
Buenas noches	Good evening
¡Hola! ¿Que tal?	Hello, how are you? (informal)
¿Como está usted?	How are you? (formal)
Adiós	Good-bye
Por favor	Please
Gracias	Thank you
Con permiso	Pardon me
De nada	You're welcome
Muy bien	Very well
Con mucho gusto	Pleased to meet you
Un placer	A pleasure
Señor	Mr.
Señora	Mrs.
Señorita	Miss
Ingeniero(a)	Engineer
Abogado(a)	Lawyer
Doctor	Doctor
Gerente	Manager

Remember, in written Spanish, questions and exclamations are also indicated at the beginning of the sentence, with an upside-down exclamation point or question mark.

Honorifics for Men, Women, and Children

Señor (Mr.) and *señora* (Mrs.), plus the family name, are an absolute must when introduced to strangers. Unless and until your Colombian colleague specifically invites you to use first names, and despite how he or she might refer to you, you must always use the family name plus the correct Spanish honorific (*señorita*—Miss—is still required for a young, unmarried woman). If you do not know whether a woman is married, use *señorita* (please note: this is the reverse from what is done in Spain, where *señora* is used when the marital status of the woman is unknown). Perhaps more so than in any other Latin American culture, in Colombia titles and rank are everything, so the term "Doctor" is used to confer rank on anyone who holds a university degree of any kind (do not, however, refer to yourself that way unless you hold a legitimate doctorate). Occasionally, the term *don* (for a man) and *doña* (for a woman) preceding the first name only will be used to indicate a person who merits great respect (due to either his or her age or power); if you are introduced to such a person this way, you must always use his or her full title (e.g., "Don Pedro," never just "Don"). *Don* and *doña* as honorifics, however, are typically used only between individuals who already have close personal relationships. Married women are not necessarily "safe" from machismo, so wearing a wedding band does not necessarily protect a woman alone; however, being a mother virtually ensures that a man will remain at a distance: bring pictures of your children. Children in Colombia are expected to be respectful and not overly conversational when speaking with adults, and must always use honorifics when referring to adults. In situations where a title is known or used, the honorific plus the title is usually employed either with or without the name (e.g., Señor Ingeniero, or Señor Ingeniero Cortez). *Licensiado* is a "title" generally used for anyone with a skill requiring some sort of diploma. "Doctor" may be safely used as a way to give respect to anyone with a university degree; as an honorific, it does not have to refer only to a Ph.D. For casual contacts (e.g., with waiters, store help, etc.), just use *señor* or *señorita* without the name. It is very important to greet people at work or in stores and restaurants with an appropriate greeting for the time of day—*buenos días, buenas tardes,* or *buenas noches*—and *adiós* upon leaving. If you speak any Spanish at all, it is important to use it, but be sure to use the formal pronoun *usted* in the beginning and do *not* switch to the *tu* (informal "you") form of speech unless and until your Colombian colleague has specifically invited you to or does so him- or herself.

Spanish family names are often hyphenated, with the mother's family name added after the father's family name. In formal speech and in written correspondence, the fully hyphenated name is used; in face-to-face introductions, usually only the father's family name is used. For example, José Ramón Mendez-Rodriguez is Señor Mendez in face-to-face introductions, with Mendez being José's father's family name and Rodriguez being José's mother's family name. Women often keep their family name when they marry, but add their husband's father's family name with the preposition *de*. For example, Señora Maria Isabel Gonzalez-Sanchez de Rodriguez is married to Señor Rodriguez, her maiden name is Gonzalez (her father's family name), and she retains her mother's family name—Sanchez—as well; in face-to-face communication she is more often referred to as Señora de Rodriguez or, very informally, as Señora Rodriguez. In Colombia, men and women often have two first names (e.g., Juan-José); the two first names may or may not be joined together with a hyphen when written. When addressing the individual, use both of the names; additionally, when writing to him or her, always write both.

The What, When, and How of Introducing People

There is a Colombian reserve that is observed between individuals who are being introduced for the first time: it is displayed by a certain formality, self-assurance, and distance that sometimes may seem off-putting to some (it is not meant to be). Always wait to be introduced to strangers before taking that responsibility upon yourself. Colombians are most comfortable with a third-party introduction whenever possible. Try to ensure that for yourself ahead of time. You will be introduced to women first, then the most senior men. Do not presume to seat yourself at a formal gathering; if possible, wait to be told where to sit. Shake hands with everyone individually in a group when being introduced and before departing; the U.S. group wave is not appreciated. Avoid ending the conversation with the American expression "Have a nice day"; it sounds controlling and insincere. Kissing is a common greeting once you have established a strong and very familiar relationship, whether between women or men and women; usually, there is a kiss on two cheeks (actually an "air kiss," first on the left side, and then the right). It is not uncommon to see men and men, and women and women, walking arm in arm down the street; they are good close friends or associates, and it usually means nothing more than that. In general, Colombians' greetings are longer and more sustained than North American greetings, which many Colombians find shallow and rushed. Take the time to inquire about your Colombian colleague's health and general well-being (without getting too personal), even on first introductions.

The use of business cards is common; if possible, you should have your business card translated into Spanish on the reverse. Be sure to put any advanced educational degrees and your full title or position on both sides of your business card. Such emblems of your status are very important to Colombians; they want to know they are doing business with an important person.

Physical Greeting Styles

The handshake is common. The Colombian version is a firm, sustained shake or two between two men, not as robustly between men and women or two women. The handshake should be accompanied by the appropriate greeting (see the list of terms outlined earlier). Smiling and other nonverbal forms of communication need not accompany the handshake when it is between people who have not met previously. Men should wait until a woman extends her hand before reaching for it, and women may take the lead in extending their hand or not. Men must remove their gloves when shaking hands with a woman, but a woman need not remove her gloves when shaking hands with a man. Between family, friends, or trusted business associates, an extra touch on the elbow or a hug (the *abrazo,* or embrace) will generally occur. This usually happens after several meetings; do not initiate it, but respond warmly in kind if it is initiated with you. Eye contact during the introduction is important, and should be maintained as long as the individual is addressing you.

Communication Styles

Okay Topics / Not Okay Topics

Okay: It is important to bone up on your knowledge of things Colombian, so that you can speak intelligently and positively about Colombian culture without falling into the negative topics of drugs, corruption, and so on. Demonstrating knowledge of and respect for Colombian history and its role as the keeper of Spanish high culture in the Americas would be a good place to start. More current, good topics include bullfighting (Colombians love it), the *cumbia* (a native Colombian dance), holiday traditions, the great phone system, the fantastic coffee, and the really cheap taxis (real proof of a technologically advanced society!), soccer, music, and art. *Not okay:* Do not inquire about a person's occupation or income in casual conversation, although that may be inquired of you. Americans often begin a conversation with "So, what do you do?"; this is too personal in Colombia, is often not the most interesting topic of conversation, and may be quite embarrassing. Do not give your opinions about the drug problem, civil disruptions, and the other difficulties. Do not talk about your tummy's adventures in Latin America; keep your health issues to yourself, because no one wants to hear about them. Also not okay: money, inquiring about private family matters (although speaking about the health and other general aspects of family life is very important). Do not go to Colombia (or Latin America) without pictures of your family, and when family is brought up (which it will be almost immediately in the conversation), use it as an opportunity to bring out the photographs. Never tell a dirty joke with a woman present.

Tone, Volume, and Speed

As you might expect, in this extremely formal culture, keeping your voice low and quietly powerful is the best way to go. Discussions between strangers usually start out politely restrained, and can remain so for some time. At meals, the wine and beer may flow, and conversation is an art; it is enjoyed, savored, and commented upon, but it never gets out of hand, and is always carried on respectfully. In business, speak softly and with restraint. This garners respect.

Use of Silence

There can be some silence, especially in formal situations, or when confrontation needs to be avoided. In general, it is probably more common than in much of the rest of Latin America, but still not that common, except in group discussions where something has been said that can cause someone a public loss of face.

Physical Gestures and Facial Expressions

The U.S. "okay" sign, made with the thumb and the forefinger, is considered vulgar and obscene, especially when wrapped around one's nose (it indicates that the person being spoken about is gay—considered a definite problem in this very macho culture): avoid it. Whistling and catcalling are common; getting the attention of a waiter, for example, may involve clapping your hands, or making a sort of *psst* sound; don't do either. Never yawn in public (if you must, cover your mouth and look away). Because Colombians are generally more reserved in public, there is less physical gesturing and physical contact during conversations. The "thumbs-up" gesture is also considered obscene, especially if accompanied by any kind of arm motion. Never stand with your hands on your hips: it is aggressive (however, there is nothing defensive about folding the arms in front of you). Tapping the bottom of the elbow indicates that the person you are talking about is cheap or making a stingy offer. Colombians have a unique way of indicating nonverbally the size of things: if you want to indicate the height of an individual, extend your arm and hold your hand vertically, with the thumb up at approximately the height you want to indicate. It is important not to hold your hand palm down, as might be done in North America, as this indicates the height of an animal, and it is insulting to refer to humans this way. Additionally, pointing with the forefinger is an aggressive action with negative connotations. Measure distance by indicating it along the length of one arm with your opposite hand.

Waving and Counting

The thumb represents the number 1, the index finger the number 2, and so on. It is insulting to beckon someone with the forefinger; instead, turn your hand so that the palm faces down and motion inward with all four fingers at once. If you need to gesture for a waiter, subtly raise your hand; never click, call, or whistle. Waving or beckoning is done with the palm down and the fingers moving forward and back in a kind of scratching motion.

Physicality and Physical Space

Colombians tend to get closer than North Americans are generally comfortable with, but never extremely so. Do not step back when your Colombian associate steps forward. Colombian men may touch each other during conversations, adjust each other's ties, dust off each other's shoulders, and the like. Never speak with your hands in your pockets; always keep them firmly at your side and stand. If men and women must cross their legs, it must never be ankle over knee (the preferred style for women is to cross ankle over ankle). Remember, even in public, formal is always better than informal until you are informed differently: no gum chewing, *ever;* no slouching, no leaning against things.

Eye Contact

Eye contact can be direct. It is a Colombian way of showing interest. Conversely, if you look away, your behavior will say to your Colombian colleague that you are disinterested, rude, or establishing yourself as the subordinate in a hierarchical relationship; none of these is a good idea. Maintain eye contact when it is made with you.

Emotive Orientation

Colombians are not often animated, physically expressive, or overly passionate in their expression with casual acquaintances. Therefore, while expressive gesturing is common, until you know people well, you want to exercise restraint, while never seeming lifeless. Colombians will always admire you if you can remain logical, formal, respectful, and diplomatic—especially at first—while being warm, open, and personable.

Protocol in Public

Walking Styles and Waiting in Lines

Expect very close physicality between strangers on the street or in public places. This is rarely an invitation to a relationship; it's just a way of pushing ahead. Resist the urge to back away; most of the time, you are not being intentionally crowded. It is more important in Colombia to maintain one's face by being first in line (and never last) than it is to maintain a queue. Don't be too distressed if someone walks right up to the front of the line at a bank, a restaurant, or a store, and gets served because of the relationship he or she has with the clerk, while you have been waiting patiently in line for forty minutes. This occurs also in response to rank based on gender and age. Remember, the need to appear helpful and courteous is strong, and if you ask for directions on the street, you will no doubt be instructed on just where to go . . . whether or not the individual actually knows!

Behavior in Public Places: Airports, Terminals, and the Market

Customer service, as a concept, is catching on, but is not fully institutionalized. Store hours are typically not designed around customer convenience (many stores are closed on weekends, certainly Sundays), although there are many malls now in Colombian cities where stores stay open late. Many stores close for lunchtime between 12 and 2 P.M. and reopen from 2 or 3 to 7 or 8 P.M. Personally thanking store owners, waiters, chefs, and hotel managers for their services is very much appreciated. In food markets, you can touch the produce; in goods stores, it may be difficult for you to return a product unless there is a flaw in it. Because of the personal nature of the culture, money is usually exchanged in the palms, not on the counter. Many indígenos and poorer people are reduced to begging in the cities, and small children and women may approach you on the street or come up to your taxi window to ask for money. It is always difficult deciding whether or not to give, but remember that the social support systems in Colombia are negligible, and begging is often the only way for these people to sustain themselves. Smoking is pervasive; if you smoke, be sure to always offer a cigarette to everyone you are talking to before you light up. In bathrooms, on the plumbing "C" means hot (*caldo*) and "F" means cold (*frío*).

When answering a phone, use the phrase *digame* (speak to me), *por favor,* or *¡A ver!* The use of cell phones is ubiquitous, and the telephone system is generally good, although many pay phones may be broken. Be sure to give both the paternal and maternal last name of the person you are looking for when calling directory assistance, as there are many people with the same last names.

Bus / Metro / Taxi / Car

Driving is on the right, but people pass very quickly on the left. Driving is difficult in the cities, and dangerous in the rural areas, and being a pedestrian is just as risky: both drivers and pedestrians really are very aggressive. Additionally, throughout Latin America, street rules are observed only sporadically (stoplights are viewed as suggestions) and drivers usually do not turn their lights on after dark (it is believed to blind the oncoming traffic), but may have them on during the day for extra safety. The best way to catch a cab is at designated taxi stands (hotels are good places, but often charge more for the same ride: a hotel surcharge is added to the meter fare, in some cases). By the way, the inexpensive taxis also do not require tips (the tip is included in the fare!). Bring food and water on board trains if your trip is a long one, as they may not have a café car. The crime situation in Colombia ebbs and flows but is generally a serious concern for travelers, and in some cities and on some intercity roads can be a considerable risk. Try to have a contact to keep you up-to-date about the crime situation, and if it sounds serious, it is. In such cases, maintaining security as a foreigner on the street is essential, and you must call a taxi only from the telephone or hotel, not from the street; additionally, avoid walking the street alone, especially at night.

Tipping

A 10 percent tip is usually sufficient in restaurants; more is considered nouveau and gauche. Porters and hotel help get the equivalent in pesos per item or service rendered, theater and bathroom attendants usually a few pesos (and in both cases, tipping in U.S. dollars, as is done throughout much of the region, is perfectly fine, actually preferred). Please double-check the current dollar/peso exchange rate, as it can vary quickly and significantly. Restaurants usually have the 10 percent tip already included on the bill, but if you are unsure, it's okay to ask whether service is included or not. Even if it is, it is still appropriate to leave a few pesos or odd change if service was particularly good. In addition, in most small shops and in markets, bargaining is very much expected. If you don't bargain well, that's okay; put a smile on your face and ask for half of what the listed price is. Stick to it and walk away if you have to, and you'll land somewhere in between. Never get angry, though, since bargaining is a game to get to know you, and it is supposed to make shopping a more pleasant experience.

Punctuality

It is perfectly acceptable—in fact, essential—to arrive at social events about an hour late. If you arrive sooner, you will be running the risk of interrupting the host or hostess as he or she gets ready. For business meetings, even in Bogotá, Medellín, or Cali, being late by five to fifteen minutes or more is usually not a problem, but it is safer for the new employee or visitor to be on time, while not being surprised if others are not. Usually, the meeting will not begin in earnest until all attendees have arrived (or at least until all the decision makers have shown up), and this may not correspond to the time listed in the agenda. Resist questioning the late ones for a reason; they always have one, usually involving an obligation with more important people, like superiors, old friends, or family.

Dress

Looking like you are the very model of a modern-day conquistador requires careful attention to style, dress, and making a good visual impression. Colombians are very serious about this; you will command respect if you dress for it. At work, men must wear very conservative, well-tailored suits of the highest quality fabrics, white shirts, and interesting and sophisticated ties; polished shoes are the order of the day, and accessories such as stylish watches, cufflinks, and tie clips are common. Men's hair must always be just cut (often it is merely brushed back and held down with some tonic). Women usually accessorize so that even the simplest of outfits stands out for its interest and style. Businesspeople may also wear, over their business clothes, a *ruana,* or a Colombian poncho-like garment; this is very traditional and formal. Women must dress very formally for work, and take care to accessorize and have well-attended coifs. For both men and women, dressing as expensively as possible has its definite rewards. On the street, informal may mean jeans and sneakers, though that is more common as clothing to wear at the gym or the beach, or while jogging (women do not wear sneakers to work); for a social gathering, informal more often than not means tastefully coordinated clothes, sometimes including a jacket and tie for men (it rarely means jeans, sneakers, and T-shirts). "Formal" usually means formal evening wear, very dressy by U.S. standards.

Seasonal Variations

One comment about life in the high altitudes of the Andean cultures: it takes a few days to adjust. Do not set about a rigorously jam-packed schedule for the first day or so: arrive, rest as much as possible, and eat lightly. Altitude sickness (*soroche,* which can be serious) is inevitable for most travelers the first day or so (you may find yourself waking up in the middle of the night for air); take it slow (no jogging!). While most of the region is mountainous, there are some very populated coastal towns; therefore, you will need to dress for warm sun and cool air in the day, plus cold nights in the mountains and tropical humidity on the coast.

Colors

Bright colors are best reserved for accessories, as offsets to the more sophisticated dark or soft hues and beiges of the outfits themselves.

Styles

Fashion for both men and women, as in many other aspects of life in Colombia, looks to Europe and not to the United States, although few people on the street can actually afford the latest trends. Nevertheless, even the average person has a heightened sense of fashion, and one should dress with the same thought and care that one should put into every aspect of his or her life. Shoes can be remarkably stylish, for both men and women.

Accessories / Jewelry / Makeup

Colombian women may wear more makeup and jewelry than women in the United States, and it is fashionable, especially in summer, not to wear stockings. Makeup, hairstyle, and accessories are very important for women.

Personal Hygiene

In Colombia, personal hygiene is very important. There is a real concern for cleanliness and smelling good; perfumes and colognes are used often. Latin men may sport facial hair, in the form of mustaches. Note that most rest room and bathroom facilities throughout Latin America do not have plumbing capable of handling paper toilet tissue; it is for this reason that there is a small receptacle next to the toilet for your used tissue: do not flush it down the bowl, but place it in the receptacle, or else you'll face the embarrassment of having to call for help when the bowl overflows. Finally, you may find that the bath is mainly a shower (full bathtubs are not as common) and that the water is heated from an electrical unit attached to the showerhead; if this is the case, it is very important never to touch the unit once the water is running!

Dining and Drinking

Mealtimes and Typical Foods

Breakfast (*el desayuno,* or *el almuerzo*) is served from about 7:30 to 9 A.M., and usually consists of the coffee, rolls, butter, and marmalade typical of the quick continental breakfast; sometimes *arepas* are served with breakfast. (An *arepa* is a kind of English muffin-cum-pancake, made out of cornmeal and white or sometimes other forms of ground flour, that lends itself to all sorts of treatment; it can be spread with jam in the morning, or sliced open and stuffed with vegetables or meat fillings for lunches, treats, appetizers, or dinner. It is ubiquitous throughout the north Andean region.) Coffee in the morning can be black, or with hot milk. Coffee is the national drink, and surprisingly, it is mild, not strong. A *tinto* is the little cup in which it is usually served; if you want your coffee with milk, it is *café perico,* and if you prefer a lot of milk with your coffee, you want *café con leche.*

Lunch (*el almuerzo*) was traditionally the main meal of the day; and even today, in busy cities, it can be an elaborate affair lasting several hours (usually an important business lunch)—or it can be a quick sandwich or a salad at a shop on the corner. Because of the altitude of Colombia, it is wise to eat lightly if you can, although lunch is often the heaviest meal. Lunch is served from 12:30 or 1 P.M. to 3 P.M. (or beyond). It usually consists of at least three courses, beginning with soup, going on to meat or fish and rice and beans, plus a dessert (usually flan) and black coffee. Even the quick business lunch often will include a main course and a dessert and coffee. On Sunday, the family day, the main meal is supper, which is usually served at lunchtime and can last well into the evening.

Dinner (*la cena*) is served from 7 P.M. on. In major cities, dinner may not start in restaurants or at dinner parties until 9 P.M. or later, even during the week, and on weekends can last till midnight or beyond. If the main meal of the day was lunch, then dinner is light, and this is often the case with families at home; it usually consists of soup, *arepas,* cheese, and vegetables, plus dessert. Drinks served with dinner at dinner parties or in restaurants are wines—usually imported from either Spain or Argentina/Chile—or beers, but at home, people typically drink water or fruit juice.

In addition to restaurants, there are *cantinas,* which serve mainly drinks and snacks (cantinas are really only for men), and *pastelerías,* where coffee, teas, and pastries are served. *Café conciertos* offer light snacks, drinks, and guitar music. Be very careful about the places you go to eat: if they don't look safe or clean, you should avoid them. Do not eat food off the street from the street stalls: this can be very dangerous to your health. Be very careful about food and drink in Colombia (and throughout Latin America); there are dangerous bugs around, and there have been cases of strangers drugging drinks in order to kidnap their guests. First, the water: Do not drink tap water anywhere in Colombia (except where *officially* noted as safe, sterilized, or "electrified"). This means no ice in any drinks (ice cubes may be made from tap water); ask for drinks *sin hielo* (without ice) when ordering. Close your mouth in the shower in the morning, and brush your teeth with bottled water. Drink only bottled water and soft drinks from bottles with intact seals opened in front of you. The fruit juices in Colombia are wonderful, but until your digestive system has adjusted, avoid them: they may have been diluted with water from the tap. Coffee and tea are generally okay, because the water is boiled first. Avoid fresh dairy products, including milk, custards, mayonnaise, and ice cream, because they all usually require refrigeration, which may be questionable in certain parts of Colombia. Definitely avoid raw shellfish and raw fish and do not eat any raw or uncooked vegetables or fruits, unless you can peel them; this means no green salad. On your first few trips to Colombia you will inevitably get the Latin American

tummy; . . . it is hard to avoid a drop of water here or there. If you have followed the above rules carefully, it is probably nothing to worry about; it will be
uncomfortable for a day or two. Eat lightly, drink lots of safe fluids, stay in or
near your room, rest, and it will pass. If a fever or vomiting develops, be sure to
seek medical attention immediately.

Regional Differences

Some Colombian modifications: The tortilla is not that common; you will usually be served *arepas*. Colombian food is not spiced, although hot sauces are
available on the side. There is a unique Colombian dessert, which is a toffee
made of milk and sugar. Throughout Latin America, milk and sugar are used in
many forms to make delicious desserts, in addition to the regional traditional
desserts of guava (or any kind of strong tart fruit) and mild white cheese. Hot
chocolate drinks are very popular (try the hot chocolate made by melting
chocolate bars into your hot milk!).

Typical Drinks and Toasting

Tequila is not a Colombian drink, so there is no Colombian tradition of salt and
lime with tequila-type liquors. The equivalent hard liquor in Colombia is *aguardiente,* a type of sugarcane firewater; take it slow (it is drunk in shots, however).
At a dinner party, predinner drinks will include hard liquor, and wine will come
with the meal (most Colombians do not drink wine at home); it is important to
accept both a hard drink (it will only be offered to the man) and wine, and be
sure to compliment the host after the first sip of either. The most common toast
is *salud* (to your health).

Table Manners and the Use of Utensils

Do not begin eating until the host says, *"¡Buen provecho!"* Referring to European traditions as they do, Colombians do not switch knives and forks, as people do in the United States. The knife remains in the right hand, and the fork
remains in the left. When you are finished, place your silverware parallel and
horizontally across the plate. If you put both utensils down on the plate for any
real length of time, it is a sign to the waitstaff that you are finished, and your
plate may be taken away from you. Alternately, if you lay your cutlery down on
either side of the plate it means you haven't finished; but if you really are, the
host might interpret this as a sign that you were not happy with the meal.

The fork and spoon above your plate are for dessert. There are often many
additional pieces of cutlery at a formal meal; if you're unsure of which utensil
to use, always start from the outside and work your way in, course by course.
Bread is sometimes served without butter; in that case, there usually will not be
a butter knife, nor will there be a bread dish: your bread is placed on the rim of
your main plate or on the table by your plate. There will be separate glasses
provided at your setting for water and white and red wine or beer (after-dinner
drink glasses come out after dinner).

When not holding utensils, your hands are expected to be visible above the
table: this means you do not keep them in your lap; instead, rest your wrists on
top of the table (never your elbows). At the table, pass all dishes to your left.

Never cut the lettuce in a salad: deftly fold it with your knife and fork into a little bundle that can be easily picked up with your fork.

Seating Plans

The most honored position is at the head of the table, with the most important guest seated immediately to the right of the host (women to the right of the host, and men to the right of the hostess). If there is a hosting couple, one will be at each end of the table. In the European tradition, men and women are seated next to one another, and couples are often broken up and seated next to people they may not have previously known. This is done to promote conversation. Men typically rise when women enter the room, and continue to hold doors for women and allow them to enter a room first. Remember, as is the case throughout the Continent, the first floor in Colombia (*PB,* or *planta baja*) is really the second floor, with the first floor usually referred to as the lobby or ground floor.

Refills and Seconds

If you do not want more food, it is okay to leave a little food on your plate in Colombia. You may always have additional beverages; drink enough to cause your cup or glass to be less than half full, and it will generally be refilled. Portions are generally equal to those in the United States, and there are usually more courses, for both lunch and dinner.

At Home, in a Restaurant, or at Work

In informal restaurants, you will rarely be required to share a table. Waitstaff may be summoned by making eye contact; waving or calling their names is very impolite (although you might see some Colombians make a kind of *pssst* sound and clap their hands; don't do it). The business dinner is not common in Colombia, as dinnertime is typically reserved for family. The business meal is generally not the time to make business decisions. Take your cue from your Colombian associates: if they bring up business, then it's okay to discuss it (more often than not, over the coffee and brandy at the end of the meal), but wait to take your lead from their conversation. No gum chewing, *ever,* at a restaurant or on the street. No-smoking sections in restaurants are still a rarity.

When you arrive at a Colombian associate's home for a formal meal, you will be told where to sit, and there you should remain. Do not wander from room to room; much of the house is really off-limits to guests. Use the toilet before you arrive, as it is considered bad form to leave the dinner party, or the table, at any time. Once you (and the group) are invited to another room, most probably the dining room, be sure to allow more senior members of your party to enter the room ahead of you: men should move aside to allow women to enter the room ahead of them. Often drinks and hors d'oeuvres are served in the living room prior to the dinner. In a private home, be careful about what and how you admire things: the host may feel obliged to give it to you! Once at the table, be sure to look for place cards, or wait until the host indicates your seat: do not presume to seat yourself, as the seating arrangement is usually predetermined. If you invite people to your home, be prepared to always have the invitation accepted, although they may not, in fact, show up; rejecting the invitation is difficult for Colombians, who seek to not offend. They may indicate their true intentions by simply responding to your invitation with "I will try."

Being a Good Guest or Host

Paying the Bill

Usually the one who does the inviting pays the bill, although the guest is expected to make an effort to pay. Sometimes other circumstances determine who pays (such as rank). Making payment arrangements ahead of time so that no exchange occurs at the table is a very classy way to host. Women, if out with men, will not really be able to pay the bill at a restaurant; if you want to, make arrangements ahead of time, and don't wait for the check to arrive at the table. The only time it is considered appropriate for a woman to pay the bill is if she is a hosting businesswoman from abroad. If a businesswoman invites a Colombian businessman to a meal, she should be sure to extend the invitation to his spouse as well, or may want to consider telling him that her (female) colleague will also be joining them (and be sure to have a female colleague along). Do not allow the Colombian male to suggest bringing one of his colleagues along (remember, the person doing the inviting can refuse the suggestion). If a Colombian male invites a businesswoman to a meeting or a meal that seems to have more than business as the subject, a businesswoman should always insist that she bring her female associate along (someone who is needed because of her role in the company); if you are a businesswoman making your first business trip to Colombia and have not yet established a relationship with your Colombian male counterparts, you are strongly advised to bring a female business associate along on the trip. Unmarried businesswomen may want to consider wearing a wedding band. If you have children, be sure to discuss that fact at some point early in the initial conversations: any aggressive macho behavior usually stops when men learn they are dealing with a *madre*.

Transportation

It's a very nice idea, when acting as the host, to inquire ahead of time as to whether your guests will require transportation. If necessary, you should arrange for taxi service at the end of the meal. When the cars arrive, be sure not to leave your spot until your guests are out of sight.

When to Arrive / Chores to Do

It is highly likely that you will be invited to someone's home for dinner; Colombians like to invite people to dinner parties at their home. When invited to a dinner party, remember to arrive at least one half hour later than the stated time and be prepared for dinner not to begin for at least another hour after you arrive, and to therefore go on well past midnight. If you are a guest staying in someone's home, be sure never to go about barefoot: Colombians always wear slippers or shoes at home. If invited to dinner at a private home, do not offer to help with the chores, nor should you expect to visit the kitchen. Middle- and upper-class Colombians often have household help for the kitchen chores. Do not leave the table unless invited to do so. Spouses do not attend business dinners without a special invitation to do so. Once you have been invited to someone's home, it is expected that you reciprocate by extending a similar invitation—sincerely—to them when they can visit you, or by hosting them at a fine restaurant as your guest on another night of your trip.

Gift Giving

A particularly Colombian variation on a common theme is that gifts usually are not opened in the presence of the giver. When gifts are given and received, it is very important to be extremely grateful and to express this openly, but the gift should not be opened just then. A good gift for a social or business thank-you is a fine bottle of brandy, liquor, or after-dinner liqueur. Good business gifts should never include items with corporate logos, which are seen as having little class in Colombia. If you bring flowers to a dinner party, be sure they are not marigolds, lilies, or other yellow flowers, which are used at funerals, or carnations, which are the national flower, and be sure to unwrap them before presenting them to the hostess when you arrive. Always be sure the bouquet is in odd numbers (an old European tradition). Red roses are fine in Colombia (unlike in many Latin American countries, in which red roses usually indicate romantic intent). In addition to the gift (and certainly if you did not send or bring one), be sure to send a handwritten thank-you note on a card the very next day after the dinner party; it is best if it is sent by messenger and not mailed.

In business, as is the case throughout most of Latin America, some chocolates or a small gift for the secretary of the person you are visiting can work wonders for future smooth sailing! If a man is giving a gift to a woman in a business setting, it is important to present it as a gift to her from his wife or sister, although perfume and other personal beauty items, which are typically regarded as very personal gifts in North America, are usually appropriate for a man to give to a woman, even as a token gift in business, in Colombia. Holiday cards are very appropriate, particularly as a thank-you for your Colombian colleague's business in the previous year, and should be mailed in time to be received the week before Christmas. Colombians celebrate Three Kings Day (as all Latin American cultures do), January 6, as the time for holiday gift giving.

If you are staying with a Colombian family, an appropriate thank-you gift would be a high-quality item that represents your country and is difficult to get in Columbia, but that is not representative of the United States in general. Small American-made electronic gadgets, a set of American bath towels (always a good gift almost everywhere, since they are usually more luxurious), or anything that reflects your host's personal tastes is appropriate.

Special Holidays and Celebrations

Major Holidays

Most Colombian workers get two weeks paid vacation; August is a popular vacation time. Business slows down from December 15 to January 6, and Holy Week is sometimes a more difficult time in which to accomplish work than Christmas.

In addition, there are many regional fiestas and saints' days throughout the year that usually close down businesses for a day or two; check with your local contacts.

January 1	*Año Nuevo* (New Year's Day)
January 6	*Día de los Reyes* (Three Kings Day; this is the gift-giving day, not Christmas)
March 19	*Fiesta de San José* (Feast of Saint Joseph)
March/April	*Semana Santa/Pasqua* (Holy Week and Easter)
May 1	*Día del Trabajo* (Labor Day)
May/June	Ascension Day (forty days after Easter)
June 29	Feast of Saints Peter and Paul
July 20	Independence Day
August 7	Celebration of the Battle of Boyaca
August 15	*Asuncíon* (Assumption)
October 12	*Día de Cristóbal Colón* (Columbus Day)
November 1	*Día de los Santos* (All Saints' Day; a somber and serious time, not like Halloween in the United States)
November 11	*Cartegena* (Independence Day)
December 8	*Imaculada Concepcíon* (Immaculate Conception)
December 25	*Navidad* (Christmas Day)

Business Culture

Daily Office Protocols

In Colombia, doors, at least those of senior management, are usually closed; knock first (this includes bathrooms) before opening doors, and when leaving a room, close the door behind you. It is not common for women to attain positions of authority in Colombia; in the traditional Colombian workplace, women are usually relegated to lower-level management and administrative support positions (although, as we have noted, women are active in politics). Women do struggle to reach the same levels of achievement as their male counterparts in Colombian business, and it is rare (though not impossible) to see women at the highest levels of business and government in Colombia. For this reason, non-Colombian businesswomen must be thoroughly professional while taking extra care not to appear bossy or inflexible, for in the macho culture of Colombia, this behavior will diminish the respect they are working so hard to garner. It is a fine and difficult line to walk. People organize their time on a daily basis according to the tasks they must accomplish, and the relationships they must depend upon in order to accomplish these tasks; the clock takes a backseat. Therefore, the day may begin slowly, but there can be much activity by day's end, and people often stay late in the office in order to finish up what needs to be done. This pattern repeats itself over larger blocks of time in regard to the accomplishment of projects and the meeting of deadlines.

Management Styles

Privacy and individual accomplishment of one's tasks are critical; workers provide what their bosses expect of them, and the preparation of plans, methods, and reports can be time-consuming and complicated efforts. Gathering the information required in order to do what your boss expects from you, or creating consensus among your colleagues in order to accomplish a particular goal, can take a long time. All of this occurs in a formal and sometimes very rigid hierarchical structure, which means that deadlines and efficiency are secondary to attention to detail, perfection of form, bureaucratic requirements, and the need to be clever in the face of limited resources in order to be effective. Because of this rigid rank and hierarchy orientation, titles in Colombia are very important; the highest ones (e.g., vice president) are usually reserved for very senior, executive-level positions, and should not be used as casually as they are in the United States. Complimenting and rewarding employees publicly is usually not done. For non-Colombians, it is essential to try to have a local contact who can tell you what is really going on after you return home, and to have a local intermediary—as well as a local lawyer and *notario* (a very responsible administrative position throughout much of Latin America)—to act as a liaison for you with the people you need to see while you are there. This needs to be set up ahead of time. This person will probably be with you throughout most of your activities in Colombia, and will insist on meeting you at the airport to get you through customs, and taking you to your plane when your trip is finished, and it's a good idea to let him or her smooth the way for you whenever possible. It is important in Colombia not to try to bribe anyone; if you decide you must, never do it directly, and leave this kind of thing to your Colombian intermediary (the one who made the essential third-party contacts for you initially). You may inadvertently insult someone, get yourself in some serious trouble, or give yourself a reputation as someone who will pay in order to get things done, which you will regret later.

Boss-Subordinate Relations

Rank most definitely has its privileges in Colombia. Pride and self-importance require that Colombians always do business with the most important people in any organization (and this should be the same for the non-Colombian working with them). Whenever possible, when visiting, stay at the best hotel you can, and when hosting at restaurants—at least for the introductory meeting or the last—choose the best restaurant you can. There is a rigid chain of command that must be respected. No matter what field you are in, there is a proper way for communicating with particular individuals, and an established procedure that one is expected to follow. Deviating from the normal channels will generally make more problems for you, even if the intent is to bypass what appear to be obstacles. Bosses are expected to provide guidance, distribute information, and make decisions; subordinates are expected to provide detailed information and follow the decisions made by the superiors.

Conducting a Meeting or Presentation

At meetings of peers, there can be open communication and sharing of ideas; in fact, these sessions often serve as information-sharing and decision-making forums in which all individuals are expected to contribute. Under these circumstances, discussions are usually vibrant, with many people speaking at once; questions are common and interruptions, even of presentations, should be expected.

In more formal, conservative organizations, meetings are often gatherings of non-peers, clearly called together by decision makers in order to gather information from below, clarify goals, and formulate action plans. In these cases, individuals often do not share ideas and are not expected to contribute to mutual problem solving. Remember, because a close personal relationship is often demonstrated through physicality in Latin cultures, the nearer your Colombian colleagues are to you, typically, the better they are responding to your proposal.

Negotiation Styles

Colombians generally play their cards close to the vest; they do not divulge information easily (it is seen as the source of power). They are usually circumspect in their communication styles, and will indicate their thoughts in indirect ways. They respect someone who comes to them with already established knowledge and experience, and will build relationships based on your level in society and the organization. Whether you are worth knowing and doing business with may be more important than the details of your proposal, and the relationship may, in fact, sustain you, despite occasionally more attractive terms from other competitors. As is the case in most relationship-based cultures—certainly throughout most of Latin America—it is unwise to introduce new members to a meeting, negotiation, or project team without careful handing off; things get done because of Colombians' trust in certain people, not only the company name. Details are important, and a carefully planned, logically organized, and beautifully presented proposal is key (graphs, charts, and good-looking handouts are appreciated). Bargaining is the essence of the negotiation, as a way to build trust; therefore, be reasonable, but do not overcompromise, as this shows weakness.

The first meeting is usually formal, with the Colombians sizing up you and your organization: it will be conducted in the office. Take copious notes afterward, but put on a warm, dignified demeanor during the meeting. Never be condescending. Expect to go out to a restaurant for lunch as a possible first meeting, as well, and to carry on a conversation around everything but business unless your Colombian colleagues bring it up; how you handle yourself as a person is, at first, more important than the terms you might offer to your Colombian colleague, revealing your breeding, background, and ability to be a trusted friend. Although the contract must be legal down to the dotted i's, it really is just a legal formality to the Colombians and can be overcome, by either party, if such a need arises later on. Plan your meetings as carefully and as well in advance as you can, but expect changes. The goal, at least for the first meeting, is the development of a good feeling of respect and mutual trust. Remember also that the meeting might start and end much later than you anticipated; nevertheless, as in most polychronic cultures, you should always arrive on time. Coffee is the universal greeting; always accept it, always serve it (in nice china, never in Styrofoam), and drink as much or as little as you can or desire. It is the gesture of acceptance and appreciation that counts (never refuse coffee, or an invitation to go with your colleague to a café and have some).

Written Correspondence

Business letters must be very formal and respectful of hierarchy. Last names are usually written in uppercase; dates are given using the day/month/year format (with periods in between, not slashes); and an honorific plus a title is as common as an honorific plus the last name. The time of day is typically written in military time; weights and measures are given in metric measurements. Monetary amounts are written so that the period breaks up the figure into tens, hundreds, and thousands, and a comma separates the pesos from the centavos.

The traditional language used in openings and closings may be convoluted and formal, and you should write your e-mails, letters, and faxes using a precise formula. Be sure to inquire first, in all communications, about your colleague's health and progress, then move on to the substance of your communication, and close with a salutation and your personal wish for his or her success and well-being (the Latin communication "sandwich"). Some important business abbreviations: "S.A." means "incorporated," a *cia* is a company, and EE.UU. is the abbreviation for the United States. If your colleagues write to you in Spanish, try to respond in Spanish, if you can, or use the services of a translator. Written addresses are usually in the following format:

> Line 1: name
> Line 2: title/position
> Line 3: company
> Line 4: street address
> Line 5: city, state

Finally, never misspell the name of the country: if you haven't noticed it yet, there is no *u* in Colombia.

VENEZUELA

Note: Refer to the preceding section on Colombia for information about general Andean and South American cultural behaviors; the material that follows describes specific Venezuelan variations on general Andean and South American customs.

Some Introductory Background on Venezuela and the Venezuelans

When the Spaniards first arrived on the coast of Venezuela, the indigenous peoples were living in houses on stilts in the numerous waterways; it reminded the Europeans of Venice, and so they named the country "little Venice," or Venezuela. Several hundred years later, those same shores oozed forth the second great national treasure of Venezuela: oil. The first great national treasure of the country is the Venezuelan hero, Simon Bolivar, who led the country and most of the continent in its struggle for independence against Spain. You can see statues of him in most every town square, in most cases appropriately named Plaza de Bolivar. Gaze on his statue respectfully and walk the square with dignity; Venezuelans take their hero very seriously, and will expect non-Venezuelans to appreciate his greatness. If you don't know his story, they will gladly tell you.

However, both the democratic republican government that freedom and sovereignty was supposed to bring and the economic independence that oil wealth was supposed to bestow are even now in Venezuela more promise than reality. Unfortunately, the political situation in Venezuela has been shaky for most of its history, due to the same initial aristocratic forces that shaped most of Latin America, but with a twist: the wealth from oil that was supposed to benefit so many has in reality benefited only the oligarchic few, the banks, and the repayment of international debts. Today, Caracas is the business and administrative center of the country, with Maracaibo specifically the manufacturing center of the oil and energy industry. Go to Caracas today and you see a very North American–looking city, but with squalid poverty in its midst; there is a clear and rigid separation of classes. Nevertheless, the proximity to North America and historical experience with North American businesses (primarily oil and energy) give Venezuelans a familiarity with and knowledge of North-American cultural styles perhaps more profound than anywhere else in the region. Wrapping itself around the Latin heart of Venezuelans is a veneer of North-American behavior, particularly in business: they can be punctual, matter-of-fact, very direct, and pointed; they have a reputation for not beating around the bush and for being able to say no and explain why they disagree with you. They like business deals to move along quickly when they have decided to move forward, and they understand, perhaps more so than others in the region, the mentality of their North-American colleagues. Still, the sometimes difficult and adversarial relationship with North America demands *personalismo,* a sense of trust, a certain formality, and the time necessary to build a long-term relationship. Decisions are made based on personal experience, and the facts over time have to be considered before the Venezuelan is completely comfortable with the North American.

Venezuela has had a difficult time with its neighbors, having waged several wars of varying degrees with Colombia, first over independence from greater Colombia (when Grancolombia became independent from Spain, Venezuela was within its territory) and more recently over what Venezuela claims to be illegal immigrants from Colombia seeking asylum and employment in Venezuela. Finally, Venezuela is very wary of the drug problem within Colombia and always on the alert to whether the problem is being brought into Venezuela by Colombian drug lords seeking new markets and distribution channels. Colombians, in turn, claim that Venezuela is just using the drug problem as an excuse for continuing its low-level war against Colombia. Venezuela has also been wary throughout its history of its large neighbor to the south, Brazil. There have been border skirmishes in the Amazonas region between Venezuela and Brazil over rights to land, oil, and minerals. Unfortunately, in these disputes, those who suffer most seem to be the indigenous peoples of the Amazonas region, whose interests are in most cases advanced little by either Venezuela or Brazil.

An Area Briefing

Religion and Demographics

The people are mainly Roman Catholic, with minority populations of Jews, Protestants, and others. There are small populations of indigenous peoples, mainly in the southern Amazonas region, and blacks along the coasts and in the cities. A large percentage of the population is mestizo, or of mixed European,

Indian, and African blood. It is a highly macho culture, with rigid rules for men and women in society, but it is more common to see women in business than in the past. It is essentially a very formal culture, represented in the day-to-day behaviors and dress of the people, although this formality is more prevalent among older Venezuelans than younger ones.

Greetings and Introductions

Language and Basic Vocabulary

Use your Spanish if you know some: it will be appreciated, and almost all Venezuelan businesspeople know some English.

Communication Styles

Most of the previous comments about Latin American communication styles apply in Venezuela; however, recognize that Venezuelans can be very direct in their opinions and ideas: they are not as high-context in their communication styles as their neighbors.

Okay Topics / Not Okay Topics

Okay: baseball (more popular, in fact than soccer!), family, Simon Bolivar, and professional occupation (yes, it is perfectly all right to discuss work soon after meeting someone). *Not okay:* Do not discuss Venezuelan politics (unless you really do know what you are talking about), or Venezuela's relations with its neighbors (Venezuelans have little good to say about Colombians—they will tell you all about how Colombians are ruining their country with drugs and illegal immigrants—don't get into this argument). Venezuelans will complain about their country to you and will view you as insincere if you don't join in; agree with them when you can about negative things, but be quick to also agree about positive things, and to voice your admiration for things Venezuelan, such as the beautiful rainforests in the south, the sophistication of the people, the tasty food, the music, and the glory of being the birthplace of Simon Bolivar, the Great Liberator (as he is referred to in Venezuela). Try to avoid discussions about Venezuela-U.S. relationships: Venezuelans will want to emphasize their immediate and personal relationship with you and not the relationship between the two countries, which is a good idea (remember, in Venezuela, you are a *Yanqui*, not a *gringo*). Finally, when saying goodbye, use *adiós* only when you are leaving and will be gone for a long period of time; if you will see the other person soon, use *hasta luego* instead.

Physical Gestures and Facial Expressions

While most of what is outlined in the previous section, with the exception of Colombian-specific behaviors, is appropriate in Venezuela, you should note that any up-and-down gesture with the hand is generally considered vulgar, so avoid it. Also, in Venezuela and Brazil, the *"figa"* sign (made by pressing the thumb between the forefinger and middle fingers while the hand is closed) is a sign of good luck (it is not considered offensive, as it is throughout the rest of the region).

Protocol in Public

Bus / Metro / Taxi / Car

Driving is hazardous; road rules are often ignored and lights are not used at night (drivers who do are often run off the road by angry drivers who don't). Crime is a serious issue in the major cities: do not take a taxi from the street— either radio call or have the hotel get you one (in these cases, the tip is usually included in the total fare). Avoid walking alone at any time in the cities, and this is especially true at night and at any time for women. Do not wear conspicuous jewelry, and try not to look like a foreigner or tourist.

Tipping

The tip in a restaurant is typically 10 percent and is usually included on your bill (no tip is required in taxis, either).

Dress

Looking like you are the very model of a modern-day conquistador requires careful attention to style, dress, and making a good visual impression. In business, men must wear very conservative, well-tailored suits, of the highest quality fabrics; hair must always be just cut. Professional women generally dress very formally for work, taking care to accessorize and have well-attended coifs. For both men and women, dressing as expensively and formally as possible has its definite rewards, even in this tropical climate. Men must never take their suit jackets off unless and until the most senior person present does so. However, for social or casual situations, a relaxed, tailored, and well-groomed informality is usually okay (this means jackets and slacks, sometimes even shorts, for men, but never T-shirts and jeans).

Dining and Drinking

Mealtimes and Typical Foods

Enjoy the ubiquitous *arepa,* an Andean specialty. It is a kind of English muffin-cum-pancake, made out of cornmeal, and white or sometimes other forms of ground flour, that lends itself to all sorts of treatment; it can be spread with jam in the morning, or sliced open and stuffed with vegetables or meat fillings for lunches, treats, appetizers, or dinner. Lunch (served around noon) is the main meal of the day, and dinner is usually eaten late, around 9 P.M. Dinner parties will usually start very late, and dinner usually will not be served until after 10 P.M.; expect to stay well past midnight. The drinks served to guests are usually wine or beer (although women rarely drink beer); draft beer is called *lisa,* and bottled beer is referred to as *tercio.* Coffee is drunk everywhere and all the time, and there are several varieties: *guayoyo* is a large cup of black coffee, usually not very strong (like "American" coffee), while *negro* is the same, but the coffee is much stronger; a *marron* is like a *guayoyo* but with lots of milk; a *negrito* is a strong demitasse cup of black coffee (like espresso), and a *marroncito* is a *negrito* with milk.

Regional Differences

The national dish is *pabellón,* which is really three dishes together: shredded beef with vegetables, rice and beans, and fried plantains. At dinner parties, the Venezuelan appetizer of choice is *tequenos,* or small, bite-sized pieces of white cheese rolled and fried in dough.

Table Manners and the Use of Utensils

You do not have to finish everything on your plate. When you want to indicate that you are finished with your meal, place your knife and fork parallel to each other with the fork tines facing 10 P.M. on the plate.

Refills and Seconds

Dining is done European style, and plates will be brought out with your food on them, so there is no problem with deciding on seconds; at formal meals, you won't be offered any.

At Home, in a Restaurant, or at Work

If you need to call a waiter, subtly raise your hand slightly, catch his eye, and say *mesonero* (*mesonera* for a waitress). Because of Venezuelans' need to develop trust, if you plan business appointments in the morning, expect to either extend an invitation for lunch or be invited for lunch. (Do not make back-to-back appointments.) Take your cue from your colleague as to when and whether or not business will be discussed over a meal: if it is, it will usually be after coffee, and not during the main course. If things go well, you might also want to anticipate returning to the office after lunch for a while. Be flexible. Business lunches are more common than business dinners, and spouses are almost never invited to business lunches (sometimes they are invited to dinners, but only if spouses of both sides are present). Once you have established a good relationship with your Venezuelan colleague, it would not be unusual to be invited to his or her home for a meal.

Gift Giving

A good gift for a social or business thank-you is a fine bottle of whiskey (which is very expensive in Venezuela), brandy, liquor, or after-dinner liqueur. Gifts are usually opened when exchanged. If you do bring flowers as a dinner gift, make them orchids, as they are the national flower and very much appreciated. Avoid handkerchiefs as a gift, for they represent sadness. Gold is a very special gift in

Venezuela; Venezuelans have a great admiration for it, and gold jewelry is highly prized (consider it carefully as a special gift and be careful wearing it as well, as it can be snatched off you in the streets). Thank-you notes, both for dinner parties at homes and for favors performed, business opportunities extended, and the culmination of a negotiation, are extremely important in Venezuela, and you should be prepared to send them whenever you feel an expression of thanks and goodwill is either necessary or useful.

Special Holidays and Celebrations

Major Holidays

August is a popular vacation time. Business slows down from December 15 to January 6, and Holy Week is sometimes a more difficult time in which to accomplish work than Christmas. In addition, there are many regional fiestas and saints' days throughout the year that usually close down businesses for a day or two; check with your local contacts. If a holiday falls on a Thursday or Tuesday, Monday or Friday is usually taken as the *puente,* or bridge day.

January 1	*Año Nuevo* (New Year's Day)
January 6	Three Kings Day
February/March	*Carnaval* (lots of street celebrations!)
March 19	*Fiesta de San José* (Feast of Saint Joseph)
March/April	*Semana Santa/Pasqua* (Holy Week and Easter)
April	Corpus Christi
May/June	Feast of the Ascension (forty days after Easter)
May 1	*Día del Trabajo* (Labor Day)
June 24	Commemoration of the Battle of Carabobo (the final battle for independence, fought by Simon Bolivar against the Spanish; know this)
July 5	Independence Day
July 24	Simon Bolivar's Birthday
October 12	*Día de Cristóbal Colón* (Columbus Day)
November 1	*Día de los Santos* (All Saints' Day)
December 8	*Imaculada Concepcíon* (Immaculate Conception)
December 17	Commemoration of the Death of Simon Bolivar
December 25	*Navidad* (Christmas Day)

ECUADOR

Note: Refer to the preceding section on Colombia for information about general Andean and South American cultural behaviors; the material that follows describes specific Ecuadoran variations on general Andean and South American customs.

Some Introductory Background on Ecuador and Ecuadoreans

Ecuador, along with Venezuela, Panama, and Colombia, was once part of the viceroy of Spain for the New World, and part of Grancolombia once the region was independent from Spain. Nevertheless, the differences between the individual countries soon created independence movements, and Ecuador struggled mightily toward its own sovereignty against the wishes of its neighbors, Colombia and Peru. Even today, after many wars and scuffles, Ecuador maintains an uneasy peace with Peru and Colombia, having already lost much disputed territory that it claims currently lies within the boundaries of its neighbors. Ecuador's traditions, like Colombia's, stem from the rigid class stratifications of the conquest; but by playing a secondary role to the leaders in Colombia, and always struggling against them, Ecuador was unable to consolidate its own strength, so there has been an almost unbroken history of internecine warfare among the various power brokers within Ecuador. Unfortunately, this climate set a precedent for unstable and often violent government, which continues today. Rigid class distinctions still exist, with the ruling class being the small minority of oligarchic landholders of European descent; more than half the population is, in fact, mestizo (of mixed Spanish and Indian blood), with about 25 percent being pure Indian (there is, additionally, a small black minority along the coast). Indians, mestizos, and the elite have little to do with one another, and although the government is nominally a democratic republic, the instability and traditions of political influence by the wealthy is so thorough that it would be irresponsible to even indicate that the country is in any way a representative democracy. The country is also split geographically, with the capital, Quito—playing the role of the cool, aristocratic, conservative bastion of elite culture—lodged in insulated isolation high up in the mountains and Guayaquil—playing the down-and-dirty role of the center of rough-and-tumble liberal bourgeoisie commerce—along the hot and humid coast. Serranos, or the Quito elite, live in guarded isolation (note the barbed-wire electric fences that ring every hacienda in the timeless and unchanging landscape of fifteenth-century Quito, named a world heritage site by UNESCO), while their costa cousins in Guayaquil get on with making new money and keeping the wheels of commerce alive. There is no love lost between the two groups, and while Quiteños are as aristocratic as they come, Guayaquilleños are not that far behind. Both are heirs to the Andean conquistador traditions, and for outsiders, the manners of the old guard and the nouveau riche are not that easy to distinguish. Perhaps the one thing that differentiates them is that many serranos believe their status by birth entitles them to their privileges, while costas are proud to admit that their grandfathers worked for them.

An Area Briefing

Religion and Demographics

It should be noted that, next to Colombia, Ecuador ranks a close second on the macho meter, and women must take extra precautions when working and socializing in Ecuador. A woman simply should not be alone in the evening or at a restaurant; she will be approached. If in Ecuador on business, women must walk a fine line between appearing too pushy and not being "professional." The relatively large, though almost completely disenfranchised, native indio population is very poor, and Indians will constantly seek your alms in Quito and elsewhere. The exception to the rampant poverty among the indios in Ecuador is the Otovalo Indians, who have become quite the businesspeople of the region, with an extraordinary market outside of Quito that attracts visitors from all over the world; the goods, especially the woolens, are exemplary. Otovalos have also become known as accomplished street musicians, playing Andean indigenous music in metros the world over, and selling their cassettes and CDs, as well. It should be noted that Ecuadoreans have a finely tuned sense of pride, stemming from the conquistador traditions, and often this heightened sense of self prompts behaviors that challenge even the all-powerful group to which they owe their position. It is not uncommon in Ecuador to hear of people's pride and self-possession getting in the way, and of the inevitable suffering they brought upon themselves and their family. As is the case in Colombia, the Indian traditions stand outside of the mainstream of Ecuadoran life, and the contrasts between rich and poor are vast.

Take your time adjusting to the altitude in Quito: it is quite high, and, as in Colombia, can be a challenge for the first day or so until your body acclimates.

Greetings and Introductions

Language and Basic Vocabulary

Spanish is the official language, but many Indian languages are also spoken, the most notable being the Quichua-derived dialect of the Andean descendants of the Incas (Quechua is the main Indian language of Peru). English is not spoken well, even among Spanish-speakers, although some of the business elite may have some English competency.

Physical Greeting Styles

Indians may be very standoffish with visitors, and usually refrain from contact; this means that unless you have their express permission, it is not appropriate to photograph them, and if they allow you to, they may ask for a fee (even if they do not, it is appropriate to offer some small change as a token of thanks). In Ecuador, men and women usually reserve kisses only for greeting well-known elders, or among young people, and if kissing is done in greeting, typically there is only one kiss on one cheek; otherwise, the typical greeting, especially in business, is a firm handshake between men, and a soft "handtouch" between women. As in Colombia, there is a bit of both physical and psychic distance in the initial greeting between strangers.

Communication Styles

Okay Topics / Not Okay Topics

Not okay: local politics, such as the revolving governments, and difficulties between Ecuador and its neighbors. Peruvians, Colombians, and Ecuadoreans do not appreciate being grouped together as Andean peoples by people from the United States; although they share a similar past, they are, in many ways, historic enemies.

Protocol in Public

Tipping

In restaurants, the tip (10 percent) is usually included in the bill. You do not need to tip taxi drivers.

Dress

Dress becomes more formal and conservative the more inland, and the higher up the mountains, you go. Quiteños in business always wear a suit, and business casual simply does not exist. Guyaquilleños can be seen as perhaps a little more casual (it is usually very humid and hot in Guayaquil, which is virtually at sea level): wear only natural fabrics in this climate as anything synthetic will wilt away on you. Men wear *guayaberas,* and women do wear sleeveless dresses in Guayaquil, but they always dress tastefully and formally. The culture is formal and invitations to a home, unless they specify casual, usually imply suits and ties for men, and cocktail dresses for women. By the way, most Panama hats are not made in Panama; they are made in Ecuador!

Dining and Drinking

Mealtimes and Typical Foods

Most Ecuadoran food, like Colombian food, is not spiced heavily (if you like your food spicier, you can add some of the *salsa picante* that is almost always available on the side). The elite usually serve foods, when they do, relatively undercooked for North American tastes (watch out for the red steaks and soft eggs!) and in small portions; indigenous peoples eat larger and well-cooked portions . . . when they can. Note that a special dish in Ecuador is roasted guinea pig; as an honored guest, you might be offered it. Drinks include *pisco,* which is like rum but is made from grapes and grapeskins; there is also an *aguardiente* concoction known as *paico,* which is a combination of anise, lemon, and *aguardiente* and is often served before meals and at dinner parties. Before dinner parties, you may be offered *trago,* which is a liquor made from sugarcane. (Although alcohol is served, typically women do not accept hard liquor drinks or beer, although they may drink wine.) Coffee is often made by boiling it down into a syrup and then mixing the syrup with hot milk; try it! Rice is the staple along the coast, and potatoes (of incredible Andean varieties) are the staple in the interior mountains. In most local restaurants, children may come up to you as you finish your meal and wait for you to leave, in order to get your leftovers; this may make you feel a bit uncomfortable, but it is an accepted practice, as it relieves the family from having to provide the children with all their daily meals. Please note that coca leaves, though readily available, are illegal in Ecuador (this is important to know if you are traveling in the region, as they *are* legal in both Peru and Bolivia and are used there extensively to combat altitude sickness, among other things).

At Home, in a Restaurant, or at Work

If you need to call a waiter in a restaurant, raise your hand subtly, catch his eye, and softly say *señor* or *mozo* (for a waiter, specifically). Contrary to the Colombian custom, you probably will not be invited into an Ecuadoran home for dinner, at least at first, but you will likely be invited into their home for a party; parties start very late, around 10 P.M., with people often not arriving until 11 P.M., and they go till and past dawn. A party is a Saturday night event, exclusively. The meal, if there is one, is usually breakfast, just before people leave after dawn has broken. The idea is to drink, dance, and have fun; have your dinner before you set out for the party because the only food there will typically be snacks and appetizers.

Special Holidays and Celebrations

Major Holidays

Because the weather is consistent throughout the year in Ecuador, vacation times vary. In addition, there are many regional fiestas and saints' days throughout the year that usually close down businesses for a day or two; check with your local contacts.

January 1	*Año Nuevo* (New Year's Day)
January 6	*Día de los Reyes* (Three Kings Day)
February/March	*Carnaval*
March/April	*Semana Santa/Pasqua* (Holy Week and Easter)
May 1	*Día del Trabajo* (Labor Day)
May 24	Anniversary of the Battle of Pichincha
July 24	Simon Bolivar's Birthday
August 10	Independence Day

October 9	Guayaquil Day (celebrated in Guayaquil only)
October 12	*Día de Cristóbal Colón* (Columbus Day)
November 1	*Día de los Santos* (All Saints' Day)
November 2	All Souls' Day
December 6	Quito Day (celebrated in Quito only)
December 24	Christmas Eve
December 25	*Navidad* (Christmas Day)

Business Culture

An important consideration when doing business in Ecuador: the bureaucracy can be maddening. It is cumbersome, self-perpetuating, and may seem to exist to exact a measure of tribute and not to protect the citizenry or the state. You will have endless papers to fill out, stamps to obtain, and authorities to answer to. Get an Ecuadorean intermediary (the ubiquitous *enchufado*) to help you through this, or else all you will achieve will be an increase in your stress level. Also, although Ecuadoreans are heirs to the aristocratic conquistador traditions, individuals are typically relaxed in business meetings, and may seem to be less reserved than their Colombian neighbors.

The South Andean Cultures: Peru and Bolivia

PERU

Note: Refer to the previous sections on Colombia and Ecuador for information about general Andean and South American cultural behaviors; the material that follows describes specific Peruvian variations on general Andean and South American customs.

Some Introductory Background on Peru and the Peruvians

Once the Spaniards discovered the New World, they quickly learned that some of its greatest wealth was concentrated in the Andes region of what later became Peru. Most of the silver that was extracted by Spain from the New World came from Peru, and Peru was, in fact, the wealthiest of Spain's colonies for many decades after the conquest. The great indigenous Inca culture, destroyed virtually overnight by Pizarro and his conquistadors, yielded a land rich in silver and opportunity, which was carved up according to privilege and relationship to the crown. Today, Peruvian society is extremely stratified, with a small elite governing society, mainly gathered in the withering glory of Lima, which was built as a testament to the conquest; any traces of the original indigenous civilization there were almost completely destroyed (compare this to, for example, Machu Picchu, which is a testament to the remarkable indigenous cultures of the Andes). Membership to the right class, and a deep respect for and profound allegiance to one's religion, provides the Peruvian with his or her worldview.

An Area Briefing

Religion and Demographics

Most Peruvians are Roman Catholic, although about 5 percent of the population is Protestant, and often the Catholicism that is practiced is mixed with indigenous elements. Demographically, Peru is an extremely young country, with almost 50 percent of the population under 25; the indigenous Indians are mostly separated from mainstream Peruvian life. There is a significant Asian immigrant population, with considerable political and economic influence in the country today.

Greetings and Introductions

Language and Basic Vocabulary

While Spanish is overwhelmingly the primary language, the indigenous population speaks either Quechua (a derivative of the main Inca language) or Aymara (spoken in the south nearer the Bolivian border). Some Indians in the cities may speak both their indigenous language and Spanish. When answering a phone, people usually say *"Alo?,"* sometimes followed by their family name.

Physical Greeting Styles

Kissing once on the cheek is a common greeting once you have established a relationship, whether between women or men and women. Ask permission before you take photographs of any indigenous people, including their children, and a tip is generally in order if they allow it.

Communication Styles

Okay Topics / Not Okay Topics

Okay: It should be noted that most non-Peruvians are effusively welcomed in Peru, so be prepared to be hosted very warmly, and to talk about how much you are enjoying your visit (this is in contrast to the somewhat cooler and generally more detached communication style of Colombians). *Not okay:* Do not discuss the political problems within the country, or the sometimes difficult historical relationships between Peru and its neighbors—Peruvians and Bolivians do not get along; they have fought wars over their border in the past, and Peruvians and Ecuadoreans have squared off around the same issues. Do not compare Peruvians with their neighbors.

Waving and Counting

Waving or beckoning is done with the arm extended, with your palm facing outward (not upward or downward); wave from side to side (it looks similar to the U.S. wave for goodbye).

Protocol in Public

Bus / Metro / Taxi / Car

Traveling around by car is definitely not advised, as roads are bad and poorly marked, and rural guerilla activity from time to time makes them very dangerous—especially at night. Consider traveling by plane internally in Peru (take the same precautions regarding safety against civil disturbances—and with food and drink—that are discussed in the section on Colombia). Crime is a serious issue in Peru, for both men and women; women must take special care not to wear any overtly expensive jewelry and should never go out at night without male companions. Men must also dress cautiously, and try not to look too much the foreign businessman. It could get you kidnapped.

Tipping

In restaurants, a 10 percent tip is usually included in the bill, and unless the taxi driver performs an extra service, there is no need for a tip.

Dress

Dress is a matter of class and topography; in general, businesspeople need to dress stylishly and with taste, men with ties and jackets (not necessarily suits— a high-quality sport jacket with tie and slacks is okay), women in skirts and dresses. Casual social dress would be the same, including, in most cases, ties for men; it is rarely okay (unless you are touring) to wear sneakers and jeans. Because indigenous people are so separated from mainstream Peruvian life, if you dress in native garb, they will think you are making fun of them, and non-indigenous Peruvians will not take you seriously; don't do it. In the cooler high-lands (and in the evenings everywhere, especially in the mountains, where it can get extremely cold at night), be prepared with a wrap or a sweater.

Personal Hygiene

Be careful of the shower in hotels and private homes; as is the case in much of South America, the water may be heated by a heating unit stuck directly on top of the showerhead, and if you accidentally touch it or any surrounding metal in the shower while the water is running, you will be in for a very nasty shock!

Dining and Drinking

Mealtimes and Typical Foods

Around 5 or 6 P.M. each day, most Peruvians take a small snack, called a *lonche,* which is a light, breakfast-like meal (it is the remnant of the post-siesta pick-me-up, intended to tide you over until dinner much later that night, and it is sometimes referred in English as "tea"). If you are invited to someone's home at that time of day, be prepared for tea, coffee, and cakes, but not dinner; dinner is a different invitation, and it can occur quite late—around 9 or 10 P.M.

Regional Differences

Mate de coca (tea made of coca leaves) is a common, legal drink in Peru, especially in the high altitudes of the Andes. (Although coca leaves and the tea made from them are perfectly legal, certain coca products, i.e., cocaine, are definitely not; stick to the law in Peru, as the penalties for drug possession are extremely harsh.) In fact, when you check into hotels in this area, you will probably receive a cup of *mate de coca;* it is said to make adjusting to altitude sickness a lot easier. Associated with this tea is the herbal hot drink *yerba luisa,* which is made of herbs and hot water, and substitutes for coffee, especially after big dinner meals. Both potatoes and corn come in a staggering variety of colors and sizes in this homeland: native blue corn and potatoes, and their derivative foods, are quite popular.

Typical Drinks and Toasting

Curiously, perhaps because of the affect of altitude on alcohol, when people drink wine or beer, they usually mix a little water in with it; don't take offense if water is mixed into your wine in front of you. Another popular drink is *pisco,* which is a kind of eau de vie made from grapes; it is very strong, and often mixed with lemon and sugar to make a "sour"-type drink. Finally, as far as drinks go, there is *chicha,* which is a fermented corn or grain drink sort of like wine (there is also a nonalcoholic version available—if you get served a purple-colored drink, you got the alcoholic variety, as the non-alcoholic variety is not purple).

Table Manners and the Use of Utensils

The quantity of food being served at a Peruvian businessperson's dinner party, because of his or her class, is usually quite a lot, even by American standards (potatoes, which are native to the Andes, will be served along with rice and bread and other starches); take it slowly! When you are finished with your meal, place your knife and fork together diagonally across the plate (tines pointing to 10 P.M. on the plate).

Seating Plans

In Peru, the host and the honored guest usually sit next to each other (males to the right of the hostess, and females to the right of the host); if there is a hosting couple they usually sit together.

Being a Good Guest or Host

If you are entertaining at a restaurant, choose the best one you can find (and stay at the best hotel you can find): Peruvians like to be impressed and know that the people they associate with are influential. Also, if you are hosting a dinner, invite spouses along, as dinner is usually a social gathering (avoid discussions of business at dinner—business talk is better left for the office, or over lunch, as long as your Peruvian colleagues bring it up first).

Gift Giving

In Peru, it is very important, if giving flowers, to only give roses; any other flower will appear as a cheap substitute for the real thing, and this is the case for dinner parties or other social events. Red roses, however, should still be avoided, unless you are signaling romance. Send an odd-numbered assortment, but avoid sending thirteen flowers, as thirteen is viewed as very unlucky (avoid thirteen of anything). Avoid linen handkerchiefs as a gift (they represent tears and sadness), and avoid cutlery (this represents the cutting of relationships; both of these are newer traditions brought over by the Asian immigrants to Peru). Finally, although gift giving in business is not common in the United States and only relatively common in most of Latin America, it is expected in Peru; Peruvians find it odd if you do not express thanks and show good feelings through a gift to your business associate. Thoughtful gifts include items that represent either the personal taste of the person to whom you are giving the gift or unusual and valuable (i.e., difficult to get in Peru) gifts that represent your home city, region, or country. "Corporate gifts" with logos are generally not significant enough.

Special Holidays and Celebrations

Major Holidays

Changes in climate are mainly topographical, not seasonal; therefore, vacation times vary. In addition, there are many regional fiestas and saints' days throughout the year that usually close down business for a day or two; check with your local contacts.

January 1	*Año Nuevo* (New Year's Day)
March/April	*Semana Santa/Pasqua* (Holy Week and Easter)
May 1	*Día del Trabajo* (Labor Day)
June 29	Feast of Saints Peter and Paul
July 28–29	Independence Day
August 30	Saint Rosa of the Americans Celebration
October 8	National Heroes' Day
November 1	*Día de los Santos* (All Saints' Day)
December 8	*Imaculada Concepción* (Immaculate Conception)
December 25	*Navidad* (Christmas Day)

Business Culture

Because of the severely rigid and macho culture, even non-Peruvian women will have an extremely difficult time conducting business with Peruvian businessmen. Be sure to travel with a female associate, and before you go to Peru, have respected men in your organization at home establish your authority to your Peruvian male counterparts. Never appear bossy, but always be perfectly professional. Businesspeople must take care never to do any manual labor or associate with workers (or household help) beyond pleasantries, lest they be viewed as demeaning their own positions in society. Business appointments are best scheduled for the morning; be prepared to spend the entire morning, and possibly be invited to lunch, as well. As is the case in much of the region, in business dealings and negotiations, Peruvians are most comfortable building personal relationships with individuals, and are less interested in having relationships with your organization; you are the face of your organization. Therefore, changing roles and responsibilities between individuals over time requires careful hand-offs and personal management, for anything less may be seen as too impersonal and disrespectful of the personal relationships that Peruvians have built with you. Finally, the polychronic cultural orientation of Peruvians means that discussions at meetings, in negotiations, and during presentations are nonsequential, and can include interruptions, "stop-and-go" style speech, deviations from the agenda, and people coming and going, with punctuality and the clock taking a backseat to the issues that the decision makers want to discuss. If your culture is not polychronic, you will need to practice the art of patience.

BOLIVIA

Some Introductory Background on Bolivia and the Bolivians

The fact that Bolivia named itself after the great liberator Simon Bolivar says a lot about its situation. Spain tenaciously resisted Bolivia's independence, perhaps more so than with any other former colony, precisely because of the enormous natural wealth that Bolivia provided, especially at a time when Spain was losing the same from its other, newly liberated colonies. It took sixteen years for Bolivia to achieve final independence from Spain, and by then, its natural preserves and economy were all but drained. Once much larger than it is today (it included a port on the Pacific at what is now Antofagasta, in northern Chile), Bolivia was reduced to a landlocked country, poorer even than neighboring landlocked Paraguay because, unlike Paraguay, Bolivia had no major rivers as access to the sea. The topography also made development difficult; Bolivia has just about the world's highest everything, including capital city, La Paz. (Be sure to build a day or two into your visit so that your body can acclimate to the altitude.) Today, Bolivia is the poorest of all nations in South America, with a rigidly stratified society made up of a small ruling elite of mainly white businesspeople, mestizos (people of mixed European and Indian blood), small merchant classes, and about 50 percent indigenous peoples, made up mainly of the Quechua and Aymara groups (modern descendants of the Incas), who also speak those languages respectively (sometimes to the exclusion of Spanish). Additionally, in the southeast, some of the indigenous people speak Guarani (see the section on Paraguay). Most whites do not speak the Indian languages, and will make a special point to tell you (especially if they are dark skinned) that they are not Indian (indigenous people in Bolivia are referred to by the term campesino, not as indios or indígenos). In fact, concern for social stratification along racial lines is so strong that an unusual reverse racism exists, wherein, due to their rarity, blacks are viewed by the white elite as "good luck"; if whites meet a black person on the street or in other circumstances, a custom is to pinch the person they are with and say, *Negro, negro, buena suerte.* Although there is little guerilla activity in Bolivia, petty crime—not kidnapping—can be an issue, in the cities and on rural roads, particularly at night. Bolivia had several wars with its neighbors (the War of the Pacific, for example, with Chile and Peru, in which it attempted to hold on to its coastal territory), all of which it lost; it is important, therefore, to avoid references and comparisons to Chile, Peru, Argentina, or Brazil when in Bolivia. Discussing Peruvians or Chileans in Bolivia is particularly problematic (if you are doing business in these countries on the same trip, don't mention it). In contrast, the relationship between the United States and Bolivia has been comparatively positive (which, in Latin America, is a distinction), and Bolivians generally have a fondness for people from the United States.

Greetings and Introductions

Physical Greeting Styles

Unlike in other countries farther north, in Bolivia, as in much of the Southern Cone, the handshake can be quite firm, and both women and men shake hands. Additionally, eye contact is direct (avoiding eye contact is considered rude), and while establishing a personal relationship (*personalismo*) is critical in order for any business to be done, Bolivians admire sincerity, earnestness, and forthrightness, as opposed to indirection and primary orientation to face-saving, in their communication style. (Note that this is in contrast to the typical communication styles of its neighbors to the north.) Women typically greet each other with two kisses (one on each cheek) once they know each other, and men greet each other with the *abrazo;* women and men, unless they are very close, greet each other with a handshake. People also greet each other casually by tapping each other on the shoulder; it is not considered too personal or intrusive, so avoid backing off if someone taps you on the shoulder (in fact, in the countryside, rural people often shake hands, tap each other's left shoulder, then shake hands again, as the standard greeting). Do not photograph Indians without their permission; they may believe, as do many indigenous peoples, that taking someone's picture may steal his or her soul. If they do let you take their picture, you may have to pay them a sucre or two to do it.

Communication Styles

Tone, Volume, and Speed

Whispering is considered suspicious; if you speak too softly or indirectly or are not understood, you could be accused of whispering, and therefore seen as untrustworthy.

Physical Gestures and Facial Expressions

The hand gesture of twisting the open palm from side to side that in the United States means "so-so," in Bolivia is a definite statement of "no" and disagreement. The *"figa"* sign (made by holding the thumb between index and middle fingers in a fist) is considered very vulgar (remember, in neighboring Venezuela, this is considered "good luck").

Protocol in Public

Tipping

You are not required to tip in taxis (but they rarely have meters, so be sure to negotiate the fare as soon as you get in).

Dress

Dress is determined by class and gender, occasion, and topography. Business dress for men usually requires a suit (the three-piece suit is very common in La Paz, the capital, as the altitude makes the extra layer comfortable; however, Santa Cruz is in the tropical lowlands, so lightweight tropical suits—and sometimes a *guayabera,* always worn outside the pants and without a tie—are appropriate). Women must never wear slacks or pants anywhere, anytime. The high mountains also drop down quickly to low, almost tropical areas, so bring a change of clothing if you are traveling through the major cities (compare mountainous La Paz and subtropical Cochabamba). Even in casual, social settings, clothes must be very clean and neat, never wrinkled or dirty, and dinners in private homes generally require ties and jackets for men, dresses for women. Never dress like indigenous peoples for whatever reason (never wear the bowler-type hat that is common among Indian women, for example); it is insulting, and you will be scorned by both indigenous people and businesspeople.

Personal Hygiene

Be careful of the shower in hotels and private homes; as is the case in much of South America, the water may be heated by a heating unit stuck directly on top of the showerhead, and if you accidentally touch it or any surrounding metal in the shower while the water is running, you will be in for a very nasty shock! The cautionary statements we have been making throughout the book about food and water apply in Bolivia as well. And remember the high altitude of Bolivia: rest very easy the first few days (avoid heavy eating and alcohol, and any kind of physical exertion), or you'll definitely suffer from altitude sickness, and be sure to wear sunscreen all the time during the day.

Dining and Drinking

Regional Differences

Mate de coca (tea made of coca leaves) is a common, legal drink in Bolivia, especially in the high altitudes of the Andes. (Remember, however, that while coca leaves are legal, cocaine is not.) In fact, when you check into hotels in this area, you will probably receive a cup of *mate de coca;* it is said to make adjusting to altitude sickness a lot easier. Another popular drink is *pisco,* which is a kind of eau de vie made from grapes; it is very strong, and is often mixed with orange juice as an apertif. Finally, as far as drinks go, there is *chicha,* which is a fermented corn or grain drink (there is also a nonalcoholic version available—the alcoholic variety has a purple color to it) and *chufle,* which is a mixture of soda water, lemon juice, and *singani* (another brandy-like distillation made from grapes). A word of caution: the food may be very spicy, due to the liberal use of hot sauces and hot peppers (look out for the red and green peppers in the food; you can move them aside on your plate); you are also not required to take advantage of the hot *llajua* and *halpahuayca* sauces that are always on the table in restaurants. Around 4 or 5 P.M. each day, most Bolivians take a small snack, which is then often repeated around 9 or 10 P.M., as the evening meal at home (lunch is the main meal of the day). There are also some uniquely Bolivian attitudes toward pouring wines (which are usually imported from Chile, Argentina, or abroad): never pour with your left hand (it is an insult), and if you pour the wine "backward" into the glass (that is, holding the bottom of the bottle, instead of the body or the neck, as you pour—a neat trick if you can do it, actually), it is a "backhanded" statement that you dislike the person for whom you are pouring; it will be taken as a severe insult.

Table Manners and the Use of Utensils

Formal dining is European style (eat nothing with your hands, except bread), so family-style meals are not common when hosting guests; your plate will be arranged in the kitchen and brought out to you.

Refills and Seconds

In Bolivia, you are expected to eat everything on your plate, and you will be offered seconds; you will need to politely refuse several times, if you do not want more, so pace yourself carefully.

Gift Giving

Business gifts are very common, but people from the United States may find it difficult to bring something from the United States that Bolivians don't already have; Bolivian trade laws make it extremely easy for many U.S. products, especially electronics and clothes, to be readily and cheaply available. Bring a high-quality item that is difficult to get in Bolivia that represents your native country, region, or city, or that reflects your host's personal tastes. A final thought about the ubiquitous "gifts" to public servants, such as police, customs officials, and so on: while it is not good to do so in the other Andean cultures, in Bolivia, providing a "tip" for services provided—as is done in Mexico and most of Centroamerica—is expected; the best way to handle this is to suggest that you do not want them to incur any expenses in the administration of their duties for you, and then ask if there is any cost that you can cover. This usually takes care of it.

When giving gifts for social occasions in Bolivia, it is very important, if giving flowers, to give only roses; any other flower will appear as a cheap substitute for the real thing. The red rose does not indicate special romantic intent here: it is taken merely as an exclusive type of thank-you (but yellow flowers should be avoided—they are sent as a sign of dislike—and purple flowers are associated with funerals).

Special Holidays and Celebrations

Major Holidays

Changes in climate are mainly topographical, not seasonal; therefore, vacation times vary. In addition, there are many regional fiestas and saints' days throughout the year that usually close down business for a day or two; check with your local contacts (a particularly important one is the Alasitas Festival in the major cities in honor of the indigenous god, Ekeko, who brings good fortune, good health, and luck).

January 1	*Año Nuevo* (New Year's Day)
February/March	*Carnaval* (be prepared for an outrageous celebration, and don't wear anything that you can't afford to get drenched, doused, paint poured on, etc.!)
March/April	*Semana Santa/Pasqua* (Holy Week and Easter)
May	Corpus Christi
August 6	Independence Day
October 12	*Día de Cristóbal Colón* (Columbus Day)
November 2	*Día de los Santos* (All Saints' Day)
December 25	*Navidad* (Christmas Day)

Business Culture

Businesswomen, once their authority is established and known, will be accepted in Bolivia, but women still need to be careful about traveling alone, especially in the evening; avoid it if possible. On the macho meter, Bolivia usually scores lower than its neighbors to the north, at least when it comes to women in business and public life. In the home, however, the roles of men and women are still strictly separated, as they are in much of the rest of the region; Friday nights, for example, are referred to throughout Bolivia as "Bachelor Fridays," on which men go out with their buddies, and women do not come along! If you are hosting business acquaintances in a restaurant, try the best Bolivian-style (not foreign) restaurant you can find; it shows you appreciate the local culture, and Bolivian businesspeople enjoy it.

CHAPTER SIX

Brazil

Some Introductory Background on Brazil and the Brazilians

What a country! This phrase is not an exaggeration when used to describe Brazil. This enormous nation, unquestionably the largest in Latin America, is also, in many significant ways, very different from all of its neighbors. For one thing, it is not Hispanic; it is a Luso-African culture, having at its heart the traditions and heritage of the Portuguese, overlayed with a powerful African influence. It is a country of eternal promise, even as it struggles to live up to its potential and to provide for all its myriad peoples. It is a multicultural mix of every conceivable race and ethnicity, and Brazilians celebrate their rainbow proudly; nevertheless, race and ethnicity profoundly determine position in society, resulting in an essentially white ruling elite, white and mestizo middle class, and African poor. In addition to the European, mixed, and African groups, there are significant populations of Japanese (São Paulo, in fact, has the largest expatriate population of Japanese), Germans, and Chinese. Native indigenous peoples comprise only a very small percentage of the total population, and are concentrated mainly in the remote Amazonas region. Ninety percent of the people live on 10 percent of the land, mainly along the coast from the center of the country south.

The triangle formed by the cities of Rio de Janeiro, São Paulo, and Brasília make up the dynamo that is Brazil today: hardworking, nose-to-the-grindstone São Paulo, cultural sophisticate and bearer of good times and Brazilian esprit Rio de Janeiro, and the administrative center of the country, Brasília. (Salvador, the capital of Bahia in the northeast, is the center of the unique African-Brazilian culture, and Manaus, the city created by the rubber barons of the nineteenth century deep in the heart of the Amazon, is the center of trade and activity in the Amazonas in the north.) Residents of Rio are known as Cariocas, or literally, "people from Rio," and have a reputation, at least from the perspective of others, for being free-spirited and ready to party in that uniquely Brazilian way or drop work on a moment's notice for a game of volleyball on Copacabana beach. On the other hand, residents of São Paulo, the business megalopolis slightly to the south and inland from Rio—known as the Manhattan of Brazil not only for its architecture but also because of the temperament of its people—are known as Paulistanos ("Paulistas" is a term used to describe anyone from the larger state of São Paulo, of which the city of São Paulo is its capital).

Paulistanos typically refer to their city as Sampas, short for São Paulo, and have a reputation for being hardworking participants in the rat-race, and far too serious for Cariocas (Cariocas, on the other hand, are generally far too frivolous for Paulistanos). Residents of Brasília (of which there are, relatively speaking, few, since the city is mainly made up of week- and day-tripping bureaucrats who travel in when necessary during the week and flee for their homes and families in São Paulo, Rio, and elsewhere on the weekends) are the civil servants of this vast and unwieldy Republic. Brasília was literally carved out of the jungle in an effort to bring people into the interior. However, the economic wealth and opportunity of the Amazon to the north is what continues to attract people to the interior, for better or for worse.

Brazil is always a "new" country, in the sense that tomorrow is always around the corner, a time when Brazilians will realize the potential of their vast land. Today, Brazil *is* new again, in that the economy is now more open for investment than it has been for most of the last half of the twentieth century. Until recently, the government idea was to develop Brazil by eliminating competition from abroad (i.e., imported goods and services). (This disastrous policy was essentially eliminated in the 1990s, allowing for investment from abroad.) This policy complemented the development of a vast government bureaucracy at the time, as the government took a greater role in controlling the direction of the economy; in part this expansion of the government bureaucracy was a planned attempt at providing jobs, and an entire population of civil servants developed. Although Brazil is now open for business, there is a legacy from this past that manifests itself as a wariness about doing business with outsiders and a complex and often debilitating bureaucracy that involves itself in almost all business ventures in some form or another. Rounding out this economic picture, the masses of unskilled laborers in Brazil themselves constitute a kind of shadow economy, with some individuals providing, among many other things, "assistance," whether needed or not, such as by helping companies get things done through the bureaucracy itself . . . for a fee, of course.

Some Historical Context

Brazil was "discovered" by the Portuguese explorer Pedro Cabral in 1500, and became the gem of the Portuguese empire. Because the immense potential wealth of the country was critical to Portugal, Brazil became the recipient of exported human labor from Africa, in the form of Portugal's slave trade, primarily from its colonies in southwest Africa. African slaves provided the labor needed by Portugal to exploit Brazil's potential, and as it conquered the land and its small indigenous population, carving out vast agricultural real estate for its European settlers, worked by its African slaves, for a while it looked as if Portugal might succeed in its venture in the Americas. But Napolean came on the scene in Europe, conquered Portugal itself, and threw the Portuguese empire into shambles. It also sent the Portuguese king and the royal family scrambling from Lisbon, and they settled in the safe harbor of Rio de Janeiro. There they ruled the remains of the Portuguese empire, including Portugal, disliked and shamed by the Brazilians themselves, and humiliated in their defeat by Napoleon into ruling the empire from the seat of one of their colonies. In 1821, the king returned to Portugal, and his son Dom Pedro remained in Brazil as regent. He became emperor in 1822, and eventually abdicated in favor of his son Pedro II, who ruled for almost fifty years in the nineteenth century. Pedro II eventually succumbed to old age, politics, and the military, which overthrew him, established a republic (ruled by a series of military dictators), and set the stage for almost a century of dictators and military coups. Only since the 1980s has Brazil experienced anything even remotely resembling democratic government. Nevertheless, Brazilians are extremely proud of their role in the Americas. The fruits of this legacy of Portuguese rule, slavery, colonial exploitation, hope and promise, and military dictatorship live on today as Brazil, and the rest of the region, continues to struggle with the difficult problems of poverty, concentrated wealth, powerful oligarchies, and unstable unrepresentative governments in its quest to fulfill its promise.

As is the case in Mexico, it is important for Americans from *Estados Unidos* to refer to themselves as "Americans from the United States" or "U.S. Americans" when speaking with anyone in Brazil (or anyone else in the western hemisphere). By the way, the term *"Yanqui"* can be either positive or negative in its connotation depending on the context: When used to describe a North American whom a Brazilian does not know, it is usually used pejoratively; if it is used to describe a North American with whom a Brazilian has a good relationship, it is being used affectionately.

An Area Briefing

Politics and Government

Nominally a federal Republic made up of states, with executive, legislative, and judicial branches, Brazil has experienced a succession of shaky governments and questionable elections since the military coups of the early to mid-twentieth century. Corruption is a continuing problem within the government; one of Brazil's most recent, and at the time admired, presidents, Fernando Collor de Mello, was subsequently impeached.

Schools and Education

Schooling is compulsory through the beginning of high school; however, in poorer rural regions and difficult urban neighborhoods, maintaining quality education and children's attendance through these grades is a challenge. Many children are pressed into working to help the family survive instead of attending school and many children, unfortunately, are simply left out in the cold. The wealthy send their children to private schools, including universities in Europe and the United States. Many of Brazil's elite have been educated at Ivy League institutions in the United States.

Religion and Demographics

The people are mainly Roman Catholic, with minority populations of Jews, Protestants, Muslims, and others. In its effort to establish a secular democratic republic, the government disestablished the church's authority, and there is an uncomfortable relationship between the power of the church in Brazil and government authority. Because of the strong influence of African traditions, the Catholicism that is practiced throughout the country usually contains many elements of African animist beliefs. *Macumba, Candomblé, Xango,* and other versions of African-based animist and spiritual religions command large followings in Brazil. (If you want to observe some of these rituals, it is important to obtain an invitation; be especially careful not to participate in or photograph any of these events without permission: they are generally considered sacred, and are often private only to observants.) Brazil today is demographically an extremely young country, with over 60 percent of the population under the age of thirty. It is also an extremely heterogeneous country, with a tolerance of, pride in, and admiration for the sometimes amazing rainbow mix that is the Brazilian population today; skin tones, physiognomy, hair type, and hair color come in all possible combinations. Nevertheless, while individual prejudice may not exist, society does stratify the population economically according to these indicators. There is still a rigid separation of the genders, more so in the less urbanized areas; even in the urban centers, women struggle with the glass ceiling at work and the need to perform "two jobs"—that of homemaker and societal nurturer, as well as businesswoman—and to do each twice as well as the macho Brazilian male. Non-Brazilian businesswomen must take extra care in order to not be judged as overly aggressive, yet must maintain extreme professionalism in order to not have their authority questioned. Consider too that Brazil, like most of the region, is economically a developing nation, and struggles with all the challenges associated with that status, including substantial poverty, inadequate and ill-serving infrastructures, and corruption. Nevertheless, Brazil has always looked to the future, and the younger generation is facing tomorrow with renewed optimism and hope.

Fundamental Cultural Orientations

1. What's the Best Way for People to Relate to One Another?

OTHER-INDEPENDENT OR OTHER-DEPENDENT?   As is the case with most countries in the region—due, in part, to the heavy influence of Roman Catholicism—Brazilian behavior is often significantly "other-dependent." Most individuals will seek, either formally or informally, the opinions and support of family, friends, and coworkers before venturing off to do or say something on their own. The family, in fact, is the most significant reference group for Brazilians, and it sustains them through all the trials of life. Most Brazilians, for example, revere the *parentela:* those individuals on both the mother's and father's side who can trace their roots back to a highly respected ancestor. This lineage creates the backbone from which individuals develop their own sense of worth and pride, and is a very strong element in Brazilian life. People are most comfortable in the "bosom" of others, and individuals are simply not part of society unless they can claim membership to or affiliation with some group, neighborhood, town, or business organization. A consequence of this, of course, is a resistance to the outsider, and a need for all outsiders to become associated with members of the in-group as soon as possible. Causing someone to lose face, or experience embarrassment, public ridicule, or criticism of any kind is a great insult in this other-dependent culture; here, how one is thought of by others is one of the most important concerns in life. Despite this strong need to look good in the eyes of others, the individual must bear responsibility for him- or herself in the world. In Brazil, every individual is unique and has the right to advance his or her own way in the world, as long as it is done with consideration for others; the proof of the value of one's individual behavior is whether and the degree to which it positively affects the lives of others.

HIERARCHY-ORIENTED OR EGALITY-ORIENTED? Certainly the younger generation, especially in the cities, feels more empowered as individuals than their elders, but the traditions of the Roman Catholic hierarchy still play a powerful role in determining who does what and when. Subsequently, the Brazilian workplace is rigidly layered, with the individuals at the top having supreme decision-making authority and support staff being required to follow step, challenge as little as possible, and solve all problems before they surface at the top. Society is basically structured with a very small wealthy elite—typically people of European descent—at the top, a large and growing middle class, and a massive underclass of poor people. The heterogeneous nature of society has developed a fairy egalitarian value system; most Brazilians, as individuals, believe in equality, based precisely on the differences that they quite freely acknowledge and celebrate. The importance of hierarchy, therefore, is deemphasized, although all acknowledge its existence and influence, in society and in the workplace.

In civic life, this means that government, which is supposed to be democratic, often fails to be; a practical example of this is the role of policemen on the street: they typically represent authority, not assistance. Women and men are rigidly separated in their social roles, as is the case more or less throughout all of Latin America, which is a very macho culture; women traditionally play the nurturing role in society, while men play the public leaders, in government and business. Of course, there are women who achieve high levels in both, but they do not represent most women. While their public role may be limited, however, women in Brazil are far from devalued; men glorify them, and they are entrusted with the most important work for the most important institution in society: nurturing the family.

RULE-ORIENTED OR RELATIONSHIP-ORIENTED? Despite the fact that Brazil (and the rest of the region) has tried valiantly to establish civil governments with rules and regulations that would apply to all, the reality mirrors the historical efforts of the Roman Catholic church, in that its authority and its rules could always be circumvented by those clever enough or with connections. One of the lasting legacies of Latin cultures is the rigid social hierarchy and the value people place on finding ingenious ways around rules and regulations in order to live their lives. Most of the time, the way one circumvented the authorities was to rely on the only true source of dependability in an otherwise cruel and difficult world: one's family, proven friends, and loyal business associates. Therefore, relationships—not rules—rule. Situations, if involving the right people and the right issues, will most always determine the behaviors of individuals, not bland laws or bureaucratic fiats. The concept of *jeteinho*, or essentially that for everything in life from taxes to getting government approvals there is a parallel way of doing things to the official way, dependent on the right people having relationships with the right people, is pervasive. The Brazilian psyche in fact makes a distinction between "the individual" and "the citizen," the citizen being someone who is responsible to the laws and systems of life, and the individual being someone of flesh and blood who must deal with others. This distinction often justifies the existence of *jeteinho* in Brazil, for one cannot only be successful as a citizen or an individual, but must balance the needs of both.

Jeteinho can lead to corruption, which can be a major difficulty in Brazil and throughout the region; some form of "payment" needs to be made in order to get something done, whether it's to void a traffic ticket or win government approval for a project. In its most innocuous form, *jeteinho* represents the need to build personal relationships in order to get things done; in its more common form, it represents the expectation on the part of some poorly paid government bureaucrats that they need to be compensated more appropriately for providing a valued service; and in its most insidious form, it is out-and-out extortion. This cultural dependence on personal relationships means that Brazilians will need time to get to know you before they will be ready to talk business. Attempts to discuss the terms of the deal or the immediate task at hand without having built the necessary personal trust and understanding is often a waste of time. Which takes us to our next concern.

2. What's the Best Way to View Time?

MONOCHRONIC OR POLYCHRONIC? Outside of the major cities, time is circular, and very polychronic; it is more monochronic in São Paulo, but even there, old agrarian patterns die hard, even if people aren't waking up and heading for the fields in the morning. In rural areas, it is easiest to work in the fields in the cool of the early morning and late afternoon; the midday heat is usually too oppressive, and provides a good opportunity to stoke up on a filling meal and a siesta before heading back out until the sun sets.

Working in Rio today still means showing up at the office around 9 A.M. but not really getting started until 9:30 or 10 (drinking coffee, checking the news, and catching up with the coworkers may take precedence). Lunch occurs around 1 or 2 P.M., and can either be a quick bite at the local sandwich shop or last for several hours at an elegant restaurant (those are post-lunch, not pre-dinner, cigars they are smoking at 5 P.M. in the restaurant lounge). After returning to the office (people would, in an earlier time, retire for a short nap after having gone home for the large main midday meal; this, by the way, is still done in some areas), workers stay as necessary, perhaps up to 8 or 9 P.M. At that point, they return home, or meet friends at a local bar for some drinks. Dinner, in either case, is usually not before 10 or 11 P.M. (especially in the summer), and can last till midnight or later.

On weekends, Friday and Saturday night revelries more often than not can last until after the sun comes up. If you really want things to occur punctually, you will need to identify the time as *a la gringa* or *Norteamericano.*

RISK-TAKING OR RISK-AVERSE? Latin cultures, in general, are risk-averse, and that is one of the driving reasons for the creation of structure and hierarchies. Brazil is no exception. Decision making can be slow and tedious, as various levels of the hierarchy need to be consulted, and as information must be made available to many, in order for it to occur. The belief is not so much to do it right the first time, but to avoid risk and personal responsibility if things go wrong. Even when individuals are empowered to make the decision, there can be a reticence to take the required final step. Nevertheless, there is a growing impatience among new entrepreneurs with the tedious risk-avoidance, and in São Paulo especially there is a palpable frustration with traditional risk-averse attitudes.

PAST-ORIENTED OR FUTURE-ORIENTED? Brazilians are proud of their country, and exude an optimism about the future, despite their awareness of the difficulties of the past and present. The country is, in many ways, all about promise, much of it yet unfulfilled. In this sense, Brazilians, in their beliefs and in their actions, are future-oriented, and do not look back. Nevertheless, there is a fatalism about the ability to control events and the future, and therefore a reticence to sacrifice what they have today for the possibility of tomorrow. Brazilians will work toward a goal, once it is identified as being worth the effort, but in considering the worth of any effort, they must factor in the price of losing the blessings of today. The optimism of Brazilians allows them to believe in the future, rarely look to the past, and cherish the best of the present.

3. What's the Best Way for Society to Work with the World at Large?

LOW-CONTEXT DIRECT OR HIGH-CONTEXT INDIRECT COMMUNICATORS?
Most Brazilians are high-context communicators; depending upon the situation at the moment in which the communication takes place, Brazilians can alternately be careful about what they say and how they say it and very direct and honest. Of course, Brazilians, like most Latinos, want smooth interpersonal working relationships, especially with outsiders, and will go the distance to reassure you that everything is okay and that all is in order—even when it may not be. This is not based on a desire to deceive but rather a need to appear capable and competent, and not to lose face in the eyes of others, particularly when it may be in one's interests to cultivate a relationship. It is critical, therefore, to always confirm information; to have multiple and independent sources "on the ground" to confirm for you what you are being told; and to be able to read between the lines without directly challenging the veracity of what the Brazilian is saying. There is a strong tolerance for, in fact dependence on, the subjective interpretation of events and reality.

PROCESS-ORIENTED OR RESULT-ORIENTED? As with other Latin cultures, there is a strong reliance on the deductive process: how things are being done is more important than the final result. But Brazilians are also very subjective, and will often fall back on what they personally believe in order to make or justify a decision. Although the future-orientation of the country provides an unyielding source of optimism about what will be, sometimes a serious lack of resources in what still is a developing country, coupled at times with the burden of a cumbersome and byzantine bureaucracy, makes it difficult for Brazilians to follow through easily with the actions required to put plans in place. Yet they may be reticent to admit this or inform you when problems develop. It is therefore that much more important for non-Brazilians to stay involved with Brazilians, helping them to implement what has been agreed to. This must be done, however, with sensitivity toward the pride that Brazilians feel in being able to handle things on their own: therefore, never be intrusive, but always be available; always be open to learning about their ways, while providing them with the resources and information they need, whenever possible, to assist them in making things happen.

FORMAL OR INFORMAL? Brazil basically has an informal culture. However, maintaining honor and personal pride is critical, and this occasionally requires a bit of formality. Never insult the honor, pride, or personal beliefs of a Brazilian or his or her family, colleagues, or associates.

Greetings and Introductions

Language and Basic Vocabulary

The language is Portuguese, not Spanish. Although many Brazilians do speak and understand Spanish, and will use it if you know Spanish and not Portuguese, it is important to demonstrate to your Brazilian colleagues that you recognize that their language is not Spanish. Therefore, if you do not know Portuguese, learn a few basic phrases, and always start your conversation in Portuguese before going into Spanish or English (assuming your Brazilian colleagues know either). If you learned your Portuguese in school or in Lisbon, please note that Brazilian Portuguese is different, and there are many regionalisms throughout the country (for example, in Bahia in the north, there is a Portuguese-laced Creole that is spoken); nevertheless, if you know Portuguese, you will be able to communicate anywhere in Brazil. Many, if not most, businesspeople in São Paulo and Rio who do business with non-Brazilians speak competent English. Portuguese has some unique sounds, including the very nasal "n" when it comes at the end of a word and "ao," which is made by passing air through the open mouth and nose at the same time. Here are the basics:

Bom dia	Good morning
Boa tarde	Good afternoon
Boa noite	Good night
Oi	Hello (casual)
Adeus	Good-bye
Faça o favor	Please
Obrigado(a)	Thank you
De nada	You're welcome
Sim	Yes
Nao	No
Com licença	Excuse me
Muito prazer	Pleased to meet you
¿Como vai?	How are you?
Senhor	Mr.
Senhora	Mrs.

Honorifics for Men, Women, and Children

Brazilians move very quickly to using first names, and avoid, almost from the beginning, the use of family names when addressing each other. Nevertheless, the first or given name is still used with the appropriate honorific in most cases outside of business; titles plus the given name, not the family name, are an absolute must when introduced to anyone. Architects, priests, and lawyers, are often referred to with their title plus their first name. Anyone with a university degree is often referred to as a doctor—*doutor*—even if he or she has neither a medical degree nor a Ph.D. When you are first introduced to someone in a business setting, use the appropriate honorific and the last (family) name; this will most probably quickly change to the use of the honorific and the first name. For example, when introduced to Senhor Carlo Garcia, it would be appropriate to refer to him first as Senhor Garcia, and then in future references as Senhor Carlo, but always with the honorific until a personal relationship is established (in Brazilian Portuguese, *senhor* is commonly pronounced as *seau*). A person who commands great respect because of his or her age, influence, or deep personal commitment to you is often referred to with the title *Senhor don* (for a man) or *dona* (for a woman), plus the first name. There is no common use in Brazil of an equivalent for the Spanish *señorita*. Married women are not necessarily "safe" from machismo, so wearing a wedding band does not always protect a woman alone; however, being a mother virtually ensures that a man will remain at a distance: bring pictures of your children. For casual contacts (e.g., with waiters, store help, etc.), just use *senhor* or *senhora* without the name. It is very important to greet people at work or in stores and restaurants with an appropriate greeting for the time of day—*bom dia, boa tarde,* or *boa noite*—and *adeus* upon leaving. If you speak any Portuguese at all, it is important to use it, but be sure to begin in the formal form, and do not switch to the informal form of speech unless and until your Brazilian colleague has specifically invited you to or does so him- or herself, which may happen fairly quickly. In contrast to the Spanish tradition, there is not a common use of two family names (from both the mother's and father's sides), and women may or may not keep their family name; if they take their husband's family name, it can be in addition to or replacing their family name.

The What, When, and How of Introducing People

Generally wait to be introduced to strangers before taking that responsibility upon yourself. Brazilians are most comfortable with a third-party introduction whenever possible, but it is not required in anything but the *most* formal situations. In this case, you will be introduced to women first, then the most senior men. Do not presume to seat yourself at a formal gathering; if possible, wait to be told where to sit (at an informal gathering, it is perfectly okay to wait a moment, and if not shown your seat, to simply find one). Shake hands with everyone individually in a group when being introduced and before departing; the U.S. group wave is not sufficient in Brazil. Avoid ending the conversation with the expression "Have a nice day"; it sounds controlling and insincere. Kissing is a common greeting once you have established a strong and familiar relationship, whether between women or men and women; usually, there is a kiss on two cheeks (actually an "air kiss," first on the left side, and then the right) if the women are married; if they are both single, it is a kiss on one cheek, and if one is married and the other is single, there are three kisses (the third is a kiss to wish for the single one to find a husband). When men who know each other meet, there can be much physicality, with backslapping and patting on the arm, back, or stomach. It is not uncommon to see men and men, and women and women, walking arm in arm down the street; they are good close friends or associates, and it usually means nothing more than that.

The use of business cards is common; if possible, you should have your business card translated into Portuguese on the reverse, but it is not essential. Be sure to put any advanced educational degrees and your full title or position on both sides of your business card. Such emblems of your status are very important to Brazilians; they want to know they are doing business with an important person.

Physical Greeting Styles

The handshake is common. The Brazilian version is done firmly between two men, and it can last quite a long time; it is not as robust between men and women or two women. The handshake should be accompanied by the appropriate greeting (see the list of terms outlined earlier) and a smile is typical when being introduced. Men should wait until a woman extends her hand before reaching for it, and women may take the lead in extending their hand or not. Men must remove their gloves when shaking hands with a woman, but a woman need not remove her gloves when shaking hands with a man. Between family, friends, or trusted business associates, an extra touch on the elbow, a pat on the tummy, or a hug (the *abraco,* or embrace) will generally occur. This can happen even as soon as the second meeting; do not initiate it, but respond warmly in kind if it is initiated with you. Eye contact during the introduction is important, and should be maintained as long as the individual is addressing you.

Communication Styles

Okay Topics / Not Okay Topics

Okay: politics, current events, anything interesting (but never to the point of being controversial at first), sports (soccer—or futbol, as it is known—is the national passion, if there is one, beyond *Carnaval*), Brazilian music, and history. Brazilians love to see you demonstrate knowledge and interest in things Brazil, but will quickly dismiss insincere admiration; in fact, they will often share their frustrations with you about things they are unhappy with in Brazil. Do not commiserate directly when this happens, but listen and try to understand. As a visitor, it is important to appreciate the positive aspects of the country, and leave discussing problems to the Brazilians. Alternately, they will freely and often express admiration for the United States, and it important to accept these statements modestly, and add your own corrections whenever necessary. *Not okay:* Do not inquire about a person's occupation in casual conversation, although that may very well be inquired of you. In fact, you may be asked many personal questions, such as whether or not you are married, how many children you have, the kind of car you drive; Brazilians will even comment on the fact that you've put on weight since the last time you visited. Brazilians like to get personal very fast, but this in no way is an effort to embarrass you or make you feel uncomfortable; it is just their way of getting to know you. By the same token, it is appropriate for you to inquire of them about family, personal likes and dislikes, and so on, but do avoid topics that may reveal significant differences in status between you and your colleagues. Do not give your opinions about the situation in the Amazon and the environment; Brazilians will be quick to inform you of their efforts made on behalf of ecology, such as using cars that run on ethanol, and to remind you that the United States is the world's greatest energy consumer. Do not assume partners are married: in Brazil, partners often live together a long time before, and sometimes in place of, getting married. *Also not okay:* discussing the AIDS problem in Brazil, street children, or your admiration for the lifestyle of Brazil's neighbors, such as Argentina, Peru, Colombia, and Venezuela. Brazil has gone to war, at some point, with almost all of these countries, and even today, relations between Brazil and most of them are shaky. Do not refer to the extraordinary racial mix or the ethnicity of anyone in any derogatory way. Brazilians are very proud of their multiracial and multiethnic heritage (alternately, do not misinterpret references to race or ethnicity made by most Brazilians about themselves or others as derogatory; more often than not, you will be surprised to note that such comments are made as a way to endear the person being observed to the speaker). Do not call Brazilians Hispanics, do not talk about their language as Spanish, do not denigrate Portugal (even though they might, as a parent who is weaker than the child); many Brazilians do not even appreciate being referred to as Latin, since in the Brazilian mind this is often a synonym for Hispanic; Brazilians would prefer being referred to as "South Americans." Do not go to Brazil (or anywhere in Latin America) without pictures of your family, and when family is brought up (which it will be almost immediately in the conversation), use it as an opportunity to bring out the photographs. Don't initiate conversations about Brazilian politics or the economic situation, never denigrate anything Brazilian that is clearly beloved (*Carnaval,* Brazilian beer and food, soccer), and never tell a dirty joke with a woman present.

Tone, Volume, and Speed

Discussions between strangers can quickly become animated and very lively, depending upon the nature of the discussion and the circumstances of the developing relationship. At meals, the beer (and *cachaça*) flows, and conversation is an art; it is enjoyed, savored, and commented upon. Sometimes it may appear to be getting out of hand, but it rarely ever does. In business, speak softly and with restraint. It garners respect.

Use of Silence

In general, silence is not common, except in group discussions where something is said that can cause someone a public loss of face. Avoid this, and enjoy the simultaneous conversations and frequent interruptions that usually define Brazilian conversation style.

Physical Gestures and Facial Expressions

Brazilians use many physical gestures. The U.S. "okay" sign, made with the thumb and the forefinger, is considered vulgar and obscene, avoid it. In addition, winking and whistling—often accompanied by a positive comment—is meant to be a friendly introduction between men and women, not an insult. If a woman is not interested, she merely need not acknowledge it. But if a woman's eyes meet a man's eyes under these circumstances, it is usually an indication of interest. Never stand with your hands on your hips: it is aggressive (however, there is nothing defensive about folding the arms in front of you). Brushing your fingers on the underside of your chin is a signal that you don't understand what was said. Squeezing your earlobe with your thumb and index finger is an indication that you like something (the person speaking, the food you are eating, what was just said, etc.); any kind of gentle physical contact, such as a pat on the shoulder or a touch of the elbow, is a sign of friendship; holding the middle and index fingers together so that they hit the thumb as you shake your hand, or snapping your fingers as you shake your hand, indicates that what is being said is very important. The *"figa"* sign (made by pressing the thumb between the index and middle fingers in a clenched fist) is a sign of good luck in Brazil (note that it is considered a vulgar sign in neighboring Argentina), and not only will you see people gesturing this way, but you will see drawings, pictures, and even jewelry of the *figa* everywhere.

Waving and Counting

The thumb represents the number 1, the index finger the number 2, and so on. It is insulting to beckon someone with the forefinger; instead, turn your hand so that the palm faces down and motion inward with all four fingers at once. If you need to gesture for a waiter, subtly raise your hand; never click, call, or whistle (although some Brazilians do a version of this while snapping their fingers). Waving or beckoning is done with the palm down and the fingers moving forward and back in a kind of scratching motion. Because of the personal nature of the culture, even money is exchanged in the palms, not on the counter.

Physicality and Physical Space

Brazilians tend to get closer than North Americans are generally comfortable with. Do not step back when your Brazilian associate steps forward. Brazilian men may touch each other during conversations, adjust each other's ties, dust off each other's shoulders, and the like. Never speak with your hands in your pockets; always keep them firmly at your side when standing. If men and women must cross their legs, it must never be ankle over knee (the preferred style for women is to cross ankle over ankle). Until the situation tells you otherwise, in public, no gum chewing, *ever,* no slouching, no leaning against things.

Eye Contact

Eye contact can be direct, and at times may be disconcerting for many Americans. It is important not to interpret this behavior as a way of intentionally trying to make you uncomfortable. It is the way Brazilians show their interest.

Conversely, if you look away, your behavior will say to your Brazilian colleague that you are disinterested, rude, or establishing yourself as the subordinate in a hierarchical relationship; none of these is a good idea. Maintain eye contact when it is made with you. If a stranger's eyes meet yours and linger, it can imply romantic interest. Act accordingly!

Emotive Orientation

Brazilians are often animated and physically expressive. Join in if you like, keep cool if you like; just remain warm, open, and personable.

Protocol in Public

Walking Styles and Waiting in Lines

It is more important in Brazil to maintain one's face by being first in line (and never last) than it is to maintain a queue. Don't be too distressed if someone walks right up to the front of the line at a bank, a restaurant, or a store, and gets served because of the relationship he or she has with the clerk, while you have been waiting patiently in line for forty minutes. This occurs also in response to rank based on gender and age. People also have a tendency to stand very close in public; this may feel uncomfortable at first. Resist the urge to back away; most of the time, you are not being intentionally crowded. Remember, the need to appear helpful and courteous is strong, and if you ask for directions on the street, you will no doubt be instructed on just where to go . . . whether or not the individual actually knows!

Behavior in Public Places: Airports, Terminals, and the Market

Customer service, as a concept, is catching on, but is not fully institutionalized. Store hours are typically not designed around customer convenience (many stores are closed on weekends, certainly Sundays, and many close for lunch between 12 and 2 P.M.), although there are many malls now in Brazil where stores stay open late. Personally thanking store owners, waiters, chefs, and hotel managers for their services is very much appreciated. In food markets, you can touch the produce; in goods stores, it may be difficult for you to return a product unless there is a flaw in it.

There is poverty in Brazil, and you will see some poorer people reduced to begging in the cities; small children and women may approach you to try to sell you small items on the street. It is always difficult deciding whether or not to give, but remember that the social support systems in Brazil are generally insufficient, and this is often the only way for these people to sustain themselves. Smoking is prevalent; if you smoke, be sure to always offer a cigarette to everyone you are talking to before you light up. In bathrooms, on the plumbing "Q" means hot (*quente*) and "F" means cold (*frío*).

When answering a phone, use the phrase *quem fala?* (who is speaking?). The use of cell phones is ubiquitous, and most pay phones—when they work—require a telecard (phone service can be intermittent and haphazard; it wasn't too many years ago that businesses would hire workers to do nothing but sit at a desk and redial a telephone number until the connection was made). Following Brazilian custom, even the telephone directories list people by their first name first.

Bus / Metro / Taxi / Car

Driving is on the right, but people pass very quickly on the left. Driving is difficult at best in the cities, and dangerous in the rural areas, and being a pedestrian is just as risky: both drivers and pedestrians really are very aggressive. Additionally, throughout Latin America, street rules are observed only sporadically (stoplights, one-way street designations, and stop signs are viewed as suggestions) and drivers usually do not turn their lights on after dark (it is believed to blind the oncoming traffic), but may keep them on during the day for extra safety. The metros shut down after midnight or 1 A.M. The best way to catch a cab is at designated taxi stands (hotels are good places, but often charge more for the same ride: a hotel surcharge may be added to the meter fare, in some cases). You can share taxis in Brazil in most places; be sure that the driver turns the meter on when you get in, and if "it doesn't work," be sure to negotiate the fare before the driver starts driving. You must call a taxi only on the telephone or from a hotel, not hail them from the street. Bring food and water on board commuter trains if your trip is a long one, as they may not have a café car. The crime situation in Brazil needs to be taken seriously. In both rural areas and cities, the grinding poverty drives crime, sometimes petty, sometimes serious. When driving, for example, always keep a safe distance between your car and the car in front of you, in case you need to quickly get out of line to avoid a carjacking, which is not uncommon in big-city traffic. Cities like Rio de Janeiro, for example, topographically mirror the economic condition of the country, with a narrow strip of great wealth along the beautiful beaches at the bottom of the hills that tower behind the city and that also house, in substandard *favellas,* the masses of poor people barely surviving in many cases. Be very careful about the neighborhoods you visit in the cities; avoid traveling alone as kidnapping is a major crime problem. Women must be especially careful to travel in groups, and neither men nor women should ever travel alone at night. Do not wear any expensive jewelry, do not carry bags or purses if you can avoid it, and never take anything that you cannot afford to lose onto the beach with you, almost anywhere. Try to have a contact in Brazil to keep you up-to-date about the crime situation (for example, the situation in Rio has recently improved, while the situation in São Paulo has generally deteriorated), and if it sounds serious, it is. In such cases, maintaining security as a foreigner on the street is essential.

Tipping

A 10 percent tip is usually sufficient in restaurants and taxis; more is considered nouveau and gauche. Porters and hotel help get the equivalent in reals per item or service rendered, theater and bathroom attendants usually one real (pronounced "hey-ow"); (in both cases, tipping in U.S. dollars, as is done throughout much of the region, is perfectly fine, actually preferred). Please double-check the current dollar/real exchange rate, as it can vary quickly and significantly. Restaurants usually have the 10 percent tip already included on the bill, but if you are unsure, it's okay to ask whether service is included or not. Even if it is, it is still appropriate to leave a few reals or odd change if service was particularly good. In addition, in most small shops and in markets, bargaining is expected, especially outside of the cities. In taxis, round up from the metered amount to the next real and that should suffice as a tip.

Punctuality

It is perfectly acceptable—in fact, essential—to arrive for social events about an hour late. If you arrive sooner, you will be running the risk of interrupting the host or hostess as he or she gets ready. For business meetings in Rio, being late by five to fifteen minutes or more is usually not a problem, but it is safer for the new employee or visitor to be on time, while not being surprised if others are not. Business time is more monochronic in São Paulo, and things typically start and stop more punctually. Usually, the meeting will not begin in earnest until all attendees have arrived (or at least until all the decision makers have shown up), and this may not correspond to the time listed in the agenda. Resist questioning the late ones for a reason; they always have one, usually involving an obligation with more important people, like superiors, old friends, or family. Entertaining in private homes usually doesn't start until quite late; dinner can be served at midnight and discussions can go on past dawn. At restaurants, dinner often isn't served until 9 P.M. or later.

Dress

Until you know otherwise, and especially for business and most social situations between adults, dress is somewhat formal at work, more informal in the restaurant or on the street, for men and women. Good taste is important, but being comfortable is important as well, and except for the upper class, Brazilians do not put much emphasis on demonstrating wealth or status through clothing. At work, men can wear very stylish suits (dark is best), white shirts, and interesting and sophisticated ties or simply sports jackets and slacks. Women usually accessorize so that even the simplest of outfits stands out for its interest and style. On the street, informal may mean jeans (universally accepted by all for all informal situations) and sneakers (although jeans are more typically worn with nice shoes or sandals, and women do not wear sneakers to work); informal for a social gathering more often than not means tastefully coordinated clothes, sometimes including a jacket and tie for men (it can also mean jeans and T-shirts, when simply among friends). "Formal" usually means formal evening wear, very dressy by U.S. standards.

Seasonal Variations

It is cooler in the south, and hotter in the north, though not by much seasonally; climatic differences are more likely based on topography: swamp, mountain, plain, seacoast, rainforest. Evenings in certain of these areas at certain times can be quite cool, so a wrap, a scarf (very popular), a jacket, or a sweater is advised. Air pollution can be a problem at times in São Paulo and in the outskirts of Rio: take your time to adjust (no jogging for the first few days).

Colors

Bright colors are not uncommon, but avoid wearing clothes that combine green and yellow: these are the national colors on the Brazilian flag, and it looks odd to wear them.

Styles

High fashion for both men and women, as in many other aspects of life in Brazil, looks to Europe and not to the United States, although few people on the street can actually afford the latest trends (and the United States definitely sets the trends for casual wear). Brazilians combine colors, weaves, textures, and designs. Both men's and women's shoes can be remarkably stylish. The *guayabera,* so popular in many other South American countries, is not typically worn in Brazil. Additionally, men in business should not wear short-sleeve shirts, no matter the weather.

Accessories / Jewelry / Makeup

The right makeup, hairstyle, and accessories are important for women. Men also accessorize.

Personal Hygiene

In Brazil, personal hygiene is very important. Brazilians at home often take several showers daily, when they can. There is a real concern for cleanliness and smelling good; perfumes and colognes are used often. Latin men may sport facial hair, in the form of mustaches and close-trimmed beards. Note that most rest room and bathroom facilities throughout Latin America do not have plumbing capable of handling paper toilet tissue; it is for this reason that there is a small receptacle next to the toilet for your used tissue: do not flush it down the bowl, but place it in the receptacle, or else you'll face the embarrassment of having to call for help when the bowl overflows. Additionally, many showers are heated with small electrical devices attached to the top of the actual showerhead, so it is critical never to touch this unit or any other metal while the water is running, or you will be in for a very nasty shock.

Dining and Drinking

Mealtimes and Typical Foods

Breakfast (*pequeno almoço*) is served from about 7:30 to 9 A.M., and usually consists of the coffee, rolls, butter, and marmalade typical of the quick continental breakfast; sometimes fruit is served as well. Coffee in the morning can be strong and black, or with hot milk (*café com leite*).

Lunch (*almoço*) was traditionally the main meal of the day; even today, in busy cities, it can be an elaborate affair lasting several hours (usually an important business lunch)—or it can be a quick sandwich or a salad at a shop on the corner. Lunch is typically served from noon to 2 P.M. It usually consists of at least three courses, beginning with soup, going on to meat, chicken, or fish and rice and beans (a universal staple), sometimes with a small salad on the side, plus a dessert (Brazilian-prepared desserts can be very, very sweet, but for lunch, dessert is more often just some fruit). *Vitaminas,* or drinks made of fruit juices, ice, milk, and sometimes sugar, are wonderful pick-me-ups, and enjoyed any time of day or night. Even the quick business lunch often will include a main course and a dessert and coffee. On Sunday, the family day, the main meal is supper, which is usually served at lunchtime and can last well into the evening.

Dinner (*jantar*) at home is served from 7:30 P.M. on. In major cities, dinner in restaurants often does not start until 9 P.M. or later, even during the week, and on weekends can last till midnight or beyond. If the main meal of the day was lunch, then dinner is light, and this is often the case with families at home; it usually consists of similar foods to those served at the large lunch. Drinks served with dinner are usually wines—usually imported from either France, Portugal, Spain, or the United States—or beers. Dinner parties usually end around midnight (but can go much later if all are having a good time). In addition to the three meals, there is a snack taken around 4 or 5 P.M., called a *lanche,* consisting of some cookies and coffee, tea, or fruit juice.

There are many different kinds of restaurants: the *rodizio* is a meat restaurant, where you choose the kind of meat you like from waiters who come around carving the meat in front of you. The *churrasqueria* is similar, but usually serves only charcoal-grilled and barbecued meats. *Padarias* are bakeries serving sweet breads and treats, as well as light snacks and sandwiches (like *pastels,* which are fried pastries filled with meats and vegetables). *Brazinhos* are bars, where drinks and small snacks are also served; women usually do not venture into these alone. There are *cafés,* of course, and *lanchonetes,* which are cafés that also offer drinks and a slightly larger menu of food to select from. Additionally, there is a growing popularity for buffet-style restaurants, where you buy food by the kilo and pay for the quantity you purchase.

Be very careful about the places you go to eat: if they don't look safe or clean, you should avoid them. Do not eat food off the street from the street stalls: this can be very dangerous to your health. Be very careful about food and drink in Brazil (and throughout Latin America); there are dangerous bugs around. First, the water: Do not drink tap water anywhere in Brazil (except where *officially* noted as safe, sterilized, or "electrified"). This means no ice in any drinks (ice cubes may be made from tap water); ask for drinks without ice (including the *vitaminas*). Close your mouth in the shower in the morning, and brush your teeth with bottled water. Drink only bottled water and soft drinks from bottles with intact seals opened in front of you; the fruit juices in Brazil are wonderful, but until your digestive system has adjusted, or until you know for sure that they haven't been diluted with water from the tap, avoid them. Coffee and tea are generally okay, because the water is boiled first. Avoid fresh dairy products, including milk, custards, mayonnaise, and ice cream, because they all usually require refrigeration, which may be questionable in certain parts of Brazil. Definitely avoid raw shellfish and raw fish, and do not eat any raw or uncooked vegetables or fruits, unless you can peel them; leave the salad alone that is often served to you on the side in Brazil. You may get the South American tummy on your first few trips to Brazil; it is hard to avoid a drop of water here or there. If you have followed the above rules carefully, it is probably nothing to worry about; it will be uncomfortable for a day or two. Eat lightly, drink lots of safe fluids, stay in or near your room, rest, and it will pass. If a fever or vomiting develops, be sure to seek medical attention immediately.

Regional Differences

Brazilian cuisine is unique; it can be hot and spicy, but more often than not, it is flavorful and filling. It is a complicated and rich cuisine, with variations reflecting the traditions of each section of the country. Throughout the country, there will be salt, pepper, and mandioca shakers on the table (mandioca root is a kind of starch with a mild flavor that is sprinkled on just about anything); in the north, near Bahia, there is far more use of hot and spicy flavorings (there, you will be seated at tables with a small bowl of *pimenta malagueta,* or hot pepper sauce, and hot it is, indeed; whatever you do, don't drink beer or water to quench the sting: it only spreads the pain (eat bread, rice, or other mild foods instead to stanch the heat). Meat of all varieties is quite common, but seafood is appreciated along the southern and eastern coasts. The *feijoada* is the typical Brazilian dish; it is a kind of stew with meats, mandioca, vegetables, black beans, and the works. Helpings are usually enormous and enormously filling. Restaurants serve it mainly on Wednesdays and Saturdays. Many foods, interestingly, are cooked in dende oil, a kind of palm oil, which gives the food a yellow-orange color. There is a very popular side dish called *farofa*—a mixture of fried mandioca, eggs, and other flavorings, also used as a stuffing for chicken (*frango*)—that you will see in many, many forms on menus throughout the country. Also, *cuzcuz,* which may sound like the North African grain dish, is in Brazil the name for a dessert (although in São Paulo it is a savory dish that does resemble its namesake).

Typical Drinks and Toasting

Beer is the drink that accompanies many a standard meal. Draft beer is referred to as *chopp.* Also common at most meals are water, fruit juice, and soft drinks (which are extremely popular, from the American colas to local varieties; by the way, never drink soft drinks out of a can or bottle, as it is considered bad form: always have them poured into a glass). A drink of *cachaça* or a *caipirinha* will probably be offered to you prior to a meal; *cachaça* is a clear brandy made from sugarcane, and when it is mixed with crushed ice, sugar, and lime juice it becomes a *caipirinha,* the potent, popular drink of Brazil. Coffee, in the form of the *cafezinho,* or espresso, is drunk after lunch and dinner, and in between: it is very strong and is usually taken black and very sweet. Brazilian coffee is some of the best in the world. The most common toast is *saúde* (to your health).

Table Manners and the Use of Utensils

Referring to European traditions as they do, Brazilians do not switch knives and forks, as people do in the United States. The knife remains in the right hand, and the fork remains in the left. When the meal is finished, the knife and fork are laid parallel to each other horizontally across the center of the plate—make sure they do not cross each other. If you put both utensils down on the plate for any real length of time, it is a sign to the waitstaff that you are finished, and your plate may be taken away from you. Alternately, if you lay your cutlery down on either side of the plate it means you haven't finished; but if you really are, the host might interpret this as a sign that you were not happy with the meal.

The fork and spoon above your plate are for dessert. There are often many additional pieces of cutlery at a formal meal; if you're unsure of which utensil to use, always start from the outside and work your way in, course by course. Bread (usually French bread) is sometimes served without butter; in that case, there usually will not be a butter knife, nor will there be a bread dish: your bread is placed on the rim of your main plate or on the table by your plate (the extensive use of mandioca root, however, minimizes the use of bread at traditional Brazilian meals). There will be separate glasses provided at your setting for water and white and red wine or beer (after-dinner drink glasses come out after dinner).

When not holding utensils, your hands are expected to be visible above the table: this means you do not keep them in your lap; instead, rest your wrists on top of the table (never your elbows). At the table, pass all dishes to your left. Never eat anything with your hands, including fruit, which is typically cut with a knife and fork when served at the end of the meal; equally, never cut the lettuce in a salad: deftly fold it with your knife and fork into a little bundle that can be easily picked up with your fork. Salad, if served, is more typically served as a side dish to the main meal, not afterward, as in Europe, and not before, as in the United States. The main course is usually meat or fish, and all meals end with a wonderfully sweet dessert. Rice and beans is a universal staple accompaniment throughout the country. Interestingly, if sandwiches are served at an informal meal, you eat them with a knife and fork in most cases.

Seating Plans

The most honored position is at the head of the table. The host or hostess will then sit to the side of the most important guest, and if there is a hosting couple, they will often sit on either side of the guest (women to the right of the guest, and men to the left). In the European tradition, men and women are seated next to one another, and couples are often broken up and seated next to people they may not have previously known. This is done to promote conversation. Men typically rise when women enter the room, and continue to hold doors for women and allow them to enter a room first. Remember, as is the case throughout the region, the first floor in Brazil is really the second floor, with the first floor usually referred to as the lobby or ground floor.

Refills and Seconds

If you do not want more food, or cannot eat everything on your plate, don't worry: it is perfectly okay to leave some food on your plate in Brazil; you inevitably will, as portions are usually big and there are generally many courses for both lunch and dinner, at least when entertaining or being entertained. You may always have additional beverages; drink enough to cause your cup or glass to be less than half full, and it will generally be refilled. If you smoke, never light up until the meal is finished, and always offer a cigarette to others before lighting up.

At Home, in a Restaurant, or at Work

In informal restaurants, you may be required to share a table. Waitstaff may be summoned by making eye contact; waving or calling their names is very impolite (although you might see some Brazilians make a kind of *shsh* sound and snap their fingers; don't do it). The business breakfast is not common in Brazil, although you do see it creeping into the business life of the major cities slowly. The business lunch (more common than dinner) and dinner are very acceptable, but, depending upon how well developed your relationship is with your Brazilian colleagues, they are generally not times to make business decisions. Take your cue from your Brazilian associates: if they bring up business, then it's okay to discuss it (more often than not, over coffee and brandy at the end of the meal), but wait to take your lead from their conversation. No gum chewing, *ever,* at a restaurant or on the street. No-smoking sections in restaurants are still a rarity.

When you arrive at a Brazilian associate's home for a formal meal, you will typically be told where to sit, and there you should remain. Remember, it is a real honor to be hosted in a Brazilian's home, as the home is very special and private; most Brazilians will prefer to host you in a restaurant (do not be offended if you are never invited to their home). Do not wander from room to room; much of the house is really off-limits to guests. Use the toilet before you arrive, as it is considered bad form to leave the dinner party, or the table, at any time. Once you (and the group) are invited to another room, most probably the dining room, be sure to allow more senior members of your party to enter the room ahead of you: men should move aside to allow women to enter the room ahead of them. Often drinks and hors d'oeuvres are served in the living room prior to the dinner. In a private home, be careful about what and how you admire things: the host may feel obliged to give it to you! Once at the table, be sure to look for place cards or wait until the host indicates your seat: do not presume to seat yourself, as the seating arrangement is usually predetermined. If you invite people to your home, be prepared to always have the invitation accepted, although they may not, in fact, show up; rejecting the invitation is difficult for Brazilians, who seek to not offend. They may indicate their true intentions by simply responding to your invitation with "I will try."

Being a Good Guest or Host

Paying the Bill

Usually the one who does the inviting pays the bill, although the guest is expected to make an effort to pay. Sometimes other circumstances determine who pays (such as rank). Making payment arrangements ahead of time so that no exchange occurs at the table is a very classy way to host. Women, if out with men, will not really be able to pay the bill at a restaurant; if you want to, make arrangements ahead of time, and don't wait for the check to arrive at the table. The only time it is considered appropriate for a woman to pay the bill is if she is a hosting businesswoman from abroad. If a businesswoman invites a Brazilian businessman to a meal, she should be sure to extend the invitation to his spouse as well, or may want to consider telling him that her (female) colleague will also be joining them (and be sure to have a female colleague along). Do not allow the Brazilian male to suggest bringing one of his colleagues along (remember, the person doing the inviting can refuse the suggestion). If a Brazilian male invites a businesswoman to a meeting or a meal that seems to have more than business as the subject, a businesswoman should always insist that she bring her female associate along (someone who is needed because of her role in the company); if you are a businesswoman making your first business trip to Brazil and have not yet established a relationship with your Brazilian male counterparts, you are strongly advised to bring a female business associate along on the trip. Unmarried businesswomen may want to consider wearing a wedding band. If you have children, be sure to discuss that fact at some point early in the initial conversations: any aggressive macho behavior usually stops when men learn they are dealing with a mother.

Transportation

It's a very nice idea, when acting as the host, to inquire ahead of time as to whether your guests will require transportation. If necessary, you should arrange for taxi service at the end of the meal. When the cars arrive, be sure not to leave your spot until your guests are out of sight.

When to Arrive / Chores to Do

If invited to dinner at a private home (again, this is not a common event in Brazil), do not offer to help with the chores, nor should you expect to visit the kitchen. Many middle- and upper-class Brazilians often have household help for the kitchen chores. Do not leave the table unless invited to do so. Spouses do not attend business dinners without a special invitation to do so.

Gift Giving

In general, gift giving is common among business associates, and it is always nice to bring a small gift from abroad if you are revisiting a business acquaintance (as, at this point, they have probably become a friend). As is the case throughout most of South America, some chocolates or a small gift for the secretary of the person you are visiting can work wonders for future smooth sailing! If a man is giving a gift to a woman in a business setting, it is important to present it as a gift to her from his wife or sister. Curiously, greeting cards—even for the holidays—are typically not appreciated or sent in Brazil: they are seen as insincere, and a too-easy substitute for a social visit; avoid sending them (unless you are truly very far away, and then you must include a substantial personal note or letter bringing the recipients up-to-date). Brazilians celebrate Three Kings Day (as all Latin American cultures do), January 6, as the time for holiday gift giving, although the U.S. tradition of gift giving on Christmas Day is understood and accepted (Brazilians are particularly fond of charming Christmas decorations and ornaments, and these make lovely social gifts for the family), and gift giving on New Year's Day, a very significant holiday in Brazil, is also common.

Gifts are definitely appreciated for social events, especially as thank-yous for private dinner parties. The best gift for these occasions is wine, champagne, a basket of strawberries or expensive flowers (in the case of flowers, it is best to have them sent ahead of time on the day of the dinner; simple floral arrangements are not appreciated). Be sure never to send purple flowers (purple is the color of mourning in Brazil) and always be sure the bouquet is in odd numbers (an old European tradition). If you must bring flowers with you to the dinner party, unwrap them before presenting them to your hostess. Other good gifts would be chocolates or a good bottle of European (not Argentinian) wine (do not bring tequila or mescal, no matter how fine).

If you are staying with a Brazilian family, an appropriate thank-you gift would be a high-quality item that represents your country and is difficult to get in Brazil, but that is not representative of the United States in general (Brazilians know a lot about the United States already; it's Americans who don't know much about Brazil, usually). Small American-made electronic gadgets, a set of American bath towels (always a good gift almost everywhere, since they are usually more luxurious), or anything that reflects your host's personal tastes is appropriate. Do not give Brazilian-made leather goods as a gift. As in other European-based cultures, gifts are generally opened at the time they are given and received.

Special Holidays and Celebrations

Major Holidays

Most Brazilian workers get at least two weeks paid vacation. August is a school holiday month, and January is the summer vacation month; avoid them for business travel, if you can. Business slows down from December 15 to January 6, and Holy Week is sometimes a more difficult time in which to accomplish work than Christmas. In addition, there are many regional fiestas and saints' days throughout the year that usually close down businesses for a day or two; check with your local contacts.

Special Note on *Carnaval*: Throughout the country, there is the great Carnival event—*Carnaval*—led by the spectacular explosion in Rio de Janeiro, although anywhere in the country it is not to be missed (*Carnaval* in Bahia, for example, is quite different, as befits the unique culture of the northeast Brazilian region); consider also that the country almost immediately goes into *Carnaval* preparations right after the Christmas and New Year holidays, so it can be, in reality, difficult to do business in Brazil from the middle of December right on through to the end of *Carnaval*. Do not go to *Carnaval* alone, do not wear or carry anything you cannot afford to lose, and do not go on the beaches or walk the streets alone, day or night, during *Carnaval*. There are essentially three elements to *Carnaval*: the Samba dancing (the dancing at the Sambadromo in Rio de Janeiro is the most spectacular), the costume balls, and the street parades. The costume balls are sponsored by various groups, ranging from local neighborhood associations to grand fraternal, social, and business organizations; each puts on a fancy costume ball, the swankiest of which is the Municipal Ball, held on the final night of *Carnaval* (*Carnaval*, by the way, begins on the weekend that precedes Ash Wednesday and ends on Mardi Gras, or "Fat Tuesday," the day before Ash Wednesday). The parade of the samba dancing groups is literally a twenty-four-hour musical bachanal of *"escolas de samba,"* or samba schools, clubs of musicians and dancers who spend much of the year practicing their steps, putting on a musical samba review, with original songs and costumes. Street parades are more often spontaneous, and the least spectacular (also the most dangerous) of the various *Carnaval* events.

Finally, the New Year's holiday is a major event throughout the country, especially in Rio de Janeiro, where on New Year's Eve, people—and not just *candomblé* believers—assemble on the great beach, mainly dressed in white, and, to the accompaniment of native music and the reflection of a million candles, at the stroke of midnight touch the water and offer sacrifices to the Goddess of the Sea, Imanje.

January 1	*Ano Novo* (New Year's Day)
January 6	Three Kings Day
January 20	Feast of Saint Sebastian
February/March	*Carnaval* (usually lasting from the Saturday before Lent to Ash Wednesday)
March/April	*Páscoa* (Easter)
May 1	*Dia do Trabalhao* (Labor Day)
May/June	*Corpo de Deus* (Ascension Day; forty days after Easter)
June 24–29	The June Festival
August 15	*Assuncao* (Feast of the Assumption)
September 7	*Dia da Liberdade* (Independence Day)
October 12	Our Lady of the Apparition Day
November 1	*Todos-os-Santos* (All Saints' Day)
November 2	All Souls' Day
November 15	*Dia de Republica* (Republic Day)
November 19	Flag Day
December 25	*Natal* (Christmas Day)
December 31	New Year's Eve

Business Culture

Daily Office Protocols

In Brazil, doors, at least for senior management, are more often kept open, and only the very senior people have private offices, typically. It has not been common for women to be in positions of authority outside of the home in Brazil in the past, and in the traditional Brazilian workplace women are usually relegated to lower-level management and administrative support positions. Women do struggle to reach the same levels of achievement as their male counterparts in Brazilian business, and it is rare (though not impossible) to see women at the highest levels of business and government in Brazil. People organize their time on a daily basis according to the tasks they must accomplish, and the relationships they must depend upon in order to accomplish these tasks; the clock takes a backseat. Therefore, the day may begin slowly, but there can be much activity by day's end, and people often stay late in the office in order to finish up what needs to be done. This pattern repeats itself over larger blocks of time in regard to the accomplishment of projects and the meeting of deadlines.

Management Styles

Workers typically provide what their bosses expect of them, and the preparation of plans, methods, and reports can be time-consuming and complicated efforts. Gathering the information required in order to do what your boss expects from you, or creating consensus among your colleagues in order to accomplish a particular goal, can take a long time. All of this occurs in a sometimes complex bureaucratic structure, which means that deadlines and efficiency are secondary to attention to detail, perfection of form, bureaucratic requirements, and the need to be clever in the face of limited resources in order to be effective. Titles do convey authority, but do not necessarily command blind or unquestioning obedience. The highest titles (e.g., vice president) are usually reserved for very senior, executive-level positions, and should not be used as casually as they are in the United States. Complimenting and rewarding employees publicly is usually not done. For non-Brazilians, it is essential to try to have a local contact who can tell you what is really going on after you return home, and to have a local intermediary (known as a *despachante,* or literally, an expediter)—as well as a local lawyer and *notario* (a very responsible administrative position throughout much of Latin America)—to act as a liaison for you with the people you need to see while you are there. This needs to be set up ahead of time.

Boss-Subordinate Relations

Brazilians like to do business with the most important people in any organization (and this should be the same for the non-Brazilian working with them). Deviating from the proper or expected way for outsiders to work within the organization will generally make more problems for you, even if the intent is to bypass what appear to be obstacles; nevertheless, there can be considerable consultation between decision makers and staff, and the egalitarian nature of personal relationships often plays itself out even in boss-subordinate relationships.

Conducting a Meeting or Presentation

At meetings of peers and even with individuals at different levels involved in the decision, there can be open communication and sharing of ideas; in fact, these sessions often serve as information-sharing and decision-making forums in which all individuals are expected to contribute. Under these circumstances, discussions are usually vibrant, with many people speaking at once; questions are common and interruptions, even of presentations, should be expected. Remember, because a close personal relationship is often demonstrated through physicality in Latin cultures, the nearer your Brazilian colleagues are to you, typically, the better they are responding to your proposal.

Negotiation Styles

Business negotiations may take a very long time, and business, in general, is typically a long-term affair that requires trust, commitment, and continuous care and nurturing. It is the result of a combination of the need for personal trust and relationship, the deductive European traditions of detail-consciousness, risk-averse attitudes toward responsibility and personal blame, and an extraordinary assemblage of bureaucracies required to approve apparently almost anything agreed upon in the negotiation. Remember, only recently has Brazil opened its economy to significant outside investment, and there is a residue of resistance and wariness to dealing with new foreign businesspeople. Brazilians can certainly play their cards close to the vest, but they often will honestly and openly discuss their needs and expect you to do the same. Brazilians will indicate their thoughts in sometimes fairly direct ways when it is to their advantage, but generally are indirect, especially when it comes to sharing information that is overtly negative, difficult, or confrontational. They will respect someone who comes to them with already established knowledge and experience, and will build relationships based on your proposal as well as your level in society and the organization. Nevertheless, details are important—and will be reviewed seemingly endlessly, and to what may be considered by many North Americans to be an agonizing degree—and a carefully planned, logically organized, and beautifully presented proposal in Portuguese—never Spanish—is key (good-looking charts, graphs, and handouts are impressive). Bargaining is the essence of the negotiation, as a way to build trust; therefore, be reasonable, but do not overcompromise, as this shows weakness.

The first meeting is usually formal, with the Brazilians sizing up you and your organization: it will generally be conducted in the office. Never be condescending, and be open to sharing details fairly quickly. The contract must be legal down to the dotted i's, and Brazilians may be tedious in their insistence on all details being carefully spelled out. Plan your meetings as carefully and as well in advance as you can, but expect last-minute changes in everything, including topics, agenda, attendees, and time. The meeting might start and end much later than you anticipated, but nevertheless, as in most polychronic cultures, you should always arrive on time. Coffee is the universal greeting; always accept it, always serve it (in nice china, never in Styrofoam), and drink as much or as little as you can or desire: It is the gesture of acceptance and appreciation that counts (never refuse coffee, or an invitation to go with your colleague to a café and have some). As you should throughout most of Latin America, if you are hosting at a restaurant, choose the finest restaurant you can, at least for the first (and last) meeting; by the same token, stay at the best hotel you can: these things carry prestige and will signal that you are someone worth doing business with.

Written Correspondence

After having met, even once, it is okay to refer to the individual to whom you are writing by his or her first name. Names are usually written in uppercase; dates are given using the day/month/year format (with periods in between, not slashes); and an honorific plus a title is as common as an honorific plus the last name. The time of day is typically written in military time; weights and measures are usually given in metric measurements. Monetary amounts are written so that the period breaks up the figure into tens, hundreds, and thousands, and the comma separates the *notas* (bills) from the *moedas* (coins). Be sure to inquire first, in all communications, about your colleague's health and progress, then move on to the substance of your communication, and close with a salutation and your personal wishes for his or her success and well-being (the Latin communication "sandwich"). If your colleagues write to you in Portuguese, try to respond in Portuguese, if you can, or use the services of a translator. Written addresses are usually in the following format:

Line 1: name
Line 2: title/position
Line 3: company
Line 4: street address
Line 5: city, state

The Western "Southern Cone" Cultures: Argentina and Chile

General Cultural Note: Southern Cone culture, both West and East, incorpo- rates far more multicultural elements than do the cultures in the rest of the region (excepting Brazil, with its roots in Portugal and Africa), having inte- grated the many immigrant cultures of Europe, both Latin and Northern (Ger- manic, in particular), into its original Hispanic base. For this reason, behaviors in this region are often characterized, relative to other Latin American behav- iors, as "cooler," more informal, more egalitarian and flexible. Keeping this in mind is important as a backdrop to understanding the behaviors of Argentines and Chileans, in particular.

ARGENTINA

Some Introductory Background on Argentina and the Argentines

Argentina is said to be a European country in the wrong continent. It is also said to be like Texas, only with European cowboys. It is, in fact, both. Sophisti- cated "Portenos" (what people from Buenos Aires call themselves) are conti- nental in attitude, dress, airs, speech, even blood. Most of them are descendants of immigrants from the continent, and continue to speak German, Italian, or French, or the Lunfardo, the unique form of Spanish that is spoken in Argentina today (a result of the influence of many European languages): for example, the "j" in Spanish most everywhere else in the Spanish-speaking world is pro- nounced as the "y" in "yellow"; in Argentina, it is pronounced like the "j" in "just," but ever-so-slightly softer. Additionally, the Spanish form most likely to be used instead of the informal *tu* in Argentina is the *voceo,* or informal *vos* form; Argentines also often use the pan-European *chau* or *ciao* as an informal way of saying goodbye. Today, the immigrants to Argentina might as likely be from the Pacific Rim as from Europe. Buenos Aires, architecturally, culturally, and even in terms of how it keeps time (business is fairly prompt, social events always require you to be late—if you want things to start and stop "on time," you must say *en punto*), is a profoundly European city, yet just outside the city, as we enter the great plains of Argentina, the pampas and the prairies, we enter cowboy country, where the local gaucho culture is still quite alive and well. This is one of the reasons, no doubt, that Argentines have the highest rate of meat consumption in the world (if you're vegetarian, you are going to have a hard time in Argentina). By the way, the people are "Argentine"; things are "Argentinian."

Some Historical Context

The history of Argentina is fractured, as it was originally largely ignored by the conquering Spaniards, who favored the more gold-rich areas of Bolivia and Peru to the north. This benign neglect, in fact, allowed Argentines to develop a bit more unfettered by Madrid than their neighbors, and was one of the reasons for the larger immigration into Argentina from many other parts of the world. By the time Spain was beginning to lose its grasp over the New World, Argentina had consolidated into a very large region dominated by Buenos Aires that included what is now Bolivia, Chile, Paraguay, and Uruguay. Although this region was one of the first to declare independence from Spain (under the name the United Provinces of Rio de la Plata), the disparate cultures that it encompassed resented the centralized rule from far away Buenos Aires (especially since this was just at the time when such autocratic rule from Madrid was being undone), and these regions began the struggle to break free from Argentina itself into their own countries. Subsequent to this, Argentina has had conflicts with all of its neighbors at one time or another, mainly involving border and territorial disputes.

An Area Briefing

Politics and Government

Though Argentina is nominally a federal democratic republic with a bicameral legislature, a president, and a judicial system, the government authority is still heavily influenced by powerful interests and the military. The political atmosphere has always been stormy, and although the country has since its independence from time to time been run by military juntas and dictators (the most famous—or infamous, depending upon your perspective—being Juan Perón), the key Latin American problems of wealth redistribution and land reform in Argentina have mainly taken the form of urban struggles between workers and the ruling business elite. Currently, Argentina is facing yet another of its periodic fiscal crises, so it is important to check on the current economic climate prior to any trip or business venture in Argentina. Most recently, and prior to the current government (which was a military junta that finally relinquished control to a civilian elected government in the face of the loss of the Falkland Islands War with the United Kingdom), the issue of the disappearance of citizens opposed to the government, still unresolved, emerged as an example of the distance Argentina still needs to go to become a stable and representative republic.

Schools and Education

Schooling is compulsory through high school; however, in some lower class and rural regions, maintaining quality education and children's attendance through these grades is sometimes a challenge. The wealthy send their children to private schools, including universities in Europe and the United States.

Religion and Demographics

The people are mainly Roman Catholic, with substantial minority populations of Jews, Protestants, and others. Despite its difficult history and tumultuous economic cycles, Argentina is still one of the wealthier nations in the region, with the largest middle class in all of South America. The indigenous population was small to begin with, resulting in a profoundly mixed and less stratified "European"-based demography, with peoples emigrating into Argentina from Germany, France, Italy, Ukraine, and Eastern Europe. Argentina has the largest Jewish community in all of Latin America (referred to often as *los Rusos,* because they originally emigrated to Argentina from Russia).

Fundamental Cultural Orientations

1. What's the Best Way for People to Relate to One Another?

OTHER-INDEPENDENT OR OTHER-DEPENDENT?　As is the case with most countries in the region—due, in part, to the heavy influence of Roman Catholicism—Argentinian behavior is often significantly "other-dependent." Most individuals will seek, either formally or informally, the opinions and support of family, friends, and coworkers before venturing off to do or say something on their own. While individuals are responsible for their decisions, the group in all its forms (extended family, work relationships, community) plays a powerful role in the decisions that individuals make. A consequence of this, of course, is a resistance to the outsider, and a need for all outsiders to become associated with members of the in-group as soon as possible. Causing someone to lose face, or experience embarrassment, public ridicule, or criticism of any kind is a great insult in this other-dependent culture; here, how one is thought of by others is an important concern in life. Despite this strong need to look good in the eyes of others, the individual must bear responsibility for him- or herself in the world. This may present itself in behavior that appears to be individualistic; however, most of the time, the motive for the behavior is group acceptance and respect.

HIERARCHY-ORIENTED OR EGALITY-ORIENTED?　Hierarchy and power are still rigidly determined, and unlike some other areas in Latin America where the church has recently played a revolutionary role, the church in Argentina is a particularly conservative institution, tied, as it was at the beginning, to the privileged class. Nevertheless, because of the significant immigration into Argentina of post-aristocracy Europeans in the nineteenth century (Europeans coming from countries that had already experienced the overthrow of aristocracies and the attempts at installing representative Republican forms of governments), there is always a struggle in Argentina between the traditional elite and the democratic masses. Subsequently, Argentine society is stratified, with individuals at the top typically having decision-making authority, but always being challenged. While machismo is still strong, women are playing an increasingly large role in business and politics.

RULE-ORIENTED OR RELATIONSHIP-ORIENTED? As in all Latin cultures, facts and rules are important in Argentina, but never exclusive to determining action. Feelings, the obligations of relationships, and subjective experience are critical, and the Argentine is always balancing all three in weighing issues and making decisions. In Argentina, time is well-spent on developing the personal relationship (trust and *simpatico,* or an implicit sense of understanding); attempts to discuss the terms of the deal or the immediate task at hand without having built the necessary personal trust and understanding is often a waste of time. Which takes us to our next concern.

2. What's the Best Way to View Time?

MONOCHRONIC OR POLYCHRONIC? Argentina is primarily polychronic, although non-Argentines would do best arriving for business on time: for social occasions, however, it is essential that you arrive at least 30 minutes to an hour later than the stated time. Outside of the major cities, time is circular, and very polychronic. For example, dinner at home rarely starts before 8 or 9 P.M., and a dinner party with guests at home will often not start until 9 or 10 P.M., even though guests may have been invited for 8 P.M. If you really want things to occur punctually, it is perfectly okay to identify the time as *en punto,* although it might be difficult to enforce. Business hours are often extremely late: upper-level managers and executives can stay in the office until 9 or 10 P.M., and meetings can last well into the evening.

RISK-TAKING OR RISK-AVERSE? Latin cultures, in general, are risk-averse, and that is one of the driving reasons for the creation of structure and hierarchies. Argentina is no exception. There are levels of bureaucracy that are breathtaking in their byzantine regulations, and in order to get things done in business and the public arena, there are usually many different officials who need to sign off at different stages. The pace can be slow, as people need to develop trust in order to do business with you, and the need for *enchufados,* or people with contacts and connections to help you through, is critical. Providing whatever details you need to in order for your Argentine associate to feel comfortable is important in this risk-averse culture, and repeated efforts often must be made to convince and motivate, especially if it means changing the way something is done. Even when individuals are empowered to make the decision, there can be a reticence to take the required final step.

PAST-ORIENTED OR FUTURE-ORIENTED? Latin American cultures, Argentina included, have seen their world turned upside down more than once with their having little or no ability to control the events. Imagine surviving inflation of 10,000 percent (as was the case in the 1970s) or military coups and assorted invasions. In Argentina, there is a strong doubt in the ability to ultimately control what happens, but the effort is always there, for to struggle is to live. Despite a strong desire to believe in their own ability to overcome the odds, there may be an equally strong acceptance of the inevitability of setbacks and failures, and an inclination to place the blame on others and in circumstances beyond one's control if things go wrong.

3. What's the Best Way for Society to Work with the World at Large?

LOW-CONTEXT DIRECT OR HIGH-CONTEXT INDIRECT COMMUNICATORS? Latin American speech patterns are typically high context and polychronic, and this is typically the case in Argentina. However, because of the immigrant mix, there can be many variations on this theme, ranging from surprisingly direct communication to a strong tendency among Argentines to say what they believe people want to hear rather than what is unpleasant. In most conversations, in business and social situations, there can be interruptions, unexpected topics, and unannounced visitors, with people speaking at the same time. This will require people from monochronic cultures to develop the fine art of patience. Argentines will be quick to assure you that all is going as planned or as you desire, or that they are eager to do as they agreed. This is not based on a desire to deceive but rather a need to appear capable, and not to lose face in the eyes of others, particularly when it may be in one's interest to cultivate a relationship. It is critical, therefore, to always confirm information; to have multiple and independent sources "on the ground" to confirm for you what you are being told, and to be able to read between the lines without directly challenging the veracity of what your Argentine colleague is saying. In a culture that has seen one truth replaced by another again and again, there is a strong tolerance for, in fact dependence on, the subjective interpretation of events and reality.

PROCESS-ORIENTED OR RESULT-ORIENTED? As with other Latinos, there is a strong reliance on the deductive process: how things are being done is as important as the final result. This is evident among the well-educated business elite. But Argentines, as we noted, are most comfortable using personal experience in order to make or justify a decision. While many Argentine businesspeople are influenced by facts and logic, persuasion is most successful when it confirms already existing beliefs.

FORMAL OR INFORMAL? Argentinian society in general (except perhaps for the upper-class ruling elite) is not as formal in a Catholic, conservative kind of way as some of the other countries in the region, but it is also not as informal in business or social life as North American society. Even the language is still divided into formal and informal forms and phrases, and personal behaviors are generally ruled by certain etiquette and protocol. Maintaining honor and personal respect is critical, and this requires a general sensitivity to the issues of protocol.

Greetings and Introductions

Language and Basic Vocabulary

The first language may be Spanish, but because of the significant historic immigration of Europeans, the second language is Italian, and the third is German (English is fourth). As is the case throughout most of South America, the term *gringo* is not commonly used; people from the United States are more often referred to as *Norteamericanos,* or pejoratively as *Yanquis.* Be sure to use any Spanish you do know; it will be appreciated. Many businesspeople, but not all, understand and also speak workable English. Additionally, the *lunfardo,* the Argentinian slang that sounds so Italian and is spoken primarily in Buenos Aires, is unique to the region, and Argentinian Spanish, in general, is quite different in accent and pronunciation from Castilian Spanish and the Spanish spoken in other parts of South America (recall the substitution of the "j" for "y" mentioned earlier, for example). Here are the basics:

Buenos días	Good morning
Buenas tardes	Good afternoon
Buenas noches	Good evening
¡Hola! ¿Que tal?	Hello, how are you? (informal)
¿Como está usted?	How are you? (formal)
Adiós	Good-bye
Por favor	Please
Gracias	Thank you
Con permiso	Pardon me
De nada	You're welcome
Muy bien	Very well
Con mucho gusto	Pleased to meet you
Un placer	A pleasure
Señor	Mr.
Señora	Mrs.
Señorita	Miss
Ingeniero(a)	Engineer
Abogado(a)	Lawyer
Doctor	Doctor
Gerente	Manager

Remember, in written Spanish, questions and exclamations are also indicated at the beginning of the sentence, with an upside-down exclamation point or question mark.

Honorifics for Men, Women, and Children

You must use *señor* (Mr.) and *señora* (Mrs.) plus the family name when introduced to strangers. Unless or until your Argentine colleague specifically invites you to use first names, and despite how he or she might refer to you, you must always use the family name plus the correct Spanish honorific (*señorita*—Miss—is still required for a young, unmarried woman). If you do not know whether a woman is married, use *señorita* (please note: this is the reverse from what is done in Spain, where *señora* is used when the marital status of the woman is unknown). Occasionally, the term *don* (for a man) and *doña* (for a woman) preceding the first name only will be used to indicate a person who merits great respect (due to either his or her age or power); if introduced to such a person this way, you must always use his or her full title (e.g., Don Pedro, never just Don). The use of *don* and *doña* as honorifics, however, is typically reserved for individuals who already have close personal relationships, and is not as common as in other countries in the region; you may hear it, but will rarely have a chance to use it yourself, unless you have established an especially close, long-term relationship. Married women are not necessarily "safe" from machismo, so wearing a wedding band does not always protect a woman alone; however, being a mother helps to ensure that a man will remain at a distance: bring pictures of your children. Children in Argentina are expected to be respectful and not overly conversational when speaking with adults, and must always use honorifics when referring to adults. In situations where a title is known or used, the honorific plus the title is usually employed either with or without the name (e.g., Señor Ingeniero, or Señor Ingeniero Cortez). *Licensiado* is a "title" generally used for anyone with a skill requiring some sort of diploma. "Doctor" may be safely used as a way to give respect to anyone with a university degree; as an honorific, it does not have to refer only to a Ph.D. (do not, however, refer to yourself that way unless you hold a legitimate doctorate). In casual contact (e.g., with waiters, store help, etc.), just use *señor* or *señorita* without the name. It is very important to greet people at work or in stores and restaurants with an appropriate greeting for the time of day—*buenos días, buenas tardes,* or *buenas noches*—and *adiós* upon leaving. If you speak any Spanish at all, it is important to use it, but be sure to use the formal pronoun, *usted,* in the beginning and do *not* switch to the *tu* (informal "you") form of speech unless and until your Argentinian colleague has specifically invited you to or does so him- or herself.

Spanish family names are often hyphenated, with the mother's family name added after the father's family name. In formal speech and in written correspondence, the fully hyphenated name is used; in face-to-face introductions, usually only the father's family name is used. For example, José Ramón Mendez-Rodriguez is Señor Mendez in face-to-face introductions, with Mendez being José's father's family name and Rodriguez being José's mother's family name. Women often keep their family name when they marry, but add their husband's father's family name with the preposition *de.* For example, Señora Maria Isabel Gonzalez-Sanchez de Rodriguez is married to Señor Rodriguez, her maiden name is Gonzalez (her father's family name), and she retains her mother's family name—Sanchez—as well; in face-to-face communication she is more often referred to as Señora de Rodriguez or, very informally, as Señora Rodriguez.

The What, When, and How of Introducing People

Always wait to be introduced to strangers before taking that responsibility upon yourself. Argentines are most comfortable with a third-party introduction whenever possible. Try to ensure that for yourself ahead of time. You will be introduced to women first, then the most senior men. Do not presume to seat your-self at a formal gathering; if possible, wait to be told where to sit. Shake hands with everyone individually in a group when being introduced and before depart-ing; the U.S. group wave is not appreciated. Avoid ending the conversation with the expression "Have a nice day"; it sounds controlling and insincere. It is not uncommon to see men and men, and women and women, walking arm in arm down the street; they are good close friends or associates, and it usually means nothing more than that.

The use of business cards is common; if possible, you should have your business card translated into Spanish on the reverse. Be sure to put any advanced educational degrees and your full title or position on both sides of your business card. Such emblems of your status are very important to Argentines; they want to know they are doing business with an important person.

Physical Greeting Styles

The handshake is common. The Argentinian version is a firm, quick shake or two between two men, less robust between men and women or two women. The handshake should be accompanied by the appropriate greeting (see the list of terms outlined earlier). Men should wait until a woman extends her hand before reaching for it, and women may take the lead in extending their hand or not. Men must remove their gloves when shaking hands with a woman, but a woman need not remove her gloves when shaking hands with a man. Between family, friends, or trusted business associates, a hug (the *abrazo,* or embrace) will generally occur. This usually happens after several meetings; do not initiate it, but respond warmly in kind if it is initiated with you. Eye contact during the introduction is important, and should be maintained as long as the individual is addressing you. Kissing is a common greeting once you have established a strong and very familiar relationship, whether between women or men and women; usually, there is a kiss on one cheek (actually an "air kiss"). There is a particularly personal aspect to Argentinian communication style, as well, which makes it perfectly acceptable for people, once they know you, to very quickly make personal, and sometimes teasingly disparaging remarks about you, your habits, dress, physical shape, and so on (e.g., "Gee, you haven't lost that weight yet, have you?"). Please do not take any of this with offense (although it is most decidedly personal), for it is just the Argentine way of joking around and being personable.

Communication Styles

Okay Topics / Not Okay Topics

Okay: Argentines love opera and soccer (fútbol), and women particularly love fashion; these are all acceptable topics to talk about. It is important to bone up on your knowledge of things Argentinian, so that you are able to speak intelli-gently and positively about the culture. Argentina's history and its place in South America as the country with the largest middle class and highest standards of living for most of the people, despite periodic difficulties, are a source of pride among Argentines and a good topic of conversation. Other good topics include children and food. Argentines will welcome your genuine interest about the tango, their national dance. Contrary to those in some other Latin American cultures, Argentines love photography and take pictures of events and people all the time; in fact, if you are visiting, taking pictures of them, and having them take pictures of you, is a nice way to share memories and gifts. ***Not okay:*** Avoid asking anyone if they are "native" or related to any indigenous peoples: Argentines are very proud of their European-based heritage. Because of the Falkland Islands war with Britain, Argentines are not very fond of Britons or things British (note that these islands are known in Argentina as the Malvinas Islands) and do not refer to them in Argentina as the Falklands. Also avoid discussing your colleagues, travel, or work in neighboring Chile and Bolivia; politics; the Perón years (and the personalities involved); and Argentina's relationships with its neighbors. Do not inquire about a person's occupation or income in casual conversation, although that may be inquired of you. Americans often begin a conversation with "So, what do you do?"; this is too personal in Argentina, and is often not the most interesting topic of conversation. Do not give your opinions about things Argentinian unless you really know what you're talking about, but do show a genuine interest in learning more. Do not talk about your tummy's adventures in Latin America; keep your health issues to yourself, because no one wants to hear about them. Also not okay: money and inquiring about private family matters (although speaking about the health and other general aspects of family life is very important). Do not go to Argentina (or anywhere in Latin America) without pictures of your family, and when family is brought up (which it will be almost immediately in the conversation), use it as an opportunity to bring out the photographs. Never tell a dirty joke with a woman present.

Tone, Volume, and Speed

Keeping your voice low and quietly powerful is the best way to go. Discussions between strangers usually start out politely restrained, especially in business, but can become quite animated when there are many people present, and interruptions are not uncommon, with unanticipated topics and people being introduced unexpectedly.

Use of Silence

There rarely is any intentional use of silence.

Physical Gestures and Facial Expressions

There are some unique Argentinian nonverbal communications: Holding the thumb to the tip of the forefinger and shaking the hand up and down means "Come on, hurry up!," or indicates that something is "a great deal." If you brush the underside of your chin with the tips of your fingers with the hand palm down, it means, "I don't know" or "I'm not interested." Finally, twisting the right hand from side to side with all fingers extended means *"comme ci, comme ça,"* or "so-so." The *"figa"* gesture, made by placing the thumb between the index and middle fingers, is considered vulgar (although in Brazil, it is a sign for good luck). Whistling and catcalling are not common. Never yawn in public (if you must, cover your mouth and look away). Never stand with your hands on your hips: it is aggressive (however, there is nothing defensive about folding the arms in front of you). Tapping the bottom of the elbow indicates that the person you are talking about is cheap or making a stingy offer, and a gentle tap on the shoulder is usually a way of indicating friendship.

Waving and Counting

The thumb represents the number 1, the index finger the number 2, and so on. It is insulting to beckon someone with the forefinger; instead, turn your hand so that the palm faces down and motion inward with all four fingers at once. Waving or beckoning is done with the palm down and the fingers moving forward and back in a kind of scratching motion. Because of the personal nature of the culture, even money is usually exchanged in the palms, not on the counter (and please note, coins are rarely used, since they are very devalued: you are not being cheated if the clerk rounds up the change to the nearest denomination in bills).

Physicality and Physical Space

Argentines tend to get closer than North Americans are generally comfortable with; do not step back when your Argentine associate steps forward. Argentine men, once they know each other, may often touch each other during conversations, adjust each other's ties, dust off each other's shoulders, and the like. Never speak with your hands in your pockets; always keep them firmly at your side when standing. If men and women must cross their legs, it must never be ankle over knee (for women, the preferred style is to cross ankle over ankle). Remember, even in public, formal is always better than informal: no gum chewing, *ever;* no slouching; no leaning against things.

Eye Contact

As in other Southern Cone and European cultures, it is very important to maintain direct eye contact when speaking with someone. It is an Argentine's way of showing interest. Conversely, if you look away, your behavior will say to your Argentine colleague that you are disinterested, rude, or establishing yourself as the subordinate in a hierarchical relationship; none of these is a good idea. Maintain eye contact when it is made with you.

Emotive Orientation

While expressive gesturing is common, until you know people well, you want to indicate restraint and coolness, while never seeming lifeless. Argentines will always admire you if you can remain logical, formal, respectful, and diplomatic—especially at first—while being warm, open, and personable.

Protocol in Public

Walking Styles and Waiting in Lines

Expect very close physicality between strangers on the street or in public places. This is rarely an invitation to a relationship, and more often a way of pushing ahead.

It is more important in Argentina to maintain one's face by being first in line (and never last) than it is to maintain a queue. Don't be too distressed if someone walks right up to the front of the line at a bank, a restaurant, or a store, and gets served because of the relationship he or she has with the clerk, while you have been waiting patiently in line for forty minutes. This occurs also in response to rank based on gender and age. People also have a tendency to stand very close in public; this may feel uncomfortable at first. Resist the urge to back away; most of the time, you are not being intentionally crowded. Remember, the need to appear helpful and courteous is strong, and if you ask for directions on the street, you will no doubt be instructed on just where to go . . . whether or not the individual actually knows!

Behavior in Public Places: Airports, Terminals, and the Market

Customer service, as a concept, is catching on, but is not fully institutionalized. Store hours are typically not designed around customer convenience (many stores are closed on weekends, certainly Sundays), although there are many malls now in Argentinian cities where stores stay open late. Some stores may still close for lunchtime between 1 and 2:30 P.M., and reopen from 2 or 3 to 7 or 8 P.M. Personally thanking store owners, waiters, chefs, and hotel managers for their services is very much appreciated. In food markets, you can touch the produce; in goods stores, it may be difficult for you to return a product unless there is a flaw in it. You will not find the kind of street begging and poverty in Argentina that you can find elsewhere in Latin America. Smoking is pervasive, and if you do smoke, be sure to always offer a cigarette to everyone you are talking to before you light up. In bathrooms, on the plumbing, "C" means hot (*caldo*) and "F" means cold (*frío*).

When answering a phone, say *"Hola."* The use of cell phones is ubiquitous, and the telephone system is generally good, although many pay phones may be broken. Be sure to give both the paternal and maternal last name of the person you are looking for when calling directory assistance, as there are many people with the same last names.

Bus / Metro / Taxi / Car

Driving is on the right, but people pass very quickly on the left. Driving is difficult in the cities, and dangerous in the rural areas, and being a pedestrian is just as risky: both drivers and pedestrians really are very aggressive. Additionally, throughout Latin America, street rules are observed only sporadically (stoplights are viewed as suggestions) and drivers usually do not turn their lights on after dark (it is believed to blind the oncoming traffic), but may have them on during the day for extra safety. The best way to catch a cab is at designated taxi stands (hotels are good places, but often charge more for the same ride: a hotel surcharge may be added to the meter fare, in some cases). Bring food and water on board trains if your trip is a long one, as they may not have a café car. The crime situation in Argentina is typically not as major an issue as it is in other Latin American countries, other than the kind of petty street crime that occurs everywhere.

Tipping

A 10 percent tip is usually sufficient in restaurants and taxis; more is considered nouveau and gauche. Porters and hotel help get the equivalent in pesos of one U.S. dollar per item or service rendered, theater and bathroom attendants usually a few pesos (and in both cases, tipping in U.S. dollars, as is done throughout much of the region, is perfectly fine, actually preferred). Please double-check the current dollar/peso exchange rate, as it can vary quickly and significantly. Restaurants usually have the 10 percent tip already included on the bill, but if you are unsure, it's okay to ask whether service is included or not. Even if it is, it is still appropriate to leave a few pesos or odd change if service was particularly good. Bargaining is not that common in most stores today.

Punctuality

It is perfectly acceptable—in fact, essential—to arrive for social events about an hour late. An invitation to dinner in someone's home will be for the time when people may begin to arrive; dinner itself will probably not actually be served until at least one to one and half hours later. If you arrive sooner, you will be running the risk of interrupting the host or hostess as he or she gets ready. For business meetings, being late by five to twenty minutes or more is usually not a problem, but it is safer for the new employee or visitor to be on time, while not being surprised if others are not. Usually, the meeting will not begin in earnest until all attendees have arrived (or at least until all the decision makers have shown up), and this may not correspond to the time listed in the agenda. Resist questioning the late ones for a reason; they always have one, usually involving an obligation with more important people, like superiors, old friends, or family.

Dress

Argentines are very serious about how people dress: you will be evaluated (from your polished shoes up) on your wardrobe, as it is a reflection of your position in society. At work, men typically wear conservative, well-tailored suits, of the highest quality fabrics, white shirts, and interesting and sophisticated ties. Women usually accessorize so that even the simplest of outfits stands out for its interest and style. Professional women typically dress very formally for work, and take care to accessorize and have well-attended coifs. For both men and women, dressing as expensively as possible has its definite rewards. The only time more casual clothes (and they still need to be smart and stylish) are worn to a social event is at an *asado,* or an outdoor barbecue at someone's home. Men often arrive in restaurants in the evening in the same formal business clothes that they wore during the day, but sometimes replace the tie with a stylish ascot. Never wear native indigenous or gaucho dress: you will be laughed at. Also, be prepared to wear very dispensable clothes during *Carnaval* (when people spray each other with water on the street!). Jeans and sneakers are typically worn only at the gym, on the beach, or while jogging (women do not wear sneakers to work), and even informal for a social gathering more often than not means tastefully coordinated clothes, sometimes including a jacket and tie for men (it rarely if ever means jeans, sneakers, and T-shirts). "Formal" usually means formal evening wear, very dressy by U.S. standards.

Seasonal Variations

Remember that Argentina has the reverse seasons of North America, so that summer, which can be hot, is between December and March, and winter is between June and September.

Colors

Bright colors are best reserved for accessories, as offsets to the more sophisticated dark or soft hues and beiges of the outfits themselves.

Styles

Fashion for both men and women, as in many other aspects of life in Argentina, looks to Europe and not to the United States, although few people on the street can actually afford the latest trends. Nevertheless, even the average person has a heightened sense of fashion, and one should dress with the same thought and care that one should put into every aspect of his or her life.

Accessories / Jewelry / Makeup

Argentine women may wear more makeup and jewelry than women in the United States, and it is fashionable, especially in summer, not to wear stockings. Among the upper class, there has been a strong tradition to have cosmetic plastic surgery, if they could afford it.

Personal Hygiene

In Argentina, personal hygiene is very important. There is a real concern for cleanliness and smelling good; perfumes and colognes are used often. Latin men may sport facial hair, in the form of mustaches. Note that most rest room and bathroom facilities throughout Latin America do not have plumbing capable of handling paper toilet tissue; it is for this reason that there is a small receptacle next to the toilet for your used tissue: do not flush it down the bowl, but place it in the receptacle, or else you'll face the embarrassment of having to call for help when the bowl overflows. Finally, you may find (and this is the case in much of South America) that the bath is mainly a shower (full bathtubs are not as common) and that the water is heated from an electrical unit attached to the showerhead; if this is the case, it is very important never to touch the unit once the water is running!

Dining and Drinking

Mealtimes and Typical Foods

For breakfast (*el desayuno*), which is served between 7 and 9 A.M., Argentines enjoy the national breads: the *medialuna,* a kind of croissant, or the *pan de leche,* a muffin with cream poured over it. The drink is coffee or *mate* (the national drink of the country).

Lunch (*el almuerzo*) is still the main meal of the day, served around 1 P.M.: the food is usually the same for lunch and dinner, only in varying combinations. The national dish is beef, or more precisely, steak of all kinds, usually served in huge quantities. *Churrasco* is grilled steak (and is served in *churrasquerías,* which are popular restaurants in which the waiters come around with all different cuts of meat throughout the night. Hint: don't fill up on the first few slices the waiter gives you, because they usually start out with the cheaper cuts first, and serve the more expensive cuts later in the meal, after you are too full to have too much). *Parillada* is a mixed grill of many different cuts and types of meats, served at *parrilladerías.* Appetizers at meals are sometimes meals in themselves: known as *matambres* (or "hunger-killers"), they can range from full-sized empanadas to steaks stuffed with peppers and cheese. The Argentines really do love their meat and love to eat. (They often use a special meat sauce, *chimichurri,* as a barbecue sauce for their meats.) Desserts are usually very sweet flans, puddings, and sweetened fruits (or sometimes sweet potatoes) served with bland cheeses (the balance is really memorable). There is often a break around 4 P.M. for *la hora del té,* or tea hour, for sweet snacks and tea or coffee.

Dinner is usually very late, from about 10 P.M. on, and is a smaller meal than lunch, if lunch was the main meal. Dinner parties usually start very late, and you are expected to stay very late (well past midnight). Although it is considered safe to drink the water in Buenos Aires, it is better to play it safer and stick to bottled water, and abide by all the rules of eating in public in Latin America that have been discussed throughout the book; this is still the case assuredly outside of Buenos Aires. Even taking the usual precautions, on your first few trips to the region you will inevitably get the Latin American tummy; it is hard to avoid a drop of water here or there. If you have followed the above rules carefully, it is probably nothing to worry about; it will be uncomfortable for a day or two. Eat lightly, drink lots of safe fluids, stay in or near your room, rest, and it will pass. If a fever or vomiting develops, be sure to seek medical attention immediately.

Regional Differences

In Argentina, meat is often served drier and more well-done than many North Americans like. It is also usually salted before it arrives at your table. Therefore, if you do not want your meat presalted, you will have to say, *"No use sal, por favor"* when you place your order. Additionally, if you want your meat rare, you say, *"Cruda, por favor,"* and if you want it medium rare, you say *"Poquito cruda, por favor."* *Bien cocida* means well-done, and *muy bien cocida* means very well-done.

Typical Drinks and Toasting

Argentinian wines are typically quite good, and wine is served with dinner and lunch. The usual predinner drink is *gancia,* a sweet vermouth, while after dinner, scotch is often the drink of preference. Note that imported liquors are very expensive, while local ones are not; if you want the local ones, add the word *nacional,* i.e., *"vino tinto nacional."* Good imported whiskey makes a wonderful gift. Don't ask for Californian wines, as they are generally considered inferior in Argentina. As in Bolivia and other Southern Cone countries, there are some important rules about pouring wine: never pour it backwards into the glass, as this means that you very much dislike the person you are pouring for, and do not use your left hand to pour the wine for the same reason. Coffee is mainly drunk black (you probably will have to ask for milk to add if that's the way you like it). There is a unique herbal tea that is drunk throughout Argentina called *mate* (the dried leaves are in fact known as *yerba mate*), which is served in a gourd, often with an elegant silver straw (a *bombilla*). It is very highly caffeinated, so it is a good replacement for coffee. The etiquette for drinking *mate* is to take a sip and pass the gourd to your neighbor; they do the same in turn. It generally, therefore, is not served in restaurants, but is reserved as an accompaniment to conversation in the home among friends. The most common toast is *salud* (to your health).

Table Manners and the Use of Utensils

Do not begin eating until the host says, *¡Buen provecho!* Referring to European traditions as they do, Argentines do not switch knives and forks, as people do in the United States. The knife remains in the right hand, and the fork remains in the left. Contrary to the custom in much of Latin America, lunch in Argentina is usually a private affair, with many people going home to lunch; business lunches, therefore, are not that common, while business dinners in restaurants are. You may not be invited to a home quickly, for Argentines, like their continental cousins, regard the home as sacred. At most meals, you will not be expected to eat everything on your plate, as the amount is usually substantial: your food will be served on your plate, typically not family-style (no seconds). If you want to cut your meat like an Argentine, hold the meat with your fork in your left hand, and cut the meat with the knife in your right hand through the tines of the fork. When you are finished with your meal, cross your knife and fork across the plate, with the tines facing downward. If you put both utensils down on the plate for any real length of time, it is a sign to the waitstaff that you are finished, and your plate may be taken away from you. Alternately, if you lay your cutlery down on either side of the plate it means you haven't finished; but if you really are, the host might interpret this as a sign that you were not happy with the meal.

The fork and spoon above your plate are for dessert. There are often many additional pieces of cutlery at a formal meal; if you're unsure of which utensil to use, always start from the outside and work your way in, course by course. Bread is sometimes served without butter; in that case, there usually will not be a butter knife, nor will there be a bread dish: your bread is placed on the rim of your main plate or on the table by your plate. There will be separate glasses provided at your setting for water and white and red wine or beer (after-dinner drink glasses come out after dinner).

When not holding utensils, your hands are expected to be visible above the table: this means you do not keep them in your lap; instead, rest your wrists on top of the table (never your elbows). At the table, pass all dishes to your left. Never cut the lettuce in a salad: deftly fold it with your knife and fork into a little bundle that can be easily picked up with your fork.

Seating Plans

The most honored position is at the head of the table, with the most important guest usually seated next to the host or hostess (women to the right of the host, men to the right of the hostess). In the European tradition, men and women are seated next to one another, and couples are often broken up and seated next to people they may not have previously known. This is done to promote conversation. Men typically rise when women enter the room, and continue to hold doors for women and allow them to enter a room first. Remember, as is the case throughout the Continent, the first floor in Argentina ("*PB*" or *planta baja*) is really the second floor, with the first floor usually referred to as the lobby or ground floor.

Refills and Seconds

If you do not want more food, it is okay to leave a little food on your plate in Argentina. You may always have additional beverages; drink enough to cause your cup or glass to be less than half full, and it will generally be refilled. Portions are generally large.

At Home, in a Restaurant, or at Work

In informal restaurants, you will rarely be required to share a table. Waitstaff may be summoned by catching their eye and saying *"Mozo"*; waving or calling their names is very impolite (although you might see some Argentines make a kind of puckering sound; don't do it). The business meal is generally not the time to make business decisions. Take your cue from your Argentine associates: if they bring up business, then it's okay to discuss it (more often than not, over the coffee and brandy at the end of the meal), but wait to take your lead from their conversation. No gum chewing, *ever*, at a restaurant or on the street. No-smoking sections in restaurants are still a rarity.

When you arrive at an Argentine associate's home for a formal meal, you will be told where to sit, and there you should remain. Do not wander from room to room; much of the house is really off-limits to guests. Use the toilet before you arrive, as it is considered bad form to leave the dinner party, or the table, at any time. Once you (and the group) are invited to another room, most probably the dining room, be sure to allow more senior members of your party to enter the room ahead of you: men should move aside to allow women to enter the room ahead of them. Often drinks and hors d'oeuvres are served in the living room prior to the dinner. In a private home, be careful about what and how you admire things: the host may feel obliged to give it to you! Once at the table, be sure to look for place cards, or wait until the host indicates your seat: do not presume to seat yourself, as the seating arrangement is usually predetermined. If you invite people to your home, be prepared to always have the invitation accepted, although they may not, in fact, show up; rejecting the invitation may be difficult for Argentines, who seek to not offend. They may indicate their true intentions by simply responding to your invitation with "I will try."

Being a Good Guest or Host

Paying the Bill

Usually the one who does the inviting pays the bill, although the guest is expected to make an effort to pay. Sometimes other circumstances determine who pays (such as rank). Making payment arrangements ahead of time so that no exchange occurs at the table is a very classy way to host. Women, if out with men, will not really be able to pay the bill at a restaurant; if you want to, make arrangements ahead of time, and don't wait for the check to arrive at the table. The only time it is considered appropriate for a woman to pay the bill is if she is a hosting businesswoman from abroad. If a businesswoman invites an Argentine businessman to a meal, she should be sure to extend the invitation to his spouse as well, or may want to consider telling him that her (female) colleague will also be joining them (and be sure to have a female colleague along). Do not allow the Argentine male to suggest bringing one of his colleagues along (remember, the person doing the inviting can refuse the suggestion). If an Argentine male invites a businesswoman to a meeting or a meal that seems to have more than business as the subject, a businesswoman should always insist that she bring her female associate along (someone who is needed because of her role in the company). Unmarried businesswomen may want to consider wearing a wedding band. If you have children, be sure to discuss that fact at some point early in the initial conversations: any aggressive macho behavior usually stops when men learn they are dealing with a *madre.*

Transportation

It's a very nice idea, when acting as the host, to inquire ahead of time as to whether your guests will require transportation. If necessary, you should arrange for taxi service at the end of the meal. When the cars arrive, be sure not to leave your spot until your guests are out of sight.

When to Arrive / Chores to Do

If invited to a private dinner party, remember to arrive at least a half hour later than the stated time and be prepared for dinner not to begin for at least another hour after you arrive and to go on well past midnight. If invited to dinner at an upper-class home where there are servants and help, do not offer to help with the chores, nor should you expect to visit the kitchen. Because there is such a large middle class in Argentina, in most homes there are no servants. Do not expect them in the average home. In a middle- or lower-class home, it is appropriate to offer to help with the chores, and your offer typically may be taken up. Do not leave the table unless invited to do so. Spouses do not attend business dinners without a special invitation to do so, but if you are hosting a business associate for a dinner, be sure to invite spouses. Once you have been invited to someone's home, it is expected that you reciprocate by extending a sincere invitation to them when they can visit you, or by hosting them at a fine restaurant as your guest on another night of your trip.

Gift Giving

In business, as is the case throughout most of Latin America, some chocolates or a small gift for the secretary of the person you are visiting can work wonders for future smooth sailing! If a man is giving a gift to a woman in a business setting, it is important to present it as a gift to her from his wife or sister, although perfume and other personal beauty items, which are typically regarded as very personal gifts in North America, are usually appropriate for a man to give to a woman, even as a token gift in business, in Argentina. Holiday cards are very appropriate, particularly as a thank-you for your Argentine colleagues' business in the previous year, and should be mailed in time to be received the week before Christmas. Argentines celebrate Three Kings Day (as all Latin American cultures do), January 6, as the time for holiday gift giving.

Gifts are expected for social events, especially as thank-yous for private dinner parties. The best gift is fine whiskey (Chivas or a single-malt scotch is much appreciated). If you are invited to a home, you may bring flowers; choose birds of paradise, as these are the most preferred. If you do bring flowers as a dinner gift, be sure to unwrap them before presenting them to the hostess when you arrive. With flowers, try be sure the bouquet is in odd numbers (an old European tradition). Avoid giving wine—Argentines have plenty of very good wine already—but you may give a woman perfume (it is not considered too personal). Chocolates are wonderful dinner gifts, as is a box of *masas,* a special kind of pastry that is appreciated by many. Leather goods are not special enough in this land of cattle, and cutlery is to be avoided because it symbolizes the severing of relationships. Good business gifts should never include items with corporate logos: they are seen as having little class in Argentina. In addition to the gift (and certainly if you did not send or bring one), be sure to send a handwritten thank-you note on a card the very next day after the dinner party; it is best if it is sent by messenger and not mailed.

If you are staying with an Argentine family, an appropriate thank-you gift would be a high-quality item that represents your country and is difficult to get in Argentina, but that is not representative of the United States in general. Small American-made electronic gadgets, a set of American bath towels (always a good gift almost everywhere, since they are usually more luxurious), or anything that reflects your host's personal tastes is appropriate.

Special Holidays and Celebrations

Major Holidays

There are many regional fiestas and saints' days throughout the year that usually close down businesses for a day or two; check with your local contacts. When a holidays falls on a Thursday or Tuesday, most people take off the Monday or Friday in between as well.

January 1	*Año Nuevo* (New Year's Day)
January 6	*Día de los Reyes* (Three Kings Day; this is the gift-giving day, not Christmas)

February/March	*Carnaval* (be prepared for major public partying and celebrations)
March/April	*Semana Santa/Pasqua* (Holy Week and Easter)
May 1	May Day
May 25	Anniversary of the May Revolution
June	Malvinas Day
June	Flag Day
July 9	Independence Day
August 17	Commemoration of the Death of General José de San Martin
September 21	Student Day
October 12	*Día de Cristóbal Colón* (Columbus Day)
December 25	*Navidad* (Christmas Day)

Business Culture

Daily Office Protocols

In Argentina, doors, at least for senior management, are usually closed; knock first (this includes bathrooms) before opening doors, and when leaving a room, close the door behind you. The business culture is very formal: both men and women dress very elegantly. Choose your clothes carefully for maximum fashion impact. Remember that despite the familiarity with European and North American ways, the Latin need to get to know each other and treat each other respectfully still prevails; therefore, anticipate that morning meetings, for example, will always be followed by a luncheon invitation (either you need to extend it or it will be extended to you), and you should open and close meetings with lots of small talk and personal conversation. Additionally, because things typically run very late, business meetings in offices can be scheduled for 7 or 8 P.M. or later. And remember, the country is still struggling with a large bureaucracy and a European orientation to detail: even the finest points will take time to hammer out. Businesswomen, once their authority is established and known, will be accepted, but businesswomen still need to be careful about walking the fine line between behaving professionally but not being bossy or appearing "too powerful." Additionally, women should avoid traveling alone, especially in the evening, and may, from time to time, have to deal with the issue of machismo in social situations.

People organize their time on a daily basis according to the tasks they must accomplish, and the relationships they must depend upon in order to accomplish these tasks; the clock takes a backseat. Therefore, the day may begin slowly, but there can be much activity by day's end, and people often stay very late in the office in order to finish up what needs to be done. This pattern can repeat itself over larger blocks of time in regard to the accomplishment of projects and the meeting of deadlines.

Management Styles

Privacy and individual accomplishment of one's tasks are critical; workers provide what their bosses expect of them, and the preparation of plans, methods, and reports can be time-consuming and complicated efforts. Gathering the information required in order to do what your boss expects from you, or creating consensus among your colleagues in order to accomplish a particular goal, can take a long time. In larger organizations, all of this occurs in a formal and sometimes very rigid hierarchical structure, which means that deadlines and efficiency are secondary to attention to detail, perfection of form, bureaucratic requirements, and the need to be clever in the face of limited resources in order to be effective. Titles in Argentina are very important; the highest ones (e.g., vice president) are usually reserved for very senior, executive-level positions, and should not be used as casually as they are in the United States. Complimenting and rewarding employees publicly is usually not done. For non-Argentines, it is essential to try to have a local contact who can tell you what is really going on after you return home, and to have a local intermediary—as well as a local lawyer and *notario* (a very responsible administrative position throughout much of Latin America)—to act as a liaison for you with the people you need to see while you are there. This needs to be set up ahead of time. Business is done efficiently (with the exception of the demands of the bureaucracy), and there is great familiarity in Argentina with modern business technology.

Boss-Subordinate Relations

Rank most definitely has its privileges in Argentina. Argentines always want to do business with the most important people in any organization (and this should be the same for the non-Argentine working with them). Bosses are expected to provide guidance, distribute information, and make decisions; subordinates are expected to provide detailed information and follow the decisions made by the superiors.

Conducting a Meeting or Presentation

At meetings of peers, there can be open communication and sharing of ideas; in fact, these sessions often serve as information-sharing and decision-making forums in which all individuals are expected to contribute. Under these circumstances, discussions are usually vibrant, with many people speaking at once; questions are common and interruptions, even of presentations, should be expected. In more formal, conservative organizations, meetings are often gatherings of nonpeers, clearly called together by decision makers in order to gather information from below, clarify goals, and formulate action plans. In these cases, individuals often do not share ideas and are not expected to contribute to mutual problem solving. Remember, because a close personal relationship is often demonstrated through physicality in Latin cultures, the nearer your Argentine colleagues are to you, typically, the better they are responding to your proposal.

Negotiation Styles

Argentines generally play their cards close to the vest, especially as they are building a relationship. They respect someone who comes to them with already established knowledge and experience. Whether you are worth knowing and doing business with may be more important than the details of your proposal, and the relationship may, in fact, sustain you, despite occasionally more attractive terms from other competitors. As is the case in most relationship-based cultures— certainly throughout most of Latin America—it is unwise to introduce new members to a meeting, negotiation, or project team without careful handing off; things get done because of Argentines' trust in certain people, not only the company name. Nevertheless, details are important, and a carefully planned, logically organized, and beautifully presented proposal is key (graphs, charts, and good-looking handouts are appreciated).

The first meeting is usually formal, with the Argentines sizing up you and your organization: it will be conducted in the office. Take copious notes afterward, but put on a warm, dignified demeanor during the meeting. Never be condescending. Plan your meetings as carefully and as well in advance as you can, but expect changes. The goal, at least for the first meeting, is the development of a good feeling of respect and mutual trust. Remember also that the meeting might start and end much later than you anticipated; nevertheless, as in most polychronic cultures, you should always arrive on time. Coffee is the universal greeting; always accept it, always serve it (in nice china, never in Styrofoam), and drink as much or as little as you can or desire. It is the gesture of acceptance and appreciation that counts (never refuse coffee, or an invitation to go with your colleague to a café and have some). Remember that coffee is rarely served with milk during the day and evening—it is more like espresso.

When visiting, stay at the best hotel you can, and when hosting at restaurants—at least for the introductory meeting or the last—choose the best restaurant you can. Your position and status will be judged by what you can afford.

Written Correspondence

Business letters must be very formal and respectful of hierarchy. Last names are usually written in uppercase; dates are given using the day/month/year format (with periods in between, not slashes); and an honorific plus a title is as common as an honorific plus the last name. The time of day is written in military time; weights and measures are given in metric measurements. Monetary amounts are written so that the period breaks up the figure into tens, hundreds, and thousands, and a comma separates the pesos from the centavos.

The traditional language used in openings and closings may be more convoluted and formal than you are used to, and you should write your e-mails, letters, and faxes using a precise formula. Be sure to inquire first, in all communications, about your colleague's health and progress, then move on to the substance of your communication, and close with a salutation and your personal wishes for his or her success and well-being (the Latin communication "sandwich"). Some important business abbreviations: "S.A." means "incorporated," a *cia* is a company, and EE.UU. is the abbreviation for the United States. If your colleagues write to you in Spanish, try to respond in Spanish, if you can, or use the services of a translator. Written addresses are usually in the following format:

Line 1: name
Line 2: title/position
Line 3: company
Line 4: street address
Line 5: city, state

CHILE

Note: Refer to the preceding section on Argentina for information about general Southern Cone and South American cultural behaviors; the material that follows describes specific Chilean variations on general Southern Cone and South American customs.

Some Introductory Background on Chile and the Chileans

Chile, like Argentina, was at one time left out of the great sphere of Spanish influence in the region, precisely because the Spaniards were much more interested in the gold and silver of Peru and Bolivia. Nevertheless, this fertile valley running west of the high Andes eventually proved irresistible to Spaniards and other immigrant groups, and the Spanish pursued the region as it did Argentina. What kept the region from being overrun with immigrants from the Continent, in addition to the Andes mountains, was the ferocity of the local Araucanian Indians; however, as late as the eighteenth century, Europeans were carving out an important niche for themselves. By 1810, a movement for independence from Spain had developed, led by Bernardo O'Higgins, the revolutionary hero of Chile; shortly thereafter, Chile obtained its independence from Spain. Bolivia and Peru soon followed suit, however, and a struggle ensued as to the ownership and rights to the lands claimed by all three, with Chile making a concerted effort to include the mineral-rich lands of the north in its sovereignty. Unfortunately for Chile, this land was at the time part of Bolivia, and provided Bolivia with an outlet to the sea, something she was not going to give up easily. This resulted in the War of the Pacific, in which Chile gained control of these northern areas and Bolivia lost its access to the sea. To this day, Bolivians and Chileans do not get along; don't tell Chilean colleagues about connections you may have with Bolivia (or Peru, for that matter). Because Chile also had to struggle for independence against Argentina, it is also advisable not to mention your activities across the border in Argentina. Most Chileans claim German and Italian heritage; there is also a very small percentage of indigenous Araucanian and Mapuche Indians. Chileans see themselves as egalitarian, possibly due to the multiethnic nature of the society and the influence of northern European cultures, perhaps more than most other Latin Americans.

An important note: Crime is typically not a great problem in Chile, and driving, in fact, can be a pleasant experience, as long as you take the usual precautions. By the way, as in the rest of the region, you are typically not required to tip in taxis. Outside of Santiago, be as careful as you would anywhere in South America in regard to the food and water.

Greetings and Introductions

Language and Basic Vocabulary

In Chile, the use of titles must be limited to those who have actually earned them: in fact, the only appropriate title to use is Doctor, and then only if you are a medical doctor, not a Ph.D. (unless you are a professor). This is in contrast to other more uniformly Latin cultures in which individuals seek status by the intentional use of title.

Physical Greeting Styles

Women who know each other well greet each other with one kiss on the right cheek; the Chilean version of the handshake is quick and firm between two men, slightly softer between men and women.

Communication Styles

Okay Topics / Not Okay Topics

Okay: Good topics of discussion include the strong economy that Chile has enjoyed relative to the rest of the region, and the strong Chilean work ethic: they are very proud of both accomplishments. *Not okay:* Because of the unstable political situations that have wracked Chile in recent history, it is best not to raise political issues, including the human rights issues of the Pinochet regime. Also, be aware of the Chilean sensitivity to not being confused with Brazilians, Argentines, and Bolivians.

Physical Gestures and Facial Expressions

Some physical gestures to avoid in Chile include holding the palm stretched out and facing up with the fingers splayed (this indicates that the other person is stupid and dull); hitting the open palm of the left hand with the clenched fist of the right hand (obscene); and the *"figa,"* made by placing the thumb between the index and middle fingers in a fist form (also extremely vulgar). Drivers behind the wheel sometimes give "the bird" to other drivers (and sometimes pedestrians!) by extending their arm out the window and holding the palm with fingers closed and the palm facing upward. Due to the brief and U.S.-aborted Allende experience, any nonverbal signs that indicate political affiliation or orientation are highly discouraged (don't raise a clenched fist, for example; it is a traditional sign for the worker's struggle of the Communist party).

Emotive Orientation

Chileans are sometimes known as the British of South America, in no small part due to their notably restrained manner of communication, at least relative to their Latin American cousins. It is, indeed, the most "northern European" of all the South American cultures. They are cool and collected, and it is important not to demonstrate any behavior that is loud, aggressive, or too demanding: Chileans will merely tune you out completely.

Protocol in Public

Behavior in Public Places: Airports, Terminals, and the Market

Because Chile is an egalitarian culture, there is typically no bargaining in any of the stores and shops in Chile, except perhaps very far out in the countryside. In fact, if a shopkeeper offers you a discount in exchange for not having to present you with a sales receipt, don't go along with the scheme: ask firmly but calmly for a receipt.

Dress

Chile has the reverse seasons of North America, so that summer, which can be hot, is between December and March, and winter is between June and September. In contrast to some of their very high-fashion neighbors, Chilean businessmen typically wear conservative, low-key, dark suits (sports jackets and slacks are not that common); anything high fashion is too flashy in Chile. Women in business may not accessorize as much as some of their Latin cousins. Even casual dress is typically conservative (no shorts on the city streets, and you will notice that subdued colors and styles are preferred).

Dining and Drinking

Mealtimes and Typical Foods

As meat is to Argentina, seafood is to Chile. There is a wonderful, almost endless assortment of it. The national dish is *caldillo de congrio,* or a soup/stew made of eel, potatoes, and onions. Along with all the *gambas* (shrimp), *langostinos* (lobster), *cholgas* (mussels), and *centolla* (crab) you can eat, be sure to try the *erizos:* small, bite-sized sea urchins, which are often eaten raw with dressing; attached to the sea urchin is usually a small live crab. (If you want to eat *erizos* this way, ask that the hawker leave the crab on for you and just pop the whole thing in your mouth.) Lunch is usually served from 1 or 1:30 to 3 P.M., and is the main meal of the day. Dinner, consisting of foods similar to those served at lunch, is served around 8:30 or 9 P.M. at home. Chileans eat three solid meals (even breakfast is a big meal, with delicious breads and cheeses, ham, and eggs). At around 5 P.M., Chileans have a snack called *onces* of tea or coffee, cheese, breads, and sweets to tide them over to dinner. Dinner parties usually start very late, and you are expected to stay very late (well past midnight).

Typical Drinks and Toasting

Chilean wine is very good; expect it for lunch and dinner. Predinner drinks include *pisco* (a kind of grape brandy) and *pinchuncho* (a mixture of pisco and vermouth); you may also be offered a *vaina,* particularly in the cooler weather, which is a mixed drink of sweetened wine with cinnamon. The preferred after-dinner drink is whiskey for men. As in Bolivia and other Southern Cone countries, there are some important considerations when pouring wine: never pour it backward into the glass, as this means that you very much dislike the person you are pouring for, and do not use your left hand to pour the wine for the same reason.

Table Manners and the Use of Utensils

When you are finished with your meal, place your knife and fork parallel to each other on the right side of the plate with the tines of the fork pointing north.

Seating Plans

The guest of honor is seated usually next to the host or hostess (women to the right of the host, and men to the right of the hostess).

Refills and Seconds

You will not be expected to eat everything on your plate. Your food will be served on your plate, usually not family-style (no seconds, even in a home, typically).

At Home, in a Restaurant, or at Work

Do not seat yourself with others in informal restaurants; in Chile, everyone usually has their own table. Chileans are usually very inclined to invite people into their homes for dinner parties, so you may expect an invitation once you establish a good relationship with your Chilean colleague (please note this is different from the typical Argentinian custom). If you are invited to a private dinner party at home, do not offer to help clean up afterward, as there is often maid service in most middle- and upper-class homes.

Gift Giving

A business gift is expected only once a long-standing relationship has been established (contrary to the custom in other countries of the neighboring region). In this case, the best gift is whiskey (Chivas or a fine single-malt is well-received).

If you are invited to a home, you may bring flowers; bring birds of paradise, as these are the most preferred (never choose yellow flowers: they are used to communicate displeasure). Avoid giving wine—Chileans have plenty of very good wine already—but you may give a woman perfume (it is not considered too personal). Chocolates are wonderful dinner-party gifts as well. It is important to call the day after you have attended a dinner party to say thank you (a note is considered too formal in more egalitarian Chile). In Chile, when girls reach fifteen, they celebrate the *quinceanera* (like a sweet sixteen party), and if you are invited, a good gift is gold jewelry.

Special Holidays and Celebrations

Major Holidays

There are many regional fiestas, street markets (*ferias*), and saints' days through-out the year that usually close down businesses for a day or two; check with your local contacts. When a holidays falls on a Thursday or Tuesday, most people take off the Monday or Friday in between as well.

January 1	*Año Nuevo* (New Year's Day)
February/March	*Carnaval* (pre-Lenten celebration)
March/April	*Semana Santa/Pasqua* (Holy Week and Easter)
May 1	*Día del Trabajo* (Labor Day)
May 21	Commemoration of the Battle of Iquique
August 15	*Asuncíon* (Assumption)
September 11	The "unofficial" commemoration of the 1973 military coup (this is a dark day in Chile; there can be street demonstrations, etc., and it is best avoided by foreigners)
September 18	Independence Day (there is lots of public celebrating, eating, drinking, and dancing—especially of the national folkdance, the *cueca*)
September 19	Armed Forces Day
October 12	*Día de Cristóbal Colón* (Columbus Day)
November 1	*Día de los Santos* (All Saints' Day)
December 8	*Imaculada Concepcíon* (Immaculate Conception)
December 25	*Navidad* (Christmas Day)

Business Culture

Chileans are generally conservative, direct, and honest (never attempt to bribe any official in Chile): the Swiss of the region, as it were. While *personalismo* is still very important in Chile in order to do business with the right people, so is direct communication of facts and situations. Despite direct communication styles, relatively monochronic scheduling and organization, and a low level of machismo (perhaps the lowest in South America), hierarchy is strong, as is rank and strati-fication, in business and in society, a reminder of the blending of both Latin and Northern European traditions in Chile. Decision making is generally done at the highest of levels, and works its way downward, so it is very important to estab-lish your credibility as someone who needs to interface with the top executives.

Because decisions are made by the highest members of the organization, despite the strong egalitarian ethos, and the country is still dealing with an unstable political and civil service infrastructure, delays and red tape are com-mon. Business is generally serious, conservative, and detail-oriented. Business-women, once their authority is established and known, will be accepted: in fact, businesswomen are accepted more easily in Chile than in perhaps any other Latin American country. Businesswomen can go out in the evenings, but should expect to encounter "assistance" from Chilean males.

Negotiation Styles

Despite the familiarity with European and North American ways (many Chileans, at least in the business community, are very sophisticated and well-educated, and have probably been abroad, if not actually lived abroad for substantial portions of their lives, perhaps more than once), Latin customs still dictate the need to get to know each other and treat each other respectfully; therefore, anticipate that morning meetings, for example, will always be followed by a luncheon invitation (either you need to extend it or it will be extended to you), and you need to open things and close things with lots of small talk and personal conversation. Stay in the best hotel possible, as your position and status will be judged by what you can afford.

The Eastern "Southern Cone" Cultures: Paraguay and Uruguay

PARAGUAY

Note: Refer to the preceding sections on Argentina and Chile for information about general Southern Cone and South American cultural behaviors; the material that follows describes specific Paraguayan variations on general Southern Cone and South American customs.

Some Historical Context

Paraguay has been isolated from much of the rest of the continent, if not the world, for most of its history. Early on, Jesuit missionaries were eager to establish Utopian communities in the country, and they ran up against the Spaniards who were also settling the region. Eventually, the Jesuit missions (*reducciones*) were destroyed and the Jesuits were driven out, but even today, Paraguay is influenced by missionary work, particularly from North America. The population is one of the most homogeneous in all of Latin America, due to the intermarriage between Spaniards and the native Guarani Indians. Today, 95 percent of the population is mestizo (of mixed European and Guarani blood); in fact, while Spanish is the primary language (definitely in Asuncíon, the capital), Guarani is spoken throughout most of the country (all government officials, in fact, must be bilingual in Spanish and Guarani). If you learn a few Guarani words, you will definitely impress your Paraguayan colleagues! English is spoken as a third language only by some businesspeople in Asuncíon.

Crime is not necessarily the major concern it is elsewhere in the urban centers of the region, but women should not go out alone at night. Driving is very hazardous anywhere in the country. In taxis, you are required to tip about 10 percent. And, as you should elsewhere in the region, be very careful about the food and water, as per previous comments.

Greetings and Introductions

Physical Greeting Styles

It is uniquely important in Paraguay to make a special point of shaking hands with everyone at a gathering when you leave; it is even more important than doing so when you arrive. Additionally, women who have met previously typically kiss in greeting (one kiss on both cheeks).

Communication Styles

Okay Topics / Not Okay Topics

Okay: Good topics of conversation are soccer (*fútbol;* remember, U.S. football is referred to as American *fútbol*), food, and the major hydroelectric dams in the country (they supply the power for the entire region and do, in fact, represent major technical achievements); ask to visit them. As in similar Latin American countries, the communication styles are very deferential to titles, position, and power. *Not okay:* Paraguay has had a string of charismatic dictators, most recently Alfredo Stroessner; this makes it very difficult for people to be open about their feelings regarding politics and the government. Resist these kinds of discussions (Paraguayans will avoid them anyway)—for they could get either or both of you in trouble (and possibly in jail). Although Paraguay is nominally a republic, criticizing the powers that be can land you in hot water. Also, do not discuss economics, because much of the economy of Paraguay is based on the trade of contraband goods and items. However, this makes for a consumer's paradise, where many goods are available at very low prices; the lifestyle of many Paraguayans is modest, but by Latin American standards, it is quite good and for some, superb. There is a tendency, therefore, not to complain or question too much, but to just get on with daily life and things. (This consumer climate also makes it difficult to select gifts, since most everything available elsewhere somehow some way is available in Paraguay . . . and at generally lower prices!)

Physical Gestures and Facial Expressions

In Paraguay, crossing the index and middle fingers for "good luck" is not: it is considered offensive, as is the *"figa"* sign (made by placing the thumb between the index and middle fingers in a fist) and the thumb-to-index-finger "okay" sign; the "thumbs-up" sign, however, means just that: okay or good. If you tilt your head back, it means you forgot something, and if you flick the underside of your chin with your fingers, it means you don't know or don't care about what is being discussed.

Dress

Dress in Paraguay is generally formal for work, but perhaps not as formal as in Argentina or other parts of the continent; men wear sport jackets and slacks to work, and also at private dinner parties. Remember that the seasons are reversed in the Southern Cone, and that there can be drastic temperature variations between day and night, especially in the higher elevations; bring extra clothing with you.

Dining and Drinking

Mealtimes and Typical Foods

Lunch is the main meal, taken around noontime, and dinner is also usually a large meal, served at about 8 P.M. *Mate* (a kind of tea made from the yerba mate leaves) is very popular. It is served with milk as a breakfast drink (*cocido con leche*) and is drunk at other times of the day and night as well. There is a special way of drinking it with friends: it is boiled and usually served in a gourd, with a straw. Since drinking *mate* is a social event, you take a sip, and then pass the gourd to your neighbor, who does the same, and so on. Sometimes *mate* is drunk cold; this is called *terere,* and sitting around on a hot and humid summer day at a café under the stars drinking *terere* with your friends from a communal gourd is a very common pastime. (If you don't develop a taste for the somewhat bitter flavor of *mate,* that's okay; just remind your colleagues that you're not Paraguayan, and they will understand.) Other beverages served with meals include coffee, juices, water, and wines. *Cana* is a type of sugarcane rum that is quite popular. Sometimes eggs are served with meats, and meats are eaten every day: if you don't want the egg, just say so when you order. The national Paraguayan dish is *sopa paraguaya* (a kind of bread pudding made with cornmeal, eggs, cheese, and mandioca starch that is always eaten with knives and forks). Another very common dish is *so'yosopy,* which is Guarani for a kind of meat preparation; it is a meat stew, often served with *sopa paraguaya.* Most Paraguayans do not eat many vegetables, so there won't be salads or cooked vegetables with most meals. Because of the large European (German) and Asian (Chinese) populations in the country, there will be associated ethnic restaurants and food products available in the cities.

At Home, in a Restaurant, or at Work

Waitstaff may be summoned by subtly raising your hand and saying, *"mozo."* Once you and your Paraguayan associate have established a relationship, you may be invited to his or her home for dinner.

Special Holidays and Celebrations

Major Holidays

There are many regional fiestas and saints' days throughout the year that usually close down businesses for a day or two; check with your local contacts. When a holidays falls on a Thursday or Tuesday, most people take off the Monday or Friday in between as well. Business vacations usually occur between December and February, so plan your trip accordingly.

January 1	*Año Nuevo* (New Year's Day)
February 3	Feast of Saint Blas (the patron saint of Paraguay)

February/March	*Carnaval* (much celebration; don't wear anything you can't afford to get water, drinks, paint, or anything else on!)
March 1	Heroes' Day
March/April	*Semana Santa/Pasqua* (Holy Week and Easter)
May 1	*Día del Trabajo* (Labor Day)
May 14–15	Independence Day celebrations
May	Corpus Christi
June 12	Chaco Armistice
August 15	Founding of Asunción Day
August 25	Constitution Day
September 29	Victory of Boqueron Day
October 12	*Día de Cristóbal Colón* (Columbus Day)
November 1	*Día de los Santos* (All Saints' Day)
December 8	Feast of the Virgin of Caacupe
December 25	*Navidad* (Christmas Day)

Business Culture

Because many businesspeople in Paraguay take their lunch at home (usually followed by a siesta), business meals are usually dinners, and usually take place at upscale hotel restaurants. Businesswomen may have a surprisingly easy time in Paraguay, not because the culture is not macho (it is), but because the unique form of Paraguayan machismo makes it difficult for men to say no to women. However, they will not share decision making or power internally, so while foreign businesswomen can be successful, Paraguayan businesswomen often have a difficult time achieving positions of authority within Paraguayan organizations. Decision making is done by the highest-ranking member of the organization; spend time building a relationship with the correct person in business, for meeting with the wrong person will only delay things. Business typically moves very slowly, in comparison to North American time frames; be patient.

URUGUAY

Note: Refer to the preceding sections on Argentina and Chile for information about general Southern Cone and South American cultural behaviors; the material that follows describes specific Uruguayan variations on general Southern Cone and South American customs.

Some Historical Context

Uruguay was founded by the Portuguese explorers who also founded Brazil. However, soon after, Buenos Aires–based Spaniards attempted to extend their control to include the area; after Napolean conquered Spain, they were able to do so with the support he provided. No sooner did Uruguay free itself from Spain's control than it fell under siege from Brazil. It wasn't until the middle of the nineteenth century that Montevideo was able to fully establish itself as the capital of an independent nation. Throughout this difficult period, Uruguayans as a people were flowering from an upsurge in immigration from a wide variety of countries in Europe. Today, most Uruguayans see themselves as direct (non-mestizo) descendants of their European immigrant forebears, making Uruguay one of the most homogeneous countries in all of Latin America, and an extremely European-based and -focused culture. (Uruguayans call themselves "easterners," or *"orientales,"* to distinguish themselves from the western-based Argentines—Buenos Aires is just across the broad Rio de la Plata—Paraguayans, and the northern Brazilians.) The economy following independence reflected a very sophisticated European business attitude; this paid off over time, as Uruguay quickly became one of the region's most successful economies (even today, there is an extensive welfare system, and the kind of grinding poverty among poorer classes that one can find throughout much of Latin America simply doesn't exist in Uruguay). At its economic height, Uruguay was often referred to as the South American Switzerland. But the mid-twentieth century was not as kind to Uruguay; for the last fifty years or so, Uruguay's economy has been in a slow decline and its politics have been very unstable. As the economy slipped in the 1950s, for example, it generated a Communist reaction, the *tupamaros,* which, in turn, prompted a heavy-handed military response. The result of this difficult time was, in part, the militarization of the nation, and many Uruguayans today are only now recovering economically and searching for a way back to a more effective democracy. Nevertheless, the country still has one of the highest standards of living in the western hemisphere.

Crime is typically not the major concern it is elsewhere in the urban centers of the region, but women should not go out alone at night. Driving is hazardous anywhere in the country. In taxis, you are required to tip about 5 percent. And, as you should elsewhere in the region, be very careful about the food and water, as per previous comments.

Communication Styles

Okay Topics / Not Okay Topics

Okay: Good topics of conversation are soccer, food, and international (not local), especially European, affairs. *Not okay:* It is important not to appear as if you are prying into the Uruguayan's personal life, such as asking about family. Uruguayans in general, remember, take their attitude and behaviors from the European continent directly. Getting personal too soon is not effective. Uruguayans are polite, conservative, and reserved. (There was a time during the military rule, when free-market economic reforms, especially after the attempted Communist revolution, were vigorously initiated; unfortunately, U.S. economists, mainly from the University of Chicago, were deeply involved in this, and their presence under the sponsorship of the repressive military is seen by many Uruguayans, even today, as collaboration with the oppressors.) Remember that the struggles of the recent past have set many Uruguayans, essentially very sophisticated businesspeople, back in their professional lives: many may not be working in positions that reflect their true capabilities. As in most European cultures, it is important to stay formal until relationships are established (Uruguayans, when they move to the informal form of speech, typically use the *voceo* form, not the *tu*).

Physical Gestures and Facial Expressions

While the "thumbs-up" sign does mean okay or good, crossing the index and middle fingers for "good luck" is not: it is considered offensive, as is the *"figa"* sign, made by placing the thumb between the index and middle fingers in a fist, and the thumb-to-index-finger "okay" sign; bringing the tips of all the fingers together so that they touch the thumb indicates doubt or resistance. Making a kind of *ch-ch* sound to get someone's attention is usually okay, but not in a restaurant. Yawning in public is considered rude.

Physicality and Physical Space

Perhaps because of their European traditions, perhaps because of their essentially conservative and reserved nature, and perhaps because of their familiarity with North American cultural behaviors as well, Uruguayans typically stand a little farther back from their colleagues than other Latin Americans, especially if they are among non-Uruguayans. The firm handshake is appreciated.

Dress

Dress in Uruguay is formal, but more conservative than in most other countries in the region. Both men and women should dress as they would in northern Europe for business, with very subdued colors and styling. Remember that the seasons are reversed in the Southern Cone, and there can be drastic temperature variations between day and night, especially in the higher elevations; bring extra clothing with you.

Dining and Drinking

Mealtimes and Typical Foods

Lunch is the main meal, taken around noontime, and dinner is also usually a large meal, served at about 10 P.M. *Mate,* the drink of the Southern Cone, is enjoyed in Uruguay, both hot and cold. You might see tortillas on the menu, but they are really substantial omelet-type dishes, and not the accompanying thin, round bread associated with Mexico. Beef is the national dish, as it is in Argentina; expect plenty of it in Uruguay (look for the word *lomo,* which indicates the finest cut of beef). As in Argentina, meat is eaten at *asados* (barbecues), in *parilladas* (mixed grill restaurants), and elsewhere. Drinks with lunch and dinner are usually wine or beer; the pre- and after-dinner drink of choice for men is whiskey (if you order a *copetin,* you get a whiskey or whiskey-based drink plus snacks to nibble with your drink).

Table Manners and the Use of Utensils

Dining is definitely done the European way; during the meal, keep your hands above the table (not in your lap), and when you are finished, arrange your knife and fork parallel to each other with the tines facing north on the rim of your plate. If there is sauce, it is usually okay to "wipe" the plate with bread.

At Home, in a Restaurant, or at Work

Waitstaff may be summoned by subtly raising your hand and saying, *"Mozo."* Once you and your Uruguayan associate have established a relationship, you may be invited to his or her home for dinner. Oftentimes following business meals taken in restaurants, you may be invited back to someone's home for coffee (if so, coffee won't be taken after the dessert in the restaurant); this will often be very late at night.

Gift Giving

Gift giving is not really done in business, but certainly, if you are invited to someone's home, a gift of flowers is much appreciated (red roses are the flower of choice).

Special Holidays and Celebrations

Major Holidays

When a holidays falls on a Tuesday or Thursday, most people take off the Monday or Friday in between as well. Business vacations usually occur between December and February, so plan your trip accordingly.

January 1	*Año Nuevo* (New Year's Day)
January 6	Three Kings Day
February/March	*Carnaval*
March/April	*Semana Santa/Pasqua* (Holy Week and Easter)
April 19	Commemoration of the Landing of the Thirty-Three "Easterners"
May 1	*Día del Trabajo* (Labor Day)
June 19	Anniversary of the Birth of Artigas (the national liberator)
July 18	Constitution Day
August 25	Independence Day
October 12	*Día de Cristóbal Colón* (Columbus Day)
November 2	*Día de los Santos* (All Saints' Day)
December 25	*Navidad* (Christmas Day)

Business Culture

The workday in Uruguay, for the businessperson, can be very long. Uruguayan executives and managers often work well into the night (perhaps that is why dinner is typically served so late!). Although there is generally a Northern European approach to business, there can still be a Latin approach to time; punctuality is admired, though not always achieved. Essentially, Uruguayans are polychronic. The business lunch is the more common venue for business entertaining than is the evening meal, and if there is an evening meal among business associates, business talk is kept to a minimum—this is a time to enjoy each other's company and build rapport and relationships. Foreign businesswomen in Uruguay should experience little difficulty, especially if their authority is clear, but Uruguayan women often have a more difficult time establishing themselves at high levels within the Uruguayan business organization. Uruguayans, perhaps more than most other groups in South America, understand both U.S. American and European business ways. Decision making is typically done by the highest-ranking member of the organization; spend time building a relationship with the correct person in business, for meeting with the wrong person will only delay things.

PART THREE

The Caribbean

Mambo, Mosaic, and Manana

An Introduction to the Region

For many people, those from the United States included, the Caribbean is a great playground of tropical islands strung together like jewels in a sparkling azure sea: a marvelous place for a midwinter escape, but not much more than that. But the Caribbean is far more than just the perfect destination for a relaxing getaway. For starters (and admittedly, we are going back pretty far here), it is believed that the Caribbean was formed a couple of million years ago when a giant asteroid smashed into the earth; not only did this event destroy the dinosaurs, but it collapsed the geographic area that is now the Caribbean Sea. Once humans arrived on the scene, the area was populated mainly by oftentimes warring indigenous peoples, the Tainos (mainly of the northern and western islands), the Arawaks (mainly of the eastern and southern islands), and the Caribs. Following the Spanish conquest, most of the native indigenous peoples, were wiped out through a combination of slavery, displacement, and disease. In an effort to perpetuate the convenient free labor system that they were used to, the conquering Europeans (and the Spaniards were not the only ones: the British, French, Dutch, and others joined in the colonization of the islands) began to import slaves from Africa into the New World; the Caribbean served as the major entrepot in the north (Brazil was the major area in the south) for the entry, sale, and enslavement of Africans by Europeans in the New World. Slaves from the Caribbean were then sent throughout the New World, mainly working the sugar, coffee, hemp, and other agricultural plantations. Slaves were imported, sugarcane was cut, much of it was turned into rum, and the goods were shipped to Europe. With the ascendance of the United States, the industrial revolution, and the demand for independence, the Caribbean colonies, each in its own way, struggled for autonomy from Europe and the United States. The struggle continues today.

Demographically, this history has resulted in one of the most incredible mixes of cultures and peoples in the world. The peoples are mainly, to varying degrees, descendants of indigenous, African, and European forebears, speaking a variety of representative languages, each having influenced the other. The diversity, while dizzying, is, of course, from time to time and place to place, problematic (for example, Haitians and Dominicans, who share the same island—Hispaniola—have long-simmering resentments); nevertheless, most inhabitants of the region share many similarities. The cultures are primarily agriculturally based (sugar and its main by-product, rum, is still the base of most economies), resulting in behaviors that are oriented around family, group-dependency, a very relaxed orientation toward time and planning, and a traditional differentiation of roles between men and women. The various cultures all share a gorgeous paradisiacal landscape, which does occasionally wreak havoc on the local life and economy in the form of earthquakes and devastating hurricanes. And they all share the mixed and terrifying legacies of conquest, slavery, and exploitation by the developed world.

Getting Oriented

This remarkably culturally diverse region can be divided mainly into three major cultural subgroups, all of which are influenced by Africa: Hispanic-African (cultures formed by Africa and the Spanish conquest), Franco-African (cultures formed by Africa and French colonization), and Anglo-African (cultures formed by Africa and British colonization). These cultural groupings do not necessarily follow the basic geographical division of the region, that being between the large islands of the Greater Antilles chain stretching in the northwest from Cuba to Puerto Rico in the northeast, to the smaller islands of the Lesser Antilles chain stretching from the Virgin Islands east of Puerto Rico south to the ABC's (Aruba, Bonaire, and Curaçao) just off the coast of Venezuela. Anglo-African, Franco-African, and Hispanic-African cultures are mixed throughout, like dominoes tossed on a tabletop. Let's begin with the major Hispanic-African cultures.

The Hispanic-African Cultures: Cuba, The Dominican Republic, and Puerto Rico

CUBA

Some Introductory Background on Cuba and the Cubans

We begin our exploration of the Hispanic-African Caribbean cultures with the most influential of the countries in this group, Cuba. (This may be a surprise for people from the United States, which has a unique and difficult relationship with Cuba, but Cuba is an active trading partner with most of Latin America, and much of the rest of the world, and has exerted significant cultural influence over the rest of the Hispanic Caribbean.) Unique among the nations of the region, Cuba, due to its Communist Socialist revolution, in one swift move determinedly swept away much of the legacy of the conquest that the rest of the region struggles profoundly with: there is no entrenched class system, land reform was "solved" by putting all private property into the hands of the government, and the problem of wealth distribution was also "solved" by effectively eliminating any (the unfortunate result of planned and centralized economies, however, is the collapse of effective economic systems). While the achievements of socialism cannot be denied (Cuba has, relative to much of the rest of the region, universal and good health care and education, and most of its people have employment and acceptable housing conditions), the failures are also apparent: a collapsed economy and a dependency on a revolutionary consciousness that prohibits the institutionalization of democracy. Still, the traditional plagues of Latin America—class-based oligarchies, unequal distribution of wealth and land, machismo and the subordination of women—do not exist in Cuba at any level similar to that found elsewhere in the region. Cubans are extremely proud of these accomplishments, and still do look to their revolution as an important step in freeing themselves from the inequities of the past; however, there is also increasing frustration with the difficulties of the present and the inability to reconcile ideology with reality.

Some Historical Context

Although U.S. citizens are currently prohibited, with a few exceptions, from trading with, spending money in, and essentially visiting Cuba, and although there is an economic embargo still in place, the United States has had significant ties with Cuba, and probably always will. Even in these difficult times, both countries have influenced each other enormously, and the Cuban-American population in Miami continues as a powerful force in U.S.-Cuban relations. The indigenous population of Taino Indians was all but destroyed when Spaniards first came to the island in the 1500s. For a brief period, the British ruled (at least in La Habana), but gave Cuba back to Spain in exchange for Florida. African slaves began arriving in the eighteenth century as the slave trade developed in the New World, primarily to work the sugar plantations (as was the case throughout the Caribbean). There were many uprisings against the Spaniards, one of the most notable being the Ten Years War in 1868. In 1895, José Marti, Cuba's great leader for independence, led another revolt, in which he died. International pressure to free Cuba from Spain finally led to the U.S. involvement in the Spanish-American War; subsequent to the war, the United States intermittently occupied the country, until U.S. interests in Cuba came to dominate economic and political life there. By the 1950s, U.S. business interests controlled much of the economy (including the illegal economy), with dictatorships keeping much of the wealth from the people. The country was ripe for revolution, and Fidel Castro Ruz led the revolt against the dictator Batista. Support came from the Soviet Union, pitting Cuba against the United States, and as Cuba became a Communist Socialist state, intimately tied to the Soviets, it represented a serious threat to U.S. interests in the region. A total political, social, and economic embargo between the United States and Cuba was established, which is in effect to this day.

An Area Briefing

Politics and Government

The Communist Party is the controlling force in all of society, and opposition parties are illegal. The country is Socialist. Legislative authority is vested in the National Assembly, members of which are elected by the people. The National Assembly, in turn, appoints the Council of State, which serves as the executive branch, and the Council selects its president and chief of state. Since 1959, Fidel Castro Ruz has governed as president and chief of state.

Schools and Education

Schooling is compulsory through early high school; however, in poorer rural regions and in difficult urban neighborhoods, maintaining quality education through these grades is a challenge. There is always a shortage of supplies, and the infrastructure for schools is poor. Nevertheless, education is highly valued, as are teachers, and Cuba, in fact, has one of the highest literacy rates in Latin America. Education at all levels, including college, is free. The education is highly ideological, as it hews to the Marxist-Communist line in all subjects.

Religion and Demographics

The people are mainly Roman Catholic, with minority populations of Jews, Protestants, Muslims, and others, although the official government line is atheism. Nevertheless, Catholic traditions are prevalent, often mixed with African animist ideas (known in Cuba as *Santería,* and there are other spiritualist groups (*Brujería,* or witchcraft, is also practiced by certain small groups). The Pope was welcomed openly and warmly on his visit in the late 1990s. Recall that in its effort to establish a secular Socialist republic, the government disestablished the church's authority, and there is an uncomfortable relationship between the legacy of the church and government authority. The roles of men and women, while different, are considered equal, and there is a considerable lack of demonstrable machismo. Women do hold positions of authority in government, education, and medicine. Non-Cuban businesswomen need not worry about not being taken seriously simply because of their gender, and typically are not subject to the kind of sexual harassment that is always a possibility in some other countries in Latin America. Consider too that Cuba is economically a developing nation, and struggles with all of the challenges associated with that status, including substantial poverty and inadequate and ill-serving infrastructures; however, there is little of the overt corruption that appears in other Latin American countries that struggle with similar problems. Over 60 percent of the population claims direct Spanish descent, with about 20 percent mestizo (of mixed European and Indian blood), and smaller percentages of Africans and even Asians (there was a moment of significant immigration of Chinese into Cuba during the nineteenth century). There is virtually no indigenous population remaining.

Fundamental Cultural Orientations

1. What's the Best Way for People to Relate to One Another?

OTHER-INDEPENDENT OR OTHER-DEPENDENT?   Roman Catholic traditions combined with the Communist ideology have created in Cuba a strong orientation toward "other-dependent" behavior. Most individuals will seek, either formally or informally, the opinions and support of family, friends, and coworkers before venturing off to do or say something on their own. Family support, particularly in periods of scarcity and difficulty, is critical. Nevertheless, there is great curiosity regarding non-Cubans, and a warm willingness to bring the non-Cuban into some kind of circle. It is difficult (and considered quite odd) to be alone in Cuba. Causing someone to lose face, or experience embarrassment, public ridicule, or criticism of any kind is a great insult in this other-dependent culture; here, how one is thought of by others is one of the most important concerns in life.

HIERARCHY-ORIENTED OR EGALITY-ORIENTED?   One of the goals of the Revolution was to eliminate the rigid class-based hierarchies that were imposed on Cuba, and much of the rest of Latin America, by the conquest. Subsequently, the typical Latin American stratifications between classes do not officially exist in Cuba, and egalitarianism is the value. Nevertheless, there is no doubt that Communist party members and government apparatchiks do constitute a privileged class, and that within these groups there is significant division of status and rank. But in society in general, people hold very egalitarian and integrated views. Businesses are typically either small with little need for internal hierarchy, or government affairs where the bureaucracy is already in place. Women and men are officially treated equally, and overt demonstrations of traditional Latin machismo are minimal.

RULE-ORIENTED OR RELATIONSHIP-ORIENTED? Again, the legacy of the rigid hierarchy of the Roman Catholic Church and the imposition of Communism drive the need for rules and order; nevertheless, the personal relationships one is able to develop with the right people can see one through difficult times. The strong egalitarian orientation and pride for the country provide most people with a rationale for balancing the need for relationships and the respect for rules. Situations, if involving the right people and the right issues, will almost always determine the behaviors of individuals, not bland laws or bureaucratic fiats. Typical petty corruption of the type one sometimes encounters elsewhere in Latin America is not prevalent in Cuba (you do not, for example, offer small payments to government officials or police). Cubans will need time to get to know you before they will be ready to talk business. Attempts to discuss the terms of the deal or the immediate task at hand without having built the necessary personal trust and understanding is often a waste of time. Which takes us to our next concern.

2. What's the Best Way to View Time?

MONOCHRONIC OR POLYCHRONIC? Time is circular, and very polychronic everywhere, perhaps slightly more so in the countryside. In rural areas, it is easiest to work in the fields in the cool of the early morning and late afternoon; the midday heat is usually too oppressive, and provides a good opportunity to stoke up on a filling meal and a siesta before heading back out until the sun sets. This pattern is repeated even in urban areas. In the workplace, this means showing up at the office around 9 A.M., but not really getting started until 9:30 or 10 (drinking coffee, checking the news, and catching up with coworkers may take precedence). Lunch occurs around noon, and can either be a quick bite at the local sandwich shop or last for an hour or slightly more (or in rural areas, might entail a visit home and a short siesta afterward). After returning to the office, workers stay as long as necessary, perhaps up to 6 P.M. Recognize also that the problems with transportation, communication, and the general infrastructure make planning and keeping to schedules difficult. Cubans can be punctual, but it is simply not a priority.

RISK-TAKING OR RISK-AVERSE? Latin cultures, in general, are risk-averse, and although the ideology of the Revolution was to work for a better tomorrow, there is a growing frustration, particularly among the young, with the disparity between ideology and reality. There has historically been less of a need for risk-avoidance in Cuba than in much of the rest of Hispanic Latin America; Cubans are open to new ideas and have, as the current period of economic difficulties demonstrates, high comfort levels with uncertainty. Typical Latin "analysis paralysis" does not exist. (Decision making, however, because of the involvement of government bureaucracies, can be long and tedious.)

PAST-ORIENTED OR FUTURE-ORIENTED? One of the powerful lessons of the Revolution was that individuals can change things. There is a strong belief in the ability to take charge of one's world, combined with the realist's awareness of certain things being beyond one's control. Cubans did, in fact, change their world, and see current difficulties more the result of forces they have no control over (the United States and its embargo, primarily) than of their own inabilities, shortcomings, or fate. The past in Cuba was forcefully rejected, the present is endured, and there is a strong belief that things will definitely change tomorrow.

3. What's the Best Way for Society to Work with the World at Large?

LOW-CONTEXT DIRECT OR HIGH-CONTEXT INDIRECT COMMUNICATORS? Most Cubans are more often high-context communicators; depending upon the situation and people involved, Cubans will be careful about what they say and how they say it. Political opinions are difficult to express openly, for example, but Cubans are very curious and opinionated about most things, and ultimately won't have trouble expressing their views. Most important, Cubans, like most Latinos, want smooth interpersonal working relationships, especially with outsiders, and will go the distance to reassure you that everything is okay and that all is in order—even when it may not be. This is not based on a desire to deceive but rather a need to appear capable and competent, and not to lose face in the eyes of others, particularly when it may be in one's interests to cultivate a relationship. It is critical, therefore, to always confirm information, to have multiple and independent sources "on the ground" to confirm for you what you are being told, and to be able to read between the lines without directly challenging the veracity of what your Cuban colleague is saying. This tendency also makes for complimentary and respectful introductory conversation, and an avoidance of anything that may strike you as unpleasant; at first, Cubans will always try to say what they think you want to hear, but they will then quickly tell you what they think.

PROCESS-ORIENTED OR RESULT-ORIENTED? As with other Latinos, there is a strong reliance on the deductive process: how things are being done is as important as the final result. But Cubans are very subjective, and will also often fall back on what they personally believe—and this may be ideology-based at times—in order to make or justify a decision. In Cuba's case, the process is the state-run organization, and because of the inefficiencies inherent in centralized economies, and a serious lack of resources in what still is a developing country, Cubans may not be able to follow through easily with the actions required to put the plans in place. Yet they will be reticent to admit this or inform you when problems develop. It is therefore that much more important for non-Cubans to stay involved with them, helping them to implement what has been agreed to. This must be done, however, with sensitivity toward the pride that Cubans feel in being able to handle things on their own, and the requirement of the government for them to do things a particular way.

FORMAL OR INFORMAL? Cuban culture is respectful of individuals and their roles, but it is not formal. Formal Latin traditions from the conquest were rejected by the Revolution, and there is an egalitarian and respectful—not casual—informality that permeates relationships. The Spanish language, however, is still divided into formal and informal forms and phrases, and personal behaviors in different situations do follow certain rules of protocol and etiquette. Never insult the honor, pride, or beliefs of a Cuban or his or her family, colleagues, and associates, or country.

Greetings and Introductions

Language and Basic Vocabulary

Spanish is the language, but there is a specific Spanish that has developed in Cuba in which many words have very different meanings than they do in other Spanish-speaking cultures, and special words have developed to handle Cuba-specific issues. For example, never use the word *papaya* (this refers to female genitalia); *guaguas* are city buses; "the special period" refers to the time after the fall of the Soviets (prior to this time, Cuba received most of its aid from the Soviet Union, and in the absence of this aid, has fallen on some very hard economic times); *adiós!* said between people passing each other on the street does not specifically mean goodbye, but is rather a sort of informal hello; *paladare* are private restaurants in people's homes (wonderful places for a decent meal, since all other restaurants in Cuba are state-run); *amarillo* refers to traffic cops and their yellow outfits; *"plan jaba"* is a government plan that allows working women time to shop; and the wonderful word *rebambaramba* means a ruckus, a free-for-all. Be sure to use any Spanish you do know, even if you learned it from a neighbor or in school: Cubans love it when you try to speak Spanish, and they will help you get it right; this often becomes a relationship-building event and can be a more important activity in the formative stages of the relationship than any substantive discussions you can have.

Here are the basics:

Buenos días	Good morning
Buenas tardes	Good afternoon
Buenas noches	Good evening
¡Hola! ¿Que tal?	Hello, how are you? (informal)
¿Como está usted?	How are you? (formal)
Adiós	Good-bye
Por favor	Please
Gracias	Thank you
Con permiso	Pardon me
Muy bien	Very well
De nada	You're welcome
Con mucho gusto	Pleased to meet you
Un placer	A pleasure
Señor	Mr.
Señora	Mrs.
Señorita	Miss
Ingeniero(a)	Engineer
Abogado(a)	Lawyer
Doctor	Doctor
Gerente	Manager

Remember, in written Spanish, questions and exclamations are also indicated at the beginning of the sentence, with an upside-down exclamation point or question mark.

Honorifics for Men, Women, and Children

Señor (Mr.) and *señora* (Mrs.) plus the last name are used when addressing foreigners or senior people; most of the time, *"compañero"* (or *compañera,* for a woman)—freely translated as "comrade"—is used. Sometimes these honorifics are used by themselves, or with the first name, but once people know each other, Cubans quickly switch to using first names only. In Cuba, as throughout most of the region, if you do not know whether a woman is married, use *señorita* (please note: this is the reverse from what is done in Spain, where *señora* is used when the marital status of the woman is unknown). Children in Cuba are expected to be respectful and not overly conversational when speaking with adults, and must always use honorifics when referring to adults. In certain situations, the title is used alone, either with or without the name (e.g., *Ingeniero,* or Ingeniero Cortez), but not necessarily with the honorific. *Licensiado* is a "title" generally used for anyone with a skill requiring some sort of diploma. "Doctor" may be safely used as a way to give respect to anyone with a university degree; as an honorific, it does not have to refer only to a Ph.D. For casual contacts (e.g., with waiters, store help, etc.), just use *señor* or *señorita* without the name. It is very important to greet people at work or in stores and restaurants with an appropriate greeting for the time of day—*buenos días, buenas tardes,* or *buenas noches*—and *adiós* upon leaving. If you speak any Spanish at all, it is important to use it, but be sure to use the formal pronoun, *usted,* at the beginning and do not switch to the *tu* (informal "you") form of speech unless and until your Cuban colleague does so him- or herself.

Spanish family names are often hyphenated, with the mother's family name added after the father's family name. In formal speech and in written correspondence, the fully hyphenated name is used; in face-to-face introductions, usually only the father's family name is used. For example, José Ramón Mendez-Rodriguez is Señor Mendez in face-to-face introductions, with Mendez being José's father's family name and Rodriguez being José's mother's family name. Women traditionally kept their family name when they married, but added their husband's father's family name with the preposition *de.* For example, Señora Maria Isabel Gonzalez-Sanchez de Rodriguez is married to Señor Rodriguez, her maiden name is Gonzalez (her father's family name), and she retains her mother's family name—Sanchez—as well; in face-to-face communication she is more often referred to as Señora de Rodriguez or, very informally, as Señora Rodriguez; this is, however, not as common in Cuba today. Common-law relationships are growing in popularity, and in these cases there is no name changing.

The What, When, and How of Introducing People

In most situations, Cubans will introduce themselves to each other; don't wait for formal third-party introductions. Do not presume to seat yourself at a formal gathering; if possible, wait to be told where to sit. If you are not shown a seat, then it is appropriate to take one, but allow seniors and women first choice.

Shake hands with everyone individually in a group when being introduced and before departing; the U.S. group wave is not appreciated. Avoid ending the conversation with the American expression "Have a nice day"; it sounds controlling and insincere. Kissing is a common greeting once you have established a strong and very familiar relationship, whether between women or men and women; usually, there is a kiss on two cheeks (actually an "air kiss," first on the left side, and then the right). It is not uncommon to see men and men, and women and women, walking arm in arm down the street; they are good close friends or associates, and it usually means nothing more than that.

The use of business cards is appreciated; if possible, you should have your business card translated into Spanish on the reverse. Be sure to put any advanced educational degrees and your full title or position on both sides of your business card. Don't expect to always receive a business card in return, however.

Physical Greeting Styles

The handshake is common. The Cuban version is brisk and firm between two men, lest robust between men and women, or two women. The handshake should be accompanied by the appropriate greeting (see the list of terms outlined earlier). Smiling and other nonverbal forms of communication often accompany the handshake. Men and women are free to greet each other as equals. Between family, friends, or trusted business associates, an extra touch on the elbow or a hug (the *abrazo,* or embrace) will generally occur. This can happen even as soon as the second meeting; do not initiate it, but respond warmly in kind if it is initiated with you. Eye contact during the introduction is important, and should be maintained as long as the individual is addressing you.

Communication Styles

Okay Topics / Not Okay Topics

Okay: baseball (it is the national sport), Cuban literature, Cuban food and drink, family (but don't get personal at first), Cuban music and dance (the chacha, mambo, and rhumba all came from Cuba, and dancing is a national passion). You can speak about current events, but be careful about politics, as people will be reticent to express controversial views openly, at least at first. Cubans will do everything possible to "educate" people from the United States about Cuban culture; be a student, go along with the effort, enjoy yourself, be appreciative and admiring, and take the opportunity as a way to build that all-important personal relationship, even when the conversation is about the strained Cuban-U.S. history and current relations. Cubans will ask Americans why the U.S. government maintains such a discriminatory and aggressive policy against Cuba. *Not okay:* Do not inquire about a person's occupation in casual conversation, although that may be inquired of you. Americans often begin a conversation with "So, what do you do?"; this can be embarrassing, and is often not the most interesting topic of conversation. Do not give your opinions about Cuban politics, Communism, or the difficult economic situation in Cuba (you will be reminded that it is a direct result of the U.S. embargo). Do not talk about your tummy, if it is on the blink; keep your health issues to yourself, because no one wants to hear about them. Also not okay: money (although you may be asked about your income, among many other questions regarding personal matters, such as your marital status and whether you have children). Do not go to Cuba (or Latin America) without pictures of your family and life in your country, and when family is brought up (which it will be almost immediately in the conversation), use it as an opportunity to bring out the photographs. Cubans love to be photographed, and sharing pictures is a major way of building personal relationships. Expect many questions about life in your country, as Cubans are extremely curious about life outside of Cuba. Avoid discussions of Miami and the Cuban-American population, as there are very mixed feelings in Cuba about them (although many people have family in Miami, many are equally frustrated over what they see as efforts by the U.S.-based Cuban population to overthrow the Cuban government; nevertheless, money and goods from the Cuban community in the United States account for much support back home on the island). Never tell a dirty joke with a woman present.

Tone, Volume, and Speed

Discussions between strangers can quickly become animated and very lively, depending upon the nature of the discussion and the circumstances of the developing relationship. At meals, the wine, tequila, and beer flow, and conversation is an art; it is enjoyed, savored, and commented upon, but it rarely gets out of hand, and is always carried on respectfully. In business, speak softly and with restraint. This garners respect.

Use of Silence

In general, silence is not that common, except in group discussions where something is said that can cause someone a public loss of face. Avoid this, and enjoy the animated, simultaneous conversations and frequent interruptions that usually define Cuban conversation style.

Physical Gestures and Facial Expressions

The U.S. "okay" sign, made with the thumb and the forefinger, is considered offensive: avoid it. In addition, winking and whistling (often accompanied by a positive comment) is meant to be a friendly introduction between men and women. Never stand with your hands on your hips: it is aggressive (however, there is nothing defensive about folding the arms in front of you). Tapping the bottom of the elbow indicates that the person you are talking about is cheap or making a stingy offer; tapping or touching the person you are speaking with is a common sign of friendship.

Waving and Counting

The thumb represents the number 1, the index finger the number 2, and so on. It is insulting to beckon someone with the forefinger; instead, turn your hand so that the palm faces down and motion inward with all four fingers at once, in a kind of scratching motion (beckoning someone with the palm facing up is insulting). If you need to gesture for a waiter, subtly raise your hand; never click, call, or whistle.

Physicality and Physical Space

Cubans tend to get closer than North Americans are generally comfortable with. Do not step back when your Cuban associate steps forward. Cuban men may touch each other during conversations, adjust each other's collars, dust off each other's shoulders, and the like. Never speak with your hands in your pockets; always keep them firmly at your side when standing. If men and women must cross their legs, it should be ankle over knee (for women, the preferred style is to cross ankle over ankle).

Eye Contact

Direct eye contact is best. It is important not to interpret this behavior as a way of intentionally trying to make you uncomfortable. It is the way Cubans show their interest. Conversely, if you look away, your behavior will say to your Cuban colleague that you are either disinterested or rude. Maintain eye contact when it is made with you.

Emotive Orientation

Cubans are often animated and physically expressive, but respectful. Therefore, while expressive gesturing is common, until you know people well, you want to indicate warmth, involvement, and respect, while never seeming lifeless.

Protocol in Public

Walking Styles and Waiting in Lines

The line is a common phenomenon of daily Cuban life, as shortages of basic supplies and state-run stores represent the current state of affairs. Cubans live with the reality of having to wait on line for practically everything, and the line becomes a place for socializing and catching up on things. Don't break the line (although as a foreigner you may be invited to the front of the line as a courtesy). People also have a tendency to stand very close in public; this may feel uncomfortable at first. Resist the urge to back away; most of the time, you are not being intentionally crowded. Remember, the need to appear helpful and courteous is strong, and if you ask for directions on the street, you will no doubt be instructed on just where to go . . . whether or not the individual actually knows (note: many urban streets have two names, one of which is the traditional name, the other a name given after the Revolution)!

Behavior in Public Places: Airports, Terminals, and the Market

Customer service, as a concept, as in most centralized state-run economies, really does not exist. Store hours are typically not designed around customer convenience (many stores are closed on Sundays), although there are many local markets with their own odd hours. Bargaining is very common in small shops and markets, but recognize that the prices may already be, in most cases, remarkably low. Basic daily supplies are typically purchased at state-run bodegas. Foreigners will be encouraged to pay in U.S. dollars (they are very much in demand, and those people who have access to U.S. dollars have far more opportunity to provide for themselves and their families); in state-run stores, even though locals pay in pesos, foreigners must pay in U.S. dollars. Use Cuban pesos in stores that are off the beaten tourist track (by the way, tourism is a fairly advanced industry in Cuba; U.S. citizens have difficulty going there, but much of the rest of the world doesn't). Personally thanking store owners, waiters, chefs, and hotel managers for their services is very much appreciated. In food markets, you can touch the produce; in goods stores, it may be difficult for you to return a product unless there is a flaw in it. Because of the personal nature of the culture, money is exchanged in the palms, not on the counter. There is little to no begging or extreme poverty. Smoking is prevalent; if you do smoke, be sure to always offer a cigarette to everyone you are talking to before you light up. In bathrooms, on the plumbing "C" means hot (*caldo*) and "F" means cold (*frio*).

When answering a phone, use the phrase *digame* (speak to me), *por favor,* or the very Cuban *Oigo* (I hear you). Cell phone use is limited, and most pay phones—when they work—require a telecard (phone service can be intermittent and haphazard; it wasn't too many years ago that businesses would have workers do nothing but sit at a desk and redial a telephone number until the connection was made). Be sure to give both the paternal and maternal last name of the person you are looking for when calling directory assistance, as there are many people with the same last names.

Bus / Metro / Taxi / Car

Driving is on the right, and driving is not a problem in Cuba, as there are so few cars. (This makes parking easy, as well.) Those who do drive are typically courteous and careful (nevertheless, roads are often unlit, and traffic lights may or may not work, so be careful!). Additionally, use caution when driving at night, as roads are full of potholes, and the infrequency of vehicles actually encourages people to occasionally camp out on the side of the road. Gas stations are often few and far between, and may or may not have gas (never accept roadside gas: it may be adulterated), so be sure your tank is topped before you head out on any car trip. There are no metros; buses are everywhere, and are usually very crowded. The public transportation infrastructure is lacking (although the roads are surprisingly good, perhaps in an effort to be able to move military vehicles around quickly), and bus reservations are essential. The best way to catch a cab is at designated taxi stands (hotels are good places). There are two types of taxis: the state-run tourist taxis (with a blue "T" on the door) and private (pirate) taxis (they have yellow license plates); both may or may not have workable meters, so negotiate the fee before the driver heads off. If traveling by bus, bring food and water onboard. Crime is typically not a problem, but with the increase in tourism, there is some petty crime in certain places: be cautious in tourist areas, and do not leave anything about in the hotel room that the maid could interpret as a "tip" left for her.

Tipping

The tip is typically not included in the bill, but it is also not expected (nor is it illegal, as is the case in certain planned economies); it is usually the equivalent of an extra U.S. dollar, in both restaurants and taxis. Hand your tip to the waiter; do not leave it on the table. Porters and hotel help get the equivalent of one U.S. dollar per item or per day. Tipping in U.S. dollars, as is done throughout much of the region, is perfectly fine—actually preferred. (Interestingly, the current state of U.S.-Cuban relations does not technically prevent Americans from visiting Cuba: the law merely prevents U.S. citizens from spending any money—literally even one penny—there.)

Punctuality

It is perfectly acceptable—in fact, essential—to arrive at social events about an hour late. If you arrive sooner, you will be running the risk of interrupting the host or hostess as he or she gets ready. For business meetings, even in La Habana, being late by five to fifteen minutes or more is usually not a problem, but it is safer for the new employee or visitor to be on time, while not being surprised if others are not. Usually, the meeting will not begin in earnest until all attendees have arrived (or at least until all the decision makers have shown up), and this may not correspond to the time listed in the agenda. Resist questioning the late ones for a reason; they always have one, usually involving an obligation with more important people, like superiors, old friends, or family. While being punctual is not a priority, it is interesting to note that the daily schedule is similar to that in North America (not uncommon throughout most of the Caribbean).

Dress

Good taste is everything, even though dress is often casual and comfortable. Clothes need to be neat and clean. At work, men wear the *guayabera,* or a jacket and tie; in general, Cuban women do dress fairly provocatively, at least by U.S. standards: this is not considered bad taste. On the street, and in most non-business situations, dress is informal and may mean jeans, a cotton shirt, and comfortable shoes or sandals. Do not wear expensive jewelry; it is considered ostentatious and makes you a possible mark for theft. "Formal," meaning formal evening wear, very dressy by U.S. standards, is rarely if ever called for.

Personal Hygiene

In Cuba, personal hygiene is very important. There is a real concern for cleanliness and not looking sloppy. Latin men may sport facial hair, in the form of mustaches. Note that most rest room and bathroom facilities throughout Latin America do not have plumbing capable of handling paper toilet tissue; it is for this reason that there is a small receptacle next to the toilet for your used tissue: do not flush it down the bowl, but place it in the receptacle, or else you'll face the embarrassment of having to call for help when the bowl overflows. Bring toilet tissue with you when you travel about. Remember also that showers may or may not be constantly running hot—or cold—water, and water may be heated by an electrical contraption placed on top of the showerhead: be very careful not to touch it or any metal while standing under the water or while wet!

Dining and Drinking

Mealtimes and Typical Foods

Breakfast (*el desayuno*) is served from about 6:30 to 7:30 A.M., and typically consists of coffee and some breads. It is usually very simple. Coffee in the morning can be strong and black, or with hot milk (*café con leche*), and Cuban coffee (usually referred to as *cafezito*) is very much like espresso, served sweet. If you ask for café Americano, you will get very diluted Cuban coffee.

Lunch (*el almuerzo,* or *la comida*) was traditionally the main meal of the day; even today, in busy cities, it can be the larger meal. Lunch, as well as dinner, must include black beans (usually with rice), fish, or meat if available (most families in Cuba have ration books, *libreta,* with which they can purchase meat in limited supplies monthly). Coffee is typically served after lunch.

Dinner (*la cena*) is served from 6 to 8 P.M. and typically consists of the same foods as those served at lunch. If the main meal of the day was lunch, then dinner is light. Drinks served with dinner are usually rum or beer, or soft drinks. Chilean and French wines are also occasionally available. Dinner parties usually end about two hours after the meal ends.

Anytime during the day, snacks and fruit juices are typically enjoyed, such as *refrescos* (fruit juice) and *batidas* (ice, milk, and fruit juice whipped together); in both cases, unless you know that tap water was not used in their preparation, avoid them. They are delicious, but can create problems for the unadjusted tummy.

There are only two kinds of restaurants: the state-run restaurants and the *paladares,* or private dining services in people's homes. The food in the state-run restaurants is typically not very good, so seek out the *paladares* when you can (you will need to make a reservation). Be very careful about the places you go to eat: if they don't look safe or clean, you should avoid them. Do not eat food off the street from the street stalls: this can be very dangerous to your health. Be very careful about food and drink in Cuba (and throughout Latin America); there are dangerous bugs around. First, the water: Do not drink tap water anywhere in Cuba (except where *officially* noted as safe, sterilized, or "electrified"). This means no ice in any drinks (ice cubes may be made from tap water); ask for drinks *sin hielo* (without ice) when ordering. Close your mouth in the shower in the morning, and brush your teeth with bottled water. Drink only bottled water and soft drinks from bottles with intact seals opened in front of you. Coffee and tea are generally okay, because the water is boiled first. Avoid fresh dairy products, including milk, custards, mayonnaise, and ice cream, because they all usually require refrigeration, which may be questionable in certain parts of Cuba. Definitely avoid raw shellfish and raw fish and do not eat any raw or uncooked vegetables or fruits, unless you can peel them; this means no green salad. You will inevitably get the Latin American tummy on your trip . . . it is hard to avoid a drop of water here or there. If you have followed the above rules carefully, it is probably nothing to worry about; it will be uncomfortable for a day or two. Eat lightly, drink lots of safe fluids, stay in or near your room, rest, and it will pass. If a fever or vomiting develops, be sure to seek medical attention immediately. (Medical services are available for all free of charge in Cuba, and usually have high standards: the problem is that medical supplies are not always available.)

Regional Differences

Empanadas, seafood along the coast, roast pig *(lechon),* and *fufu* (pork rinds mixed with fried plantains) are all very popular. Rice and beans is universal, practically for every meal; *Moros y Cristianos* ("Moors and Christians," or rice with red beans) is a very common version. Try *crillos,* which is a combined dish of meat and beans and rice. Cuban food can be spicy or not, depending on the dish. Curiously, lobster and other seafood delicacies are abundant, and as with most food, inexpensive. There are many, often very sweet, desserts, such as versions of the ubiquitous flan and *tres leches,* which are milk and sugar puddings, some mixed with coconut and other flavorings. A favorite dessert is guava paste and a soft, cream-cheese-like cheese.

Typical Drinks and Toasting

Rum—light and clear, or dark and heavy—is the national drink, if there is one. Beer is also drunk. Soft drinks are popular. The rum and Coke originated in Cuba. The famous *mojito,* a drink of rum, lime juice, sugar, and bitters, also originated in Cuba. The most common toast is *salud* (to your health).

Table Manners and the Use of Utensils

Do not begin eating until the host says *"¡Buen provecho!"* Referring to European traditions as they do, Cubans do not switch knives and forks, as people do in the United States. The knife remains in the right hand, and the fork remains in the left. When the meal is finished, the knife and fork are laid parallel to each other across the right side of the plate. If you put both utensils down on the plate for any real length of time, it is a sign to the waitstaff that you are finished, and your plate may be taken away from you. Alternately, if you lay your cutlery down on either side of the plate it means you haven't finished; but if you really are, the host might interpret this as a sign that you were not happy with the meal. There will be separate glasses provided at your setting for water and white and red wine or beer (after-dinner drink glasses come out after dinner).

When not holding utensils, your hands are expected to be visible above the table: this means you do not keep them in your lap; instead, rest your wrists on top of the table (never your elbows). At the table, pass all dishes to your left. Fruits and fresh vegetables may be scarce, so treat them respectfully if they are served by always using a knife and fork to cut them (salads are not common, nor are fruits for dessert).

Seating Plans

The most honored position is at the head of the table, with the most important guest seated immediately to the right of the host (women to the right of the host, and men to the right of the hostess). If there is a hosting couple, one will be at each end of the table. Men typically rise when women enter the room, and continue to hold doors for women and allow them to enter a room first. Remember, as is the case throughout the region, the first floor in Cuba ("*PB*" or *planta baja*) is really the second floor, with the first floor usually referred to as the lobby or ground floor.

Refills and Seconds

If your food is served family-style, it is important to take only what you will eat, and eat everything you take. Sharing food is common in a land of shortages, but wasting it is not. You will always be invited to a meal in people's homes, especially if you turn up during a time when someone is eating. In a restaurant, do not leave food on your plate. You will be offered seconds in a home, but guests usually decline. You may always have additional beverages; drink enough to cause your cup or glass to be less than half full, and it will generally be refilled.

At Home, in a Restaurant, or at Work

In informal restaurants, you will rarely be required to share a table. Waitstaff may be summoned by making eye contact; waving or calling their names is very impolite. The business breakfast is not uncommon in Cuba, although the business lunch is more common (more common than dinner—which is usually reserved for family). Inviting a business associate to lunch is typically done after the second meeting. Whenever the business meal occurs, it is generally not the time to make business decisions. Take your cue from your Cuban associates: if they bring up business, then it's okay to discuss it (more often than not, over the coffee at the end of the meal), but wait to take your lead from their conversation. No gum chewing at a restaurant or on the street. No-smoking sections in restaurants are still a rarity.

Most meals hosted at home are informal. When you arrive at a Cuban associate's home for a formal meal, you will be told where to sit, and there you should remain. Do not wander from room to room; much of the house is really off-limits to guests. Once you (and the group) are invited to another room, be sure to allow more senior members of your party to enter the room ahead of you: men should move aside to allow women to enter the room ahead of them. There are usually not predinner drinks. In a private home, be careful about what and how you admire things: the host may feel obliged to give it to you and this may cause great difficulty for them. If you invite people to your home, be prepared to always have the invitation accepted, although they may not, in fact, show up; rejecting the invitation is difficult for Cubans, who seek to not offend. They may indicate their true intentions by simply responding to your invitation with "I will try." Please note that conversation at the table may be secondary to enjoying the food . . . dining is not necessarily a time for the usual lively Cuban discussion (that is more typically saved for after the meal, over coffee or drinks, a game of dominoes, etc.).

Being a Good Guest or Host

Paying the Bill

Usually the one who does the inviting pays the bill, although the guest is expected to make an effort to pay, especially in Cuba, where it is recognized that for visitors the expense is minimal. Sometimes other circumstances determine who pays (such as rank). Women can equally offer to pay the bill, and to host, as long as their professional authority is understood.

Transportation

It's a very nice idea, when acting as the host, to inquire ahead of time as to whether your guests will require transportation. If necessary, you should arrange for taxi service at the end of the meal. When the cars arrive, be sure not to leave your spot until your guests are out of sight.

When to Arrive / Chores to Do

If invited to dinner at a private home, you may offer to help with the chores and you should expect to visit the kitchen. Spouses do not attend business dinners without a special invitation to do so, and typically this does not happen.

Gift Giving

In general, gift giving is not common in business (and it is absolutely forbidden when working with civil servants).

A good gift to bring to a dinner would be a nice bottle of wine. If the host has children, definitely bring something for them; appreciated gifts include Spanish-language storybooks, English-Spanish dictionaries, and chocolates. Especially valuable as gifts are items that are difficult to come by in Cuba: small kitchen appliances, school supplies, and calculators are all welcome, and much more appreciated than flowers. Many Cubans celebrate Three Kings Day (as all Latin American cultures do), January 6, as the time for holiday gift giving. Do not give gifts that reflect the United States necessarily. Do not give Cubans rum as a gift. As in other European-based cultures, gifts are generally opened at the time they are given and received, although Cubans may not openly say thank you for gifts received (they are, nevertheless, very appreciative, and also very generous).

Special Holidays and Celebrations

Major Holidays

There is no one specific vacation time, and work does not necessarily stop for all holidays; additionally, the times of special events often change, so please be sure to have a contact to confirm any activities you plan to do.

January 1	Liberation Day (New Year's Day)
January 2	Victory Day
January 6	Three Kings Day
January 28	José Marti's Birthday
February 24	Anniversary of the Second War of Independence
March 8	International Women's Day
March 13	Anniversary of the Students' Attack on the Presidential Palace
April 19	Bay of Pigs Victory
May 1	*Día del Trabajo* (Labor Day)
July 25–27	National Revolution Days (coincides with the celebration of *Carnaval*)
July 30	Day of the Martyrs of the Revolution
October 8	Anniversary of Che Guevara's Death
October 10	Anniversary of the First War of Independence
October 28	Memorial Day for Camilio Cienfuegos
December 2	Anniversary of the Landing of the Granma
December 7	Memorial Day for Antonio Macco
December 25	*Navidad* (Christmas Day—reinstated after the visit of the Pope in 1997)

Business Culture

Daily Office Protocols

It is common for women to be in positions of authority outside of the home in Cuba, but this is in addition to their traditional roles as nurturers of the family. People organize their time on a daily basis according to the tasks they must accomplish, and the relationships they must depend upon in order to accomplish these tasks; the clock takes a backseat. Therefore, the day may begin slowly, but there can be much activity by day's end, and people can stay late in the office in order to finish up what needs to be done. This pattern repeats itself over larger blocks of time in regard to the accomplishment of projects and the meeting of deadlines.

Management Styles

People share responsibilities and work best in teams; workers provide what their bosses expect of them, and the preparation of plans, methods, and reports can be time-consuming and complicated efforts. Gathering the information required in order to do what your supervisor expects from you, or creating consensus among your colleagues in order to accomplish a particular goal, can take a long time. All of this occurs for most people within a governmental or state-run hierarchy, which means that deadlines and efficiency are often secondary to attention to detail, perfection of form, bureaucratic requirements, and the need to be clever in the face of limited resources in order to be effective. Titles are typically not critical. Complimenting and rewarding people publicly is usually not done. For non-Cubans, it is essential to try to have a local contact who can tell you what is really going on after you return home, and also to have a local intermediary to act as a liaison for you with the people you need to see while you are there. This person is typically from the government.

Conducting a Meeting or Presentation

At presentations and meetings, discussions can be vibrant, with many people speaking at once; questions are common and interruptions, even of presentations, should be expected. Remember, because a close personal relationship is often demonstrated through physicality in Latin cultures, the nearer your Cuban colleagues are to you, the better they are responding to your proposal. The best time to schedule meetings and presentations is in the morning; by 3 or 4 P.M., most people are more focused on getting home. In general, the best presentation is one that shows how your business will benefit Cuban society in general: remember, the profit system of capitalism is not the basis of this centralized, state-run, planned economy. Additionally, be sure to make your presentation in Spanish if you can, and have handouts in Spanish, and in enough supply for more than the number of people you anticipate (again, shortages make it difficult to duplicate on-site).

Negotiation Styles

Cubans will respect someone who comes to them with already established knowledge and experience, and will build relationships based on your expertise and the opportunities to the society in general that you bring. Bargaining is not the essence of the negotiation, but things will move slowly, as you must build trust; do not appear as if your major concern is to make lots of money from the deal. Never be condescending. Once the contract is in place, it is respected as a formal agreement between you and the Cuban government. Plan your meetings as carefully and as well in advance as you can, but expect changes. The goal, at least for the first meeting, is the development of a good feeling of respect and mutual trust. Remember also that the meeting might start and end later than you anticipated; nevertheless, as in most polychronic cultures, you should always arrive on time. Coffee is the universal greeting; always accept it, always serve it (in nice china, never in Styrofoam), and drink as much or as little as you can or desire. It is the gesture of acceptance and appreciation that counts (never refuse coffee, or an invitation to go with your colleague to a café and have some).

Written Correspondence

Last names (with honorifics when writing, even if you use first names without honorifics when speaking) are usually written in uppercase; dates are given using the day/month/year format (with periods in between, not slashes). The time of day is written in military time; weights and measures are given in metric measurements. Monetary amounts are written so that the period breaks up the figure into tens, hundreds, and thousands, and a comma separates the pesos from the centavos. Be sure to inquire first, in all communications, about your colleague's health and progress, then move on to the substance of your communication, and close with a salutation and your personal wishes for his or her success and well-being (the Latin communication "sandwich"). If your colleagues write to you in Spanish, try to respond in Spanish, if you can, or use the services of a translator. Written addresses are usually in the following format:

Line 1: name
Line 2: title/position
Line 3: company
Line 4: street address
Line 5: city, state

THE DOMINICAN REPUBLIC

Note: Refer to the preceding introduction to this section for information about general Hispanic-African Caribbean and Latin American cultural behaviors; the material that follows describes specific Dominican variations on general Hispanic-African Caribbean and Latin American customs.

Some Introductory Background on the Dominican Republic and the Dominicans

Dominicans (the people of the Dominican Republic; residents of the small island of Dominica, which is part of the Anglo-African Caribbean, refer to themselves as Dominicans as well, so there may be some confusion around this; the context usually quickly determines which Dominican one is referring to) are very familiar with the United States and things "American." More than once, the United States has sent Marines into the Dominican Republic to quell unrest and to restore, ostensibly, order to a disrupted civil life. And the Dominican Republic has sent many of its sons to the United States, some to become famous baseball stars (the national sport and passion, next to merengue and salsa music, is baseball)! In fact, one in eight Dominicans is a resident of New York City, and returns to the island several times during a year. Whole neighborhoods of Santo Domingo, the capital city (known as Ciudad Trujillo during the infamous dictator's lifetime), are referred to with the names of barrios (neighborhoods) in New York City (New York City–residing Dominicans are referred to as Dominican Yorks). The Dominican Republic shares the small island of Hispaniola with its neighbor, Haiti, a member of the Franco-African Caribbean group, and their relationship has been stormy, at best. (Nevertheless, there is a significant Haitian population living and working in the Dominican Republic, as it is, relatively speaking, still the more economically advantaged of the two countries.) Many Dominicans know much about life in the United States, though many Americans know little about Dominicans.

Some Historical Context

The Arawak and Taino Indians (who generally fought constantly whenever they came in contact with each other) occupied the island as indigenous peoples (it seems the island has always experienced an ethnic separation of one kind or another). When the Spaniards came (Christopher Columbus, in fact, was the first colonizing European for most of the Caribbean), they overcame the Tainos and Arawaks almost immediately, and set about importing slaves from Africa for labor (the first European settlement in the New World was Santo Domingo, and even today, the glory of its colonial section remains). With the French attempt at colonizing the Caribbean came conflict, and after losing several battles, the Spaniards ceded half the island to the French (this half became Haiti). However, Haiti experienced the New World's first slave revolt, which quickly spread to Santo Domingo, thereby spreading Haiti's influence over the Dominicans. This ensured a legacy of mistrust and hatred that lingers even today between Haitians and Dominicans. Dominicans struggled against Haitian domination, and as Haiti slid into economic depression, Dominicans declared their independence from Haiti and from Spain as well. Although Spain attempted several times to reinstate control, in 1918 U.S. Marines finally ended Spanish rule and freed Dominicans from Madrid. This is one of the main reasons for the affinity between Dominicans and Americans. But U.S. interests also saw to it that no policies would be instituted in the country that went against their goals, and the political dictatorship of Rafael Trujillo ensured U.S. interests in the country while exacerbating the hatred between Haitians and Dominicans. When Trujillo was assassinated in 1961, political unrest ensued and the United States sent in the Marines, again, in 1965. Eventually, order was restored, and presidential elections have occurred, nominally, ever since.

An Area Briefing

Schools and Education

Schooling is compulsory through high school; however, in poorer rural regions and in difficult urban neighborhoods, maintaining quality education and children's attendance through these grades is a challenge. Many children are pressed into working to help the family survive instead of attending school. Wealthier people send their children to private schools (*colegios*) in the cities. There is generally a shortage of good school supplies, teachers, and basic infrastructure.

Religion and Demographics

The people are mainly Roman Catholic, with minority populations of Jews, Protestants, Muslims, Evangelical Protestants, Mormons, and others. There is a significant spiritualist following, as well. The Dominican Republic today is demographically an extremely young country, with more than one-third of the population under the age of sixteen. There is still a rigid separation of the genders in the Dominican Republic, more so in the less urbanized areas; even in Santo Domingo, women struggle with the glass ceiling at work and the need to perform "two jobs"—that of homemaker and societal nurturer, as well as businesswoman, and to do each twice as well as the Dominican male. Non-Dominican businesswomen must take extra care in order to not be judged as overly aggressive, yet must maintain extreme professionalism in order to not have their authority questioned. Consider too that the Dominican Republic, like most of the region, is economically a developing nation, and struggles with all of the challenges associated with that status, including substantial poverty, inadequate and ill-serving infrastructures, and corruption.

Fundamental Cultural Orientations

1. What's the Best Way for People to Relate to One Another?

OTHER-INDEPENDENT OR OTHER-DEPENDENT? As is the case with most countries in the region—due, in part, to the heavy influence of Roman Catholicism—Dominican behavior is often significantly "other-dependent." Most individuals will seek, either formally or informally, the opinions and support of family, friends, and coworkers before venturing off to do or say something on their own. People are most comfortable in the "bosom" of others, and individuals are simply not part of society unless they can claim membership to or affiliation with some group, neighborhood, town, or business organization. The extended family—cousins, aunts, uncles—typically lives under one roof, or very nearby (there is sometimes no distinction made between members of the nuclear family and the extended family members). A consequence of this, of course, is a resistance to the outsider, and a need for all outsiders to become associated with members of the in-group as soon as possible. To be alone in the Dominican Republic is to live a sad and difficult life (in fact, it is odd to claim time alone, as being alone is always associated with sadness; people typically stop in to socialize with each other throughout the day). Because of this strong need to look good in the eyes of others, the individual must bear responsibility for him- or herself in the world.

HIERARCHY-ORIENTED OR EGALITY-ORIENTED? Certainly the younger generation, especially in the cities, feels more empowered as individuals than their elders, but the traditions of the Roman Catholic hierarchy still play a powerful role in determining who does what and when. Subsequently, the Dominican workplace is heavily dependent upon the leader, who has supreme decision-making authority, and with the support staff being required to follow step, challenge as little as possible, and solve all problems before they surface at the top. Society is rigidly stratified, with the large poorer classes on the bottom, some middle classes in the middle, and a small elite at the top; this division is often reflected racially, with the elite generally being lighter skinned and the poor being darker. Women and men are rigidly separated in their social roles, as is the case more or less throughout all of Latin America, in this macho culture; women traditionally play the nurturing role in society, while men play the public leaders, in government and business.

RULE-ORIENTED OR RELATIONSHIP-ORIENTED? There is an established pattern of behavior that encourages the circumvention of rules from above by those clever enough or with connections. One of the lasting legacies of Latin cultures is the rigid social hierarchy and the value people place on finding ingenious ways around the rules and regulations in order to live their lives. Most of the time, the way one circumvented the authorities was to rely on the only true source of dependability in an otherwise cruel and difficult world: one's family, proven friends, and loyal business associates. Therefore, relationships—not rules—rule. Situations, if involving the right people and the right issues, will almost always determine the behaviors of individuals, not bland laws or bureaucratic fiats. This can lead to corruption; in its more common form, it represents the expectation on the part of some poorly paid government bureaucrats that they need to be compensated more appropriately for providing a valued service; and in its most insidious form, it is out-and-out extortion. This cultural dependence on personal relationships means that Dominicans will need time to get to know you before they will be ready to talk business. Attempts to discuss the terms of the deal or the immediate task at hand without having built the necessary personal trust and understanding is often a waste of time. Which takes us to our next concern.

2. What's the Best Way to View Time?

Monochronic or Polychronic?   Time is circular, and very polychronic; more so in the rural areas. Even in the major cities, old agrarian patterns die hard, even if people aren't waking up and heading for the fields in the morning. In rural areas, it is easiest to work in the fields in the cool of the early morning and late afternoon; the midday heat is usually oppressive, and provides a good opportunity to stoke up on a filling meal and a midday siesta before heading back out until the sun sets.

Working in Santo Domingo today still means showing up at the office around 9 A.M., but not really getting started until 9:30 or 10 (drinking coffee, checking the news, and catching up with coworkers may take precedence). Lunch occurs around noon, and can either be a quick bite at the local sandwich shop or last several hours at an elegant restaurant. After returning to the office (people would, in an earlier time, retire for a short nap after having gone home for the large main midday meal), workers stay as long as necessary, perhaps up to 7 P.M. or later. At that point, they return home, or meet friends at a local bar for some drinks. Dinner, in either case, is usually not before 8 P.M. On weekends, Friday and Saturday night revelries more often than not last well past midnight. If you really want things to occur punctually, it is perfectly okay to identify the time as *"en punto."*

Risk-Taking or Risk-Averse?   Latin cultures, in general, are risk-averse, and that is one of the driving reasons for the creation of structure and hierarchies. The Dominican Republic is no exception. Decision making can be slow and tedious, as various levels of the hierarchy need to be consulted, and as information must be made available to many in order for it to occur. The belief is to analyze everything carefully—several times, if necessary—and to debate all aspects of a decision until everything is clear and agreed upon. Even when individuals are empowered to make the decision, there can be a reticence to take the required final step. Nevertheless, there is a growing impatience with the tedious risk-avoidance among new entrepreneurs and the young (particularly among the Dominican Yorks).

Past-Oriented or Future-Oriented?   Latin American cultures have seen their world turned upside down more than once with their having little or no ability to control the events. In the Dominican Republic, there is a strong doubt in the ability to control what happens, but the effort is always there, for to struggle is to live. *Si Dios quiere* (if God wills) is a common expression that reveals a certain fatalism, and a sense that one can only do what one can do, given one's position in the world. Dominicans, therefore, look to their family and friends for stability and dependability, and are generally wary about the ultimate outcome of things. Despite a strong desire to believe in their own ability to overcome the odds, there is an equally strong acceptance of the inevitability of setbacks and failures, almost a fatalistic expectation of it, and a resistance to identify individuals for blame when and if things go wrong.

3. What's the Best Way for Society to Work with the World at Large?

LOW-CONTEXT DIRECT OR HIGH-CONTEXT INDIRECT COMMUNICATORS? Most Dominicans are high-context communicators; nevertheless, they are demonstrative, warm, and gregarious, and they love good conversation. Once it gets going, expect forthright and direct communication. Dominicans can be proud and aggressive when it comes to competitive situations, and in those circumstances will often let you know what they are thinking. Yet as they build their relationships with people they like, Dominicans, like most Latinos, want smooth interpersonal working relationships, especially with outsiders, and will go the distance to reassure you that everything is okay and that all is in order—even when it may not be. This is not based on a desire to deceive, but rather on a need to appear capable, and not to lose face in the eyes of people from cultures with greater resources. It is critical, therefore, to always confirm information, to have multiple, independent, and reliable sources to verify or interpret what you are being told, and to be able to read between the lines. This tendency also makes for complimentary and respectful introductory conversation, and an avoidance of anything that may strike you as unpleasant; Dominicans will always try to say what they think you want to hear.

PROCESS-ORIENTED OR RESULT-ORIENTED?   As with other Latino cultures, there is a strong reliance on the deductive process: how things are being done is as important as the final result. But Dominicans are very subjective, and will also often fall back on what they personally believe in order to make or justify a decision. Because there is great admiration for a good plan, but sometimes a serious lack of resources in what still is a developing country, coupled at times with the burden of an unpredictable bureaucracy, Dominicans may not be able to follow through with the actions required to put the plans in place. Yet they will be reticent to admit this or inform you when problems develop. It is therefore that much more important for non-Dominicans to stay involved with them, helping them to implement what has been agreed to. This must be done, however, with sensitivity toward the pride that Dominicans feel in being able to handle things on their own; therefore, never be intrusive, but always be available; always be open to learning about their way, while providing them with the resources and information they need, whenever possible, to assist them in making things happen. They will be very clever about making the end result happen, but the way they get there may be very different from the original plan.

FORMAL OR INFORMAL?   The Dominican Republic has an informal and relationship-oriented culture. Family members relate to one another according to rules that respect traditional family roles (*el papa, la madre, el niño, la niña, mi amigo*). This does not have to be artificial or contrived; in fact, it is often loving and spontaneous. Even the language is divided into formal and informal forms and phrases, and personal behaviors are ruled by etiquette and protocol. Maintaining honor and personal pride is important. *Never* insult the honor, pride, or personal beliefs of a Dominican or his or her family, colleagues, or associates.

Greetings and Introductions

Language and Basic Vocabulary

Spanish is the language, but there are many words that are specifically Dominican Spanish, filled with Caribbean flavorings. For example, instead of saying *un poquito* (a little), people will say, *un chin;* accents vary and Creole is spoken in areas with Haitian populations (typically near the border with Haiti). Be sure to use any Spanish you do know, even if you learned it from a neighbor or in school: Dominicans love it when you try to speak Spanish, and they will help you get it right; this often becomes a relationship-building event, and can be a more important activity in the formative stages of the relationship than any substantive discussions you can have.

Here are the basics:

Buenos días	Good morning
Buenas tardes	Good afternoon
Buenas noches	Good evening
¡Hola! ¿Que tal? or *Saludos*	Hello, how are you? (informal)
¿Como está usted?	How are you? (formal)
Adiós	Good-bye
Por favor	Please
Gracias	Thank you
Con permiso	Pardon me
De nada	You're welcome
Muy bien	Very well
Con mucho gusto	Pleased to meet you
Un placer	A pleasure
Señor	Mr.
Señora	Mrs.
Señorita	Miss
Ingeniero(a)	Engineer
Abogado(a)	Lawyer
Doctor	Doctor
Gerente	Manager

Remember, in written Spanish, questions and exclamations are also indicated at the beginning of the sentence, with an upside-down exclamation point or question mark.

Honorifics for Men, Women, and Children

You must use *señor* (Mr.) and *señora* (Mrs.) plus the family name when introduced to strangers. Unless and until your Dominican colleague specifically invites you to use first names, and despite how he or she might refer to you, you should always use the family name plus the correct Spanish honorific (*señorita*—Miss—is still required for a young, unmarried woman) at first, although titles are typically dropped quickly, and first names used often. If you do not know whether a woman is married, use *señorita* (please note: this is the reverse from what is done in Spain, where *señora* is used when the marital status of the woman is unknown). *Don* (*doña* for an unmarried woman) is a special title of respect, typically used before and with the first (given) name only, and usually used only by people who know each other well and desire to show great respect. In the *campo* (countryside), people sometimes greet each other with *compadre* replacing *señor,* and *comadre* replacing *señora* and *señorita.* Married women are not necessarily "safe" from machismo, so wearing a wedding band does not always protect a woman alone; however, being a mother virtually ensures that a man will remain at a distance: bring pictures of your children. Children may typically greet their parents or other significant adults, like aunts and uncles, by "asking for blessings" (*"Benedición, Mama"*); the response is, *"Dios te bendiga"* (God bless you). In situations where a title is known or used, the honorific plus the title is usually employed, either with or without the name (e.g., Señor Ingeniero, or Señor Ingeniero Cortez). *Licensiado* is a "title" generally used for anyone with a skill requiring some sort of diploma. "Doctor" may be safely used as a way to give respect to anyone with a university degree; as an honorific, it does not have to refer only to a Ph.D. For casual contacts (e.g., with waiters, store help, etc.), just use *señor* or *señorita* without the name. It is very important to greet people at work or in stores and restaurants with an appropriate greeting for the time of day—*buenos días, buenas tardes,* or *buenas noches*—and *adiós* upon leaving. If you speak any Spanish at all, it is important to use it, but be sure to use the formal pronoun *usted* at the beginning and do *not* switch to the *tu* (informal "you") form of speech unless and until your Dominican colleague has specifically invited you to or does so him- or herself.

Spanish family names are often hyphenated, with the mother's family name added after the father's family name. In formal speech and in written correspondence, the fully hyphenated name is used; in face-to-face introductions, usually only the father's family name is used. For example, José Ramón Mendez-Rodriguez is Señor Mendez in face-to-face introductions, with Mendez being José's father's family name and Rodriguez being José's mother's family name. Women often keep their family name when they marry, but add their husband's father's family name with the preposition *de.* For example, Señora Maria Isabel Gonzalez-Sanchez de Rodriguez is married to Señor Rodriguez, her maiden name is Gonzalez (her father's family name), and she retains her mother's family name—Sanchez—as well; in face-to-face communication she is more often referred to as Señora de Rodriguez or, very informally, as Señora Rodriguez.

The What, When, and How of Introducing People

In most formal situations, it is okay to introduce yourself to others, if you have not been introduced to them by a third party. (In the latter case, you will be introduced to women first, then the most senior men.) Similarly, do not presume to seat yourself at a formal gathering at first, but if you are not shown a seat, then, after allowing seniors and women to select a seat, go ahead and select one for yourself. Shake hands with everyone individually in a group when being introduced and before departing; the U.S. group wave is not appreciated. Avoid ending the conversation with the expression "Have a nice day"; it sounds insincere. Kissing is a common greeting once you have established a strong relationship, whether between women or men and women; it usually consists of a kiss on both cheeks (actually an "air kiss," first on the left side, and then the right). It is not uncommon to see men and men, and women and women, walking arm in arm down the street; they are good close friends or associates, and it means nothing more than that.

The use of business cards is common; if possible, you should have your business card translated into Spanish on the reverse. Be sure to put any advanced educational degrees and your full title or position on both sides of your business card. Such emblems of your status are very important to Dominicans (especially if you are from the United States or New York due to the likely possibility of their having connections with family and friends there); they want to know they are doing business with an important person.

Physical Greeting Styles

The handshake is common. The Dominican version is firm between two men, but not as robust between men and women or two women. The handshake should be accompanied by the appropriate greeting (see the list of terms outlined earlier). Men should wait until a woman extends her hand before reaching for it, and women may take the lead in extending their hand or not. Between family, friends, or trusted business associates, an extra touch on the elbow or a hug (the *abrazo,* or embrace) will generally occur. This can happen even as soon as the second meeting; do not initiate it, but respond warmly in kind if it is initiated with you. Eye contact during the introduction is important, and should be maintained as long as the individual is addressing you.

Communication Styles

Okay Topics / Not Okay Topics

Okay: politics, current events, anything interesting (but never to the point of being controversial at first), baseball (and the unique contribution made by Dominicans to the sport), New York City, family, dominoes, merengue (the original national dance) and Dominican music, cockfighting (a national passion—don't criticize it). *Not okay:* Do not inquire about a person's occupation or income in casual conversation, although it may be inquired of you. Americans often begin a conversation with "So, what do you do?"; this is too personal in the Dominican Republic, and is often not the most interesting topic of conversation. Do not give your opinions about Haiti or Dominican politics (unless you really know what you are talking about). Do not talk about your Latin American tummy; keep your health issues to yourself, because no one wants to hear about them. Also not okay: money, inquiring about *private* family matters (although speaking about the health and other general aspects of family life is very important). Do not go to the Dominican Republic (or Latin America) without pictures of your family, and when family is brought up (which it will be almost immediately in the conversation), use it as an opportunity to bring out the photographs. Never tell a dirty joke with a woman present.

Tone, Volume, and Speed

Discussions can quickly become animated and very lively, depending upon the nature of the discussion and the circumstances of the developing relationship. At meals, afterward, during a simple visit, or sitting in *mesadoras* (rocking chairs) on the porches at night (a very common way of socializing) conversation is an art; it is enjoyed, savored, and commented upon, but it never gets out of hand, and is always carried on respectfully. In business, speak softly and with restraint. It garners respect.

Use of Silence

In general, silence is not that common, except in group discussions where something has been said that can cause public loss of face. Avoid this, and enjoy the simultaneous conversations and frequent interruptions that usually define Dominican conversation style.

Physical Gestures and Facial Expressions

Typically, indicating direction or selecting something is done with the lips: you pucker your lips and make a slight head movement in the direction of the object you are referring to. If you want to indicate that you don't like someone or something, you point with your lips as discussed above, while rolling your eyes. Winking and whistling—often accompanied by a positive comment—is meant to be a friendly introduction between men and women. Tapping the bottom of the elbow indicates that the person you are talking about is cheap or making a stingy offer. If you wrinkle your nose in response to something, it means you do not understand it. Rubbing your index finger and thumb together indicates money. People will *psst* at you when they want your attention, and oftentimes in conversations, there can be a tap on the shoulder and much touching: this typically indicates friendship.

Waving and Counting

The thumb represents the number 1, the index finger the number 2, and so on. It is insulting to beckon someone with the forefinger. If you need to gesture for a waiter, subtly raise your hand; never click, call, or whistle. Waving or beckoning is done with the palm down and the fingers moving forward and back in a kind of scratching motion.

Physicality and Physical Space

Dominicans tend to get closer than North Americans are generally comfortable with, but never extremely so. Do not step back when your Dominican associate steps forward. Dominican men may touch each other during conversations, adjust each other's ties, dust off each other's shoulders, and the like. Don't speak with your hands in your pockets; always keep them firmly at your side when standing. If men and women must cross their legs, it should never be ankle over knee (the preferred style for women is to cross ankle over ankle). Remember, even in public, formal is always better than informal: no gum chewing, *ever;* no slouching; no leaning against things.

Eye Contact

Eye contact can be direct, and at times may be disconcerting for many Americans. It is important not to interpret this behavior as a way of intentionally trying to make you uncomfortable. It is the way Dominicans show their interest. Conversely, if you look away, your behavior will say to your Dominican colleague that you are disinterested, rude, or establishing yourself as the subordinate in a hierarchical relationship; none of these is a good idea.

Emotive Orientation

Dominicans are often animated and physically expressive. Join in if you like, but keep your cool if you can. Dominicans will always admire you if you can remain logical, formal, respectful, and diplomatic while staying warm, open, and personable.

Protocol in Public

Walking Styles and Waiting in Lines

Don't be too distressed if someone walks right up to the front of the line at a bank, a restaurant, or a store and gets served because of the relationship he or she has with the clerk, while you have been waiting patiently in line for forty minutes. People also have a tendency to stand very close in public; this may feel uncomfortable at first. Resist the urge to back away; most of the time, you are not being intentionally crowded. Remember, the need to appear helpful and courteous is strong, and if you ask for directions on the street, you will no doubt be instructed on just where to go . . . whether or not the individual actually knows!

Behavior in Public Places: Airports, Terminals, and the Market

Most stores are closed on Sundays, and many small stores *(colmados)* close each day at midday for lunch and a short siesta. Personally thanking store owners, waiters, chefs, and hotel managers for their services is very much appreciated. In food markets, you can touch the produce; in goods stores, it may be difficult for you to return a product unless there is a flaw in it. Because of the personal nature of the culture, money is usually exchanged in the palms, not on the counter. In addition, in most small shops and in markets, bargaining is very expected. If you don't bargain well, that's okay; put a smile on your face and ask for half of what the listed price is. Stick to it and walk away if you have to, and you'll land somewhere in between. Never get angry, though, since bargaining is a game to get to know you, and it is supposed to make shopping a more pleasant experience. Always offer a fair price, as the amount you pay goes to the support of a family.

Because of the high poverty rate, small children and women may approach you on the street or come up to your taxi window to ask for money. It is always difficult deciding whether or not to give, but remember that the social support systems are negligible, and this is often the only way for these people to sustain themselves. Smoking is pervasive; if you do smoke, be sure to always offer a cigarette to everyone you are talking to before you light up. In bathrooms, on the plumbing "C" means hot (*caldo*) and "F" means cold (*frío*).

Bus / Metro / Taxi / Car

Driving is on the right, but people pass very quickly on the left. Driving may be difficult in the cities, and dangerous in the rural areas, and being a pedestrian is just as risky: both drivers and pedestrians really are very aggressive. Additionally, throughout Latin America, street rules are observed only sporadically (stoplights are viewed as "suggestions") and drivers usually do not turn their lights on after dark (it is believed to blind the oncoming traffic). There are no metros, but *guaguas,* buses, and *carros publicos* (public cars, or taxis that follow specific routes) are common. The best way to catch a cab is at designated taxi stands (hotels are good places, but often charge more for the same ride: a hotel surcharge may be added to the meter fare, in some cases). When hailing a taxi, extend your hand with the number of fingers indicating the number of passengers you have to go with you. The crime situation in areas where visitors typically travel is minimal, typically petty crime in the tourist areas.

Tipping

A 10 percent tip is usually sufficient in restaurants (it is usually included in the bill); you need only tip the equivalent of one U.S. dollar in taxis. Porters and hotel help get the equivalent in pesos of one U.S. dollar per item or service rendered (tipping in U.S. dollars, as is done throughout much of the region, is perfectly fine, actually preferred). Please double-check the current dollar/peso exchange rate, as it can vary quickly and significantly.

Punctuality

It is perfectly acceptable—in fact, essential—to arrive for social events about an hour late. If you arrive sooner, you will be running the risk of interrupting the host or hostess as he or she gets ready. For business meetings, being late by five to fifteen minutes or more is usually not a problem, but it is safer for the new employee or visitor to be on time, while not being surprised if others are not. Usually, the meeting will not begin in earnest until all attendees have arrived (or at least until all the decision makers have shown up), and this may not correspond to the time listed in the agenda. Resist questioning the late ones for a reason; they always have one, usually involving an obligation with more important people, like superiors, old friends, or family.

Dress

Being well-groomed and dressing with respect for yourself and others is important. Being on top of fashion is considered very good. While much of Latin America looks to Europe for fashion, Dominicans typically look to New York. Casual wear includes jeans and skirts (dresses and blouses in the countryside); even T-shirts and sneakers are okay if they are in good condition and neat and clean. Business dress includes suits and ties for men, dresses and blouses for women; sometimes the *chacabana* (the Dominican version of the Latin American *guayabera*) is worn by older Dominican men in business. Clothes, especially for social get-togethers, tend to be flashy and colorful, and the use of jewelry is always admired (however, be careful where and when you wear fine jewelry, as you can also make yourself a mark for theft). Dominican women may wear more makeup and jewelry than women in the United States, and it is fashionable, especially in summer, not to wear stockings. Women do not wear sneakers to work.

Personal Hygiene

In the Dominican Republic, personal hygiene is very important. There is a real concern for cleanliness and smelling good; perfumes and colognes are used often. Latin men may sport facial hair, in the form of mustaches.

Note that most rest room and bathroom facilities throughout Latin America do not have plumbing capable of handling paper toilet tissue; it is for this reason that there is a small receptacle next to the toilet for your used tissue: do not flush it down the bowl, but place it in the receptacle, or else you'll face the embarrassment of having to call for help when the bowl overflows. Take paper tissue with you if you travel about. Remember also that the water in showers may be heated by a little electrical device placed above the showerhead: never touch it or any metal when wet!

Dining and Drinking

Mealtimes and Typical Foods

Breakfast (*el desayuno*) is served from about 7:30 to 9 A.M., and usually consists of some bread and coffee. Coffee in the morning can be strong and black, or with hot milk (*café con leche*).

Lunch (*la comida*) was traditionally the main meal of the day; even today, in busy cities, it can be an elaborate affair lasting several hours (usually an important business lunch)—or it can be a quick sandwich or salad at a shop on the corner. Lunch is usually served from noon to 2 P.M. It usually consists of rice and beans, which is eaten practically every day. Typically some vegetables, such as yucca and plantains, and some meat or chicken are also served. Sometimes fish (*baccalao,* or salt cod, is a favorite) is served at special meals. Meals often end with a sweet dessert, or fresh tropical fruits. *Sancocho* is the national specialty dish, and is served on special occasions; it is a big meat and vegetable stew. Even the quick business lunch often will include a main course and a dessert and coffee. On Sunday, the family day, the main meal is supper, which is usually served at lunchtime and can last well into the evening. The food is typically not very spicy.

Dinner (*la cena*) is served from 6:30 P.M. on. If the main meal of the day was lunch, then the family dinner at home is light; it usually consists of the same kinds of foods as those served for lunch. Drinks served with dinner are usually beer, water, fruit juices, or soft drinks. Coffee, typically strong, black, and sweet, is always served after dinner.

Be very careful about the places you go to eat: if they don't look safe or clean, you should avoid them. Do not eat food off the street from the street stalls: this can be very dangerous to your health. Be very careful about food and drink in the Dominican Republic (and throughout Latin America); although in tourist areas, it is probably safer than elsewhere, there are dangerous bugs around. First, the water: Do not drink tap water anywhere (except where *officially* noted as safe, sterilized, or "electrified," as in the resort hotels). This means no ice in any drinks (ice cubes may be made from tap water); ask for drinks *sin hielo* (without ice) when ordering. Close your mouth in the shower in the morning, and brush your teeth with bottled water. Drink only bottled water and soft drinks from bottles with intact seals opened in front of you; the fruit juices in the Dominican Republic are wonderful, but until your digestive system has adjusted, avoid them: they may have been diluted with water from the tap. Coffee and tea are generally okay, because the water is boiled first. Avoid fresh dairy products, including milk, custards, mayonnaise, and ice cream, because they all usually require refrigeration, which may be questionable in certain parts of the Dominican Republic. Definitely avoid raw shellfish and raw fish and do not eat any raw or uncooked vegetables or fruits, unless you can peel them; this means no green salad. You will inevitably get the Latin American tummy on your first few trips . . . it is hard to avoid a drop of water here or there. If you have followed the above rules carefully, it is probably nothing to worry about; it will be uncomfortable for a day or two. Eat lightly, drink lots of safe fluids, stay in or near your room, rest, and it will pass. If a fever or vomiting develops, be sure to seek medical attention immediately.

Typical Drinks and Toasting

Beer and rum are the national drinks. *Habichuelas con dulce* is a special sweet drink made from beans that is often served around Eastertime. There are also many local brandies made from sugarcane, which can vary from mild to incredibly strong (be warned), and which are offered as pre- or post-meal drinks. The most common toast is *salud* (to your health).

Table Manners and the Use of Utensils

Do not begin eating until the host says, *"¡Buen provecho!"* Knives and forks can be used U.S. style (switching) or European style (keeping the fork and knife in the same hands throughout the entire meal). When the meal is finished, the knife and fork are laid parallel to each other across the plate. If you put both utensils down on the plate for any real length of time, it is a sign to the waitstaff that you are finished, and your plate may be taken away from you. Alternately, if you lay your cutlery down on either side of the plate it means you haven't finished; but if you really are, the host might interpret this as a sign that you were not happy with the meal.

When not holding utensils, your hands are expected to be visible above the table: this means you do not keep them in your lap; instead, rest your wrists on top of the table (never your elbows). At the table, pass all dishes to your left.

Seating Plans

The most honored position is at the head of the table, with the most important guest seated immediately to the right of the host (women to the right of the host, and men to the right of the hostess). If there is a hosting couple, one will be at each end of the table. In the European tradition, men and women are seated next to one another, and couples are often broken up and seated next to people they may not have previously known. This is done to promote conversation. Men typically rise when women enter the room, and continue to hold doors for women and allow them to enter a room first. Remember, as is the case throughout the region, the first floor (*PB,* or *planta baja*) is really the second floor, with the first floor usually referred to as the lobby or ground floor.

Refills and Seconds

If you do not want more food, or cannot eat everything on your plate, it is okay to leave some food on your plate, but try to eat most of it (wasting food is not appreciated). If serving yourself family style, take only what you will eat. You may always have additional beverages; drink enough to cause your cup or glass to be less than half full, and it will generally be refilled. Portions are generally equal to or greater than those in the United States, especially when it comes to rice.

At Home, in a Restaurant, or at Work

In informal restaurants, you will rarely be required to share a table. Waitstaff may be summoned by making eye contact; waving or calling their names is very impolite. The business breakfast is not common, although you do see it creeping into the business life of the major cities slowly. The business lunch (more common than dinner) and dinner are very acceptable, but, depending on how well developed your relationship is with your Dominican colleagues, they are generally not times to make business decisions. Take your cue from your Dominican associates: if they bring up business, then it's okay to discuss it (more often than not, over the coffee and brandy at the end of the meal), but wait to take your lead from their conversation. No gum chewing, *ever,* at a restaurant or on the street. No-smoking sections in restaurants are still a rarity.

Meals at home are typically informal affairs, and people who drop by at mealtimes are always expected to have a bite and stay a while if they can. When you are invited to a Dominican associate's home, do not wander from room to room; much of the house is really off-limits to guests. Use the toilet before you arrive, as it is considered bad form to leave the table before the meal is over. If it is a formal meal, once you (and the group) are invited to another room, most probably the dining room, be sure to allow more senior members of your party to enter the room ahead of you: men should move aside to allow women to enter the room ahead of them. In a private home, be careful about what and how you admire things: the host may feel obliged to give it to you, and this could be a great inconvenience. If you invite people to your home, be prepared to always have the invitation accepted, although they may not, in fact, show up; rejecting the invitation is difficult for Dominicans, who seek to not offend. They may indicate their true intentions by simply responding to your invitation with "I will try."

Being a Good Guest or Host

Paying the Bill

Usually the one who does the inviting pays the bill, although the guest is expected to make an effort to pay. Sometimes other circumstances determine who pays (such as rank). Making payment arrangements ahead of time so that no exchange occurs at the table is a very classy way to host. Women, if out with men, will not really be able to pay the bill at a restaurant; if you want to, make arrangements ahead of time, and don't wait for the check to arrive at the table. The only time it is considered appropriate for a woman to pay the bill is if she is a hosting businesswoman from abroad. If a businesswoman invites a Dominican businessman to a meal, she should be sure to extend the invitation to his spouse as well, or may want to consider telling him that her (female) colleague will also be joining them (and be sure to have a female colleague along). Do not allow the Dominican male to suggest bringing one of his colleagues along (remember, the person doing the inviting can refuse the suggestion). If a Dominican male invites a businesswoman to a meeting or a meal that seems to have more than business as the subject, a businesswoman should always insist that she bring her female associate along (someone who is needed because of her role in the company); if you are a businesswoman making your first business trip to the Dominican Republic and have not yet established a relationship with your Dominican male counterparts, you are strongly advised to bring a female business associate along on the trip. Unmarried businesswomen may want to consider wearing a wedding band. If you have children, be sure to discuss that fact at some point early in the initial conversations: any aggressive macho behavior usually stops when men learn they are dealing with a *madre*.

Transportation

It's a very nice idea, when acting as the host, to inquire ahead of time as to whether your guests will require transportation. If necessary, you should arrange for taxi service at the end of the meal. When the cars arrive, be sure not to leave your spot until your guests are out of sight.

When to Arrive / Chores to Do

If invited to dinner at a private, upper-class home, do not offer to help with the chores, nor should you expect to visit the kitchen. Upper-class Dominicans often have household help for the kitchen chores. Do not leave the table unless invited to do so. Spouses typically do not attend business dinners without a special invitation to do so. You may be invited into a Dominican home fairly quickly. Be sure to reciprocate by hosting your colleague in your home when and if he or she comes to your country or at a nice restaurant on another night of your trip.

Gift Giving

In general, gift giving is not common in business, although it is nice to bring a small gift from abroad if you are revisiting a business acquaintance (as, at this point, they have probably become a friend). One exception: as is the case throughout most of Latin America, some chocolates or a small gift for the secretary of the person you are visiting can work wonders for future smooth sailing! If a man is giving a gift to a woman in a business setting, it is important to present it as a gift to her from his wife or sister. Holiday cards are very appropriate, particularly as a thank-you for your Dominican colleagues' business in the previous year, and should be mailed in time to be received the week before Christmas. Dominicans celebrate Three Kings Day (as all Latin American cultures do), January 6, as the time for holiday gift giving.

Gifts are not expected if you are invited to a dinner or social event, although it is nice to bring something appropriate along. The best gift for these occasions is wine, chocolates or a dessert pastry, or something for the children. Avoid flowers (they are already abundant). Gifts are generally opened at the time they are given and received.

Special Holidays and Celebrations

Major Holidays

August is a leading vacation time, and business slows down from December 15 to January 6. Holy Week is sometimes a more difficult time in which to accomplish work than Christmas. In addition, there are many regional fiestas and saints' days throughout the year that usually close down businesses for a day or two; check with your local contacts. As you establish personal relationships with your Dominican colleagues, you may be invited to special family events, such as a wedding or a baptism; be sure to go, and bring an appropriate gift.

January 1	*Año Nuevo* (New Year's Day)
January 6	*Día de los Reyes* (Three Kings Day; this is the gift-giving day, not Christmas)
January 21	Our Lady of High Gratitude Day
January 26	Duarte's Birthday (founder of the independent Dominican nation)
February/March	*Carnaval* (a special time just before Lent, celebrated with outrageous street pageants, pranks, and partying: do not wear anything you cannot afford to lose or get wet, painted on, etc.)
February 27	Independence Day

March/April	*Semana Santa/Pasqua* (Holy Week and Easter)
May 1	*Día del Trabajo* (Labor Day)
August 16	Corpus Christi / Restoration of Independence Day
September 24	Our Lady of Mercies Day
October 12	*Día de Cristóbal Colón* (Columbus Day)
December 25	*Navidad* (Christmas Day)

Business Culture

Daily Office Protocols

It is not common for women to attain positions of authority in the Dominican Republic; in the traditional Dominican workplace, women are usually relegated to lower-level management and administrative support positions. Women do struggle to reach the same levels of achievement as their male counterparts in Dominican business, and it is rare (though not impossible) to see women at the highest levels of business and government in the Dominican Republic.

People organize their time on a daily basis according to the tasks they must accomplish, and the relationships they must depend upon in order to accomplish these tasks; the clock takes a backseat. Therefore, the day may begin slowly, but there can be much activity by day's end, and people often stay late in the office in order to finish up what needs to be done. This pattern repeats itself over larger blocks of time in regard to the accomplishment of projects and the meeting of deadlines.

Management Styles

Gathering the information required in order to do what your boss expects from you, or creating consensus among your colleagues in order to accomplish a particular goal, can take a long time. All of this occurs in a formal and sometimes very rigid hierarchical structure, which means that deadlines and efficiency are secondary to attention to detail, perfection of form, bureaucratic requirements, and the need to be clever in the face of limited resources in order to be effective. Titles are very important, and the highest ones (e.g., vice president) are usually reserved for very senior, executive-level positions, and should not be used as casually as they are in the United States. Complimenting and rewarding employees publicly is usually not done. For non-Dominicans, it can be important to have a local contact who can tell you what is really going on after you return home, and to have a local intermediary—as well as a local lawyer and *notario* (a very responsible administrative position throughout much of Latin America)—to act as a liaison for you with the people you need to see while you are there. This needs to be set up ahead of time.

Boss-Subordinate Relations

Rank most definitely has its privileges in the Dominican Republic. Pride and self-importance require that Dominicans always do business with the most important people in any organization (and this should be the same for the non-Dominican working with them). Bosses are expected to provide guidance, distribute information, and make decisions; subordinates are expected to provide detailed information and follow the decisions made by the superiors.

Conducting a Meeting or Presentation

At meetings of peers, there can be open communication and sharing of ideas; in fact, these sessions often serve as information-sharing and decision-making forums in which all individuals are expected to contribute. Under these circumstances, discussions are usually vibrant, with many people speaking at once; questions are common and interruptions, even of presentations, should be expected. In more formal, conservative organizations, meetings are often gatherings of nonpeers, clearly called together by decision makers in order to gather information from below, clarify goals, and formulate action plans. In these cases, individuals often do not share ideas and are not expected to contribute to mutual problem solving. Remember, because a close personal relationship is often demonstrated through physicality in Latin cultures, the nearer your Dominican colleagues are to you, typically, the better they are responding to your proposal.

Negotiation Styles

Dominicans generally play their cards close to the vest; they do not divulge information easily (it is seen as the source of power). They will respect someone who comes to them with already established knowledge and experience, and will build relationships based on your position in society and the organization. Whether you are worth knowing and doing business with may be more important than the details of your proposal. Nevertheless, details are important, and a carefully planned, logically organized, and beautifully presented proposal is key. Bargaining is the essence of the negotiation, as a way to build trust; therefore, be reasonable, but do not overcompromise, as this shows weakness.

The first meeting is usually formal, with the Dominicans sizing up you and your organization: it will be conducted in the office. Although the contract must be legal down to the dotted i's, it really is just a formality to the Dominicans and can be overcome, by either party, if such a need arises later on. Plan your meetings as carefully and as well in advance as you can, but expect changes. The goal, at least for the first meeting, is the development of a good feeling of respect and mutual trust. Remember also that the meeting might start and end much later than you anticipated; nevertheless, as in most polychronic cultures, you should always arrive on time. Coffee is the universal greeting; always accept it, always serve it (in nice china, never in Styrofoam), and drink as much or as little as you can or desire. It is the gesture of acceptance and appreciation that counts (never refuse coffee, or an invitation to go with your colleague to a café and have some). As is the case throughout most of Latin America, if you are hosting at a restaurant, choose the finest restaurant you can, at least for the first (and last) meeting; by the same token, stay at the best hotel you can: these things carry prestige and will signal that you are someone worth doing business with.

Written Correspondence

Business letters can be very formal and respectful of hierarchy. Last names are usually written in uppercase; dates are given using the day/month/year format (with periods in between, not slashes); and an honorific plus a title is as common as an honorific plus the last name. The time of day is written in military time; weights and measures are given in metric measurements. Monetary amounts are written so that the period breaks up the figure into tens, hundreds, and thousands, and the comma separates the pesos from the centavos.

Be sure to inquire first, in all communications, about your colleague's health and progress, then move on to the substance of your communication, and close with a salutation and your personal wishes for his or her success and well-being (the Latin communication "sandwich"). Some important business abbreviations: "S.A." means "incorporated," a *cia* is a company, and EE.UU. is the abbreviation for the United States. If your colleagues write to you in Spanish, try to respond in Spanish, if you can, or use the services of a translator. Written addresses are usually in the following format:

Line 1: name
Line 2: title/position
Line 3: company
Line 4: street address
Line 5: city, state

PUERTO RICO

Note: Refer to the previous section on the Dominican Republic for information about general Hispanic-African Caribbean and Latin American cultural behaviors; the material that follows describes specific Puerto Rican variations on general Hispanic-African Caribbean and Latin American customs.

Some Introductory Background on Puerto Rico and the Puerto Ricans

Puerto Rico, unique among most of the Caribbean (and much of the rest of the world), is a culture still in colonial status: it is technically a commonwealth of the United States. As is the case with many of the islands in the Caribbean, it was "discovered" by Christopher Columbus, and was subsequently subsumed into the Spanish Empire through the conquest. The original inhabitants were the indigenous Taino people, who were quickly either killed or enslaved (curiously, the men were annihilated, but the women remained to continue what little there was left of the culture: today, there is still some Taino heritage and blood in the Puerto Rican population). Puerto Rico became an entrepot for the slave trade, with the slaves mainly working the sugarcane fields. In 1897, Spain granted self rule to Puerto Rico, and Luis Muñoz Rivera became governor. The United States invaded a few years later during the Spanish-American War, dismissing the Spanish "protectors," and Puerto Rico officially became a U.S. territory. It wasn't until 1952 that it became a commonwealth of the United States, and very quickly opposition to this status erupted, both on the island and in the United States (several congressmen were shot during a disturbance over this issue in the U.S. Congress in 1954). The status of the island today is a source of major political debate. Several plebescites have been held, asking the population to decide whether to remain a commonwealth, become a U.S. state, or declare independence as a separate or affiliated Republic; as of this writing, maintaining the current status narrowly won in the last plebescite. Political parties on the island mainly reflect these three positions. Unless and until one has a clear understanding of the repercussions of any of these positions, it is best to avoid stating an opinion about any of them when speaking with Puerto Ricans. Puertoriqueños are sensitive, warm, and easily offended by individuals, particularly "mainlanders" (the term used to describe U.S. citizens from the fifty states) who state opinions about their status, one way or the other.

It is important to note that nearly one-third of the population lives in New York City; in fact, many Puerto Ricans move to New York, and develop a life with the goal of returning back to the island some day (many do; many do not). These people are referred to as *Newyoricans.*

Greetings and Introductions

Language and Basic Vocabulary

Because both English and Spanish are spoken (both are currently official languages of the island), there is a unique local blending of the two, known as *Spanglish.*

Honorifics for Men, Women, and Children

It is interesting to note that women on the island do not typically take their husband's name after marriage. Also, in terms of names, as is the case with much of the rest of the region, people use both their father and mother's family names in formal address, but may also carry two given names (using both the first and "middle" name): it is important if introduced to someone with two "first" names to use both of them: ("Teresa Maria" must never be shortened to just "Teresa").

Communication Styles

Socializing with friends and family is the main source of pleasure in life, and it is typically informal and relaxed; friends often drop in (sometimes unannounced) in the early evening for an hour or so to chat. Extended family members typically live very close to one another, but not necessarily under the same roof.

Okay Topics / Not Okay Topics

Okay: Baseball is the great national sport, and Puerto Ricans are very proud of the unique role that their culture has played in the arts: Puerto Rican music, in the form of salsa and Latin jazz, is world-renowned, and Puerto Rican poetry, literature, and painting have a worldwide following. Be sure to inquire in conversation about these achievements.

Physical Gestures and Facial Expressions

Wiggling the nose generally means, "Hey, what's going on?"

Dining and Drinking

The dining schedule for the island is similar to that of North America, and the food and water, in most populated places, is fairly safe to eat and drink (it is always safer to take the precautions we have outlined throughout the book regarding food and water in the region, however, especially in the countryside). Rice and beans is the universal dish, but *arroz con pollo* (rice and chicken) is a close second, and fried vegetables (*frituras*), sometimes mixed with meats (*alcapurrias,* or plantains mixed with meat), are tasty snacks and alternatives. The Puerto Rican bread eaten with all formal meals is *pan sabao.* Seafood and fish, interestingly, are not as commonly eaten as meat and vegetables.

Special Holidays and Celebrations

Major Holidays

U.S. national holidays, Puerto Rican holidays, and local fiestas (typically, celebrations of local saints) are all celebrated in Puerto Rico. The holidays in Puerto Rico are:

January 1	New Year's Day
January 6	Three Kings Day (this typically ends the three-week Christmas celebration, and is the preferred day for gift giving, at least for children)
January 11	Eugenio Maria de Hostos's Birthday
January	Martin Luther King, Jr.'s, Birthday (celebrated on the third Monday of the month)
February/March	*Carnaval* (just before the beginning of Lent—this is a major celebration time with street parades of *vejigantes,* or monsters, usually made out of papier-mâché, wearing costumes, bells, and decorations; they "threaten" the celebrants on the streets, and, in turn, children try to steal the bells off their costumes. Great fun for all!)
March 22	The Abolition of Slavery
March/April	Easter (Holy Week is very special in Puerto Rico, and there is generally a weeklong slowdown between Palm Sunday and Easter Sunday)
April	José Diega's Birthday (celebrated on the third Monday of the month)
July 4	U.S. Independence Day

July 17	Luis Muñoz Rivera's Day
July 25	Constitution Day
July 28	José Celos Barbosa's Birthday
September	Labor Day (celebrated on the first Monday of the month)
November 2	All Souls' Day
November 19	Discovery of Puerto Rico Day
November	Thanksgiving (celebrated on the fourth Thursday of the month)
December	Christmas holidays include the tradition of *parrandas,* when groups of friends go singing door to door, and are invited into each home briefly for some food and drink.
December 25	Christmas Day

CHAPTER TEN

The Franco-African Cultures: Haiti

Some Introductory Background on Haiti and the Haitians

Haitians are familiar with the United States and things American. For one thing, their recent history has been intimately tied to the United States: There is a significant Haitian population in New York City (in fact, New York City has the largest West Indian community outside of the Caribbean in the world; London is second) and Miami, and several times in the recent past, U.S. troops have been sent to Haiti to restore order. But Haitians also look to their past history with France and Africa for their moorings. The roots of many typically Haitian behaviors and attitudes can be found in both the French and African traditions. Haiti shares the small island of Hispaniola with its neighbor, the Dominican Republic, a member of the Hispanic-African Caribbean group, and their relationship has been stormy at best. (There is a significant Haitian population living and working in the Dominican Republic, as it is, relatively speaking, still the more economically advantaged neighbor of the two countries.) Haiti is one of the world's poorest countries, with over one-third of its people living in extreme poverty; funding for health care and education is severely strained, and the base of the economy is agricultural—coffee, cocoa, sugar—producing barely enough for the people to survive (there are nearly no exports). The country is very small—smaller than Maryland—and therefore very limited in its economic potential. The challenging topography, with mountains rising dramatically out of the sea and plunging into deep, rich valleys, has kept Haitians, as a people, separated from each other, creating a strong dependency on immediate family and neighbors. In fact, southern Haiti and northern Haiti were only reunited into one nation in the nineteenth century—and this with difficulty. Complicating the economic difficulties, and no doubt a contributing factor to them, is the remarkable legacy of political instability of the country: rarely has there been leadership that has not been threatened with violent rebellion, and that period of stability that Haiti did enjoy in the mid-twentieth century was one of tyrannical and terrorist rule by the infamous François Duvalier ("Papa Doc") and his torturous secret police, the Tontons Macoutes. Nevertheless, there is a certain measured grace to the people and the country, no doubt a result of the French and African influences, and the Haitian people remain friendly, open, and generous, despite their hardships. Haitians are proud of their past, despite the difficulties of the present; they will quickly and proudly remind you that the first major revolt against slavery in the New World occurred in Haiti and was led by a Haitian.

Some Historical Context

The Arawaks and Tainos (who fought constantly whenever they came in contact with each other) occupied the island as indigenous peoples (it seems the island has always experienced an ethnic separation of one kind or another). When the Spaniards came (Christopher Columbus, in fact, was the first colonizing European for most of the Caribbean), they vanquished the Tainos and Arawaks almost immediately, and set about importing slaves from Africa for labor. Within just a few years, African slaves made up over 80 percent of the population. Spain ceded the western half of Hispaniola to France at the end of the seventeenth century, in response to European politics at the time, and within a few years, the entire island was ceded to France. With the shift, the slave population saw an opportunity, and launched the New World's first major slave revolt, led by Toussaint L'Ouverture, who is now a hero in Haiti and among many other African populations around the world; interestingly, he was captured by the French and died in prison, and the revolt succeeded under the final leadership of Jean-Jacques Dessalines. Haiti declared independence from France and Dessalines became emperor of Haiti. The slave revolt quickly spread to Santo Domingo, on the Hispanic side of the island, thereby spreading Haiti's influence over the Dominicans. This ensured a legacy of mistrust and hatred between Haitians and Dominicans that lingers even today. From Dessalines's rule forward, Haiti has experienced political insurrection after political rebellion, often with the leaders themselves being either killed or exiled, going right on through into the twentieth century, forcing the United States to intervene from time to time. Most recently, Jean-Bertrand Aristide led the country in its first democratic election, only to be ousted in a military coup. To date, the political climate remains as unstable as the economy.

An Area Briefing

Schools and Education

Schooling is compulsory through high school, and mirrors the French school system; however, in poorer rural regions and difficult urban neighborhoods, maintaining quality education and children's attendance through these grades is a challenge. Many children are pressed into working to help the family survive instead of attending school; the threat of political disturbances also keeps children from attending school. A lack of supplies and infrastructure is a serious problem. Those who can afford to do so send their children to private school, and most of the schools in Haiti are private schools. It is important to note that the school system, having French traditions, does emphasize the importance of process and conceptualization, which acts as a counterbalance to the reliance by much of the unschooled population on subjective experience and past precedence for decision making.

Religion and Demographics

The people are mainly Roman Catholic, with minority populations of Protestants, Muslims, Evangelical Protestants, Pentecostalists, and others. However, all religions, especially Catholicism, are heavily influenced by spiritualist and animist beliefs, which come out of the African traditions. The most powerful of these is voodoo, which—while officially rejected by the Catholic church—is in reality incorporated significantly into Catholic worship. Many people practice voodoo exclusively, and the superstitions and associated beliefs of voodoo (for example the cult of the zombie) are commonly held throughout the island by the majority of the population.

There is a rigid separation of the genders in Haiti, more so in the less urbanized areas; women mainly sell the crops and wares in the market, while men work the fields and at manufacturing jobs in small shops. Women do hold "two jobs"— that of homemaker and societal nurturer, as well as the seller of goods in the marketplace. Machismo is strong in Haitian society; many men have children by several different women, and the divorce rate is high. The society is highly stratified, with a very small urban elite of wealthy, politically influential families; the rest of the country struggles in extreme poverty. There is virtually no middle class, and rural and urban people often do live in two separate worlds.

Fundamental Cultural Orientations

1. What's the Best Way for People to Relate to One Another?

OTHER-INDEPENDENT OR OTHER-DEPENDENT?   As is the case with most countries in the region—due, in part, to the heavy influence of Roman Catholicism and African traditions—Haitian behavior is often significantly "other-dependent." Constant political and economic instability reinforces this orientation and most individuals will seek, either formally or informally, the opinions and support of family, friends, and coworkers before venturing off to do or say something on their own. People are most comfortable in the "bosom" of others, and individuals are simply not part of society unless they can claim membership to or affiliation with some group, neighborhood, town, or business organization. The extended family, including cousins, aunts, and uncles, typically lives under one roof, or very nearby (there is sometimes no distinction made between members of the nuclear family and the extended family members, and typically even married children live with parents under the same roof). A consequence of this, of course, is a resistance to the outsider, and a need for all outsiders to become associated with members of the in-group as soon as possible in order to be accepted. In Haiti, to be alone is to be sad and vulnerable. People typically stop in to socialize with each other throughout the day: this form of visiting is, in fact, the primary socializing activity.

HIERARCHY-ORIENTED OR EGALITY-ORIENTED? Roman Catholic hierarchy and the emphasis that French culture places on organization and structure have combined in Haiti to play a powerful role in determining individual roles in society. Society is rigidly stratified, with the poor on the bottom and the very small controlling elite at the top. Egalitarian traditions are weak, although distinctions between roles, it should be noted, are not made along racial lines (as is the case in much of Latin America), since virtually all people, poor or elite, are descendants of African slaves.

RULE-ORIENTED OR RELATIONSHIP-ORIENTED? The circumvention of rules by those clever enough or with connections is a way of life. No system of rules was ever beneficial to the population, and African traditions strongly emphasize the need for relationship and consensus-building among all people involved in an issue. Most of the time, the way one circumvented the authorities was to rely on the only true source of dependability in an otherwise cruel and difficult world: one's family, proven friends, and loyal business associates. Therefore, relationships—not rules—rule. Situations, if involving the right people and the right issues, will almost always determine the behaviors of individuals, not bland laws or bureaucratic fiats. This leads to corruption on a massive scale; nobody believes that the government can provide what the people need, or do so in any way that is representative of the people's interests. This cultural dependence on personal relationships means that Haitians will need time to get to know you before they will be ready to talk business. In fact, there is little distinction made between socializing and doing business: they are often one and the same.

2. What's the Best Way to View Time?

MONOCHRONIC OR POLYCHRONIC? Time is circular, and very polychronic; more so in the rural areas. Old agrarian patterns die hard, even if people aren't waking up and heading for the fields in the morning. In rural areas, it is easiest to work in the fields in the cool of the early morning and late afternoon; the midday heat is usually too oppressive, and provides a good opportunity to stoke up on a filling meal and take a midday rest before heading back out to work until the sun sets.

RISK-TAKING OR RISK-AVERSE? Latin cultures, in general, are risk-averse, and that is one of the driving reasons for the creation of structure and hierarchies. Haiti is no exception, except for the fact that the economic and personal situation of most people is so extremely poor that oftentimes a risk does not involve the possibility of losing anything, and is therefore worth taking. However, the decision to move forward is often made after careful consultation with others whom one trusts and has confidence in (often elders or other members of the family).

PAST-ORIENTED OR FUTURE-ORIENTED? Latin American and African cultures have seen their world turned upside down more than once with their having little or no ability to control the events. Haitians can express a strong skepticism as to their ability to control their future when dealing with outsiders, but there is an equally powerful streak of self-reliance and optimism, and a belief in their own power and strength. They are proud of their past, and rely on it for the strength to work hard for the future, despite the fact that they will often attribute their current condition to the will of God.

3. What's the Best Way for Society to Work with the World at Large?

LOW-CONTEXT DIRECT OR HIGH-CONTEXT INDIRECT COMMUNICATORS?
Most Haitians are high-context communicators; nevertheless, they are demonstrative, warm, and gregarious, and they love good conversation. Once it gets going, expect forthright and direct communication. Haitians want smooth interpersonal working relationships, especially with outsiders, and may sometimes reassure you that everything is okay and that all is in order—even when it may not be. This is not based on a desire to deceive, but rather on a need to appear capable, and not to lose face in the eyes of people from cultures with great resources. It is critical, therefore, to always confirm information; to have multiple, independent, and reliable sources to verify or interpret what you are being told; and to be able to read between the lines. Once relationships are established, Haitians, in the best French tradition, can speak their mind, and in the best African tradition, use language artistically and metaphorically, to add color, emphasis, and beauty to what is being said.

PROCESS-ORIENTED OR RESULT-ORIENTED? In the French tradition, there is a strong reliance on the deductive process; how things are being done is as important as the final result. However, Haitians are also very subjective, and will often fall back on what they personally believe or have experienced, even if it is counter to the evidence or deductive logic, in order to make or justify a decision. Because of the serious problems facing them in day-to-day life, Haitians may not be able to follow through with the actions required to put the plans in place. Yet they may be reticent to admit this or inform you when problems develop, partly because they may assume you understand this. It is therefore that much more important for non-Haitians to stay involved with them, helping them to implement what has been agreed to.

FORMAL OR INFORMAL? Haitian culture is relationship-oriented, in a slightly formalized way. This does not mean it is unrelaxed; it is very casual. However, roles are more clearly prescribed and the responsibilities between individuals are often seen as obligations. This need to establish formal roles between people even extends to the way individuals greet each other: respect must be demonstrated for age, gender, and relationships (for example, even children who are unrelated to certain adults will refer to them as "auntie" or "uncle"). This is, unsurprisingly, in keeping with more formal French and African traditions. This is never artificial or contrived; in fact, it is often loving and spontaneous. Nevertheless, once roles are clear and honored, interactions are often very casual and relaxed.

Greetings and Introductions

Language and Basic Vocabulary

Creole (specifically, Haitian Creole, which is a mix of certain African languages and French) is the day-to-day language, with French being the language of business and government. More and more people are beginning to understand English through the media and visits to relatives in the United States. Certainly, if you know any Caribbean Patois, use it, and if you speak French, of course use it; doing so will help you to advance your relationships more quickly.

Honorifics for Men, Women, and Children

You must use *monsieur* (Mr.) and *madame* (Ms. or Mrs.) plus the family name when introduced to anyone of importance or rank, or individuals whom you want to show particular respect or admiration, and this is certainly the case in all business encounters. In all other situations, it is perfectly okay to refer to people by their first names, and without a title. (*Mademoiselle*—Miss—is still required for a young, unmarried woman.) If you do not know whether a woman is married, use Madame (as you would in France) for anyone who is not obviously very young. Married women are not necessarily "safe" from machismo, so wearing a wedding band does not always protect a woman alone; however, being a mother virtually ensures that a man will remain at a distance: bring pictures of your children. In situations where a title is known or used, the honorific plus the title is usually employed, either with or without the name (e.g., Monsieur l'Avocat, or Monsieur Avocat Ducasse). For casual contacts (e.g., with waiters, store help, etc.), just use *monsieur* or *mademoiselle* without the name, but always use the honorific. It is very important to greet people you pass on the street, at work, in stores, and restaurants with an appropriate greeting (*bonjour,* or *bonjour, kouman ou ye?*—hello, how are you?). If you speak any French at all, it is important to use it, but be sure to use the formal pronoun, *vous,* at the beginning and do not switch to the *tu* (informal "you") form unless and until your Haitian colleague has specifically invited you to or does so him- or herself (which may be rather quickly).

Women when they marry often keep their family name.

The What, When, and How of Introducing People

In most formal situations, it is okay to introduce yourself to others, if you have not been introduced to them by a third party. In the latter case, you will be introduced to women first, then the most senior men. Similarly, do not presume to seat yourself at a formal gathering at first, but if you are not shown a seat, then, after allowing seniors and women to select a seat, go ahead and select one for yourself. Shake hands with everyone individually in a group when being introduced and before departing: the U.S. group wave is not appreciated in formal settings. It is very important to greet people whenever the opportunity arises, and this means not only at social gatherings, but even when passing strangers on the street. You can simply nod your head in an upward fashion, but it is better to say *bonjour.* Avoid ending any introductory conversation with the expression "Have a nice day": it sounds insincere. Kissing is a common greeting once you have established a strong relationship, whether between women or men and women; it usually consists of one kiss on one cheek. It is not uncommon to see women and women (but typically not men and men) walking arm in arm down the street; they are good close friends or family, and if your arm is taken, it is a sign of friendship.

Physical Greeting Styles

The handshake is common. The Haitian version is firm between two men, not as robust between men and women or two women. The handshake should be accompanied by an appropriate greeting. Men should wait until the woman extends her hand before reaching for it, and women may take the lead in extending their hand or not. Between family, friends, or trusted business associates, an extra touch on the elbow, a hug, and an embrace similar to the Hispanic *abrazo* will generally occur. This can happen as soon as the second meeting; do not initiate it, but respond warmly in kind if it is initiated with you. Eye contact during the introduction is important, and should be maintained as long as the individual is addressing you.

The use of business cards is common; if possible, you should have your business card translated into French on the reverse. Be sure to put any advanced educational degrees and your full title or position on either side of your business card. Such emblems of your status are very important to Haitians, especially if you are from the United States or New York: they want to know they are doing business with an important person.

Communication Styles

Okay Topics / Not Okay Topics

Okay: soccer, life in your country, the gorgeous weather, your family, food, relatives in New York City or Miami, politics back home, and Haitian music. *Not okay:* Do not inquire about a person's occupation or income in casual conversation, although that, and other personal matters, may be inquired of you. Americans often begin a conversation with "So, what do you do?"; this is too personal in Haiti. Do not give your opinions about Haitian politics or the economy unless you really know what you are talking about; do not compare Haitians with Dominicans, and do not disparage Haitian relations with the Dominican Republic. Do not talk about your Latin American tummy; keep your health issues to yourself, because no one wants to hear about them. Although you may inquire honestly regarding voodoo, offer no opinions, and be prepared for the question to be deflected. Do not try to attend a voodoo ceremony on your own, as many are intentionally private events, and uninvited visitors are truly unwelcome. Also not okay: money and inquiring about *private* family matters (although speaking about the health and other general aspects of family life is very important). Do not go to Haiti (or anywhere in Latin America) without pictures of your family, and when family is brought up (which it will be almost immediately in the conversation), use it as an opportunity to bring out the photographs. Never tell a dirty joke with a woman present.

Tone, Volume, and Speed

Discussions can quickly become animated and very lively, depending upon the nature of the discussion and the circumstances of the developing relationship. Haitians can speak very loudly and very quickly, and laugh loudly, in general conversation. None of this should be taken as a sign of aggression or displeasure. You will know when they are angry. Conversation is an art: it is enjoyed, savored, and commented upon.

Use of Silence

In general, silence doesn't happen. Enjoy the simultaneous conversations and frequent interruptions that usually define Haitian conversation style.

Physical Gestures and Facial Expressions

Typically, indicating direction or selecting something is done with the lips: you pucker your lips and make a slight head movement in the direction of the object you are referring to. If you want to indicate that you don't like someone or something, you point with your lips as discussed above while rolling your eyes. If you wrinkle your nose in response to something, it means you do not understand it. Rubbing the tips of your index finger and thumb together indicates money. People will *psst* at you when they want your attention, and oftentimes in conversations, there can be a tap on the shoulder and much touching: this typically indicates friendship.

Waving and Counting

The thumb represents the number 1, the index finger the number 2, and so on. It is insulting to beckon someone with the forefinger. Nevertheless, when Haitians want to make a point, they can wag their finger in close proximity to your face. Waving or beckoning is done with the palm down and the fingers moving forward and back in a kind of scratching motion. If you need to gesture for a waiter, subtly raise your hand; never click, call, or whistle.

Physicality and Physical Space

Haitians tend to get closer than North Americans are generally comfortable with. Resist the urge to step back when your Haitian associate steps forward. Haitian men may often touch each other during conversations, adjust each other's shirt, dust off each other's shoulders, and the like. Never speak with your hands in your pockets; always keep them firmly at your side when standing. If men and women must cross their legs, it should never be ankle over knee (the preferred style for women is to cross ankle over ankle). Remember, even in public, formal is always better than informal. No gum chewing, *ever;* no slouching; no leaning against things.

Eye Contact

Eye contact can be direct, and at times may be disconcerting for many Americans. It is important not to interpret this behavior as a way of intentionally trying to make you uncomfortable. It is the way Haitians show their interest. Conversely, if you look away, your behavior will say to your Haitian colleague that you are disinterested, rude, or establishing yourself as the subordinate in a hierarchical relationship; none of these is a good idea.

Emotive Orientation

Haitians are often animated and physically expressive. Join in if you like, but keep cool if you can. Always remain warm, open, and personable.

Protocol in Public

Walking Styles and Waiting in Lines

Don't be too distressed if someone walks right up to the front of the line at a bank, a restaurant, or a store, and gets served because of the relationship he or she has with the clerk, while you have been waiting patiently in line for forty minutes. People also have a tendency to stand very close in public; this may feel uncomfortable at first. Resist the urge to back away; most of the time, you are not being intentionally crowded. Remember, the need to appear helpful and courteous is strong, and if you ask for directions on the street, you will no doubt be instructed on just where to go . . . whether or not the individual actually knows!

Behavior in Public Places: Airports, Terminals, and the Market

Most stores are closed on Sundays, and many small stores close each day either at midday for lunch and a short siesta or around 3 or 4 P.M. Personally thanking store owners, waiters, chefs, and hotel managers for their services is very much appreciated. In food markets, you can touch the produce; in goods stores, it may be difficult to return a product unless there is a flaw in it. Because of the personal nature of the culture, even money is usually exchanged in the palms, not on the counter. In addition, in most small shops and in markets, bargaining is very much expected. If you don't bargain well, that's okay; put a smile on your face and ask for half of what the listed price is. Stick to it, walk away if you have to, and you'll land somewhere in between. Never get angry, though, since bargaining is a game to get to know you, and is supposed to make shopping a more pleasant experience. Always offer a fair price, as the amount you pay goes toward the support of a family.

Because of the high poverty rate, small children and women may approach you on the street or come up to your taxi window to ask for money. It is always difficult deciding whether or not to give, but remember that the social support systems are negligible, and this is often the only way for these people to sustain themselves. Smoking is pervasive, and if you do smoke, be sure to always offer a cigarette to everyone you are talking to before you light up. In bathrooms, on the plumbing "C" means hot (*chaud*) and "F" means cold (*froid*).

Bus / Metro / Taxi / Car

Driving is on the right, but people pass very quickly on the left. Driving is not risky in the sense that there are virtually no private cars on the road (people simply do not own them), but is risky in the sense that roads are usually in disrepair, driving at night is treacherous, and many people are walking on the roads all the time and do not anticipate cars. There are no metros, but *tap-taps,* or cars or vans that follow specific routes, ferry people about; they are always crowded. Believe it or not, most people get around simply by walking from place to place. If you need a taxi, they are best found at designated taxi stands (hotels are good places, but often charge more for the same ride: a hotel surcharge is added to the meter fare). The crime situation in areas where visitors typically travel is minimal, mostly petty crime in the tourist areas.

Tipping

The equivalent of one U.S. dollar or so is usually sufficient in restaurants and taxis. Porters and hotel help get the equivalent in *gourdes* (the Haitian currency) of one U.S. dollar per item or service rendered (and in both cases, tipping in

U.S. dollars, as is done throughout much of the region, is perfectly fine, actually preferred). Please double-check the current dollar/gourde exchange rate, as it can vary quickly and significantly.

Punctuality

It is perfectly acceptable—in fact, essential—to arrive for social events about an hour late. If you arrive sooner, you will be running the risk of interrupting the host or hostess as he or she gets ready. For business meetings, being late by five to fifteen minutes or more is usually not a problem, but it is safer for the new employee or visitor to be on time, while not being surprised if others are not. Usually, the meeting will not begin in earnest until all attendees have arrived (or at least until all the decision makers have shown up), and this may not correspond to the time listed in the agenda. Resist questioning the late ones for a reason; they always have one, usually involving an obligation with more important people, like superiors, old friends, or family.

Dress

Being clean and well-groomed and dressing with respect for yourself and others is important whenever possible (understand that rampant poverty can make this even basic requirement difficult). Casual wear includes jeans and skirts (dresses and blouses in the countryside); even T-shirts and sneakers are okay if they are in good condition and neat and clean. Business dress includes suits and ties for men, dresses and blouses for women; women in particular wear colorful clothes (often with head wraps in the same fabric), and jewelry—especially gold—for both men and women is a real status symbol.

Personal Hygiene

In Haiti, it is very important to be clean and neat whenever possible. Note that most rest room and bathroom facilities throughout Haiti, where they exist, do not have plumbing capable of handling paper toilet tissue; it is for this reason that there is a small receptacle next to the toilet for your used tissue: do not flush it down the bowl, but place it in the receptacle, or else you'll face the embarrassment of having to call for help when the bowl overflows. Take paper tissue with you if you travel about. Remember also that the water in showers may be heated by a little electrical device placed above the showerhead: never touch it or any metal when wet!

Dining and Drinking

Mealtimes and Typical Foods

Breakfast (*le petit dejeuner*) is served from about 7:30 to 9 A.M., and usually consists of some bread (usually *cassave,* which is bread made with manioc root) and coffee. Coffee in the morning can be strong and black, or with hot milk (*café au lait*). Many Haitians have two meals per day, the second after breakfast either being lunch or dinner.

Lunch (*le dejeuner*) was traditionally the main meal of the day; and even today, in busy cities, it can still be the main meal. It certainly is in rural areas. Lunch is usually served from noon to 2 P.M. It usually consists of rice and beans, which is eaten practically every day. Typically some vegetables, such as yucca and plantains, and some meat or chicken are also served. Haitians like spiced foods (watch out for the *piman zwazo,* or small, fiery peppers that are served with most dishes), so dishes are often highly seasoned or marinated. Pork is the most popular meat, but almost any kind of available meat is used. Goat is a close second in preference. Some seafood is eaten, and there are wonderful tropical fruits for dessert. On Sunday, the family day, the main meal is supper, which is usually served at lunchtime and can last well into the evening.

Dinner (*le dîner*) is served from 6:30 P.M. on, if at all. It is typically a light meal, especially if lunch was the heavier, main meal of the day, and consists of the same kinds of foods served at lunch. Drinks served with dinner are usually beer, water, fruit juices, or soft drinks. If there are guests, the meal will also generally end with coffee.

Be very careful about the places you go to eat: if they don't look safe or clean, you should avoid them. Do not eat food off the street from the street stalls: this can be very dangerous to your health. Be very careful about food and drink in Haiti (and throughout Latin America); there are dangerous bugs around. First, the water: Do not drink tap water anywhere (except where *officially* noted as safe, sterilized, or "electrified"). This means no ice in any drinks (ice cubes may be made from tap water). Close your mouth in the shower in the morning, and brush your teeth with bottled water. Drink only bottled water and soft drinks from bottles with intact seals opened in front of you; the fruit juices in Haiti are wonderful, but until your digestive system has adjusted, avoid them: they may have been diluted with water from the tap. Coffee and tea are generally okay, because the water is boiled first. Avoid fresh dairy products, including milk, custards, mayonnaise, and ice cream, because they all usually require refrigeration, which may be questionable in certain parts of Haiti. Definitely avoid raw shellfish and raw fish, and do not eat any raw or uncooked vegetables or fruits, unless you can peel them; this means no green salad. You will inevitably get the Latin American tummy on your first few trips . . . it is hard to avoid a drop of water here or there. If you have followed the above rules carefully, it is probably nothing to worry about; it will be uncomfortable for a day or two. Eat lightly, drink lots of safe fluids, stay in or near your room, rest, and it will pass. If a fever or vomiting develops, be sure to seek medical attention immediately.

Typical Drinks and Toasting

Beer, rum, fruit juice, and soft drinks are the drinks of choice. There are also some local brandies made from sugarcane, which can vary from mild to incredibly strong (be warned), and which may be offered; usually these are home-brews. The most common toast is *salud* (to your health).

Table Manners and the Use of Utensils

Do not begin eating until the host says, *"Bon appetit!"* Knives and forks are used the European way (the knife remains in the right hand, and the fork remains in the left throughout the meal). When the meal is finished, the knife and fork are laid parallel to each other across the right side of the plate. If you put both utensils down on the plate for any real length of time, it is a sign to the waitstaff that you are finished, and your plate may be taken away from you.

When not holding utensils, your hands are expected to be visible above the table: this means you do not keep them in your lap; instead, rest the wrists on top of the table (never the elbows). At the table, pass all dishes to your left. Meals in both restaurants and private homes are often served family style. Take as much as you are offered, but eat all that you take. Leaving food uneaten is wasteful. Be sensitive to the fact that as a guest, you will always encouraged to take more, even if your doing so might be a sacrifice for the family.

Seating Plans

The most honored position is at the head of the table, with the most important guest seated immediately to the right of the host (women to the right of the host, and men to the right of the hostess). If there is a hosting couple, one will be at each end of the table. In the European tradition, men and women are seated next to one another, and couples are often broken up and seated next to people they may not have previously known. This is done to promote conversation. Men typically rise when women enter the room, and continue to hold doors for women and allow them to enter a room first. Remember, in buildings, the first floor is really the second floor, with the first floor usually referred to as the lobby or ground floor.

At Home, in a Restaurant, or at Work

In informal restaurants, you may be required to share a table. Waitstaff may be summoned by making eye contact; waving or calling their names is very impolite. Any meal is an opportunity for business, and vice versa, although while eating is generally not the time to make business decisions. Take your cue from your Haitian associates: if they bring up business, then it's okay to discuss it (more often than not, over the coffee at the end of the meal), but wait to take your lead from their conversation. No gum chewing, *ever,* at a restaurant or on the street. No-smoking sections in restaurants are still a rarity.

Meals at home are typically informal affairs, and people who drop by at mealtimes are always expected to have a bite and stay a while if they can. When you are invited to your Haitian colleague's home, do not wander from room to room; much of the house is really off-limits to guests. Use the toilet before you arrive, as it is considered bad form to leave the table during the meal. If it is a formal meal, once you (and the group) are invited to the table, be sure to allow more senior members of your party to enter ahead of you: men should move aside to allow women to enter ahead of them. In a private home, be careful about what and how you admire things: the host may feel obliged to give it to you, and this could be a great inconvenience. If you invite people to your home, be prepared to always have the invitation accepted, although they may not, in fact, show up; rejecting the invitation is difficult for Haitians, who seek to not offend, and they may be very uncomfortable about coming into your home. They may indicate their true intentions by simply responding to your invitation with "I will try."

Being a Good Guest or Host

Paying the Bill

Usually the one who does the inviting pays the bill, although the guest is expected to make an effort to pay. Sometimes other circumstances determine who pays (such as rank). Making payment arrangements ahead of time so that no exchange occurs at the table is a very classy way to host. Women, when out with men, will not really be able to pay the bill at a restaurant: if you want to, make arrangements ahead of time, and don't wait for the check to arrive at the table. The only time it is considered appropriate for a woman to do this is if she is a hosting businesswoman from abroad. Women should not host Haitian men at a business meal without another woman associate present.

When to Arrive / Chores to Do

If invited into a private, upper-class home for a formal meal, do not offer to help with the chores, nor should you expect to visit the kitchen. Upper-class Haitians often have household help for the kitchen chores. Do not leave the table unless you are invited to. Spouses do not attend business dinners without a special invitation to do so.

Gift Giving

In general, gift giving is a common way in business to thank people for their help and to demonstrate appreciation for the relationship. It is nice to bring a small gift from abroad if you are revisiting a business acquaintance (as, at this point, they have probably become a friend), and any other important person, such as an assistant, if there is one. If a man is giving a gift to a woman in a business setting, it is important to present it as a gift to her from his wife or sister. Holiday cards are very appropriate, particularly as a thank-you for your Haitian colleagues' business in the previous year, and should be mailed in time to be received the week before Christmas.

Gifts are not expected if you are invited to a dinner or social event, although it is nice to bring something appropriate along. The best gift in this case is chocolates or a dessert pastry, something for the children, or something useful, such as small kitchen devices (non-electric), household items (towels or unusual and interesting foodstuffs), school supplies of any kind (there are always children who need them), calculators, and picture books. Avoid flowers (they are already abundant). Gifts are generally opened at the time they are given and received.

Special Holidays and Celebrations

Major Holidays

Business slows down from December 15 to January 6, and Holy Week is sometimes a more difficult time in which to accomplish work than Christmas. In addition, there are many regional fiestas and saints' days throughout the year that usually close down businesses for a day or two: check with your local contacts. As you establish personal relationships with your Haitian colleagues, you may be invited to special family events, such as a wedding or a baptism; be sure to go, and bring an appropriate gift.

January 1	*Le Jour de l'An* (New Year's Day— also Independence Day)
January 2	National Heroes' Day
January 6	Three Kings Day
February/March	*Carnaval* (carnival—a special time just before Lent, celebrated with street parades and street dancing for several days: do not wear anything you cannot afford to lose or get wet, painted on, etc.). In addition, in the countryside, from mid-January right up to Easter there are parades of *raras,* or local bands; this is in lieu of *Carnaval,* which is typically not celebrated in the countryside.
February 7	Freedom from Duvalier Day
March/April	*Pâques* (Holy Week and Easter)
May 18	Flag Day
June	*Fête Dieu* (Corpus Christi; celebrated on the first Thursday of the month)
October 15	Return of Aristide
November 2	*Fête Gede* (All Souls' Day)
December 25	*Noël* (Christmas Day)

Business Culture

Daily Office Protocols

It is not common for women to attain positions of authority in Haiti; their role outside of the home is usually limited to selling crops and wares in the marketplace. People organize their time on a daily basis according to the tasks they must accomplish, and the relationships they must depend upon in order to accomplish these tasks; the clock takes a backseat. Therefore, the day may begin slowly, but there can be much activity by day's end. This pattern repeats itself over larger blocks of time in regard to the accomplishment of projects and the meeting of deadlines.

Management Styles

For office-type businesses, gathering the information required in order to do what your boss expects from you, or creating consensus among your colleagues in order to accomplish a particular goal, can take a long time. Deadlines and efficiency are often secondary to attention to detail, perfection of form, bureaucratic requirements, and the need to be clever in the face of limited resources in order to be effective. Titles are important, and the highest ones (e.g., vice president) are usually reserved for very senior, executive-level positions, and should not be used as casually as they are in the United States. For non-Haitians it can be important to try to have a local contact who can tell you what is really going on after you return home, and to have a local intermediary—usually a local lawyer—to act as a liaison for you with the people you need to see while you are there. This needs to be set up ahead of time.

Boss-Subordinate Relations

Rank most definitely has its privileges in Haiti. Do business only with the most important people in any organization, whenever possible. Bosses are expected to provide guidance, distribute information, and make decisions; subordinates are expected to provide detailed information and follow the decisions made by their superiors.

Negotiation Styles

Haitians generally play their cards close to the vest; they do not divulge information easily (it is seen as the source of power). They will respect someone who comes to them with established knowledge and experience, and will build relationships based on your level in society and the organization. Whether you are worth knowing and doing business with may be more important than the details of your proposal. Nevertheless, details are important, and a carefully planned, logically organized, and beautifully presented proposal is key. Bargaining is the essence of the negotiation, as a way to build trust; therefore, be reasonable, but do not overcompromise, as this shows weakness; how you handle yourself as a person is, at first, more important than the terms you might offer to your Haitian colleague. Plan your meetings as carefully and as well in advance as you can, but expect changes. The goal, at least for the first meeting, is the development of a good feeling of respect and mutual trust. Remember also that the meeting might start and end much later than you anticipated; nevertheless, as in most polychronic cultures, you should always arrive on time. Coffee is the universal greeting; always accept it, always serve it, and drink as much or as little as you can or desire. It is the gesture of acceptance and appreciation that counts (never refuse coffee, or an invitation to go with your colleague to a café and have some). As is the case throughout most of Latin America, if you are hosting at a restaurant, choose the finest restaurant you can, at least for the first (and last) meeting; by the same token, stay at the best hotel you can: these things carry prestige and will signal that you are someone worth doing business with; in Haiti these choices will be automatic and apparent.

Written Correspondence

Last names are often written in uppercase; dates are given using the day/month/year format (with periods in between, not slashes); and an honorific plus a title is as common as an honorific plus the last name. The time of day is written in military time; weights and measures are usually given in metric measurements. Monetary amounts are written so that the period breaks up the figure into tens, hundreds, and thousands, and the comma separates the gourdes from the centimes. Be sure to inquire first, in all communications, about your colleague's health and progress, then move on to the substance of your communication, and close with a salutation and your personal wishes for his or her success and well-being. If your colleagues write to you in French or Creole, try to respond in French, if you can, or use the services of a translator. Written addresses are usually in the following format:

Line 1: name
Line 2: title/position
Line 3: company
Line 4: street address
Line 5: city, state

The Anglo-African Cultures: Jamaica, Barbados, and Trinidad and Tobago

JAMAICA

Some Introductory Background on Jamaica and the Jamaicans

Jamaicans are very familiar with the United States and things American, as well as Britain and things British. This is due not only to the British heritage, but to the fact that there are as many Jamaicans living outside of Jamaica (mainly in New York City and other east coast United States cities, and in London) as there are Jamaicans living on the island (over 2.5 million)! Jamaica is undoubtedly the largest English-speaking country in the Caribbean, and one of the most culturally influential; its influence—especially in the form of reggae music and Rastafarian culture—is felt throughout the rest of the Anglo-African Caribbean. Jamaicans have a strong reputation for being independent, opinionated, and risk-taking . . . some qualities that are not typically associated with Latin America. That's because Jamaicans (and the rest of the Anglo-African Caribbean world) are not Latin: their behavior, attitudes, and beliefs come from a unique combination of African and British traditions, and it sets Jamaicans apart from their Franco-African and Hispanic-African Caribbean neighbors.

Some Historical Context

The Arawaks were the primary indigenous people of the island, and they named it Xaymaca, which in Arawak means "land of wood and water." When the Spaniards came (Christopher Columbus, in fact, was the first colonizing European for most of the Caribbean), they vanquished the Arawaks almost immediately, only to lose the island to the invading British in the seventeenth century. (Officially, the invaders were from the British navy; unofficially, British pirates who roamed the Caribbean whittled away at the Spanish possession, making life miserable for both Spaniards and the indigenous natives, and softening them up for the final assault.) Once the British had established their authority, they quickly set to the business of importing slaves from Africa for labor in the sugar plantations and the manufacture of rum. By the time slavery ended in the early 1800s, a significant number of Spaniards still remained on the island, intermarrying as they did with African slaves, to create the *maroons;* today, maroon culture is quite different from the mainstream Jamaican culture, and maroons typically are thought of as a singularly autonomous group (maroons and maroon culture can be found in other parts of the south Caribbean as well, particularly along the coasts of Guyana, central America, and Venezuela). Interestingly, Jamaica also has a significant Jewish population, which traces its roots back to some of Columbus's shiphands, who were escaping the persecution of the Spanish inquisition. Although slavery was abolished, a social system was put in place on the island that still reflected significant stratification between day laborers and landowners, and this tension erupted periodically in the form of serious labor and social unrest. Norman Manley is a hero on the island, as a progressive who forced a great deal of social change. When the island finally achieved full independence in the 1960s, the fight for social and economic justice passed from Britain to two local political parties, whose competition for the people's votes often become goals, not unlike between political parties elsewhere, in and of themselves. The parties (the conservative Jamaican Labor Party and the socialist People's National Party) have instituted themselves as representatives of various neighborhoods, literally staking out ownership of communities that are beholden to them for their economic survival. The almost ganglike atmosphere of these garrison constituencies, as they are known, has highlighted the problems with the current party system and its inability to address the real underlying issues that Jamaicans face. The nature of the ganglike system itself and the frustration with its inability to solve the deeper problems are an explosive combination that periodically erupts into social unrest.

An Area Briefing

Schools and Education

Schooling is compulsory through early high school; however, in poorer rural regions and difficult urban neighborhoods, maintaining quality education and children's attendance through these grades is a challenge. Many children are pressed into working to help the family survive instead of attending school. Secondary education (after the age of twelve) is restricted to those who pass selective qualifying exams, and more and more, girls occupy these positions, while boys are relegated to the trades or unemployment. Local colleges and a university are available to students who qualify.

Religion and Demographics

Most Jamaicans are Christian, and the largest Christian denomination is the Anglican Church (the Church of England); Anglicans make up just over half the total Jamaican population, with another 5 percent being Roman Catholic, and the remaining people subscribing to other Protestant affiliations, Judaism, Islam, and Rastafarianism. (In Jamaica, the term "Christian" is typically used to define anyone who is Protestant.) African influences have integrated themselves into the practices of the churches, giving Christianity a uniquely Jamaican flavor. The Rastafarians ("Rastas," for short) are a unique Jamaican religious group, who believe that Africa is the promised land and that the late Emperor Haile

Selassie I of Ethiopia was, and is, "the living God" ("the Lion of Judah"). Some of the major Rastafarian traditions include observing the Old Testament, viewing marijuana as a sacred herb that allows the attainment of a spiritual state, and wearing dreadlocks (not cutting the hair) as a sign of group membership. Although the actual number of Rastafarians relative to the rest of the population is small, their influence both in Jamaica and culturally throughout the entire Caribbean has been profound. Because of the many different groups living on the island, there is a tolerance of spirit, at least when it comes to religious differences, among Jamaicans, which is not always found elsewhere in the region.

The demography of the island is mainly African (over 75 percent), with a significant population of Asians and a small population of Europeans (less than 5 percent). There is a separation of gender roles, more so in the less urbanized areas; women handle the traditional nurturing roles of society and men handle the business and administrative affairs, although women often operate the business in the local markets. There are, however, some Jamaican women making strides into the workplace and higher governmental positions. The separation of gender roles is reflected in a macho approach to women by many men, resulting in, among other things, "Baby Fathers" and "Baby Mothers" (respectively, fathers and mothers with children conceived out of wedlock who are often cared for by extended families). Consider too that Jamaica, like most of the region, is economically a developing nation, and struggles with all of the challenges associated with that status, including substantial poverty, inadequate and ill-serving infrastructures, and corruption.

Fundamental Cultural Orientations

1. What's the Best Way for People to Relate to One Another?

OTHER-INDEPENDENT OR OTHER-DEPENDENT? Family and friends play a powerful role in the lives of most Jamaicans; nevertheless, the deeper value system is the individual's responsibility to provide for the family and fulfill obligations to friends (and in turn achieve respect in their eyes). So while individuals seek the counsel of friends and family, they are respected not so much for staying within their orbit, but for branching out and achieving on their own. Jamaicans value hard work, individual effort, honesty, and financial security. A consequence of this, of course, is a generally quicker acceptance of the outsider, once he or she has proven themselves to be trustworthy and reliable. Individual Jamaican pride, based on one's role, achievements, and level in society, is strong, a representation of one's role in the larger society, and must always be respected.

HIERARCHY-ORIENTED OR EGALITY-ORIENTED? Certainly the younger generation, especially in the cities, feels more empowered as individuals than their elders. However, because individuals feel empowered in certain areas of life and work, there is a consistent need in Jamaican business and social life to challenge the "man," and a reluctance to automatically respect authority or structure just because it is there. This is supported by a strong tradition of labor and union strength, and a historical struggle by the working class to achieve its rights against privilege. Nevertheless, society is still stratified, with the large poorer classes on the bottom, a small middle or merchant class, and a very small elite at the top; this division is typically not reflected racially, as the majority of the population is African.

RULE-ORIENTED OR RELATIONSHIP-ORIENTED? There is an established pattern of behavior that encourages the circumvention of rules by those clever enough or with connections. Therefore, relationships—not rules—rule. Situations, if involving the right people and the right issues, will almost always determine the behaviors of individuals, not bland laws or bureaucratic fiats. This tends to lead to corruption. This cultural dependence on personal relationships means that Jamaicans will need time to get to know you before they will be ready to talk business. Attempts to discuss the terms of the deal or the immediate task at hand without having built the necessary personal trust and understanding is often a waste of time. Which takes us to our next concern.

2. What's the Best Way to View Time?

MONOCHRONIC OR POLYCHRONIC? Time is circular, and very polychronic; more so in the rural areas. Old agrarian patterns die hard, even if people aren't waking up and heading for the fields in the morning. In rural areas, it is easiest to work in the fields in the cool of the early morning and late afternoon; the midday heat is usually too oppressive, and provides a good opportunity to stoke up on a filling meal and a midday nap before heading back out to work until the sun sets. "Soon come," a common phrase, means things will happen eventually, and it is important to try not to stress about it. If you really want things to occur punctually, it is perfectly okay to identify the time as "North American," but it might not have that much of an effect.

RISK-TAKING OR RISK-AVERSE? This is one of the areas where Jamaicans differ substantially from their neighbors in the region: they can be great risk takers. There is a flexible approach to life, and when a situation is regarded as an opportunity, Jamaicans can move very quickly. They are often willing to overlook obstacles and rise to the challenge, if they perceive a possible advantage. You will often hear the phrase "No problem, man" in response to a situation requiring a decision or action, and Jamaicans will say it even when there is no immediate decision or solution in sight. Nevertheless, something eventually will be done, often more quickly than not. Jamaicans will generally not waste time with details if they perceive an advantage in moving forward, or if they believe in the relationship they have built with the individuals involved.

PAST-ORIENTED OR FUTURE-ORIENTED? Jamaicans can be future-oriented, and will often be willing to sacrifice both the difficulties and comforts of the past and present if they believe doing so will lead to a better tomorrow. While they are not blind to their difficulties, they do display a belief in their ability to change their destiny, and individuals are often held accountable for their achievements and their failings.

3. What's the Best Way for Society to Work with the World at Large?

LOW-CONTEXT DIRECT OR HIGH-CONTEXT INDIRECT COMMUNICATORS? Most Jamaicans are less high-context communicators than their neighbors in the region. They can be pointedly opinionated, and will not pass up an opportunity for a good debate. They are typically very gregarious (at least with people they have relationships with) and animated in their conversation style. They will more likely tell you the bad news than not, if there is any. As relationships are still critical to success, direct and low-context communication always occurs with sensitivity to how it impacts the individuals involved. If you have built the all-important relationship, you do not necessarily need to be concerned that you aren't getting the whole story with Jamaicans, as you will probably hear the good, the bad, and the ugly, as well as the glorious.

PROCESS-ORIENTED OR RESULT-ORIENTED?   The British tradition provides Jamaicans with a strong education in inductive logic: if you find something that works, and it has proven itself in the past, then this becomes the way for doing things in the future. This tradition, in combination with the Jamaican experience of associative thinking (that is, evaluating something by comparing it to something similar in one's past experience), results in Jamaicans' being able to move quickly with something once it is evaluated as having proven itself in past similar circumstances. There is little conceptual requirement, and combined with a willingness to take risks, predisposes Jamaicans to proven plans and precedent. Nevertheless, a serious lack of resources in what still is a developing country means that Jamaicans may not be able to follow through with the actions required to put the plans in place. Jamaicans will be very clever about making the end result happen; the way they get there, however, may be very different from the original plan.

FORMAL OR INFORMAL?   Jamaican culture is essentially informal and spontaneous. People socialize best in informal meetings on the street or in front of someone's home ("meet and greets"); business is often done in similar fashion. While schedules may be less important than the individuals and circumstances of the moment, decision making can be quick and informal.

Greetings and Introductions

Language and Basic Vocabulary

English is the primary language, but it has been so heavily influenced by African languages, syntax, and style, that a unique, rhythmic, and musical Jamaican Patois, or Creole, has developed, which, depending upon one's familiarity with it, may be almost incomprehensible to the average non-Caribbean English speaker.

Honorifics for Men, Women, and Children

Mr., Mrs., and Miss are commonly used between individuals who have not yet established personal relationships, and should be used when meeting people, socially or in business, for the first time. You may quickly be invited to use the first name, but do not presume to do so until invited. It is important to quickly add a welcome whenever using the honorific in a greeting, such as "Good morning, Mr. . . ." or "Good evening, Miss. . . ." In situations where a title is known or used, the honorific plus the title is usually employed, either with or without the name (e.g., Mr. Foreman, or Attorney Smith). For casual contact (e.g., with waiters, store help, etc.), just use Mr. or Miss without the name. It is very important to greet people you pass on the street, at work, in stores, and in restaurants with an appropriate greeting for the time of day—good morning, good afternoon, or good evening—and goodbye upon leaving (more typically, goodbye is expressed "Later," "tomorrow, then," or "Me we see you"). Once personal relationships are established, first names are typically used, and often nicknames that reflect personal attributes of the individual; don't be offended if you are referred to as "fatty," or "whitey" (if you are white—don't respond in kind, since referring to Jamaican blackness by a white person carries too much historical baggage, and risks being insulting). Sometimes nicknames are referred to as "pet names" or "yard names" when they take the form of diminutives of the original given name (e.g., "Jimmy" for Jim).

The What, When, and How of Introducing People

In most formal situations, it is okay to introduce yourself to others, if you have not been introduced to them by a third party. In the latter case, you will sometimes be introduced to women first, then the most senior men. Similarly, do not presume to seat yourself at a gathering at first, but if you are not shown a seat, then, after allowing seniors and women to select a seat, go ahead and select one for yourself. Shake hands with everyone individually in a group when being introduced and before departing; the U.S. group wave is not appreciated except in the most informal settings. Avoid ending the conversation with the U.S. expression "Have a nice day"; it sounds insincere. Kissing is a common greeting between women once they have established a strong relationship; it usually consists of a kiss on both cheeks (actually an "air kiss," first on the left side, and then the right). It is not uncommon to see women and women (but not men and men) walking arm in arm down the street; they are good close friends or family, and it usually means nothing more than that.

Physical Greeting Styles

The handshake is common, but there can be much additional physical expression to greetings. Sometimes the hand is held for a long time after it is shaken, as if to make the point of being extremely pleased to meet; additional touching, on the shoulder, arm, or body (but usually only between members of the same sex, and not between men and women) is also common. Men should wait until the woman extends her hand before reaching for it, and women may take the lead in extending their hand or not. Between family, friends, or trusted business associates, an extra touch on the elbow or a hug may occur, but rarely an embrace, especially in public. You may not want to initiate any of these extra physical gestures, but do react warmly if they are initiated with you. Eye contact during the introduction is extremely important, and should be maintained as long as the individual is addressing you.

The use of business cards is a good idea, though not essential (you may not receive one from your Jamaican business colleague, at least not at first). Go ahead and put any advanced educational degrees and your full title or position on your business card. Such emblems of your status are important sources of information for your Jamaican colleagues, although they will not necessarily be impressed only by your credentials: who you are as a person will ultimately be more important.

Communication Styles

Okay Topics / Not Okay Topics

Okay: politics, current events, anything interesting, cricket or soccer (the two national games), family, dominoes (a favorite pastime), reggae (the uniquely Jamaican contribution to music) and soca ("social calypso") music, and Jamaican food (usually very tasty and spicy). *Not okay:* Do not inquire about a person's occupation or income in casual conversation, although that, and other personal matters, may be inquired of you. Americans often begin a conversation with "So, what do you do?"; this is not necessarily bad in Jamaica, but avoid it as an opener. Do not give your opinions about poverty, women, or Jamaican politics (unless you really know what you are talking about). Do not talk about your travel tummy; keep your health issues to yourself, because no one wants to hear about them. Do not go to Jamaica without pictures of your family, and when family is brought up (which it will be rather quickly in the conversation), use it as an opportunity to bring out the photographs. Never tell a dirty joke with a woman present.

Tone, Volume, and Speed

Discussions can quickly become animated and very lively, depending upon the nature of the discussion and the circumstances of the developing relationship. Conversation can be loud, and, at times, "in your face." At meals, and afterward, or just during a simple visit, conversation is an art, and Jamaicans love to have a good time: laughing and fooling around with friends is the ultimate entertainment. In business, speak softly and with restraint. It garners respect.

Use of Silence

In general, silence is not that common, except in group discussions where something is said that can cause someone a public loss of face. Avoid this, and enjoy the simultaneous conversations and frequent interruptions that usually define Jamaican conversation style.

Physical Gestures and Facial Expressions

Typically, the hands add emphasis to just about anything that is being verbally said. When two individuals each make a fist and quickly touch their fists, it indicates that they approve or agree with what is being said. Winking or whistling—often accompanied by a positive comment—is meant to be a friendly introduction between men and women. Rubbing your index finger and thumb together indicates money. People will *psst* at you when they want your attention, and oftentimes in conversations, there can be a tap on the shoulder and much touching: this typically indicates friendship. Sucking air in through clenched teeth is an expression of frustration and can be freely translated as, "Oh, come on!"

Waving and Counting

The thumb represents the number 1, the index finger the number 2, and so on. It is insulting to beckon someone with the forefinger. Waving or beckoning is done with the palm down and the fingers moving forward and back in a kind of scratching motion. If you need to gesture for a waiter, subtly raise your hand; never click, call, or whistle.

Physicality and Physical Space

Jamaicans tend to get closer than North Americans are generally comfortable with; sometimes, depending on what is being discussed, extremely so. Do not step back when your Jamaican associate steps forward. Jamaican men may touch each other during conversations, adjust each other's ties, dust off each other's shoulders, and the like. Avoid speaking with your hands in your pockets; always keep them firmly at your side when standing. If men and women must cross their legs, it should never be ankle over knee (the preferred style for women is to cross ankle over ankle). No gum chewing, *ever;* no slouching; no leaning against things.

Eye Contact

Eye contact can be direct, and may at times be disconcerting for many U.S. Americans. If you look away, your behavior will say to your Jamaican colleague that you are either disinterested or rude.

Emotive Orientation

Jamaicans are often animated and physically expressive. Join in if you like but keep cool if you can. Jamaicans will always admire you if you can remain coolly logical while staying warm, open, and personable.

Protocol in Public

Walking Styles and Waiting in Lines

Lines aren't really taken seriously, although there will be much talk of "the queue." Don't be too distressed if someone walks right up to the front of the line at a bank, a restaurant, or a store, and gets served because of the relationship he or she has with the clerk, while you have been waiting patiently in line for forty minutes. People also have a tendency to stand very close in public; this may feel uncomfortable to non-Caribbeans at first. Resist the urge to back away; most of the time, you are not being intentionally crowded. Remember, the need to appear helpful and courteous is strong, and if you ask for directions on the street, you will no doubt be instructed on just where to go . . . whether or not the individual actually knows!

Behavior in Public Places: Airports, Terminals, and the Market

Most stores are closed on Sundays, and many small stores close each day for lunch. Personally thanking store owners, waiters, chefs, and hotel managers for their services is very much appreciated. In food markets, you can touch the produce; in goods stores, it may be difficult to return a product unless there is a flaw in it. Because of the personal nature of the culture, money is exchanged in the palms, not on the counter. In addition, in most small shops and in markets, bargaining is very expected. If you don't bargain well, that's okay; put a smile on your face and ask for half of what the listed price is. Stick to it and walk away if you have to, and you'll land somewhere in between. Never get angry, though, since bargaining is a game to get to know you, and it is supposed to make shopping a more pleasant experience. Always offer a fair price, as the amount you pay goes toward the support of a family.

Because of the high poverty rate, small children and women may approach you on the street or come up to your taxi window to ask for money. It is always difficult deciding whether or not to give, but remember that the social support systems are negligible, and this is often the only way for these people to sustain themselves. Smoking is pervasive, and if you do smoke, be sure to always offer a cigarette to everyone you are talking to before you light up. If you buy food from a street vendor (not a good idea for health reasons) you should not eat while walking: it is considered impolite; eat your food at the stand where you bought it.

Bus / Metro / Taxi / Car

Driving is on the left, British style. Driving may be difficult in certain neighborhoods in the cities, and being a pedestrian is just as risky: both drivers and pedestrians can be very aggressive. The main roads are surprisingly good, but smaller roads can be treacherous. There are no metros, but buses traverse the cities and connect the towns. There are also public cars, or route taxis, that follow specific routes. The best way to catch a cab is at designated taxi stands (hotels are good places, but often charge more for the same ride: a hotel surcharge is added to the meter fare, in some cases). The crime situation varies from neighborhood to neighborhood and town to town: check with a local contact before venturing out into unknown areas on the island, as you can run the risk of being a victim of more than the usual petty street crime.

Tipping

A 10 percent tip is usually sufficient in restaurants and taxis. Restaurants usually have the 10 percent tip included in the bill; however, this practice is not universal throughout the island, so ask if it is not explicitly indicated on the bill when you get it. Even if it is, it is still appropriate to leave some odd change if the service was particularly good. Porters and hotel help get the equivalent of one U.S. dollar per item or service rendered (tipping in U.S. dollars, as is done throughout much of the region, is perfectly fine, actually preferred). Please double-check the current U.S. dollar/Jamaican dollar exchange rate, as it can vary quickly and significantly.

Punctuality

It is perfectly acceptable—in fact, essential—to arrive for social events about one hour late. If you arrive sooner, you will be running the risk of interrupting the host or hostess as he or she gets ready. For business meetings, being late by five to fifteen minutes or more is usually not a problem, but it is safer for the new employee or visitor to be on time, while not being surprised if others are not. Usually, the meeting will not begin in earnest until all attendees have arrived (or at least until all the decision makers have shown up), and this may not correspond to the time listed in the agenda. Resist questioning the late ones for a reason; they always have one, usually involving an obligation with more important people, like superiors, old friends, or family.

Dress

In Jamaica, being well-groomed and dressing with respect for yourself and others are important. Nevertheless, the individualist streak in Jamaican culture extends to clothes, so Jamaicans can be quite iconoclastic about dress. Some (particularly the youth) follow U.S. music and popular trends, others (particularly older women) are more traditional and conservative in their dress. Casual wear includes jeans and skirts (dresses and blouses in the countryside); even T-shirts and sneakers are okay. Business dress can include suits and ties for men, dresses and blouses for women (many businesses issue uniforms to women), and can range from very individualistic in style to unassuming business standard. Rastafarians often dress in the colors of their religion (green, red, and gold), and this color scheme is also adopted by many Jamaicans who are not Rastas themselves.

Personal Hygiene

Jamaicans are very concerned about cleanliness and smelling good. Dreadlocks are either worn long and down the back or gathered up on top of the head under a kind of hat, which holds the hair in place. Note that most rest room and bathroom facilities do not have plumbing capable of handling paper toilet tissue; it is for this reason that there is a small receptacle next to the toilet for your used tissue: do not flush it down the bowl, but place it in the receptacle, or else you'll face the embarrassment of having to call for help when the bowl overflows. Take paper tissue with you if you travel about. Remember also that the water in showers may be heated by a little electrical device placed above the showerhead: never touch it or any metal when wet!

Dining and Drinking

Mealtimes and Typical Foods

Breakfast is served from about 7:30 to 9 A.M., and usually consists of some bread and coffee or tea (please note, all hot drinks in Jamaica, whether tea or coffee or anything else, are referred to first as tea, and then you specify). Jamaican food is often spicy and very tasty; even at breakfast, *ackee,* a sweet red fruit, is often eaten with the national dish, salt fish. Coffee in the morning can be strong and black, or with hot milk.

Lunch was traditionally the main meal of the day, and even today, in busy cities, it can be an extended affair—or it can be a quick sandwich or a salad at a shop on the corner. Lunch is usually served from noon to 2 P.M. It usually consists of rice and "peas" (which are really red beans), which is eaten practically every day, especially on Sundays. Stews and curries (made with different kinds of meat, such as chicken, beef, goat, etc.) are very popular. *Jerk,* which is a spicy barbecue of meats, originally cooked over an open pit, is also very popular. Bread, sometimes made of cassava root (*bammy* bread), is common with every meal, and the typical blandness of the bread is intentional to offset the spice of the food. Another popular combination is "fish and festival" (fish and fried dough). Typically a vegetable, such as plantains, is served with meat or fish as well. There is often a fresh salad to accompany the meal. Meals often end with fresh tropical fruits. Don't be surprised to see a lot of Asian foods in Jamaica: Jamaicans love Chinese food.

Dinner is served from 6:30 P.M. on. It is typically a light meal, especially if lunch was the heavier, main meal of the day, and consists of the same kinds of foods as those served for lunch. Drinks served with dinner are usually beer, water, fruit juices, or soft drinks, and there is always the ubiquitous rum.

Be very careful about the places you go to eat: if they don't look safe or clean, you should avoid them. Do not eat food off the street from the street stalls: this can be very dangerous to your health. Be very careful about food and drink in Jamaica (and throughout Latin America): although in tourist areas, it is probably safer than elsewhere, there are dangerous bugs around. First, the water: Despite the official line that piped water is safe to drink, at least in the major cities, it is safer still not to drink tap water anywhere (except where *officially* noted as safe, sterilized, or "electrified," as in the resort hotels). This means no ice in any drinks (ice cubes may be made from tap water). Close your mouth in the shower in the morning, and brush your teeth with bottled water. Drink only bottled water and soft drinks from bottles with intact seals opened in front of you; the fruit juices in Jamaica are wonderful, but until your digestive system has adjusted, avoid them: they may have been diluted with water from the tap. Coffee and tea are generally okay, because the water is boiled first. Avoid fresh dairy products, including milk, custards, mayonnaise, and ice cream, because they all usually require refrigeration, which may be questionable in certain parts of the island. Definitely avoid raw shellfish and raw fish and do not eat any raw or uncooked vegetables or fruits, unless you can peel them; this means no green salad. You will inevitably get the Latin American tummy on your first few trips . . . it is hard to avoid a drop of water here or there. If you have followed the above rules carefully, it is probably nothing to worry about; it will be uncomfortable for a day or two. Eat lightly, drink lots of safe fluids, stay in or near your room, rest, and it will pass. If a fever or vomiting develops, be sure to seek medical attention immediately.

Typical Drinks and Toasting

Beer and rum are the national drinks. Nonalcoholic drinks include all sorts of tisanes (herbal infusions), coffee, teas, cocoa, and soft drinks. There are also many local brandies made from sugarcane, which can vary from mild to incredibly strong (be warned), and which are offered as pre- or post-meal drinks. The most common toast is "cheers."

Table Manners and the Use of Utensils

Do not begin eating until the host says something like "Let's eat" or "Please begin!" Knives and forks are typically used European style (the knife remains in the right hand and the fork remains in the left throughout the meal). When the meal is finished, the knife and fork are laid parallel to each other across the right side of the plate. If you put both utensils down on the plate for any real length of time, it is a sign to the waitstaff that you are finished, and your plate may be taken away from you.

When not holding utensils, your hands are expected to be in your lap as they are in Britain (note that this is the reverse from what is done throughout most of the region).

Seating Plans

At formal meals, the most honored position is at the head of the table, with the most important guest seated immediately to the right of the host (women to the right of the host, and men to the right of the hostess). If there is a hosting couple, one will usually be seated at each end of the table. In the European tradition, men and women are seated next to one another, and couples are often broken up and seated next to people they may not have previously known (this is done to promote conversation), although at informal gatherings, men often sit with men and women with women. Men typically rise when women enter the room, and continue to hold doors for women and allow them to enter a room first.

Refills and Seconds

If you do not want more food, or cannot eat everything on your plate, it is okay to leave some food on your plate, but eat most of it (wasting food is not appreciated). If serving yourself family style, take only what you will eat. You may always have additional beverages; drink enough to cause your cup or glass to be less than half full, and it will generally be refilled. Portions are often equal to or greater than those in the United States, especially when it comes to rice.

At Home, in a Restaurant, or at Work

In informal restaurants, you will rarely be required to share a table. Waitstaff may be summoned by making eye contact; waving or calling their names is very impolite. The business breakfast is not common, although you do see it creeping into the business life of the major cities slowly. The business lunch (more common than dinner) and dinner are very acceptable, but, depending on how well developed your relationship is with your Jamaican colleagues, may or may not be the time to make business decisions. Take your cue from your Jamaican associates: if they bring up business, then it's okay to discuss it. No gum chewing, *ever,* at a restaurant or on the street. No-smoking sections in restaurants are still a rarity.

Meals at home are typically informal affairs, and people who drop by at mealtimes are always expected to have a bite and stay a while if they can. Dropping by unannounced is usually perfectly okay between friends, but until you have established that kind of relationship, it's best to always plan your visits. When invited to a home for a formal meal, do not wander from room to room.

Use the toilet before you arrive, as it is considered bad form to leave the table at any time. If it is a formal meal, once you (and the group) are invited to another room, most probably the dining room, be sure to allow more senior members of your party to enter the room ahead of you: men should also move aside to allow women to enter the room ahead of them. If you invite people to your home, be prepared to always have the invitation accepted, although they may not, in fact, show up; rejecting the invitation may be difficult for Jamaicans, who seek to not offend. They may indicate their true intentions by simply responding to your invitation with "I will try."

Being a Good Guest or Host

Paying the Bill

Usually the one who does the inviting pays the bill, although the guest is expected to make an effort to pay. Sometimes other circumstances determine who pays (such as rank). Making payment arrangements ahead of time so that no exchange occurs at the table is a very classy way to host. Women, if out with men, will not really be able to pay the bill at a restaurant; if you want to, make arrangements ahead of time, and don't wait for the check to arrive at the table. The only time it is considered appropriate for a woman to do this is if she is a hosting businesswoman from abroad. If a businesswoman invites a Jamaican businessman to a meal, she should be sure to extend the invitation to his spouse as well, or may want to consider telling him that her (female) colleague will also be joining them (and be sure to have a female colleague along). Do not allow a Jamaican male to suggest bringing one of his colleagues along (remember, the person doing the inviting can refuse the suggestion). If a Jamaican male invites a businesswoman to a meeting or a meal that seems to have more than business as the subject, a businesswoman should always insist that she bring her female associate along (someone who is needed because of her role in the company). Unmarried businesswomen may want to consider wearing a wedding band. If you have children, be sure to discuss that fact at some point early in the initial conversations, although this may not have the same effect of discouraging men as it can in Hispanic Latin America.

Transportation

It's a very nice idea, when acting as the host, to inquire ahead of time as to whether your guests will require transportation. If necessary, you should arrange for taxi or car service at the end of the meal. When the cars arrive, be sure not to leave your spot until your guests are out of sight.

When to Arrive / Chores to Do

If invited to dinner at a private home for a formal meal, do not offer to help with the chores, nor should you expect to visit the kitchen. Do not leave the table unless invited to do so. Spouses typically do not attend business dinners without a special invitation to do so. You may not be invited into a Jamaican home that quickly, as it is usually a private place for only the closest family and friends. If you are, be sure to reciprocate by hosting your colleague in your home when and if he or she comes to your country or at a fine restaurant on another night of your trip.

Gift Giving

In general, gift giving is not common among business associates, although it is nice to bring a small gift from abroad if you are revisiting a business acquaintance (as, at this point, they have probably become a friend). One exception: as is the case throughout most of the region, some chocolates or a small gift for the secretary of the person you are visiting can work wonders for future smooth sailing! If a man is giving a gift to a woman in a business setting, it is important to present it as a gift to her from his wife or sister. Holiday cards are very appropriate, particularly as a thank-you for your Jamaican colleagues' business in the previous year, and should be mailed in time to be received the week before Christmas.

Gifts are not expected if you are invited to a dinner or social event, although it is nice to bring something appropriate along. The best gift for these occasions is wine, chocolates or a dessert pastry, or something for the children. Avoid flowers (they are already abundant). Gifts are generally opened at the time they are given and received.

Special Holidays and Celebrations

Major Holidays

January 1	New Year's Day
January 6	Maroon New Year's Day
March/April	Holy Week and Easter
May 23	Labor Day (Labor Day in Brooklyn, New York— in September—by the way, is a huge carnival-like celebration of the world's largest West Indian community outside of the Caribbean)
August	Independence Day (celebrated on the first Monday of the month)
October	National Heroes' Day (celebrated on the third Monday of the month)
December 25	Christmas Day
December 26	Boxing Day

Business Culture

Daily Office Protocols

While it is becoming more and more common for women to attain positions of authority in Jamaica, women do struggle to reach the same levels of achievement as their male counterparts in Jamaican business, and it is rare (though not impossible) to see women at the highest levels of business and government.

People organize their time on a daily basis according to the tasks they must accomplish, and the relationships they must depend upon in order to accomplish these tasks; the clock takes a backseat. Therefore, the day may begin slowly, but there can be much activity by day's end, and people often stay late in the office in order to finish up what needs to be done. This pattern repeats itself over larger blocks of time in regard to the accomplishment of projects and the meeting of deadlines.

Management Styles

Gathering the information required in order to do what your boss expects from you, or creating consensus among your colleagues in order to accomplish a particular goal, can take a long time. Deadlines may be secondary, but efficiency and accomplishing the task is important. Titles are very important, and the highest ones (e.g., vice president) are usually reserved for very senior, executive-level positions, and should not be used as casually as they are in the United States. Complimenting and rewarding employees publicly are usually not done. For non-Jamaicans, it can be important to have a local contact who can tell you what is really going on after you return home, and to have a local intermediary—as well as a local lawyer—to act as a liaison for you with the people you need to see while you are there. This should be set up ahead of time.

Boss-Subordinate Relations

Decision making is usually reserved for individuals, so it is important that both you and your Jamaican colleague be the decision makers in the business at hand. Bosses are expected to provide guidance, distribute information, and make decisions; subordinates are typically expected to provide detailed information and follow the decisions made by their superiors.

Conducting a Meeting or Presentation

At most meetings, even when there are people of different ranks at the table, there can be open communication and sharing of ideas. In fact, these sessions often serve as information-sharing and decision-making forums in which all individuals are expected to contribute. Under these circumstances, discussions are usually vibrant, with many people speaking at once; questions are common and interruptions, even of presentations, should be expected.

Negotiation Styles

Jamaicans generally start out playing their cards close to the vest, but quickly will provide information when it is perceived that there is an advantage to working together and moving forward. They will respect someone who comes to them with established knowledge and experience, and will build relationships because of your expertise. Whether you are worth knowing and doing business with may be more important than the details of your proposal. While a carefully planned, logically organized, and well-presented proposal is important, it need not cover every minute detail (although the contract should). Bargaining is the essence of the negotiation, as a way to build trust; therefore, be reasonable, but do not overcompromise, as this shows weakness.

The first meeting is usually an informal meeting in the office. Expect to go out to a restaurant for lunch or dinner soon thereafter, where you may or may not continue the business discussion (take your cue from your Jamaican colleague). The contract must be legal down to the dotted i's, and is regarded as a binding document, as it is in North America. Plan your meetings as carefully and as well in advance as you can, but expect changes and unexpected additions and adjustments to the agenda. Remember also that the meeting might start and end later than you anticipated; nevertheless, as in most polychronic cultures, you should always arrive on time. Tea, coffee, or a cola is the universal business meeting drink; always accept it, always serve it (in nice china, never in Styrofoam), and drink as much or as little as you can or desire. It is the gesture of acceptance and appreciation that counts (never refuse coffee, or an invitation to go with your colleague to a café and have some). You need not host in the absolute best restaurant around, nor need you stay in the top hotel in order to signal that you are someone worth doing business with.

Written Correspondence

Letters should be businesslike without being overly formal or convoluted. Dates are given using the day/month/year format (with periods in between, not slashes); use an honorific plus the last name. The time of day is written in military time; weights and measures are usually given in metric measurements. Monetary amounts are written as they are in the United States. Be sure to inquire first, in all communications, about your colleague's health and progress in a short personal opening statement, then move on to the substance of your communication, and close with a salutation and your personal wishes for his or her success and well-being. Your colleagues will most likely write to you in English. Written addresses are usually in the following format:

Line 1: name
Line 2: title/position
Line 3: company
Line 4: street address
Line 5: city, state

BARBADOS

Note: Refer to the preceding section on Jamaica for information about general Anglo-African Caribbean and Latin American cultural behaviors; the material that follows describes specific Barbadian variations on general Anglo-African Caribbean and Latin American customs.

Some Introductory Background on Barbados and the Barbadians

If you look at the map, you will notice the first anomaly about Barbados: it juts out of the far eastern Caribbean into the Atlantic Ocean, and is, in fact, the easternmost of all the islands in the Caribbean. Look into the island itself and you will notice a few other anomalies: there are no rivers (Barbados gets all its potable water from rainfall—and yes, you can drink the water from the tap in Barbados!), and the soil itself is a fertile cover that sits atop a coral base that has risen from the sea over time. Culturally, Barbados is a bit of an anomaly in the region as well: it is the wealthiest of all Caribbean nations. It has an 85 percent school attendance rate, the most compulsory schooling (until age sixteen), and the highest GDP of the region (most families own at least one car, and more families own homes than anywhere in the region). In fact, Barbadians are extremely proud of their economic achievements and relative political and economic stability. They value their independence, their Anglo-African heritage, and their success. This also has given them a reputation for being slightly standoffish, at least as they relate to their Caribbean neighbors. Barbadians are warm and generous people, but interpersonally, they may appear to be a bit distant at first. Well, look at that map: they are a bit out of the way, after all.

The history of Barbados differs from that of their neighbors as well; when the British claimed the island from the Portuguese, who first discovered it, the indigenous Arawaks had already mysteriously disappeared from the island. While the island did become a major slave entrepot, there was no legacy of a conquered or enslaved indigenous people, and the African and British traditions that were subsequently imported into the island became the core of what was to become Bajan culture (Barbadians typically refer to themselves and their culture by shortening Barbadian to Bajan).

The language spoken is an English threaded with the influence of African languages, resulting in a lilting patois referred to locally as "Broken English." The majority of Bajans are Christian, with approximately half being members of the Anglican Church and the other half Methodist and other Protestant denominations. Women make up the bulk of the churchgoing populations (in fact, a favorite pastime for men is to visit each other or meet at a local shop and catch up and socialize on Sunday mornings while the women are in church). Christianity has exercised a strong influence over the island (meals are often begun with grace, and school activities and all public functions typically open with a prayer). Education is highly valued, and approximately half the school population is female, providing women with an opportunity to enter the workforce that is unparalleled in the rest of the region. In fact, women do make up approximately 50 percent of the workforce in Barbados, and can attain positions of authority in business and government. (Barbados was the first Caribbean nation to give women the right to vote.) Non-Bajan businesswomen should have no problem doing business in Barbados, as long as their authority and credibility have been established ahead of time with the individuals they will be doing business with (particularly if they are businessmen—there is a certain level of Bajan machismo).

Greetings and Introductions

Greetings are important, even when passing people on the street: always acknowledge someone with a "Good morning" or "Hello." When you are introduced to people, begin using last names and honorifics; once a relationship is established, Bajans typically move to first names quickly, even in business. Children typically address adults with whom they are familiar with "auntie" or "uncle," even if they are not technically related. Young males sometimes greet each other by tapping the top of each other's clenched fists.

Communication Styles

Okay Topics / Not Okay Topics

Okay: cricket (the national sport), draughts (like checkers, the national pastime), Bajan music ("wukking-up" is a typical form of Bajan calypso), and Bajan food. *Not okay:* marriage (there are high rates of divorce and cohabitation, and single-mother families are common).

Physical Gestures and Facial Expressions

Sucking air in through the teeth resulting in something that sounds like *chppsss* signals annoyance and frustration. Sitting with arms folded is typically not a defiant posture (standing with hands on hips, however, is)—it usually indicates, "I am listening, go on."

Physicality and Physical Space

One difference between Bajans and their Caribbean neighbors is the issue of personal space: Bajans typically like some distance between individuals, similar to the custom in North America, and in general, personal space is respected.

Eye Contact

Eye contact is occasional, and not steady; the North American pattern of making intermittent eye contact when speaking with someone is preferred.

Dress

Dress is neat and clean, and even in business, can be casual and comfortable. The "shirt-jac" for men (typically a light, square-cut jacket and open collar shirt underneath, sometimes worn outside of the pants) is acceptable everywhere; most women wear long, colorful dresses. Bajans do dress up for social events, and for church; women especially will be seen wearing their finest to both events, usually including very fashionable hats. Among younger people, jeans, T-shirts, and sneakers are fine for casual events, but they should always be neat and clean. As is the case throughout most of the region, beachwear is only for the beach.

Dining and Drinking

Bajans eat three meals a day, scheduled as they are in North America, and foods can include the national dish (flying fish and *cou-cou,* which is a combination of okra and cornmeal), rice, vegetables, peas (really beans or any beanlike vegetable), potatoes, meats, and fish. Popular foods include pepperpot (a spicy stew), jug-jug (pasta and peas), and conkies (spices, sweet potatoes, and raisins steamed together in a banana leaf—you unwrap the leaf and toss it: do not eat the banana leaf!). Tea is the term used for all hot drinks, and tea, as it is known in Britain, is drunk at most meals. You will be offered the Bajan rum: try it.

Special Holidays and Celebrations

January 1	New Year's Day
January 21	Errol Barrow Day
March/April	Easter
May 1	May Day
August	Whitmonday/Kadooment Day (celebrated on the first Monday of the month)
August 3	Emancipation Day
October	United Nations Day (celebrated on the first Monday of the month)
November 30	Independence Day
December 25	Christmas Day
December 26	Boxing Day

Additionally, there are four major celebrations on the island:

- The Holetown Festival, held for three days in February, celebrates the arrival of the first settlers.
- The Oistins Fish Festival usually occurs over Easter and honors the fishing industry and fishermen.
- The Crop-Over Festival (sometime between June and the end of July) celebrates the end of the sugarcane harvest (Kadooment Day is the last day of the Crop-Over festival, and is like Carnival, with street parades and music throughout the island).
- The National Independence Festival of Creative Arts is held island-wide around Independence Day in November; everyone is expected to display their handiwork and creative spirit.

TRINIDAD AND TOBAGO

Note: Refer to the previous sections on Jamaica and Barbados for information about general Anglo-African Caribbean and Latin American cultural behaviors; the material that follows describes specific Trinidadian variations on general Anglo-African Caribbean and Latin American customs.

Some Introductory Background on Trinidad and the Trinidadians

Yes, the official language is English. Yes, the British institutionalized many of the patterns of daily life in T&T (as it is commonly referred to). Nevertheless, T&T is perhaps the most multicultural of all the cultures in the Caribbean. In fact, it is a culture that is Anglo-African only in the sense that the British were perhaps the most influential of all the European groups to have claimed the island at one time (certainly Britain had the longest and strongest claim prior to T&T's independence); while Africans make up the majority of the population. The history of T&T reads like a constant struggle between most European nations for control over these islands: the Spanish arrived in Trinidad with Columbus, but very quickly the British settled in Tobago; Spaniards invaded Tobago, France and Holland claimed Tobago, even Latvia (!) attempted an invasion of Tobago; back and forth the islands switched between Spain, Britain, and France, ultimately becoming a British colony at the end of the eighteenth century. By this time, it served as yet another major entrepot for the slave trade, but as the slaves rioted (more than once, and T&T proudly claims—along with Haiti—some of the earliest and most influential slave riots in the New World), Britain was forced to look elsewhere for its labor source; given the multicultural influences already existing on the island, it encouraged immigration by indentured servants from its other colonies, especially India. The subsequent tide of Indian immigration was followed by immigration into the island from other parts of Asia, resulting today in a population descended from Africans, Europeans (Spaniards, French, and others), Indians, Indonesians (and other East Asians), and Arabs. There is a strong influence from this Asian immigration on all aspects of life, from religion (there is a large population of Hindus from India, and a significant Muslim population from other parts of East Asia, the Middle East, and Africa), food, dress (people from these different groups often dress as such, with Hindu women, for example, wearing sarilike dresses), music, pastimes (everything from cricket to calypso to soca to Indian movies), and language (English is the lingua franca, but the various languages continue to be spoken). Each group in T&T typically retains its own cultural identity, and proudly so, and the islands pride themselves on being tolerant and heterogeneous. This tolerance and flexibility are also evident in business, which is usually conducted with a relaxed but businesslike focus; the multicultural legacy also provides most Trinidadians with an increased familiarity with foreign business practices, and the very dominant oil and petroleum industry (among other things such as a very strong local economy) has exposed most businesspeople to doing business with non-Caribbeans.

T&T is not alone in being an incredible cultural mosaic in this very southern part of the Caribbean. The three-island chain of the "ABC's" (Aruba, Bonaire, and Curaçao), running along the northern coast of Venezuela, has also been significantly influenced by all of the above groups, although the Dutch, not the British, were the primary European colonial power, and these islands today thrive primarily on tourism.

Special Holidays and Celebrations

January 1	New Year's Day
February/March	Carnival (a major celebration in T&T!)
February/March	*Phagwa/Holi* (Hindu Festival of Color)
February/March	Ramadan (Muslim holy month)
March/April	Easter

June 19	Labor Day
August 1	Emancipation Day
August 31	Independence Day
September 24	Republic Day
December 25	Christmas Day
December 26	Boxing Day
Variable	*Eid Ul Fitr* (Muslim religious festival)
Variable	*Divali* (Hindu Festival of lights)

Index

address, forms of. *See* honorifics
African influence
  Barbados, 271
  Belize, 58
  Brazil, 11, 136
  Caribbean cultures, 197, 198
  Haiti, 239, 240, 241, 243
  Jamaica, 255–56, 259
  Trinidad and Tobago, 273, 274
alcohol. *See* drinks and toasts
Amazonas cultures, 89. *See also* Brazil
"Americans," use of term, 11, 14
Andean cultures, 11, 89. *See also* Bolivia;
    Colombia; Ecuador; Peru; Venezuela
Anglo-African cultures, 198. *See also*
    Barbados; Jamaica; Trinidad and
    Tobago
Argentina, 162-82
  background and history, 91, 162–64
  business culture, 173, 177, 178, 180–82
  communication styles, 166, 169–71
  cultural orientations, 164–66
  dining and drinking, 174–78
  dress, 173–74
  economic conditions, 163, 164
  European influence, 162, 167, 170
  gift giving, 179
  greetings and introductions, 167–69
  guests and hosts, 178
  holidays and celebrations, 179–80
  politics and government, 163

  public behavior, 171–73
  religion and demographics, 164
  schools and education, 164
  transportation, 172, 178
  women's roles, 165, 178, 180
Asian influence
  Peru, 126–27, 130
  Trinidad and Tobago, 274
Aztecs, 13, 14, 90

Barbados, 270-73
  African influence, 271
  background and history, 270–71
  British influence, 271
  business culture, 271
  communication styles, 272
  dining and drinking, 272–73
  dress, 272
  economic conditions, 271
  greetings and introductions, 271–72
  holidays and celebrations, 273
  religion and demographics, 271
  women's roles, 271
bargaining, in stores
  Argentina, 173
  Chile, 185
  Costa Rica, 83
  Cuba, 209
  Dominican Republic, 226–27
  Guatemala, 48
  Haiti, 247

bargaining, in stores *(continued)*
  Jamaica, 263
  Mexico, 25
  Nicaragua, 73–74
bathing. *See* personal hygiene
begging
  Argentina, 172
  Brazil, 148
  Colombia, 104
  Cuba, 209
  Dominican Republic, 227
  Ecuador, 122
  Guatemala, 48
  Haiti, 247
  Jamaica, 263
  Mexico, 25
  Nicaragua, 74
Belize, 58-60
  African and British influences, 58
  background and history, 58
  business culture, 60
  cultural orientations, 58–59
  dining and drinking, 59–60
  greetings and introductions, 59
  guests and hosts, 60
  holidays and celebrations, 60
  public behavior, 59
  women's roles, 58, 60
Bolivar, Simon, 93, 115, 131
Bolivia, 131-35
  background and history, 90, 131–32
  business culture, 135
  communication styles, 132
  crime, 131
  demographics, 131
  dining and drinking, 133–34
  dress, 133
  economic conditions, 131
  gift giving, 134
  greetings and introductions, 132
  holidays and celebrations, 135
  public behavior, 133

  Spanish influence, 131
  U.S. relations, 132
  women's roles, 135
boss-subordinate relations. *See* business
  culture
Brasília, 136, 137
Brazil, 136-61
  African influence, 11, 136
  background and history, 89, 90–91,
    136–38
  business culture, 137, 141, 150, 152,
    155–56, 158–61
  communication styles, 142, 145–48
  cultural orientations, 139–43
  dining and drinking, 151–55
  dress, 150–51
  economic conditions, 137, 139, 148, 149
  European influence, 136
  gift giving, 156–57
  greetings and introductions, 143–45
  guests and hosts, 155–56
  holidays and celebrations, 157–58
  Luso-African culture, 11, 91, 136
  politics and government, 137, 138, 140
  public behavior, 148–50
  religion and demographics, 138–39
  schools and education, 138
  transportation, 148, 149, 156
  women's roles, 139, 140, 149, 155–56,
    158
British influence
  Barbados, 271
  Belize, 58
  Jamaica, 255
  Trinidad and Tobago, 273, 274
Buenos Aires, 162
buses. *See* transportation
business cards
  Argentina, 169
  Brazil, 145
  Colombia, 101
  Cuba, 206

Dominican Republic, 224
Guatemala, 45
Haiti, 245
Jamaica, 260
Mexico, 22
Nicaragua, 71
business culture
   Argentina, 173, 177, 178, 180–82
   Barbados, 271
   Belize, 60
   Bolivia, 135
   Brazil, 137, 141, 150, 152, 155–56, 158–61
   Chile, 187–88
   Colombia, 109, 110, 112–15
   Costa Rica, 85
   Cuba, 210, 213, 215–17
   Dominican Republic, 220, 228, 230, 233–35
   Ecuador, 125
   Guatemala, 49, 53, 55–57
   Haiti, 248, 250, 252–54
   Jamaica, 266, 268–70
   Mexico, 31, 34–37
   Nicaragua, 74–75, 78, 80–82
   Panama, 88
   Paraguay, 192
   Peru, 130–31
   Trinidad and Tobago, 274
   Uruguay, 195–96
   Venezuela, 116, 119
   See also business cards; dress; punctuality

Cabral, Pedro, 137, 138
cabs. *See* transportation
cantinas
   Colombia, 107
   Mexico, 28
Caracas, 116
Caribbean cultures, 11, 197–98. *See also* Barbados; Cuba; Dominican Republic; Haiti; Jamaica; Puerto Rico; Trinidad and Tobago
Carnaval, 157–58, 173
cars. *See* transportation
Castro Ruz, Fidel, 200
Catholic Church. *See* Roman Catholic Church
celebrations. *See* holidays and celebrations
Centroamerica, 38. *See also* Belize; Costa Rica; El Salvador; Guatemala; Honduras; Nicaragua; Panama
children. *See* honorifics; schools and education
Chile, 183-88
   background and history, 91, 183
   business culture, 187–88
   communication styles, 184
   crime, 183
   dining and drinking, 185–86
   dress, 185
   European influence, 183, 184, 187
   gift giving, 186–87
   greetings and introductions, 183–84
   holidays and celebrations, 187
   politics and government, 184
   public behavior, 185
   Spanish influence, 183
   women's roles, 187–88
clothing. *See* dress
Colombia, 90-115
   background and history, 90, 93–95
   business culture, 109, 110, 112–15
   communication styles, 97–98, 101–103
   crime, 94, 104
   cultural orientation, 95–98
   dining and drinking, 97, 106–108
   dress, 105–106
   gift giving, 111
   greetings and introductions, 98–101
   guests and hosts, 110–11
   holidays and celebrations, 111-12
   land reform issues, 94

Colombia (*continued*)
  politics and government, 94, 95
  public behavior, 103–105
  religion and demographics, 95
  schools and education, 95
  Spanish influence, 93
  transportation, 104, 110
  women's roles, 96, 99–100, 110, 112
communication styles
  Argentina, 166, 169–71
  Barbados, 272
  Bolivia, 132
  Brazil, 142, 145–48
  Chile, 184
  Colombia, 97–98, 101–103
  Costa Rica, 84
  Cuba, 203, 206–208
  Dominican Republic, 221, 224–26
  Ecuador, 123
  Guatemala, 42, 45–47
  Haiti, 243, 245–46
  Jamaica, 258–59, 261–62
  low-context vs. high-context, 7
  Mexico, 22–24
  Nicaragua, 68, 71–73
  Panama, 87
  Paraguay, 190
  Peru, 127
  Puerto Rico, 236–37
  Uruguay, 193
  Venezuela, 117–18
Communism, in Cuba, 199, 200
conversational topics, acceptable and not
  acceptable
  Argentina, 169–70
  Barbados, 272
  Brazil, 145–46
  Chile, 184
  Colombia, 101–102
  Cuba, 206–207
  Dominican Republic, 224–25
  Ecuador, 123

  Guatemala, 45–46
  Haiti, 245
  Jamaica, 261
  Mexico, 22–23
  Nicaragua, 71–72
  Panama, 87
  Paraguay, 190
  Peru, 127
  Puerto Rico, 236–37
  Uruguay, 193
  Venezuela, 117
Costa Rica, 82-85
  background and history, 83
  business culture, 85
  communication styles, 84
  dining and drinking, 84
  European influence, 83
  gift giving, 84–85
  greetings and introductions, 83–84
  holidays and celebrations, 85
  politics and government, 83
  public behavior, 84
  U.S. relations, 83
  women's roles, 85
counting. *See* waving and counting
crime
  Bolivia, 131
  Chile, 183
  Colombia, 94, 104
  Cuba, 209
  Dominican Republic, 227
  Haiti, 247
  Jamaica, 263
  Mexico, 26
  Nicaragua, 74
  Paraguay, 189
  Peru, 128
  Uruguay, 193
  Venezuela, 118
Cuba, 199-217
  background and history, 199–201
  business culture, 210, 213, 215–17

communication styles, 203, 206–208
Communism in, 199, 200
crime, 209
cultural orientations, 201–204
demographics, 201
dining and drinking, 211–13
dress, 210–11
economic conditions, 199, 200, 201, 204
gift giving, 214
greetings and introductions, 204–206
guests and hosts, 214
holidays and celebrations, 214–15
politics and government, 199, 200
public behavior, 208–10
religion, 200–201
schools and education, 200
transportation, 209, 214
U.S. relations, 199, 200, 206, 207
women's roles, 200–201, 214, 215
cultural orientations
    Argentina, 164–66
    Belize, 58–59
    Brazil, 139–43
    Colombia, 95–98
    Cuba, 201–204
    defined, 5–7
    Dominican Republic, 219–22
    Guatemala, 40–43
    Haiti, 241–43
    Honduras, 62
    Jamaica, 257–59
    Mexico, 16–19
    Nicaragua, 66–69
    Trinidad and Tobago, 274
culture, defined, 3–4

demographics
    Argentina, 164
    Bolivia, 131
    Brazil, 139
    Caribbean cultures, 197
    Colombia, 95
    Cuba, 201
    Dominican Republic, 218
    Ecuador, 121–22
    Guatemala, 40
    Haiti, 241
    Jamaica, 257
    Mexico, 15–16
    Nicaragua, 66
    Peru, 126–27
    Trinidad and Tobago, 274
    Venezuela, 116–17
dining and drinking
    Argentina, 174–77
    Barbados, 272–73
    Belize, 59–60
    Bolivia, 133–34
    Brazil, 151–55
    Chile, 185–86
    Colombia, 97, 106–108
    Costa Rica, 84
    Cuba, 211–13
    Dominican Republic, 220, 228–31
    Ecuador, 123–24
    Guatemala, 42, 50–53
    Jamaica, 264–67
    Mexico, 6, 17–18, 28–31
    Nicaragua, 67, 75–78
    Panama, 87
    Paraguay, 191
    Peru, 128–29
    Puerto Rico, 237
    Uruguay, 194
    Venezuela, 6, 118–19
Dominican Republic, 217–35
    background and history, 217–18
    business culture, 220, 228, 230, 233–35
    communication styles, 221, 224–26
    crime, 227
    cultural orientations, 219–22
    dining and drinking, 220, 228–31
    dress, 228

Dominican Republic *(continued)*
  economic conditions, 218, 227
  gift giving, 232
  greetings and introductions, 222–24
  guests and hosts, 231–32
  Haitians and, 217, 218, 239
  holidays and celebrations, 232–33
  politics and government, 217, 218
  public behavior, 226–27
  religion and demographics, 218
  schools and education, 218
  U.S. relations, 217, 218
  women's roles, 218, 219, 231, 233
dress
  Argentina, 173–74
  Barbados, 272
  Bolivia, 133
  Brazil, 150–51
  Chile, 185
  Colombia, 105–106
  Cuba, 210–11
  Dominican Republic, 228
  Ecuador, 123
  Guatemala, 49–50
  Haiti, 248
  Honduras, 61
  Jamaica, 264
  Mexico, 26–27
  Nicaragua, 75
  Panama, 87
  Paraguay, 190–91
  Peru, 128
  Trinidad and Tobago, 274
  Uruguay, 194
  Venezuela, 118
drinks and toasts
  Argentina, 175
  Brazil, 153
  Chile, 186
  Colombia, 108
  Cuba, 212
  Dominican Republic, 229

  Guatemala, 51–52
  Haiti, 249
  Jamaica, 265
  Mexico, 29
  Nicaragua, 76
  Peru, 129
driving. *See* transportation
drug trade, in Colombia, 94, 116

eastern Southern Cone cultures.
    See Paraguay; Uruguay
eating. *See* dining and drinking
economic conditions
  Argentina, 163, 164
  Barbados, 271
  Bolivia, 131
  Brazil, 137, 139, 148, 149
  Centroamerica, 38
  Cuba, 199, 200, 201, 204
  Dominican Republic, 218, 227
  Ecuador, 122
  El Salvador, 63
  Guatemala, 39, 40
  Haiti, 240, 247
  Honduras, 61
  Jamaica, 257, 263
  Mexico, 15–16
  Nicaragua, 73–74
  Paraguay, 190
  Uruguay, 193
  Venezuela, 116
Ecuador, 120-25
  background and history, 90, 121
  business culture, 125
  communication styles, 123
  demographics, 121–22
  dining and drinking, 123–24
  dress, 123
  economic conditions, 122
  greetings and introductions, 122
  holidays and celebrations, 124–25
  politics and government, 121

public behavior, 123
  women's roles, 121–22
education. *See* schools and education
egality-oriented cultures, 6
El Salvador, 63–64
emotive orientation
  Argentina, 171
  Brazil, 148
  Chile, 184
  Colombia, 103
  Costa Rica, 84
  Cuba, 208
  Dominican Republic, 226
  Guatemala, 47
  Haiti, 246
  Jamaica, 262
  Mexico, 24
  Nicaragua, 73
entertaining. *See* dining and drinking; gift
    giving; guests and hosts
European conquest, 10, 39, 89–90, 197
European influence
  Argentina, 162, 167, 170
  Belize, 58
  Brazil, 136
  Caribbean cultures, 197
  Chile, 183, 184, 187
  Costa Rica, 83
  Jamaica, 255–56
  Trinidad and Tobago, 273, 274
  Uruguay, 192–93, 196
  See also Spanish influence
eye contact
  Argentina, 171
  Barbados, 272
  Brazil, 147–48
  Colombia, 103
  Costa Rica, 84
  Cuba, 208
  Dominican Republic, 224, 226
  Guatemala, 47
  Haiti, 246

  Jamaica, 262
  Mexico, 22, 24
  Nicaragua, 73

facial expressions. *See* physical gestures
    and facial expressions
flowers, as gifts. *See* gift giving
food. *See* dining and drinking; mealtimes
    and typical foods
food markets. *See* stores and food markets
formal cultures, 7
Franco-African cultures, 198. *See also* Haiti
French, influence on Haiti, 239, 240, 242,
    243–44
future-oriented cultures, 7

gestures. *See* physical gestures and facial
    expressions
gift giving
  Argentina, 179
  Bolivia, 134
  Brazil, 156–57
  Chile, 186–87
  Colombia, 111
  Costa Rica, 84–85
  Cuba, 214
  Dominican Republic, 232
  Guatemala, 54–55
  Haiti, 251
  Jamaica, 268
  Mexico, 32–33
  Nicaragua, 79
  Peru, 129–30
  Uruguay, 195
  Venezuela, 119–20
government. *See* politics and government
Grancolombia, 90, 93–94
Greater Antilles, 198
greetings
  Argentina, 167, 167–69
  Barbados, 272–73
  Belize, 59

greetings *(continued)*
  Bolivia, 132
  Brazil, 143–45
  Chile, 183–84
  Colombia, 98–101
  Costa Rica, 84–85
  Cuba, 204–206
  Dominican Republic, 222–224
  Ecuador, 122
  Guatemala, 43–45
  Haiti, 243–45
  Jamaica, 259–60
  Mexico, 20–22
  Nicaragua, 69–71, 72
  Panama, 87
  Paraguay, 190
  Peru, 127
  Puerto Rico, 236
  Venezuela, 117
Guatemala, 38-57
  background and history, 38–39
  business culture, 49, 53, 55–57
  communication styles, 42, 45–47
  cultural orientations, 40–43
  dining and drinking, 42, 50–53
  dress, 49–50
  economic conditions, 39, 40
  gift giving, 54–55
  greetings and introductions, 43–45
  guests and hosts, 53–54
  holidays and celebrations, 55
  politics and government, 39–40
  public behavior, 47–49
  religion and demographics, 40
  schools and education, 40
  Spanish influence, 39
  transportation, 48–49, 54
  women's roles, 41, 46, 55
guests and hosts
  Argentina, 178
  Belize, 60
  Brazil, 155–56
  Colombia, 110–11

  Cuba, 214
  Dominican Republic, 231–32
  Guatemala, 53–54
  Haiti, 251
  Jamaica, 267–68
  Mexico, 30–32
  Nicaragua, 78–79
  Peru, 129
  See also dining and drinking; gift giving
gum chewing prohibitions
  Argentina, 177
  Brazil, 155
  Colombia, 109
  Cuba, 213
  Dominican Republic, 230
  Guatemala, 53
  Haiti, 250
  Jamaica, 262, 266
  Mexico, 31
  Nicaragua, 78

Haiti, 239-54
  African influence, 239, 240, 241, 243
  background and history, 239–40
  business culture, 248, 250, 252–54
  communication styles, 243, 245–46
  crime, 247
  cultural orientations, 241–43
  dining and drinking, 248–50
  Dominicans and, 217, 218, 239
  dress, 248
  economic conditions, 240, 247
  French influence, 239, 240, 242, 243–44
  gift giving, 251
  greetings and introductions, 243–45
  guests and hosts, 251
  holidays and celebrations, 251–52
  politics and government, 239, 240
  public behavior, 246–48
  religion and demographics, 241
  schools and education, 240–41
  U.S. relations, 239, 240
  women's roles, 241, 244, 251, 252

handshakes. *See* physical greetings
hierarchy-oriented cultures, 6
high-context communicators, 7
Hispanic-African cultures, 198. *See also*
    Cuba; Dominican Republic; Puerto
    Rico
Hispanic cultures, 11
holiday cards. *See* gift giving
holidays and celebrations
    Argentina, 179–80
    Belize, 60
    Bolivia, 135
    Brazil, 157–58
    Carnaval, 157–58, 173
    Chile, 187
    Colombia, 111–12
    Costa Rica, 85
    Cuba, 214–215
    Dominican Republic, 232–33
    Ecuador, 124–25
    El Salvador, 64
    Guatemala, 55
    Haiti, 251
    Honduras, 62
    Jamaica, 268
    Mexico, 33–34
    Nicaragua, 80
    Panama, 87
    Paraguay, 191–92
    Peru, 130
    Puerto Rico, 237–38
    Trinidad and Tobago, 274–75
    Uruguay, 195
    Venezuela, 120
Honduras, 61–62
honorifics
    Argentina, 167–68
    Barbados, 271
    Belize, 59
    Brazil, 144
    Colombia, 99–100
    Cuba, 205
    Dominican Republic, 222–23

    Guatemala, 44–45
    Haiti, 244
    Jamaica, 259–60
    Mexico, 20–21
    Nicaragua, 70
    Puerto Rico, 236
hosts. *See* guests and hosts
hugging. *See* physical greetings
hygiene. *See* personal hygiene

Incas, 90, 126
informal cultures, 7
introductions
    Argentina, 167–69
    Barbados, 272–73
    Belize, 59
    Bolivia, 132
    Brazil, 143, 144–45
    Chile, 183–84
    Colombia, 100–101
    Cuba, 205–206
    Dominican Republic, 223–24
    Ecuador, 122
    Guatemala, 45
    Haiti, 244
    Jamaica, 260
    Mexico, 21–22
    Nicaragua, 70–71
    Paraguay, 190
    Peru, 127
    Puerto Rico, 236
    Venezuela, 117

Jamaica, 255-70
    African influence, 255–56, 259
    background and history, 255–57
    British influence, 255
    business culture, 266, 268–70
    communication styles, 258–59, 261–62
    crime, 263
    cultural orientations, 257–69
    demographics, 257
    dining and drinking, 264–67

Jamaica *(continued)*
    dress, 264
    economic conditions, 257, 263
    gift giving, 268
    greetings and introductions, 259–60
    guests and hosts, 267–68
    holidays and celebrations, 268
    politics and government, 256
    public behavior, 262–64
    religion, 256–57
    schools and education, 256
    transportation, 263, 267
    U.S. relations, 255
    women's roles, 257, 267, 268
jewelry. *See* dress

kissing. *See* physical greetings

language and basic vocabulary
    Argentina, 162, 167
    Bolivia, 131
    Brazil, 143
    Chile, 183–84
    Colombia, 93, 98–99
    Costa Rica, 83–84
    Cuba, 204–205
    Dominican Republic, 222
    Ecuador, 122
    Guatemala, 43
    Haiti, 243–44
    Jamaica, 259
    Mexico, 20
    Nicaragua, 69
    Paraguay, 189
    Peru, 127
    Puerto Rico, 236
    Venezuela, 117
La Paz, 131
Latin America
    culture and history, 4, 9–10, 89–91
    influence on United States, 9
Lesser Antilles, 198

lines, waiting in. *See* walking styles and
    waiting in lines
low-context communicators, 7
Luso-African cultures, 11, 91, 136.
    See also Brazil

"magical realism," 19
makeup. *See* dress
management styles. *See* business culture
markets. *See* stores and food markets
mate, drinking, 191
Mayans, 14, 38–39, 40, 90
mealtimes and typical foods
    Argentina, 165, 174
    Belize, 59
    Bolivia, 134
    Brazil, 141, 151–53
    Chile, 185
    Colombia, 97, 106–108
    Cuba, 211–12
    Dominican Republic, 220, 228
    Ecuador, 123–24
    Guatemala, 42, 50–51
    Haiti, 248–49
    Jamaica, 264–65
    Mexico, 6, 17–18, 28–31
    Nicaragua, 67, 75–76
    Paraguay, 191
    Peru, 128
    Uruguay, 194
    Venezuela, 6, 118–19
    See also dining and drinking
meetings and presentations. *See* business
    culture
megacultures, defined, 4
Mesoamerica, 11. *See also* Mexico
metros. *See* transportation
Mexico, 13–37
    background and history, 13–16, 90
    business cards, 22
    business culture, 31, 34–37
    communication styles, 18–19, 22–24

crime, 26
cultural orientations, 16–19
dining and drinking, 6, 17–18, 28–31
dress, 26–27
economic conditions, 15–16
gift giving, 32–33
greetings and introductions, 20–22
guests and hosts, 30–32
holidays and celebrations, 33–34
physical gestures and facial expressions,
    23
politics and government, 15
public behavior, 24–26
religion and demographics, 15–16, 17
schools and education, 15
transportation, 25–26, 32
U.S. relations, 14
women's roles, 15, 16–17
Mexico City, 11, 13
money
    Argentina, 173
    Brazil, 149
    Colombia, 105
    Cuba, 209
    Dominican Republic, 226, 227
    Haiti, 247–48
    Jamaica, 263
    Mexico, 25
monochronic cultures, 6

names, Spanish family. *See* honorifics
negotiation styles. *See* business culture
Nicaragua, 65-82
    background and history, 65–66
    business culture, 74–75, 78, 80–82
    communication styles, 68, 71–73
    crime, 74
    cultural orientations, 66–69
    dining and drinking, 75–78
    dress, 75
    economic conditions, 73
    gift giving, 79

    greetings and introductions, 69–71
    guests and hosts, 78–79
    holidays and celebrations, 80
    land reform issues, 65
    politics and government, 65–66
    public behavior, 73–75
    religion and demographics, 66
    schools and education, 66
    transportation, 74, 79
    U.S. relations, 65, 66, 71
    women's roles, 67, 70, 71–72, 78, 80
nonverbal behavior. *See* eye contact;
    physical gestures and facial
    expressions; physical greetings;
    physicality and physical space;
    silence; waving and counting
north Andean cultures. *See* Colombia;
    Ecuador; Venezuela
northern Centroamerican cultures.
    See Belize; El Salvador; Guatemala;
    Honduras

office protocols. *See* business culture
organization-oriented cultures, 6
other-dependent and other-independent
    cultures, 6

Panama, 86-88
    background and history, 86
    business culture, 88
    communication styles, 87
    dining and drinking, 87
    dress, 87
    holidays and celebrations, 87–88
    U.S. relations, 86, 87
Panama Canal, 86
Paraguay, 189-92
    background and history, 91, 189–90
    business culture, 192
    communication styles, 190
    crime, 189
    dining and drinking, 191

Paraguay *(continued)*
  dress, 190–91
  economic conditions, 190
  greetings and introductions, 190
  holidays and celebrations, 191–92
  politics and government, 190
  transportation, 189
  women's roles, 192
past-oriented cultures, 7
personal hygiene
  Bolivia, 133
  Brazil, 151
  Colombia, 106
  Cuba, 210–11
  Dominican Republic, 228
  Guatemala, 50
  Haiti, 248
  Jamaica, 263
  Mexico, 27
  Nicaragua, 75
  Peru, 128
Peru, 126-31
  Asian influence, 126–27, 130
  background and history, 90, 126
  business culture, 129, 130–31
  communication styles, 127
  crime, 128
  dining and drinking, 128–29
  dress, 128
  gift giving, 129–30
  greetings and introductions, 127
  guests and hosts, 129
  holidays and celebrations, 130
  politics and government, 126
  public behavior, 127–28
  religion and demographics, 126–27
  Spanish influence, 126
  transportation, 127–28
physical gestures and facial expressions
  Argentina, 170
  Barbados, 272
  Bolivia, 132
  Brazil, 147

Chile, 184
Colombia, 102
Cuba, 207
Dominican Republic, 225
Guatemala, 46
Haiti, 246
Jamaica, 261
Mexico, 23
Nicaragua, 72
Panama, 87
Paraguay, 190
Puerto Rico, 237
Uruguay, 194
Venezuela, 117–18
See also physical greetings
physical greetings
  Argentina, 169
  Barbados, 272
  Bolivia, 132
  Brazil, 145
  Chile, 184
  Colombia, 101
  Costa Rica, 84
  Cuba, 206
  Dominican Republic, 224
  Ecuador, 122
  Guatemala, 45
  Haiti, 244–45
  Jamaica, 260
  Mexico, 22
  Nicaragua, 71, 72
  Panama, 87
  Paraguay, 190
  Peru, 127
physicality and physical space
  Argentina, 171
  Barbados, 272
  Brazil, 147
  Colombia, 103
  Cuba, 208
  Dominican Republic, 225–26
  Guatemala, 47
  Haiti, 246

Jamaica, 262
Mexico, 24
Nicaragua, 72
Uruguay, 194
politics and government
Argentina, 163
Brazil, 137, 138, 140
Centroamerica, 38
Chile, 184
Colombia, 94, 95
Costa Rica, 83
Cuba, 199, 200
Dominican Republic, 217, 218
Ecuador, 121
El Salvador, 63
Guatemala, 39–40
Haiti, 239, 240
Honduras, 61
Jamaica, 256
Mexico, 15
Nicaragua, 65–66
Paraguay, 190
Peru, 126
Puerto Rico, 235–36
Uruguay, 193
Venezuela, 116
polychronic cultures, 6
Portugal, 90, 137, 138, 193
process-oriented cultures, 7
public behavior
Argentina, 171–73
Belize, 59
Bolivia, 133
Brazil, 148–50
Chile, 185
Colombia, 104
Costa Rica, 84
Cuba, 208–10
Dominican Republic, 226–27
Ecuador, 123
Guatemala, 47–49
Haiti, 246–48
Jamaica, 262–64

Mexico, 24–26
Nicaragua, 73–75
Venezuela, 118
Puerto Rico, 235-38
background and history, 235–36
communication styles, 236–237
dining and drinking, 237
greetings and introductions, 236
holidays and celebrations, 237–38
politics and government, 235–36
U.S. relations, 235, 236
punctuality
Argentina, 162, 165, 173
Belize, 60
Brazil, 141, 150
Colombia, 105
Cuba, 202, 210
Dominican Republic, 220, 227
Guatemala, 49
Haiti, 248
Jamaica, 258, 263–64
Mexico, 18, 26
Nicaragua, 67, 74–75
Uruguay, 196

Quito, 121, 122

Rastafarians, 256–57
relationship-oriented cultures, 6
religion
Argentina, 164
Barbados, 271
Brazil, 138–39
Colombia, 95
Cuba, 200–201
Dominican Republic, 218
El Salvador, 63
Guatemala, 40
Haiti, 241
influence on Latin America, 10
Jamaica, 256–57
Mexico, 15
Nicaragua, 66

religion *(continued)*
  Peru, 126
  Trinidad and Tobago, 274
  Venezuela, 116
restaurants
  Argentina, 173, 175, 177, 182
  Bolivia, 135
  Brazil, 149, 152, 155, 160
  Chile, 186
  Colombia, 107, 109, 114
  Cuba, 204, 211, 213
  Dominican Republic, 229, 230, 234
  Ecuador, 124
  Guatemala, 53
  Haiti, 249, 250, 253
  Jamaica, 265, 266, 270
  Mexico, 28, 31
  Nicaragua, 75, 76, 77–78
  Paraguay, 191
  Peru, 129
  Uruguay, 194, 195
results-oriented cultures, 7
Rio de Janeiro, 136, 137, 157, 158
risk-averse and risk-taking cultures, 7
Roman Catholic Church
  Argentina, 164
  Brazil, 138–39, 140
  Colombia, 95
  Cuba, 201
  Dominican Republic, 219
  El Salvador, 63
  Guatemala, 40
  Haiti, 241, 242
  Mexico, 15, 16, 17
  Venezuela, 116
rule-oriented cultures, 6

Santo Domingo, 217, 218
São Paulo, 136, 137
schools and education
  Argentina, 164
  Barbados, 271
  Brazil, 138

  Colombia, 95
  Cuba, 200
  Dominican Republic, 218
  Guatemala, 40
  Haiti, 240–41
  Jamaica, 256
  Mexico, 15
  Nicaragua, 66
seating arrangements. *See* dining and
  drinking
silence, use of
  Argentina, 170
  Brazil, 146
  Colombia, 103
  Cuba, 207
  Dominican Republic, 225
  Guatemala, 46
  Haiti, 245
  Jamaica, 261
  Mexico, 23
  Nicaragua, 72
slang. *See* language and basic vocabulary
smoking
  Argentina, 172, 177
  Brazil, 148, 155
  Colombia, 104
  Cuba, 209, 213
  Dominican Republic, 227, 230
  Guatemala, 48
  Haiti, 247, 250
  Jamaica, 263, 266
  Mexico, 25
  Nicaragua, 74
South America, 89–91. *See also* Argentina;
  Bolivia; Brazil; Chile; Colombia;
  Ecuador; Paraguay; Peru; Uruguay;
  Venezuela
south Andean cultures. *See* Bolivia; Peru
southern Centroamerican cultures.
  See Costa Rica; Panama; Nicaragua
Southern Cone cultures, 11, 89, 91. *See*
  also Argentina; Chile; Paraguay;
  Uruguay

Spanish conquest, 10, 39, 89–90, 126, 197
Spanish influence
  Bolivia, 131
  Chile, 183
  Colombia, 93
  El Salvador, 63
  Guatemala, 39
  Peru, 126
stores and food markets
  Argentina, 172, 173
  Brazil, 148
  Chile, 185
  Colombia, 104
  Cuba, 208–209
  Dominican Republic, 226–27
  Guatemala, 48
  Haiti, 247
  Jamaica, 262–63
  Mexico, 25
  Nicaragua, 73–74

table manners
  Argentina, 176
  Belize, 60
  Bolivia, 134
  Brazil, 153–54
  Chile, 186
  Colombia, 108
  Cuba, 212–13
  Dominican Republic, 229–30
  Guatemala, 52
  Haiti, 249
  Jamaica, 266
  Mexico, 30
  Nicaragua, 77
  Peru, 129
  Uruguay, 194–95
  Venezuela, 119
taxis. *See* transportation
telephone use
  Argentina, 172
  Belize, 59
  Brazil, 148–49

  Colombia, 104
  Cuba, 209
  Guatemala, 48
  Mexico, 25
  Peru, 127
tequila, 29
thank-you gifts and notes. *See* gift giving
time perspectives, 6–7. *See also* punctuality
tipping
  Argentina, 173
  Belize, 59
  Bolivia, 133
  Brazil, 149–50
  Chile, 183
  Colombia, 104–105
  Costa Rica, 84
  Cuba, 210
  Dominican Republic, 227
  Ecuador, 123
  Guatemala, 49
  Haiti, 247–48
  Jamaica, 263
  Mexico, 26
  Nicaragua, 74
  Paraguay, 189
  Peru, 128
  Uruguay, 193
  Venezuela, 118
titles. *See* business culture; honorifics
toasts. *See* drinks and toasts
transportation
  Argentina, 172, 178
  Brazil, 148, 149, 15
  Chile, 183
  Colombia, 104, 110
  Cuba, 209, 214
  Dominican Republic, 227, 231
  Guatemala, 48–49, 54
  Haiti, 247
  Jamaica, 263, 267
  Mexico, 25–26, 32
  Nicaragua, 74, 79
  Paraguay, 189

transportation *(continued)*
   Peru, 127–28
   Uruguay, 193
   Venezuela, 118
Trinidad and Tobago, 273–75

United States, Latin America's influence
   on, 9
United States, relations with
   Bolivia, 132
   Costa Rica, 83
   Cuba, 199, 200, 206, 207
   Dominican Republic, 217, 218
   Haiti, 239, 240
   Jamaica, 255
   Mexico, 14
   Nicaragua, 65, 66, 71
   Panama, 86, 87
   Puerto Rico, 235, 236
   Uruguay, 193
Uruguay, 192-96
   background and history, 91, 192–93
   business culture, 195–96
   communication styles, 193–94
   crime, 193
   dining and drinking, 194–95
   dress, 194
   economic conditions, 193
   European influence, 192–93, 196
   gift giving, 195
   holidays and celebrations, 195
   politics and government, 193
   transportation, 193
   U.S. relations, 193
   women's roles, 196
"U.S. Americans," use of term, 14, 138
utensils, use of. *See* table manners

Venezuela, 115-20
   background and history, 90, 115–17
   business culture, 116, 119

communication styles, 117–18
crime, 118
dining and drinking, 118–19
dress, 118
economic conditions, 116
gift giving, 119–20
greetings and introductions, 117
holidays and celebrations, 120
politics and government, 116
public behavior, 118
religion and demographics, 116–17
viceroys, in South America, 90, 93
vocabulary. *See* language and basic
   vocabulary
voodoo, in Haiti, 241

walking styles and waiting in lines
   Argentina, 171–72
   Brazil, 148
   Colombia, 103
   Cuba, 208
   Dominican Republic, 226
   Guatemala, 47
   Haiti, 245–46
   Jamaica, 262
   Mexico, 24–25
   Nicaragua, 73
waving and counting
   Argentina, 171
   Brazil, 147
   Colombia, 102–103
   Cuba, 207–208
   Dominican Republic, 225
   Guatemala, 46–47
   Haiti, 246
   Jamaica, 262
   Mexico, 23–24
   Nicaragua, 72
   Peru, 127
western Southern Cone cultures, 162.
    See also Argentina; Chile

women, role of
  Argentina, 165, 178, 180
  Barbados, 271
  Belize, 58, 60
  Bolivia, 135
  Brazil, 139, 140, 149, 155–56, 158
  Chile, 187–88
  Colombia, 96, 99–100, 110, 112
  Costa Rica, 85
  Cuba, 201–202, 214, 215
  Dominican Republic, 218, 219, 231, 233
  Ecuador, 121–22
  Guatemala, 41, 46, 55
  Haiti, 241, 244, 251, 252
  Jamaica, 257, 267, 268
  Mexico, 15, 16–17
  Nicaragua, 67, 70, 71–72, 78, 80
  Paraguay, 191
  Uruguay, 196
written correspondence. *See* business
  culture